W9-BKZ-604

NATIONAL GEOGRAPHIC
TRAVELER

IRELAND

NATIONAL GEOGRAPHIC
TRAVELER

IRELAND

by Christopher Somerville

National Geographic
Washington, D.C.

DEC 0 3 2019

SOUTH COUNTRY LIBRARY
22 STATION RD
BELLPORT, NY 11713

CONTENTS

▪ Pages 2–3: Medieval Blarney Castle, home of the famous stone, near Cork
▪ Opposite: Beautifully embroidered designs based on ancient Celtic symbols adorn the dress of a young dancer in County Kerry.

TRAVELING WITH EYES OPEN

Alert travelers go with a purpose and leave with a benefit. If you travel responsibly, you can help support wildlife conservation, historic preservation, and cultural enrichment in the places you visit. You can enrich your own travel experience as well.

To be a geo-savvy traveler:

- Recognize that your presence has an impact on the places you visit.

- Spend your time and money in ways that sustain local character. (Besides, it's more interesting that way.)

- Value the destination's natural and cultural heritage.

- Respect the local customs and traditions.

- Express appreciation to local people about things you find interesting and unique to the place: its nature and scenery, music and food, historic villages and buildings.

- Vote with your wallet: Support the people who support the place, patronizing businesses that make an effort to celebrate and protect what's special there. Seek out local shops, restaurants, and inns. Use tour operators who love their home—who love taking care of it and showing it off. Avoid businesses that detract from the character of the place.

- Enrich yourself, taking home memories and stories to tell, knowing that you have contributed to the preservation and enhancement of the destination.

That is the type of travel now called geotourism, defined as "tourism that sustains or enhances the geographical character of a place—its environment, culture, aesthetics, heritage, and the well-being of its residents." To learn more, visit National Geographic's Center for Sustainable Destinations at *nationalgeographic.com/maps/geotourism.*

NATIONAL GEOGRAPHIC
T R A V E L E R

IRELAND

❙ ABOUT THE AUTHOR

■ **Christopher Somerville** is one of Britain's best known travel writers, with some 35 books to his name—including *National Geographic Traveler: Great Britain.* He writes regularly for the travel sections of the *Times* and the *Irish Independent* and also broadcasts on radio. His love affair with Ireland was kindled on his first trip to the island, an 800-mile (1,280 km) walk through the rugged and romantic west of Ireland. Since then, he has written four books and countless words of travel journalism about the country, and returns whenever he can to hook up with old friends, walk the mountains and coasts, play traditional music, and continue his search for that place "just around the corner, now," where the *craic* is mighty, the whiskey is warming, and the pub never closes.

CHARTING YOUR TRIP

With its charming towns, cozy pubs, sheep-dotted hills, and friendly and quick-witted locals, it's easy to see Ireland only as depicted in the emerald-green pages of a tourist brochure. But Ireland is not all about soft-focus romanticism.

Alongside the donkey cart, sometimes overtaking it rather brashly, you'll see the 4x4 of modern progress and the sheen of a youthful, forward-pressing republic. This bracing, sometimes challenging, and always fascinating mix will be readily on show as you take in the justly famous sights and landscapes, even if you have only a short time to explore this rich and surprisingly complex land.

Ireland's extensive bus and rail systems make it easy to move about the country, but many people find the freedom and flexibility afforded by a car the best way to go. Car rental agencies abound in all cities and most sizable towns. But remember to drive on the left.

How to Visit: If You Have a Week

Even if you have only a week in Ireland, spend a day or two in the capital city, **Dublin,** on the country's east coast. Join one of the guided walks for some flavor of this spellbinding place, a nursery for writers, artists, musicians, rogues, and rebels. The **National Museum of Ireland–Archaeology** boasts dazzling ancient and medieval relics and an account of the nation's long road to independence from Britain. Other can't-miss attractions include the wonderfully illuminated **Book of Kells** (A.D. 800) at Trinity College and the grim but gripping tour of **Kilmainham Gaol,** key to understanding Ireland's revolutionary history and spirit.

Then head to Ireland's **southwest**—the country's most visited region—for two or three days. Travel by way of **Killarney National Park** (190 miles/300 km southwest of Dublin), a wonderfully preserved ring of lakes and mountains, on your way to explore the spectacularly wild shores and mountains of **Cork** and **Kerry,** where the restless Atlantic breaks up the seaboard into jagged green peninsulas—especially Iveragh with its famous **Ring of Kerry** drive (best out of season) and the green and hilly **Dingle Peninsula** in central west Kerry.

Heading north two or three hours up the west coast from Kerry takes you through the bare gray hills of County Clare's **Burren** region, famous for its spectacular late-spring and early-summer carpets of wildflowers. An hour northwest of the Burren, make a day circuit of the large west Galway peninsula, better known as **Connemara,** the iconic heart of "wild Ireland." Then carry on north another hour into rugged

■ A statue in Cobh commemorates Irish emigration.

County Mayo for a night in the pubs of **Westport,** a peerless town for traditional musical sessions.

You could then return to Dublin (160 miles/260 km from Westport) across the vast **peat bogs** of the Irish midlands, many now being conserved for their wild-life. You can also stop off en route to visit the round towers and beautifully carved buildings of **Clonmac-noise** on the banks of the River Shannon in County Offaly to cap off your week.

If You Have More Time . . .

. . . then lucky you! It's a great pity to rush through such a laid-back country. The suggested itinerary below follows some of the same route as the one-week version above, but ventures more off the beaten tourist trail and explores more of the island.

Around Dublin: There are several regions near the capital worth exploring. About 30 miles (48 km) north of Dublin in County Meath lies the extraordi-nary Stone Age necropolis of **Brú na Bóinne** with its great 5,000-year-old tombs, including **Newgrange.** The riding stables and famous horse-racing tracks of the **Curragh** of Kildare beckon 40 miles (65 km) southwest of Dublin; here you'll also find the eastern edge of the wide flat boglands. Then turn southeast to the **Wicklow Moun-tains** to stroll by the supremely beautiful twin lakes of **Glendalough,** about 40 miles (65 km) south of Dublin. With a 1,500-year-old monastery as part of the setting, a walk here–in the early morning or late evening to avoid the crowds–gives insight into the "Irish soul" as few places do.

Southwest & Western Ireland: From Glendalough in the Wicklow Mountains, an 80-mile (130 km) drive south along the sandy, warm southeast coast brings you to **Waterford,** where the famous crystal factory offers tours, and the showroom exhibits and sells exquisite handcrafted glassware. From Waterford, it's another 80 miles (130 km) southwest to ring the **Bells of Shandon** on a tour of historic **Cork**

NOT TO BE MISSED:

The beautiful Book of Kells at Dublin's Trinity College 54–55

Going for a dawn or evening walk at Glendalough 98–103

A boat trip to the Blasket Islands off the Dingle Peninsula 156

The spectacular Burren 168-173

A music session in Westport 190–191

The views over Yeats Country from Knocknaree 210–211

Sailing down the River Shannon to Clonmacnoise 250–251

A Black Taxi tour of the murals of Belfast 285–290

Cruising to the islands in Lower Lough Erne 323

Visitor Information

Faílte Ireland *(discoverireland.ie)* is your one-stop center for travel information for Ireland, while the excellent **Northen Ireland Tourism Bureau** *(discovernorthern ireland.com)* covers the North. You'll also find thousands of suggestions for places to stay and things to do at the **Tourism Ireland** website *(ireland.com).*

Information on bus travel within the Republic can be found at **Bus Éireann** (Irish Bus; *buseireann.ie),* and at **Ulsterbus** *(trans-link.co.uk/Services/Ulsterbus-Service-Page)* for schedules within Northern Ireland. For rail schedules and reservations, contact **Irish Rail** *(irishrail.ie)* or **Northern Ireland Rail-ways** *(translink.co.uk/Services/NI-Railways).*

When to Go

There's no guarantee of either sunny or wet weather in any season, so the question of when to visit Ireland depends on what you want to do there. Many go to enjoy the St. Patrick's Day celebrations on March 17, especially the big parade in Dublin. In the months of April through June, everything is particularly green, the wildflowers are out, the birds are singing, and tourist facilities have reopened after winter.

To experience Ireland's festivals (see p. 44 & Travelwise p. 342), visit in July or August. It's crowded, and the rain can fall as prices rise, but at least the sea is swimmable. There's often clear, cool weather in September and October, as the colors change and prices begin to fall, while winter is for fans of the outdoors—walkers and mountaineers out to enjoy crisp, frosty days—and for lovers of a cozy pub, a blazing fire, and a timeless session of talk.

city. Just outside Cork, you can guarantee yourself the gift of the gab by kissing the **Blarney Stone** at Blarney Castle before heading a couple of hours west to the famed west Cork and Kerry coasts (see p. 8).

From the southwest peninsulas, travel north of the Burren and Connemara to the western Irish counties of **Clare, Galway,** and **Mayo,** each about 150 miles (240 km) west of Dublin. The west is a stronghold of great traditional music: Try **Ennistymon** and **Doolin** in County Clare, **Galway city,** and almost any town or village—just ask around. Hill-climbing and walking are also wonderful here, especially the **Twelve Bens** and **Maumturks** of Connemara and the remote **Nephin Beg** of Mayo. Mountains with a special spiritual significance are **Mullaghmore** in the Burren region of Clare and the famous pilgrimage mountain of **Croagh Patrick** on the shores of Clew Bay. And don't miss a trip out to the glorious **Aran Islands** to glimpse a more traditional way of life.

Central & Northwest Ireland: The flat central midlands nestled between Dublin and the wild west, mostly bog and meadows, have their own understated charm. Take a cruise along the **River Shannon** from **Athlone** or **Carrick-on-Shannon,** or walk the bog roads and trails of **Longford, Offaly,** or **Laois** to appreciate it. In the northwest of the country, the shadows of the Yeats brothers, poet William and painter Jack, lie long through

What to Pack

Generally, dress in Ireland is quite informal. But, since the country lies right in the track of Atlantic weather patterns, its climate is notably damp. You will probably see everything from soft, freckling, pervasive moisture to good honest rain while you're here. So you'll need to bring a good waterproof jacket and pair of pants, footwear that will stand a soaking, a collapsible umbrella, and a good hat with a brim. These will make all the difference to your enjoyment of Ireland, no matter what time of year you visit, and will prevent you having to search endlessly—and pay through the nose—for decent weatherproof gear.

If you plan on playing golf, don't forget your favorite shoes, and bring sturdy walking boots if you want to do any hiking. Small, light binoculars are a boon for admiring birds or the scenery.

Take some cards printed with your name and contact details to give to new friends, and pack a sense of humor and irony—the Irish deal in little else. (See Travelwise p. 342 for more information.)

■ On the beach below Mussenden Temple in County Londonderry, Northern Ireland

mountainous **Sligo** (135 miles/215 km from Dublin), while an Irish-speaking, rugged atmosphere pervades the moors and lonely coasts of **Donegal** (about 50 miles/80 km north of Sligo). Here on the cliffs of **Slieve League,** or out in the **Rosses,** you will feel truly away from it all.

Northern Ireland: Don't neglect Northern Ireland, an unmissable part of your Irish experience. Take a walking tour of the city of **Belfast** (100 miles/160 km or two hours by rail from Dublin), embark on a **Black Taxi tour** to see the remarkable "political" murals, and visit **Titanic Belfast** (see pp. 291–293), the stunning new exhibition on the ill-fated Belfast-built liner, R.M.S. *Titanic.* Then drive north up the **Antrim Coast,** a breathtaking display of volcanic cliff scenery, to the famed **Giant's Causeway** promontory of basalt. **Londonderry** (68 miles/110 km northwest of Belfast) has its walled city and gorgeous beaches, while in **County Fermanagh,** in Northern Ireland's southwest, you can cruise the island-dotted waters of Lough Erne. In the southeast, climb the noble hills—the mountains of **Mourne** in County Down, South Armagh's **Slieve Gullion**—for mighty views before you head south again the 70 miles (115 km) back to Dublin.

Tipping

No one is entitled to a tip, and the only service providers who might mutter to themselves if one isn't forthcoming would be taxi drivers and waiters and waitresses in restaurants. For a taxi ride, tipping the driver 10 percent of the fare is plenty. In a restaurant, look to see whether service has been added to your final bill. If it hasn't, whether or not to leave a tip is entirely up to you. A tip of 10 percent of the final bill would be fine, 15 percent would be very generous. (See Travelwise p. 347 for more information.)

HISTORY &
CULTURE

▪ The pennywhistle drives many
an Irish jig.
▪ Opposite: Dublin's Temple Bar area is
the capital's hub of nocturnal revelry.

IRELAND TODAY

A leather-faced countryman in a cloth cap and an old patched jacket, pitch-forking his hay in a tiny stone-walled field against a timeless backdrop of mountains and sea: That's Ireland today. His green-haired daughter striding out of a Dublin cappuccino bar, networking to the United States on her cell phone: That's today's Ireland, too, on the move and on the change.

Romance with a Hard Edge

Romantics have no trouble at all finding what they're looking for in Ireland. Few countries project such a seductive image as this rainwashed little island off the north-west coast of Europe, and few fulfill their visitors' dreams so faithfully—the green fields, the soft rain, the quick-tongued and openhanded people, the Guinness-drinking and laughter against that eternal backdrop of irresistible Irish music.

But there is a hard edge, too, not far underneath the fun and fancy. During the past 25 years, no western European country has undergone such a profound economic and social change as Ireland. Everywhere people talk of the Celtic Tiger, the boom economy that saw business and optimism swell in the Republic in the 1990s. "Ireland of the Welcomes," the laid-back land where hospitality is the watchword and no one's in a hurry, still flourishes, of course, as much in visitors' minds as anywhere. You can feel more relaxed, more welcome here than in almost any other country in the world. Ireland is famous for just this atmosphere, with good reason. Back at the turn of the millennium, though, the signs of change were all around —money jingling in Dubliners' pockets, farmland sliced by superhighways built with European Union development grants, extravagant

> **You can feel more relaxed, more welcome here than in almost any other country in the world. Ireland is famous for this atmosphere, with good reason.**

modern houses sprouting on remote hillsides, and a confidence in the attitudes of youngsters who no longer needed to emigrate to find a good job and some freedom to live their lives as they saw fit.

The image of Ireland as a gently backward, rural, and mystical land, and of the Irish as a rustically humorous community of God-fearing, thrifty peasants (seeded with a few erratically brilliant novelists and poets), was deliberately fostered in the 1930s and '40s for nationalistic reasons by Eamon de Valera, prime minister of the newly and proudly independent Eire. It wasn't without a basis in truth. And it served the Irish tourist industry well, fixing southern Ireland in the world's mind as the ideal soft landing for an escape from reality. What it disguised, though, was an all-too-real rural poverty, economic and social, which drove young, vigorous men and women to emigrate in droves up to the mid-1990s. In the first decade of the 21st century, many were returning to Ireland, or had never had to leave in the first place.

This new, shiny-faced, and thrusting young republic, transformed into one of Europe's most dynamic economies, was built on a foundation of development money from the European Union and from the International Fund for Ireland. Agricultural and pharmaceutical chemicals and information technology were particularly big players. Tax breaks enticed multinational corporations to open headquarters in cities throughout the island, where they had the added benefit of a high quality workforce whose native language was English. Today, Ireland's high standard of livability and its appealing job market have made it a country that attracts young people from all over Europe.

Dublin shines at dusk along the River Liffey.

Troublesome Tiger

Despite this newfound reputation, the Celtic Tiger has turned out to be a troublesome, uncertain, and some would say toothless economic beast. Too many of these new high-tech industries have been found to flit out from under when times get tough or when the global market gives a twitch, with little sense of loyalty to their host country or workforce. Older homegrown industries such as textiles, car assembly, and agriculture haven't done so well. Some visitors find an un-Irish offhandedness and arrogance in the new breed of entrepreneurial young highfliers. Indeed, the Irish are not unquestioning Europeans. On June 12, 2008, they voted to reject ratification of the Treaty of Lisbon, which established a Europe-wide constitution in everything but name. In October 2009, though, after reassurances on taxation and autonomy, the Irish reversed that decision.

That same year, worldwide economic overconfidence caused the collapse of much of Europe's banking system and brought recession and enormous economic uncertainty to the Republic. The Celtic Tiger had been footed on a boom in the construction industry, itself shakily propped up by unsustainable borrowing and economic aid. Building works halted overnight, and housing and business park projects stood unfinished. After two decades of prosperity, Irish youngsters once more prepared to emigrate in search of work.

In November 2012, with unemployment at 15 percent and emigration soaring (mostly of the best and brightest), Ireland was forced to request help from the European Union and the International Monetary Fund (IMF). A loan of €85 billion was eventually agreed upon, and an "age of austerity" began. This has proved unpalatable, naturally, but the medicine has begun to work. By the end of 2013 the strict controls imposed by the IMF and the European lenders had been eased. This made it possible for Ireland to bounce back quickly and in the five years that followed, from 2014 to 2018, it became one of Europe's driving economies and had one of its highest growth rates. When the multinational corporations took advantage of low tax rates and invested in the country, unemployment plunged to an extreme low while salaries and consumer figures rose. Nevertheless, Ireland's economy is still strongly connected to Great Britain's and making predictions about the effects that Brexit will have on the country when the U.K.'s exit from the European Union (EU) becomes effective is difficult.

> **Despite this newfound reputation, the Celtic Tiger has turned out to be a troublesome, uncertain, and some would say toothless economic beast.**

New Hope for the North

The island of Ireland contains 32 counties. The six northernmost counties of Antrim, Derry, Tyrone, Fermanagh, Armagh, and Down make up the province of Northern Ireland, which remained politically a part of the United Kingdom when the other 26 counties of Ireland split away to form the Irish Free State in

■ **Fans of the Irish national soccer team celebrate a goal by the home team.**

1921 after the Irish War of Independence (see pp. 32–33). You may hear Northern Ireland called Ulster—the six counties formed part of the ancient Irish province of that name. Ancient Ulster contained three additional counties (Donegal, Cavan, and Monaghan), but these joined the infant Free State (later the Irish Republic) in 1921 and have remained politically apart from Northern Ireland ever since.

Almost everyone in Northern Ireland in the mid-1990s would have given their eyeteeth to enjoy an image as benign, if misleading, as the Republic's leprechaun winsomeness, instead of the dour and deadly reputation—equally false—that they had been cursed with through the activities of a few bitter bigots. Thirty years of being unwillingly strapped to the careering headless horse of sectarian and politically motivated terrorism made all moderate folk—and they constitute the majority of people in the North—heartily sick of being classified with extremists. They knew only too well the damage it was doing to their province's economy, with visitors and overseas investors reluctant to come to a place tarred with the deep-staining brush of violence and intolerance. The North's traditional heavy industry, following a pan-European trend, was in decline, the economy stagnant. Emigration of bright, ambitious youngsters, always seen as a purely southern Irish scourge, was getting a grip of Northern Ireland, too.

With all its flaws and uncertainties, the Good Friday Agreement of April 10, 1998 (see p. 289), brought about a new perspective on Northern Ireland. The outside world, looking in, began to see growing shoots of hope for peace and a settled society, rather than yet more uprooted aspirations. In 2005, the IRA declared its campaign over after 35 years of the Troubles, during which the paramilitary republican group had sought to bomb and shoot the British Army out of Northern Ireland and to establish by violent means a reunification of the island of Ireland. Few onlookers could quite believe the cessation, and the subsequent process of decommissioning the IRA's arsenal of weapons was fraught with mistrust. Loyalist paramilitary groups took some time to follow suit. Since then a number of splinter groups have caused trouble and concern, but they are tiny and have no voter endorsement.

Peace on the streets of Northern Ireland depends on the existence of a credible form of devolved government for the North. The Northern Ireland Assembly, based at Stormont Castle just outside Belfast, has had a troubled genesis since first elected in June 1998–it has been suspended several times already in its short existence.

■ Old-fashioned traditions are still practiced in many isolated pockets of rural Ireland.

The pacification process between the parts was favored by both nations' membership in the EU since it removed the restrictions on the free exchange of goods between the Republic of Ireland and Northern Ireland. However, if the U.K.'s exit from the EU after the Brexit referendum brings about the re-establishment of the borders, the demand for a united Ireland could become strong again and exacerbate the relationship between the two political factions.

Rural Charm & City Buzz

Few enough visitors yet know about Northern Ireland's gorgeous secret countryside or the warmth of the welcome in the music pubs and bed-and-breakfast houses of the province. Their expectations are vague, their image of the North distorted by the Troubles (see p. 35). But south of the border it's a different story. Over three million visitors a year flock to the Republic, almost one tourist for every inhabitant. Tourism is big business here.

Visitors planning a trip to southern Ireland have a seductive image in mind—the beauty of the mountains and seacoasts of the west and southwest, the sophistication and humor of Dublin, outdoor fun on golf courses, horse tracks, and fishing lakes, and the laid-back pleasures of the talk, the music, and the general lifestyle everywhere. Famous beauty spots and tourist honeypots lie thick on the ground, and those who come to Ireland to find the fantasy island of the Leprechauns don't go home disappointed. Buying shamrocks and shillelaghs in the crowded gift shops of Killarney, crawling bumper to bumper around the Ring of Kerry's overpopular scenic route, fighting for a table in a Kinsale fish restaurant, or watching stage Irishwomen at their spinning wheels in Bunratty Folk Park, you could be forgiven for thinking that all Ireland was out to sell itself lock, stock, and barrel to the tourist trade.

> ### EXPERIENCE:
> ## Take the Time to Yarn
>
> "Every gateway holds a farmer, and every farmer holds a story." You'll find the truth of that old saw when you travel through backcountry Ireland—but not if you race through, cocooned in your rental car. Rent a bike for a day, or better yet, set out on foot. Irish folk are notably friendly and inquisitive, and the more rural the situation, the more they will be ready for a good chat. That's the best way to hear the stories, the legends, and the scandals, not to mention opinions both well informed and "original." Find hundreds of downloadable walking routes, from country rambles to jaunts through Ireland's bustling cities, at *discoverireland.ie/walking* and *walkni.com*.

The real living country, you'll find, lies along the lane just off the main road, in the street behind the harbor, ten minutes' walk up the mountain track, out along the bog road. Explorers and wanderers get the best out of Ireland—so do talkers and listeners, hikers and bikers, laughers and quaffers, and those who like the odd angle and the elliptical way.

That easygoing image, of course, is only half the story. It's true that there are still thousands of small traditional farms in rural Ireland, especially out in the Irish-speaking Gaeltacht areas of the west, working their picturesquely tiny, intensely green stone-walled fields, with EU subsidies to prop up the businesses. Country towns still tend to be charming and sleepy in equal proportion, retaining their old-fashioned grocers' and butchers' shops and tiny dark pubs. But cities such as Galway and Cork, where many of the Celtic Tiger youngsters have injected a healthy dash of loud life, buzz with modern energy these days.

Keeping an Eye on Things

Irish politics, both local and national, have always been riven by scandal. Bribes, cronyism, and deals behind closed doors were so much the order of the day by the early 1990s that they were becoming an embarrassment to the Irish themselves, as well as an international talking point. The Ethics in Public Office Act was passed in 1995 to try to get a grip on this shady side of things, with mixed success to date.

> **Change is sweeping through Irish life, and nowhere is this more clearly shown than in the rise in status that women achieved during the last decade of the 20th century.**

During the same period, a very noticeable growth in concern for the environment, both built and natural, has led to lively debate about planning, development, and design, notoriously unchecked until recently. Traveling through rural areas you'll hardly fail to spot the much reviled "Irish hacienda" style of architecture—a sprawling ranch-style bungalow fronted by an enormous prairie of slate patio behind raw brick arches, usually posed on an otherwise pristine hillside. Around city streets the main culprit has been the use of garish plastic and eyeball-tingling paint. In areas of outstanding natural beauty and historical interest, European development money has paid for several interpretive centers of often obtrusive design. Few would have raised a murmur 20 years ago; now, thanks to the emergence of a better educated and more sophisticated electorate, the powers-that-be are obliged to take notice of objectors. Perhaps the most telling example of this newfound consciousness is the growing protest over the destruction of the vast boglands by Bord na Móna, the Peat Board (see pp. 254–255). Seen until recently as barren wastelands fit only to be exploited for cheap fuel, the boglands are now regarded by many as a wonderful, strangely beautiful refuge for wildlife.

Women to the Fore

Change is sweeping through Irish life, and nowhere is this more clearly shown than in the rise in status that women achieved during the last decade of the 20th century. When Mary Robinson, a liberal-minded barrister with strong feminist allegiances, was elected president of the Republic of Ireland in 1990, she became an inspiration to many women, who were still taking pretty much a backseat in Irish political and business life, and they quickly became much more assertive and self-confident. Robinson proved an indefatigable traveler in her own country and through the wider world, keen to gain a hearing for unpopular or ticklish subjects such as unmarried mothers, drug abuse, gay rights, and religious intolerance. By her warm and genuine personality she raised the profile of the presidency and of Ireland, and especially of Irish women. In 1997, Robinson was replaced by another woman—Mary McAleese, a Roman Catholic law lecturer from Northern Ireland—who served as president until 2011, when Michael D. Higgins took over the office.

A Church in Crisis

The business of who lines up on which side of the religious divide has come to mean less and less in modern Ireland. In Eamon de Valera's backwoods Ireland of the 1930s, the Roman Catholic Church was king of the castle, dispensing welfare and education and laying down strict rules of behavior that the largely poor and rural populace disregarded at their peril. Anyone who crossed a priest in some country parish would become an untouchable. Respect for the Church and adherence to Christianity—Church of Ireland or Roman Catholic—was almost universal.

But social change, greater affluence, international travel, and a wider education have put an end to all that. These days, after a series of scandals, the Roman Catholic Church is in a very reduced state. There have been two very clear signs of the great changes taking place in an ever more liberal, multicultural Irish society. The first was the referendum of May 22, 2015, that approved changing the constitution to extend civil marriage rights to same-sex couples and the second was the referendum of May 25, 2018, which repealed the Constitution's 8th amendment that prohibited abortion. ■

The Grand Canal Dock area in Dublin represents Ireland's modern face. It has become known as "Silicon Docks" for it houses the headquarters of many high-tech companies.

FAUNA, FLORA, & CLIMATE

Ireland's climate is famously mild and wet, with rain falling somewhere almost every day of the year. In the west, on what locals euphemistically term "soft" summer days, it can seem as if most of it is falling on you. The prevailing damp westerly airstream off the Atlantic is what makes Ireland so beautifully green.

Ireland is like a great geological wheel, with a hub of carboniferous limestone filling the interior within a rim of ancient volcanic rock. You'll find schist and gneiss in western Connemara and parts of the far north, spectacular basalt formations along the Antrim coast, and granite along the north shore of Galway Bay, in west Donegal, and southwest of Dublin. The famed bogs that formed in the central region are still cut and milled for turf—as the Irish call their horticultural and fuel peat—but exploitation is in its final phase now (see pp. 254–255).

Ten thousand years ago the meltwaters of Ice Age glaciers heaped parts of the landscape with eskers (long ridges) and drumlins (round hillocks) of rubble, now greened over to form bumpy little hills and islets. All of these areas support a variety of wildlife (famously lacking in snakes), though Ireland's four-legged creatures—wild goats, hares, deer—can be difficult to spot. The spectacular seabird colonies of the west coast cliffs and islands are matched by tremendous gatherings of overwintering wildfowl on east coast estuaries such as Strangford Lough, east of Belfast, and the North Slobs mudflats and marshes near Wexford. It's the mountains and moorlands of Ireland that will give you the best opportunity to spot birds of prey, including hen harriers, peregrines, merlins, and wheeling buzzards. The boglands offer the chance to spot buntings and warblers, while along the hayfields around Killala Bay where Sligo meets Mayo, and in remote Inishowen in northern Donegal, you might just hear the grating *crex-crex* of the elusive corncrake.

As for wildflowers, you'll find beautiful pink bogbean, insect-eating sundews, and wonderfully colored rushes and grasses in the bogs, primroses in the narrow country lanes in springtime, and bloodred fuchsia in the hedges of the southwestern counties in summer. Ireland's showpiece for wildflowers, however, is the Burren in County Clare (see pp. 168–173), a unique environment of limestone pavement where acid- and lime-loving plants and Arctic and Mediterranean flowers abound. ∎

EXPERIENCE:

Conserving Resources

Over the past half century, intensive farming, greenbelt development, and neglect have damaged wildlife and despoiled vast acreages of bogs. But things are improving as government agencies and private organizations across the island move to place conservation at the top of the agenda.

The **Irish Wildlife Trust** *(iwt.ie)* offers many educational programs and volunteer activities for those wanting to pitch in. **The Conservation Volunteers** *(conservation volunteers.ie)* encourages people to get involved in local conservation projects such as saving wildflower seeds in County Clare's Burren region, tree-planting and hedge-laying in Galway, cutting back invasive rhododendron in Dublin, or carrying out plant and animal surveys in the wilds of Donegal.

▤ Blocks of turf, dug from the boglands of Achill Island, laid neatly in long rows to dry

HISTORY OF IRELAND

Ireland's spiritual influence and artistic achievement reached their zenith more than a thousand years ago, bolstered by a rich mythic tradition and a flowering of passionate Christianity. Echoes of that magnificence sustained the Irish over the ensuing centuries and through the long, bitter struggle for independence from the British. The stories of Ireland and Britain, uneasy neighbors and bedfellows, have been intimately bound up together for the past ten centuries.

Immemorial myth, that potent source of national identity and pride, has Ireland's ancient inhabitants, the Firbolgs, being overcome by a race of mystical and magical conquerors known as Tuatha de Danaan, the People of Danu, Mother of the Gods. This version of the island's story gets off to a flying start with tales of wooings, betrayals, battles, feasts, and mighty deeds of derring-do by heroes and heroines such as Fionn MacCumhaill (Finn McCool), Diarmuid and Gráinne (see p. 262), Deirdre of the Sorrows, and Cúchulainn (see pp. 334–335).

More prosaically, it was a hardy bunch of fishermen and food-gatherers who first crossed to the Antrim coast from Scotland about 10,000 years ago, at the end of the last Ice Age. Little is known about this thin population who made their settlement by lakeside and seashore.

By the time the first Celts from central Europe began to arrive around 500 B.C., Irish culture had progressed through Stone, Bronze, and Iron Ages that left the landscape scattered with splendid chambered tombs, stone circles, and field systems. Irish became the universal language in a country divided among rival noble families who elected their own kings from among themselves. Families lived in wooden homesteads surrounded by earth banks, well strengthened with stone walls. Land was held in common; cattle became the main measure of wealth, with cattle-raiding endemic. Warfare between family "kingdoms" was a way of life.

> 66 **The stories of Ireland and Britain, uneasy neighbors and bedfellows, have been intimately bound up together for the past ten centuries.** 99

Balance and a sense of justice were encouraged by the liberal set of rules known as Brehon Law—the experts who codified the law were known as brehons—by which society more or less abided.

Coming of Christianity

Into this fertile, vigorous society came Christianity, brought to Ireland by the itinerant preacher Patrick in A.D. 432. By now Ireland had divided into the four major kingdoms, or provinces, of Ulster (north), Connacht (west), Leinster (east), and Munster (south), each ruled by its own king. St. Patrick and the early Christian missionaries wisely decided to work with, not against, the established druidic religion of the Irish Celts. They built many of their churches and monasteries on sites already considered holy and showed respect for the leaders of Irish society. Their reward was to see Ireland embrace Christianity fervently.

Golden Age

Along with Christianity came literacy and a flowering of the arts. Monasteries became centers of culture, from which Irish monks went out to spread the word all over Europe and far beyond. Poetry, song, stone-carving, and the arts of jewelry and gold-working all flourished. The seventh and eighth centuries were Ireland's golden age, culminating in the production of such glorious works of art as the Ardagh Chalice and the Tara Brooch, both from the eighth century (now in the National Museum of Ireland–Archaeology, see pp. 56–59), and the incomparable Book

■ **Around Lough Gur lie the remains of buildings that span 5,000 years of human occupation.**

of Kells around 800 (which is now in Trinity College, Dublin, see pp. 54–55). The Vikings were unwelcome visitors from around that time onward; Brian Boru, High King of Ireland, finally defeated them and broke their power at the Battle of Clontarf in 1014. Another century was to pass before even more effective invaders began to cast their eyes across the Irish Sea.

Settlers from England

The Normans had occupied mainland Britain in 1066, but it took another hundred years for them to invade Ireland. They came to support Dermot MacMurrough, King of Leinster, who had been banished by Rory O'Connor, High King of Ireland (for stealing the wife of one of the king's friends). At first the Normans made a great show of force, building castles on land they seized. But after various military setbacks, with the passing of centuries and some intermarriage, they settled down—mostly in a strip of land around Dublin known as the Pale, defended with palings, or palisades—to a more or less neighborly accommodation with the Irish.

Repression & Rebellion

Fearing a Roman Catholic invasion of the mainland from Irish soil, King Henry VIII of England and then his daughter Queen Elizabeth I set the fire under the cauldron of Ireland in the 16th century with a series of punitive taxes, confiscations, and legal exclusions of influential Irish Catholic families. In 1541, Henry had himself proclaimed King of Ireland and unleashed a wave of repression that in its turn bred resentment and rebellion. The Catholic countries of Europe, keen to blunt the supremacy of England on the high seas and to bring the newly Protestantized country back into the Roman Catholic fold, saw Catholic Ireland as a potential springboard for the invasion and subjection of the British mainland. A mixed Spanish and Italian landing on the Dingle Peninsula in 1580 was defeated with savagery by Elizabeth's Crown forces, and more repressions followed. Repression bred rebellions, each put down with the mailed fist. The last uprising of this period, an insurrection headed by Hugh O'Neill, Earl of Tyrone, and backed by 4,500 Spanish soldiers, was crushed in 1601.

■ **Oliver Cromwell earned an everlasting reputation for brutality for his savage repression of Irish insurgents.**

By 1610, the leaders of the great families of Ulster had fled overseas, and in what was known as the Plantation of Ulster, Protestant farmers from Scotland and England were encouraged with grants of money and land to settle all over the north of Ireland in order to keep land and influence out of Catholic hands.

If things were bad for Irish Catholics, they got a great deal worse in the mid-17th century when sparks from the English Civil War ignited more trouble in Ireland. After ten years of confused fighting, Oliver Cromwell arrived with his battle-hardened Ironsides and instituted a repression that put even the Elizabethan brutalities in the shade. Towns such as Drogheda and Wexford were sacked; rebels were executed en masse. Catholic landowners all over the country were stripped of their property and rights and driven west across the River Shannon "to Hell or Connacht," to the poorest land in the west, while "planters" took their place in the fat lands of the east and the midlands.

From Penal Times to Swaggering Dan

The infamous penal times continued through the late 18th century. After the Cromwellian repressions, there was a surge of Catholic hope when King James II, the Roman Catholic monarch deposed from the English throne, tried to gain support for his cause in Ireland. Though James was defeated at the Battle of the Boyne on July 12, 1690, his conqueror, King William III, seemed to hold out promise of better and more equal opportunities for Irish Catholics. But William soon went back on his word, and within a few years the miserable penal laws had been introduced.

The penal laws enshrined Catholic disenfranchisement; no Catholic was allowed to vote, to educate his children as Catholics, or to hold property. The intention of the penal laws was clear—to perform a kind of ethnic cleansing on the Catholic majority by squeezing them out of political, social, and economic life. The ban that really hurt, though, was that on celebrating Mass. Roman Catholicism became a clandestine faith, practiced in out-of-the-way places, its priests in fear of death, its adherents increasingly politicized through poverty and desperation. Risings came and went, each harshly suppressed. Rebel groups formed in secret, plotting insurrection. The United Irishmen mounted the final rebellion of the 18th century in 1798, bolstered by 1,100 Frenchmen who landed at Killala Bay on the Sligo/Mayo border. It started successfully, with a crushing defeat of the English at Castlebar, but ended, as all the other uprisings had, in defeat for the rebels and death for their leaders.

Heritage Sites

The best way to enrich your understanding of Ireland's long and extraordinary history is to relive it at the country's Heritage Sites. Ranging in date from the end of the last Ice Age to as recently as the 20th century, Heritage Sites include everything from Stone Age monuments and early Christian monasteries to looming castles and national parks.

Ireland's **National Monuments Service** (archaeology.ie) provides a guide to nearly 1,000 historical places and buildings around the country. To find out which sites are open to the public, visit **Heritage Ireland** (heritageireland.ie). There you can also purchase a Heritage Card, which allows for unlimited free admission to most of Ireland's Heritage Sites for one year from the date of purchase.

Intolerance of Catholics as a general practice had been softening toward the end of the 18th century. The penal laws were not being applied as rigorously as they had been at the outset. In 1782, a qualified parliamentary independence was granted, but the 1798 Rising put an end to all that. The new century opened with the 1801 Act of Union that abolished the Irish parliament and imposed direct rule from London. Discrimination against Catholics was tightened, not to be relaxed again until the forceful Kerry lawyer Daniel O'Connell won his famous long-drawn-out struggle to force Westminster to attend to the grievances of the Irish poor. "Swaggering Dan," or "the Liberator" as his followers styled him, finally gained a seat in Parliament as a Catholic MP (member of Parliament) in 1828.

The Great Famine

The history of 19th-century Ireland—and 20th-century Ireland, too—was shaped by the overarching tragedy of the Great Famine of 1845 to 1849. The potato fungus *Phytophthora infestans* struck a country with a population of nine million, the majority of them poor, illiterate peasants living in enormous families on tiny patches of rented land in remote regions, entirely dependent on the potato for food. When the fungus turned their potatoes to black slime in the ground four seasons out of five, they had no defense against the disaster.

   The British government's response has frequently been condemned as cruelly indifferent, even deliberately so. Initially, in fact, measures were taken to relieve the famine. Food depots were established, corn was put on the market, hospitals were opened, and relief works started. But the authorities were soon overwhelmed by the scale of the catastrophe, the sheer numbers of people involved, the lack of infrastructure—hospitals, relief centers, port facilities, even roads—within rural Ireland, and the rapidity with which

■ During the famine, overcrowded workhouses and hospitals turned away the starving.

disease and death spread. A hard-hearted change of policy after the first year of the famine saw the government at Westminster throw much of the responsibility for dealing with the disaster onto the shoulders of local Poor Law Unions, charitable organizations, and individual landlords.

It is tempting today to see all the landlords as absentee exploiters, feathering their own nests and harshly evicting those tenants who failed to pay their rent. Some certainly fitted that bill. Others, such as the Marquess of Sligo, however, suspended rents and sold their own possessions to aid their tenants. But it was the peasants of Ireland who paid the highest price for the government's past policy and present pragmatism. Workhouses and temporary hospitals were filled to overflowing. Sick and starving people were turned away. Typhus, cholera, relapsing fever, and diarrhea spread like wildfire through the crowded cabins and hovels of the rural poor and through the unsanitary streets of the towns. Families

> **The history of 19th-century Ireland—and 20th-century Ireland, too—was shaped by the overarching tragedy of the Great Famine of 1845 to 1849.**

died where they lay together, unattended by doctor or priest. It is impossible to collect accurate figures, but a million men, women, and children probably died during the five years of the Great Famine—either from disease or literally starving to death.

Emigration & Anger

Emigration, which had been a means of escape from poverty for the rural Irish for a century or more, swelled to a flood during and after the famine. Anyone who could scrape up the price of a ticket boarded one of the emigration ships—leaky, dirty old buckets as many of them were—in hopes of a better life elsewhere, especially in mainland Britain, the U.S., Canada, and Australia. The Irish diaspora spread all over the world during the following century, draining the young and active lifeblood of Ireland, especially in the poor rural west. Today the population of the Irish Republic is about 4.8 million—just over half its pre-famine level.

As the emigrants picked up the threads of strange new lives, powerful feelings of attachment to their homeland were mingled in many cases with bitterness and anger toward Britain, the country they held responsible for their plight. This mixture of sentiment and politics grew stronger as time went on. It was to fuel the activities of 19th-century anti-British organizations such as the Fenian Brotherhood, established in the U.S. in the 1850s, and sees its expression today in support among many expatriate Irish communities for extremist causes in Northern Ireland.

Land Reform & Home Rule

As for the movement for political change in post-famine Ireland, it continued down its well-worn track of clandestine groupings organizing boycotts, sporadic attacks on landlords and their agents, and a string of brief and unsuccessful risings. But the grievances of poor Catholic Ireland were coming more and more to the fore in mainstream politics. Michael Davitt's nonviolent Land League movement eventually forced a Land Act, passed in 1881, which ensured fair rents and security of tenure for tenants. And the ever more vociferous Home Rule movement found a powerful mouthpiece in one of the Land Act's keenest supporters, Charles Stewart Parnell (see sidebar, left), heir to Daniel O'Connell's crown as champion of the Catholic poor.

Parnell was brought down by a sexual scandal in 1890, but the impetus he gave to the Home Rule movement meant that the government could no longer consign the issue to the back burner. As the new century dawned, militant pressure for independence from Britain grew irresistible. Yet in Northern Ireland the Protestant people, descendants of the 17th-century planters with a clear interest in preserving the status quo, were lining up behind charismatic Dublin MP Sir Edward Carson to repudiate the notion of political severance from the United Kingdom. Their stance was made far worse in the eyes of many Northern Catholics by Carson's decision to agree to the establishment of an Ulster that excluded three of the nine counties of the historic province. Catholic voters were in a majority in Monaghan, Cavan, and Donegal, and Protestant dominance of those three counties looked uncertain. So they were "let go" to the putative independent free state of southern Ireland. Their Protestant inhabitants were not happy to be included in what appeared to them a hostile and backward country.

"Uncrowned King"

Charles Stewart Parnell (1846–1891) was a wealthy Protestant landowner and MP. Although he had little in common with his Irish Catholic countrymen, Parnell was nevertheless a keen proponent of land redistribution, which he felt was the first step toward Irish self-government. His denunciation of the 1882 assassination of two British officials helped subordinate radical nationalist factions to his own more moderate fight for Home Rule. Under his leadership, the Land League became the wildly popular Irish National League, while Parnell himself was familiarly known as Ireland's "uncrowned king."

Home Rule–minded Catholics in Antrim, Derry (called Londonderry by Protestants), Tyrone, Fermanagh, Armagh, and Down, the Six Counties of the proposed Ulster, resented being severed from the political freedom that their southern brethren seemed about to enjoy. The seeds of cross-border bitterness and resentment were sown.

A compromise Home Rule Act, excluding the Ulster counties of Antrim, Londonderry, Tyrone, Fermanagh, Armagh, and Down, was passed in 1914. But this effective partition of Ireland was then immediately suspended upon the outbreak of World War I. This was the final straw as far as radical Home Rule advocates were concerned. They drew together under the umbrella of the Irish Republican Brotherhood (first formed in the 1850s in the aftermath of the Great Famine) and began preparations for an armed rebellion.

The Easter Rising

The Easter Rising of 1916 was planned by a small group of people dedicated to gaining independence from Britain. They were organized and led by socialist trade unionist James Connolly and Christian schoolteacher Padraic Pearse. They argued, philosophized, organized, and drilled their small bands of volunteers, looking for

Dublin's post office building became a powerful symbol of freedom after the Easter Rising.

the right moment to act. "England's difficulty is Ireland's opportunity," ran the republican mantra. On the eve of the planned uprising, the activists dispatched Sir Roger Casement to Germany, looking for support. Casement's assessment was that they could expect no help and should call off the rising. But they went ahead anyway, hoping for simultaneous action from 10,000 sympathizers all over Ireland.

Owing to confusion, poor coordination, and lack of communication among widely scattered groups, only 2,000 rebels joined the rising, with almost all the action taking place in Dublin. The initial action that Easter Monday morning took the authorities by surprise, and about 1,000 armed insurgents installed themselves in various key administrative buildings across the city. Standing on the steps under the portico of the General Post Office (GPO) on O'Connell Street, Pearse read out the rebels' proclamation: "We hereby proclaim the Irish Republic as a Sovereign Independent State, and we pledge our lives and the lives of our comrades in arms to the cause of its freedom, of its welfare and of its exaltation among the nations."

> **In 1921 the Anglo-Irish Treaty put an end to the fighting and established an independent Irish Free State that excluded the contentious six counties of Northern Ireland.**

Fine words and fine aspirations—which were soon crushed. The rebels had the bravery but not the resources to withstand the British Army for long, once it had recovered from its shock and rolled its troops and hardware into action. A week of bombardment, and many deaths on both sides, saw the GPO shattered by shellfire and the activists forced to surrender. If the British government had played it cool from then on, benefiting from a wartime public mood in Ireland that initially saw the rebels as misguided hotheads—if not downright traitors—rather than heroes, a lot of subsequent bloodshed would have been avoided. Instead they enshrined the insurgents as martyrs by shooting 15 of the leaders, drawing out the executions over the following weeks in a manner that outraged decent opinion.

Two Wars

Republican sentiment coalesced around Sinn Féin (Ourselves Alone), a small political sect that quickly grew to wield real power. Immediately after the end of World War I in 1919, with half its MPs in jail, it forced Ireland to the top of the British government's agenda again by declaring independence, forming its own parliament under Eamon de Valera, and making a demand that Westminster could not agree to: a withdrawal of all British troops from Ireland. There followed two years of war between the official military forces of Britain and the irregular battalions of the nationalists' Irish Republican Army (IRA), of bombs and ambushes, interrogations, and ransackings. During this period the British paramilitary force known as the Black and Tans gained notoriety for its brutality, and republican leader Michael Collins developed from a dashing, romantic Robin Hood–style guerrilla fighter into a charismatic political figure. In 1921 the Anglo-Irish Treaty put an end to the fighting and established an independent Irish Free State that excluded the contentious six counties of Northern Ireland.

Now came a split between followers of Collins, reluctantly prepared to accept the partition of Ireland—and even the prospect of basing some British troops there in time of war— and the less accommodating republicans behind de Valera, who held out for a united Ireland and denial of all military

concessions to Britain. The Civil War that broke out between the two factions in July 1922 claimed the lives of thousands more Irish men and women, including Collins himself, generated internecine bitterness that lasts to this day, and ended in May 1923 with defeat for the hard-line republicans.

From Free State to Republic: Decades in a Rural Backwater

Eamon de Valera went to jail, and the brand-new Irish nation began to lick its wounds. In 1924, de Valera was released, and in 1926, he quit Sinn Féin and started his own Fianna Fail (Soldiers of Destiny) party. Six years later, Fianna Fail came to power, and de Valera started a mammoth term as Taoiseach (prime minister) that would last until well after World War II. The Free State renamed itself Eire, a good indication of the folksy-nationalist direction in which it was heading—a direction inspired by de Valera's vision of "a land whose countryside would be bright with cozy homesteads, whose fields and villages would be joyous with the sounds of industry, with the rompings of sturdy children, the contests of athletic youths and the laughter of comely maidens, whose firesides would be forums for the wisdom of serene old age." Fianna Fail abolished the oath of allegiance to the Crown and claimed sovereignty over the North

■ In the 1970s, IRA terrorist attacks (and the ensuing loyalist reprisals) rocked Belfast.

(a bone of contention not resolved until the Good Friday Agreement of 1998; see p. 289). Meanwhile the Roman Catholic Church tightened its grasp on all aspects of life south of the border. In the North, Protestantism stayed in the ascendancy while the economy took a nosedive along with the rest of the industrial world.

Eire declared itself neutral for the duration of World War II, though thousands of men and women from both sides of the border volunteered to fight in the Allied cause. Belfast was badly bombed—in one terrible night in April 1941 more than 700 civilians were killed. In 1949, Eire—now calling itself the Republic of Ireland—left the British Commonwealth. Through the 1950s it stagnated, stuck in an agricultural and social backwater, with increasing censorship of books, films, and plays by a church and state unwilling to come to terms with the modern world. Emigration soared as younger Irish people left to find better-paid work and greater artistic, sexual, and moral freedom than small-time farming or backwoods town life in Ireland could provide. To many Protestants and Catholics north of the border, too, life in the Republic seemed backward and unappealing.

Progress in the Republic

In the 1960s, the Republic became a more energetic and outward-looking place under the leadership of Taoiseach Sean Leamass. In the 1970s, the country joined the European Union and began to benefit from a flow of economic development

Two Bloody Sundays

Two separate incidents have each come to be known as "Bloody Sunday." On November 21, 1920, during the Irish War of Independence, IRA units killed 14 British undercover agents in Dublin. Shortly afterward, 14 civilians attending a Gaelic football match at Croke Park in the city were killed by the Royal Irish Constabulary, aided by Auxiliary and Black and Tan units of the British forces. In the evening three IRA prisoners in Dublin Castle were killed by their interrogators.

Derry's notorious "Bloody Sunday" took place on January 30, 1972, when out-of-control Parachute Regiment

soldiers, in an action subsequently labeled by British prime minister David Cameron as "unjustified and unjustifiable," shot 26 civilians at a civil rights march in the city—14 of whom died, then or later.

In the early 1980s, the historically charged term would give the Dublin band U2 the title for a globally popular song: "Sunday Bloody Sunday" was inspired by Ireland's Troubles and by singer Bono's early experience of watching his parents go to churches of different denominations throughout his childhood.

money and a healthy agricultural economy. The 1980s saw a faltering in progress and a rise in emigration, but the following decade became a gallop to economic glory on the back of the Celtic Tiger and a remarkable boom in tourism and popularity around the world. The deep recession of the early 21st century (see p. 16) knocked confidence badly—but the support of the European Union together with national policies that included low corporate tax rates encouraged foreign investments and Ireland's economy began to grow rapidly once again, as it attracted more and more multinational corporations.

■ Tibetan spiritual leader the Dalai Lama leads a walk across the Peace Bridge, Derry, during his visit to Northern Ireland in 2013.

Northern Ireland Through the Troubles

As for Northern Ireland in the 1970s, '80s, and '90s, rarely can a country have undergone such a thoroughly publicized roller-coaster ride through such depths of misery and despair. Discrimination against Roman Catholics in the workplace, in housing, and in health, education, and social services had been enshrined since 1921—and for centuries before that, too. The civil rights movements of the late 1960s aimed to force change through popular protest, in as peaceful a way as possible. But with so much mutual mistrust and bitterness, contempt, and bigotry on hand, the marches became the flash point for full-blown civil strife. From the moment in August 1969 that British troops were deployed on the streets of Londonderry and Belfast, the Troubles were on every television set and radio. They were to stay center stage, making Northern Ireland a byword for sectarian hatred and terrorism for almost 30 years (see pp. 286–289), until the historic paramilitary cease-fires and the signing of the Good Friday Agreement in 1998.

No one would claim that all the problems of the North have been solved, particularly in the political climate of uncertainty that was created by the June 23, 2016, referendum, when 51.9 percent of voters in the U.K. supported Brexit, their country's exit from the European Union. Northern Ireland is doubtlessly undergoing a series of positive changes; people of differing political traditions and loyalties are learning to live together. The country has become an appealing tourist destination once again due, in part, to the substantial investments made to valorize the territory but thanks also to the breathtaking beauty of the landscape that can be seen more and more often as the set for movies and television series. ■

FOOD & DRINK

Irish food was once famous for its plainness, but affluence and tourism have changed all that. In the 1990s, the number of restaurants serving international cuisine—and fast-food outlets, too—witnessed phenomenal growth. Homespun Irish dishes fell into disfavor. Recently that trend has reversed with the onset of a new sophistication and a more demanding class of visitor.

Schools such as the Ballymaloe Cookery School in County Cork offer an array of courses in Irish cuisine.

Today's young chefs use the very best that Ireland has to offer, including wild Atlantic salmon, mountain lamb, shellfish, and organically grown vegetables and herbs. They take pleasure in adding a touch of modern magic to such traditional Irish fare as *champ* (mashed potatoes and scallions), *drisheen* (black pudding), *colcannon* (potatoes, cabbage, onions, and cream), *brack* (fruity tea bread), or the famous Irish stew that can have pretty much

anything in it along with the four vital ingredients: neck of mutton, potatoes, onions, and a pinch of serendipity.

Cooking schools are flourishing—the Allen family's Ballymaloe House *(ballymaloe.com)*, County Cork; Catherine Fulvio's Ballynocken Cookery School *(thecookeryschool.ie)*, County Wicklow; and Belle Isle *(belle-isle.com)* near Enniskillen, County Fermanagh, are three of the best known. Celebrity chefs such as Paul

Flynn and Neven Maguire, TV shows like *The Great Irish Bake-Off*, and food festivals such as the Waterford Festival of Food have all helped popularize Irish cooking.

INSIDER TIP:

For Irish boxty, stir eggs and milk into a "well" of flour and salt. Add mashed potato, herbs, and seasoning for a pancake batter, with sliced mushrooms, leeks, and spring onions on top. Mmmm!

—CHEF NEVEN MAGUIRE
Head chef and proprietor of the MacNean House and Restaurant.

Visitors with their preconceptions still intact are always surprised to learn that the Irish national drink is not Guinness but tea. God alone knows how much tea is drunk in Ireland every day, but it would probably fill Boston Harbor. In the cities these days you can also get a very respectable cup of coffee, from cappuccino to espresso with all the continental variations in between. As far as alcoholic drink is concerned, there is a small but good selection of Irish whiskeys (County Antrim's Bushmills and Jameson's of Cork head the smoother brands, generally sweeter than their Scottish counterparts) and a growing number of "real ales" or unpasteurized,

unfiltered beers brewed by small, independent breweries and served from a hand pump.

But it's the famous strong black stout with its creamy head, poured with ritual slowness from a tap rather than a bottle, that rules the pub roost. Murphy's (favored in Cork) is sweeter, Guinness heavier and more bitter. What the Irish tell foreigners about Guinness is absolutely true: If you have tried it in your own country and disliked it, give it another go when you visit Ireland. Guinness drunk in an Irish pub is one of the world's most nectarous delights.

■ **On a cold Irish night, a pint of Guinness and a roaring fire always warm the heart.**

Top Food & Drink Guides

Time was, not so long ago, when Irish cuisine was the object of suspicion, if not outright derision. Bacon, cabbage, potatoes, and then what? But that's all in the past. These days Ireland is well known for its great food and drink, and there are plenty of resources to guide you to the best the country has to offer.

One of the most reliable is **Georgina Campbell's Ireland** *(ireland-guide.com)*, an online guide to Ireland's restaurants,

pubs, and hotels. Search for places to eat by location, budget, and dietary needs.

An online guide to the best in Irish cuisine is **John and Sally McKennas' Guides** *(guides.ie)*, which is styled as "a local guide to local places." **The Taste of Ireland** *(tasteofireland.com)* is also full of tips. **The Taste**'s website *(thetaste.ie)* offers suggestions about nightlife and dining and has a section dedicated to traditional recipes.

ARTS & CULTURE

Novelists, playwrights, poets, short-story writers; rock bands, fiddle players, opera stars, singers; TV soap stars and comedians; film directors and actors; dancers, painters, street performers ... Ireland has them all, in numbers and of a quality that would be the envy of a country ten times the size. James Joyce, W. B. and Jack Yeats, U2, Enya, and Riverdance merely scratch the surface.

The oral tradition of Irish folktales dates back 2,000 years or more and is embedded deeply in the national sense of identity. It's not by random selection that the influential traditional music group De Dannan named itself after a mythical race of magic makers or that the cultural activities center in Mullaghbane in County Armagh is named Tí Chulainn, the House of Chulainn, after the legendary blacksmith of nearby Slieve Gullion mountain. Such names, and the tales that are associated with them, still carry considerable power.

The Mighty Deeds of Fionn MacCumhaill

The best known Irish hero must be Fionn MacCumhaill—Finn McCool—not in fact a giant, although his mighty deeds make him seem one. Stories about him began to be told in the fourth and fifth centuries. Fionn's most famous act was to establish the band of knightlike heroes known as the Fianna, the Warriors. Entry requirements were tough. Anyone wanting to join the Fianna had to be able to defend himself against nine spears hurled simultaneously, while buried up to his waist in the ground and armed only with a hazel stick. Candidates also had to prove themselves capable of escaping a band of the Fianna while running through the woods, without cracking any twig or having a single hair dislodged from their braids. While running full tilt they must also leap over a head-high stick, duck under a knee-high one, and pick a thorn out of the sole of their foot. And, of course, each aspirant member had to show himself brave and honest, while also producing perfectly polished poetry. There were not many Fianna.

> **The oral tradition of Irish folktales dates back 2,000 years or more and is embedded deeply in the national sense of identity.**

Perhaps the best tale of all concerns Fionn MacCumhaill's love in old age for the beautiful Gráinne, daughter of Cormac, the High King of Tara (see p. 262), and his pursuit of her after she eloped with handsome young Fianna member Diarmuid. This is a great chase saga, and you'll find rocks and hollows known as "Diarmuid and Gráinne's Bed" all over Ireland. Fionn got his woman in the end, but only after wreaking his revenge on the dying Diarmuid (see pp. 214–215) on Benbulben Mountain.

From Telling to Writing

Tales like these were the bedrock on which Ireland's long-standing tradition of fire-side storytelling was based. Literacy, education, and modern ways of entertainment have all but eclipsed such domestic tale-spinning, although it is reviving in a new generation of "*cèilidh* houses" in which people gather to swap songs and stories. But when this lyrical talent with words hits the page, it deepens into a characteristic Irish magic. Ireland has produced four winners of the Nobel Prize for Literature— William Butler Yeats (1923), George Bernard Shaw (1925), Samuel Beckett (1969), and Seamus Heaney (1995)—a truly astonishing accolade for such a small country. The writer whom most regard as the greatest of the lot, James Joyce (1882–1941), never won a Nobel Prize: His output was far too controversial. But it was Joyce with his dense, convoluted, and brilliant 1922 masterwork *Ulysses*—unbelievably daring with its sexual frankness and open challenge to the "Celtic Twilight" quaintness of most Irish writing of the time—who set the stage for the modern novel.

James Joyce may head Ireland's roll call of 20th-century literary genius, but it bulges with talent. Among short-story writers of note are Liam O'Flaherty (1896–1984), Sean

■ **Musicians take the floor in a pub in Galway.**

O'Faolain (1900–1991), Frank O'Connor (1903–1966), with his superb stories of the 1919–1921 War of Independence such as "Guests of the Nation," and the Kerry pub owner and gentle humorist John B. Keane (1928–2002). Older-guard novelists who have caught the nuances of Irish life include Brian Moore (1921–1999), Edna O'Brien (born 1932), the subtle John McGahern (1934–2006), and the masterfully funny Flann O'Brien (1911–1966), pen name of Brian O'Nolan.

Struggle for Literary Freedom

These groundbreakers did not have it easy in the repressive cultural atmosphere of the Ireland of their day. Edna O'Brien's 1960 novel, *The Country Girls,* was banned for encouraging immorality, while John McGahern's novel *The Dark,* treating as it did homosexual child abuse, was likewise banned in 1966. James Joyce himself wrote and published *Ulysses* abroad in self-imposed artistic exile—publication in its home country of what many regard as the most influential novel ever written would have been unthinkable. When Joyce died in 1941, his countrymen would have to wait two more decades to buy his masterpiece in Ireland.

Later writers to benefit from the freedom of expression won by these trailblazers include Roddy Doyle (born 1958) with *The Commitments, The Snapper, The Van,* and *The Guts* his sharp working-class Dublin novels; Eoin McNamee (born 1960) with the dark Troubles novel *Resurrection Man;* Frank McCourt (1930–2009), awarded the Pulitzer Prize in 1997 for *Angela's Ashes;* John Banville (born 1945), whose novel *The Sea* won the 2005 Man Booker Prize for Fiction; Anne Enright (born 1962), another Booker winner in 2007 with *The Gathering;* and Anna Burns (born 1962), the first Northern Irish author to win the Man Booker prize, in 2018, for her novel, *Milkman.*

The biographies of three native Irish-speakers from County Kerry's remote Blasket islands—Tomás O'Crohan's *The Islandman* (1929), Maurice O'Sullivan's *Twenty Years A-Growing* (1933), and Peig Sayers's *Peig* (1936)—represented an astonishing flowering of talent within a tiny, culturally isolated, and largely illiterate community.

The Irish Renaissance

Alongside the political struggle for self-government that defined the late 19th and early 20th centuries, Ireland witnessed the flowering of a movement that came to be known as the Irish Renaissance or Celtic Revival. Inspired by the folktales, legends, and mythology of ancient Ireland, poet W. B. Yeats and young dramatists like Sean O'Casey and J. M. Synge revitalized popular interest in traditional Irish culture and language and sparked the development of a distinct national identity. Dublin's famed Abbey Theatre, which produced plays that helped establish Ireland's literary reputation, was inaugurated by Yeats and playwright Lady Augusta Gregory in 1904.

Poetry—From Yeats to Heaney

As for poetry—the line from William Butler Yeats (1865–1939) through Patrick Kavanagh (1904–1967) to Seamus Heaney (1939–2013) glints with genius. Much of Yeats's poetry is now undergoing a recession in popularity; many see him as important as much for his catalytic effect on the Gaelic Revival of the late 19th century, and his articulation of an Irish sense of nationhood, as for his actual verses. In fact, the poet's painter brother Jack (1871–1957) is seen nowadays as far more of an innovator, with his vivid expressionist art so profoundly influenced by the landscapes of Sligo where the Yeats boys spent much of their childhood.

Kavanagh's poetry, expressive of the backbreaking work and rural poverty—financial and spiritual—of his native County Monaghan, cut away the myth of the dignified, happy peasant Ireland so dear to Eamon de Valera's heart and opened the way for the uncomplicated yet profound insights of Heaney's work.

Heaney, Nobel Laureate and world-acclaimed poet, was a man of the people, his melodious facility with language grounded in the earthy images and dialect words of his native County Derry. He found ways of exploring the tensions and anxieties of the Troubles without climbing onto an overtly political soapbox, and he left a legacy of poetic cameos of rural life and journeys through the nature of faith and humanity. When he died in August 2013 there was a spontaneous outpouring of grief throughout Ireland at the loss of a warm man, a poetic genius who took time with everyone he met.

■ **Poet Seamus Heaney**

The Stage . . .

Among Irish playwrights to have influenced the world stage are household names such as Oscar Wilde (1854–1900), George Bernard Shaw (1856–1950), Sean O'Casey (1880–1964), with his great trilogy *Shadow of a Gunman, Juno and the Paycock,* and *The Plough and the Stars,* the irreverent and tumultous Brendan Behan (1923-1964), and the man who became James Joyce's secretary in 1932 before finding one or two things to say on his own account—Samuel Beckett (1906–1989), author of the world's least understood famous play, *Waiting for Godot.*

. . . and the Screen

The classic early Irish film documentary, Robert Flaherty's (1884–1951) *Man of Aran,* came out in 1934. But it wasn't until the establishment of the Irish Film Board in 1981 that Ireland really came into its own as a filmmaking country. Neil Jordan (born 1950) has triumphed with a tale of an IRA man tormented over his execution of a hostage (*The Crying Game,* 1992), a biography of War of Independence leader (*Michael Collins,* 1996, starring Liam Neeson), and an adaptation of Patrick McCabe's fable of small-town oppression (*The Butcher Boy,* 1998).

Meanwhile, Jim Sheridan's (born 1949) star rose to international acclaim with his version of Christy Brown's *My Left Foot* (1989), starring Daniel Day-Lewis; John B. Keane's sardonic rural parable *The Field* (1990), filmed in the spectacular mountains around Killary Harbour on the Mayo/Galway border; and *In the Name of the Father* (1993), the story of the unjust imprisonment of the Guildford Four for an IRA bombing they did not commit, also starring Day-Lewis and partly set in the grim surroundings of Dublin's Kilmainham Gaol (see pp. 75–79).

Three sprightly, very funny films were made of Roddy Doyle's novels, *The Commitments* by Alan Parker in 1991, and *The Snapper* (1993) and *The Van* (1996), both by

Stephen Frears. Director John Carney's independent movie, *Once* (2006), was filmed in the streets of Dublin and despite its limited budget, it received great acclaim. Ken Loach's movie about the Irish War of Independence, *The Wind that Shakes the Barley* (2006), won the Palme d'Or at the Cannes film festival. Meanwhile Hollywood has embraced the photogenic nature of Ireland's landscape—Mel Gibson filmed some "Scottish" scenes for *Braveheart* (1995) around Trim in County Meath, while the beaches of County Wexford took a pounding during Steven Spielberg's 1997 D-Day epic, *Saving Private Ryan*. In more recent years, the wild landscapes of Northern Ireland were home to the warring kingdoms of the television series *Game of Thrones* (2011–2019) and the small, unspoiled island of Skelling Michael off the coast of Kerry was the set of a number of scenes from the *Star Wars* movies, *The Force Awakens* (2015) and *The Last Jedi* (2017).

Irish as She Is Spoken & Played

The Irish language, after a post-famine decline to the point where barely one in ten could speak it, has undergone a revival thanks to its place in the school curriculum. These days, while only 3 percent of people in the Irish Republic use Gaelic as their first language, about 30 percent are fluent, and most educated people have at least a smattering. The language's strongholds—including west Donegal, northwest Mayo, Connemara and the Aran Islands, and west Kerry—are termed Gaeltacht areas and receive subsidies to prop up their Gaelic-speaking communities. That's where you are most likely to hear Gaelic, although you'll read it all over the Republic in the form of place-names on bilingual road signs. Connemara's Radio na Gaeltachta and Teilifís (TV) na Ghaeilge, cater specifically to Gaelic-speakers.

The revival of the language is one symbol of pride in Irish nationhood. Another is the huge popularity of traditional Irish games such as hurling and Gaelic football, administered by the powerful, and chiefly Catholic, Gaelic Athletic Association (see sidebar below). You'll see children playing with hurley (wooden stick) and sliotar (leather ball) in

EXPERIENCE: Attending a Gaelic Athletic Match

Founded in 1884, the Gaelic Athletic Association (GAA; *gaa.ie*) ensures that traditional Irish sports survive and thrive. Two sports dominate its calendar—Gaelic football and hurling. Gaelic football is a superfast, thrilling, and passionately supported game in which the 15 players of each team run and score with the ball in hand or at foot. In hurling, the oldest team sport in Europe, the *sliotar* or ball travels at ferocious speed, propelled by a thwack of the *camán* or hurley (stick made of ash wood). Players of both games, who are all amateurs, must be extremely brave, quick, and determined. Crowds are noisy,

knowledgeable, and ready to cheer (and sometimes jeer) their local heroes. Dublin's **Croke Park** *(Jones Rd., Dublin 3, tel 01/819-2300, crokepark.ie)* is the home of the GAA and site of many great matches, including the All-Ireland finals in September, when the national champions from the island's 32 counties are crowned. "Croker" (in Dublinese) is also home to the **GAA Museum** *(crokepark.ie/gaa-museum, $ museum only, $$ stadium tour)*, dedicated to the culture and history of Gaelic games, as well as the **Ericsson Skyline** *($$$)* the highest public roof terrace that offers views of the city.

■ Blood, guts, and determination: Cork and Clare hurlers battle for All-Ireland glory.

most town parks on weekends. However, this traditionalism hasn't prevented soccer from becoming a ruling passion throughout Ireland, with the Republic's team reaching the World Cup finals of 1990, 1994, and 2002, and only failing to qualify for the 2010 tournament because of France's infamously disputed "Hand of Gaul" goal.

Another very popular pastime around south Armagh and in rural County Cork—to name it formally a "sport" might be stretching a point—is road bowling, in which players have to project an iron ball along the road for an agreed distance (up to a couple of miles in some cases) using as few throws as possible. If, on your travels, you find an informal roadblock set up, the chances are that one of these keenly contested matches is going on. Take the opportunity and hop out of your car to see a very Irish bit of sport.

On the Horses

Big bets can be laid at a road bowling match, but not as big as when thousands of people gather for horse racing, Ireland's grand sporting passion. The Curragh in County Kildare is the place to go (see p. 94), but you have your pick of nearly 30 courses and dozens of meetings countrywide, from the thrill of Laytown Races on the beach near Drogheda and the genial holiday atmosphere of Galway Races to the "dukes-and-dustmen" democracy of the Irish Derby at the Curragh in June.

A FESTIVALS SAMPLING

Specific dates can vary from year to year. Consult *ireland.com/events* for details.

■ Dublin bursts into color on March 17, with the capital's world-famous St. Patrick's Day Parade.

January
New Year's Day Festival—Marching bands from around the world convene on Dublin. *visitdublin.com*

March
St. Patrick's Day, March 17—The world's favorite party throughout Ireland, but Dublin hosts the biggie. *stpatricksday.ie*

April
City of Belfast Spring Fair—Magnificent floral displays go on show. *belfastcity.gov.uk*

May
Fleadh Nua, Ennis, late May—The cream of Irish traditional music and dance is in Clare. *Tel 065/682-4276, fleadhnua.com*

June
Bloomsday, June 16—A literary Dublin pub crawl in commemoration of Leopold Bloom, hero of *Ulysses. bloomsdayfestival.ie*
Cork Midsummer Festival, late June—Ten days of arts, dance, drama, music, and film. *corkmidsummer.com*
Irish Derby, late June—Lords and layabouts rub shoulders at the Curragh for Irish racing's Big Day Out. *Tel 045/441-205, curragh.ie*

July
Orangemen's Day, July 12—With flute and drum, Protestants in Belfast and throughout Northern Ireland celebrate the victory of "King Billy," William III, at the Battle of the Boyne in 1690. *visitbelfast.com*

July/August
Galway Races *(tel 091/700-100, galwayraces .com)* and **Galway Arts Festival** *(tel 091/509-700, giaf.ie)*—Fun at the track spills over into music, theater, and films around the city.

September
Lisdoonvarna Matchmaking Festival—In county Clare, a chance for single men and women to get together via expert advice. *Tel 065/707-4005, matchmakerireland.com*
Fringe Festival—Theater, live art, dance, and music in the streets of Dublin. *Tel 01/670-6106, fringefest.com*

October
Kinsale Gourmet Festival, mid-October—A celebration of food in a beautiful County Cork coastal location. *Tel 087/167-1004, kinsalerestaurants.com*

November
Wexford Festival Opera, late October/ early November—Some of the great names of opera perform in front of a highly enthusiastic audience. *Tel 053/912-2144, wexfordopera.com*

December
Galway Continental Christmas Market, mid-December—Crafts, live music, and good cheer in Eyre Square and around. *christmasmarketgalway.com*
Dingle Wren, December 26—Boisterous fun in Dingle, with extravagant costumes and wild music. *Tel 066/915-1188, dingle-peninsula.ie*

Traditional Music—Alive & Kicking

Of all branches of art, it's the country's traditional music that most ostensibly carries the flag for Irish culture today—that infectious, irresistible forward rush of tunes that were originally created simply to help dancers keep in time but proved to have a joyful life of their own as performance and "all-join-in" pieces.

The Dubliners and the Clancy Brothers promulgated Irish songs and ballads in the 1960s, the Chieftains burst onto the scene with brilliant musical dexterity in the early 1970s and still play to worldwide acclaim, and younger bands such as De Dannan, Planxty, the Bothy Band, Dervish, Lúnasa, Danú, and Patrick Street found they could make a living by playing their native music all over the world. Masters of their craft such as uilleann pipers Liam O'Flynn and Davy Spillane, singers Dolores Keane, Mary Black, Cara Dillon, and Cathal McConnell, and fiddlers Tommy Peoples, Kevin Burke, and the dynamic Martin Hayes command a reverence among aficionados of the music. And young musicians such as brothers Bréanainn and Cormac Begley and their cousins Niall and Eoin Begley from west Kerry, fiddler Caoimhin Ó Raghallaigh and piper Seán McKeon, and bands like Gráda and Teáda are carrying on the tradition in tremendous form.

The astonishing international rise of interest in Irish traditional music in recent years has a lot to do with the sheer size and geographical spread of the Irish diaspora. Modern media have been enormously influential, too. Slick shows such as Riverdance and Lord of the Dance have made a huge impact, drawing worldwide attention not only to the costumes and dancing but also to the wild music that drives the whole thing along. And when listeners and watchers decide to come over to Ireland, they find that the music has never been more alive.

Pleasures of the Session

Well-honed music by professional troupes is laid on at Bunratty Castle and other commercial venues that cater to the tourist trade. You may also find some of the big names in concert in the main towns and cities. But you'll find the best and most enjoyable traditional music—rough edges, occasional blemishes, and all—in the sessions that take place in pubs all over the country. Anyone in the town or village can tell you where and when you'll find a session. They tend to start around 9:30 in the evening and go on till 11:30 (or much later); they may be entirely spontaneous but will probably be based around one or two local musicians. The instruments will tend to be some combination of fiddle, flute, squeezebox, bodhran (round goatskin drum), tin whistle, traditional

---

EXPERIENCE:
Storytelling at Tí Chulainn

Ireland's storytellers may be less well known than the country's rich tradition of singers, musicians, poets, and writers, but they are just as important to the island's cultural heritage. South Armagh especially cherishes its traditional Irish roots. The **Tí Chulainn Cultural Activity Centre** *(tel 028/3088-8828, tichulainn.com)*, in the village of Mullaghbane, gives a stage and an audience not only to the musicians and poets of the area but also to those with a talent for "telling the tale." The storytellers of Tí Chulainn are just as likely to put a hilarious spin on some recent event as they are to recount heroic feats of the mythological past. For news of proper old-fashioned storytelling sessions in other parts of Ireland, consult **Storytellers of Ireland** *(storytellersofireland.org)*.

uilleann (literally "elbow") pipes, guitar, bouzouki, and banjo. Anyone is welcome to join in, provided they have the courtesy to ask first. Session music frequently touches great heights, giving birth to a roaring beast of a medley that gathers its own unstoppable momentum, or a heart-meltingly emotional song or air that produces a pin-drop silence in a crowded bar. At such moments you wouldn't want to be anywhere else in the world.

Ireland is an inexhaustible breeding ground for rock and pop performers—superstar Van Morrison from Belfast, boy bands Boyzone and Westlife, women singers such as Mary Black and Sinead O'Connor, pop acts from the Corrs to Snow Patrol, rock bands from Rory Gallagher's R&B outfits to world-straddling U2 and the Cranberries with their the biting, mournful music, maverick wildman rock poets like Shane MacGowan of the Pogues and Phil Lynott of Thin Lizzy. Great things can happen, too, when innovators mix traditional music with rock (The Pogues), jazz (Moving Hearts), ambient (Enya), or classical influences (Michael O'Súilleabháin). ■

■ **Riverdance is in step with both traditional and modern Irish culture.**

A thought-provoking introduction to the country's history, fabulous collections of national treasures, or just a roaring good time

DUBLIN

Georgian door knocker, Dublin

DUBLIN

The best thing about Dublin is that there is no one best thing. Each of a hundred aspects of Ireland's agreeable national capital helps to build a picture of a city that has seen a lot of history—hard times and prosperity, dignified consolidation and brash expansion—while somehow retaining a manageable pace and scale.

■ **Molly Malone, The Tart with the Cart is how Dubliners refer to the statue of the celebrated fishmonger that inspired a traditional song.**

Those who remember Dublin "in the rare old times" will tell you that it has lost the cozy intimacy and humanity that inspired James Joyce. Certainly Ireland's wild turn-of-the-millennium ride to economic boom time on the back of the Celtic Tiger has transformed the center of the once sleepy city on the River Liffey into a place rattling with new money and businesses and stiff with the chic kind of eateries, wine bars, and dance clubs that young go-getters love to frequent.

Equally, there is still poverty in parts of the city where the new money doesn't reach and the tourists don't go. But those who come to Dublin as first-time visitors will be delighted to discover a city bustling with confidence and energy, yet still conserving its time-warp pockets of peace in traditional backstreet pubs and out-of-the-way gardens.

One of the key factors in Dublin's favor is that everything around the city center is built

low, with the great Georgian and Victorian civic buildings such as the General Post Office, the Custom House, and the buildings of Trinity College dominating the scene, rather than anonymous modern office buildings. This helps put visitors in the mood for the mythic Dublin that so many expect to find—the Joycean old city where there's always time for another pint and a bit more chat.

Another advantage the city enjoys is its relationship with the River Liffey. They used to tell you that the superiority of Guinness over other porters and stouts was due to the use of Liffey water in its brewing. You might even believe it if you have never seen the muddy waterway—rather more turbid than limpid. However, the Liffey, immortalized in the Anna Livia Plurabelle passage of Joyce's *Finnegan's*

NOT TO BE MISSED:

Area of map detail

Belfast

Dublin

CENTRAL IRELAND *p. 233*

6 kilometers
3 miles

Balscaddan
Balbriggan

Rockabill

R122
R127

Naul
M1

Skerries
St. Patrick's Island

R127
R128

Shenick's Island

Garristown

R130

Loughshinny

Irish Sea

R108
Ballyboghil

Lusk
N1
R128
Rush

Oldtown
R122

Broad Meadow Water

Portraine
Lambay Island

Killsallaghan
Ward

Donabate

M2
Swords
N1
Malahide
Malahide Castle

St. Margaret's
Dublin Airport
Cloghran
Kinsaley
Portmarnock
Ireland's Eye

D U B L I N
N2
M50
M1
N32

Howth Harbour

M3
Tolka
N3
Corduff
Santry
Coolock

Mulhuddart
Blanchardstown
Killester
Sutton
Howth

National Botanic Gardens
ST. ANNE'S PARK
R105

Glasnevin Cemetery
Marino
Clontarf
North Bull Island

Farmleigh House
PHOENIX PARK
Royal Canal
Liffey

Lucan
M4
N4
R136

See map pp. 50-51
EPIC

EAST IRELAND *p. 87*

DUBLIN
Dublin Bay

R131
Isle of Man
Holyhead, Liverpool

Grand Canal
M50
Rathgar
R118
Booterstown

Clondalkin
R120
N7
R113
N81
Rathfarnham
N11
N31

Newcastle
Dún Laoghaire
James Joyce Tower & Museum
Sandycove
Archbold's Castle

Tallaght
Ballyboden
Dalkey
153m
Killiney Hill
Dalkey Island

Rathcoole
Saggart
Dodder
Ballinteer
R113
Killiney

R113
M50
N11
Killiney Bay

N81
R114
R115
Stepaside
R119

Brittas
582m
Glendoo Mountain
Golden Ball
Shankill

THE WICKLOW WAY
R116
R117
M11
to Bray, Greystones

648m
Seahan
618m
Corrig Mountain
Glencullen

752m
Kippure

EAST IRELAND
p. 87

A B C D

■ **Grafton Street is the beating heart of Dublin. It's always pulsating with tourists and street artists, particularly on the weekend.**

Wake, is close to Dubliners' hearts. The river makes a fine spectacle as it flows through the heart of the city, between handsome old quays and beneath a series of fine bridges on its eastward journey to Dublin Bay. Favorite meeting places, Dublin's bridges are more like lively thoroughfares than mere river crossings.

Central Dublin is small enough to visit almost everything on foot or using the Luas light railway, and most of its celebrated attractions—Trinity College, St. Stephen's Green, St. Patrick's Cathedral, shops and cafés on Grafton Street, the trendily renovated quarter of Temple Bar—lie south of the Liffey. North of the river you can enjoy the sassy market vendors of Moore Street and Mary's Lane.

East of the city center, the Liffey quays take you into an area that boasts a number of fine eating and drinking places with wonderful views of the river. To the west, you come to the great national monument of Kilmainham Gaol—a must-visit place—and Europe's largest urban green space, the magnificent open miles of Phoenix Park, a marvelous place to unwind.

Although the city of Dublin is far and away the main attraction, the Irish capital is not the be-all and end-all of County Dublin. The DART, Dublin's swift suburban railway, will take you out of the city center to Dublin's outer pleasures. To the north, you can enjoy walking in St.

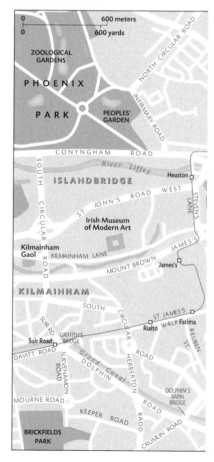

Anne's Park at Killester or around the promontory of Howth Head—the Howth Head walk in particular is a beauty, with very fine views over miles of mountains and green countryside as well as far prospects out to sea. Rhododendron season at Howth Castle is a famous day out for Dubliners.

Moving on northward, you'll find the handsome town of Malahide, known for good restaurants. Malahide Castle, home of the Talbot family for nearly eight centuries, is a romantic dream of battlements and turrets, on a core of late Norman work. Northward again is Skerries,

a pretty fishing town with fine sea views.

South of the city, the DART runs through some handsome Georgian and Victorian seaside towns. Dun Laoghaire is a pleasant place to idle, while Dalkey, with its narrow streets, still retains something of an old-fashioned village air.

Other delights of south County Dublin are visiting the James Joyce Tower & Museum at Sandycove and spotting the millionaire residents of Killiney from the top of Killiney Hill. At the end of the DART you can pick up the flavor of a traditional Irish day by the sea at the old resort town of Bray and Greystones. ■

TRINITY COLLEGE

Trinity College claims not only the finest set of university buildings in Ireland but also a roll call of alumni that embraces fierce polemicist Jonathan Swift and Ireland's first female president, Mary Robinson, satirical humorists Oscar Wilde and Brian O'Nolan (Flann O'Brien), rebel leader Wolfe Tone and statesman Edmund Burke, and writers Bram Stoker and Samuel Beckett. It also houses the Book of Kells, judged by many to be the most beautiful book in the world.

■ Undergraduates mix with tourists in the courtyards of Dublin's oldest university, Trinity College.

Dublin

🗺 49 B3–C3

Visitor Information

✉ Dublin Tourism Centre, 25 Suffolk St., Dublin 2

☎ 01/850-230330

visitdublin.com

Trinity College faces College Street, its entrance a low doorway far more modest than the grand buildings beyond. After the buzz of modern-day Dublin, everything just seems more peaceful inside the cobbled quadrangles and university buildings spanning four centuries.

Queen Elizabeth I founded Trinity in 1592. Her aim was "to civilize Ireland with both learning

and the Protestant religion, for the reformation of the barbarism of this rude people." Although in practice Catholics have studied at Trinity from the early 19th century, the Roman Catholic Church did not officially approve until the 1960s. The admission of women under-graduates as long ago as 1904, however, shows that the university was far from hidebound over gender discrimination.

University Chapel

On your left as you enter the first quadrangle is the university chapel, a peaceful paneled church with beautiful painted windows under a stucco ceiling of subtle grays and greens. The chapel was built in 1798, the momentous year when the United Irishmen launched their doomed rebellion (see p. 27).

The Old Library

On the far side of the quad you pass a 100-foot-high (30 m) Victorian campanile before heading right into the Old Library, a fine early 18th-century building. Inside, on the first floor, a permanent exhibition, **Turning Darkness into Light,** explains the technicalities of how religious manuscripts were written and illustrated, preparing you for the kernel of the exhibition, the **Book of Kells** (see pp. 54–55).

On the upper floor of the Old Library is the truly impressive **Long Room,** a vast shadowy tunnel some 210 feet (65 m) long under a barrel-vaulted roof whose pillars turn out on close inspection to be huge stacks of books—about a quarter of a million in all.

The busts of fourteen great philosophers and authors adorn the hall but two objects in particular attract the attention of visitors as they cross the wide central hallway. The first is an antique harp in oak and willow wood, constructed in the 1400s (even though folklore says it's much older) for Ireland's legendary sovereign, Brian Boru. It served as the model for the creation of the symbol of Ireland.

The other historic treasure here is an evocatively tattered and roughly printed poster, a rare original copy of the Proclamation of the Republic of Ireland, pasted up around Dublin by the rebels during the Easter Rising of 1916 (see pp. 30–32): "The Provisional Govern-

---

INSIDER TIP:

While admittedly austere, the Trinity College dorms offer unique accommodations as well as a jump start on the line for the Book of Kells the next day.

—ROBIN CURRIE
National Geographic author

---

ment of the Irish Republic, to the People of Ireland. . .We declare the right of the people of Ireland to the ownership of Ireland, and to the unfettered control of Irish destiny, to be sovereign and indefeasible. . .

We hereby proclaim the Irish Republic as a Sovereign Independent State, and we pledge our lives and the lives of our comrades in arms to the cause of its freedom, of its welfare, and of its exaltation among the nations."

Science Gallery

Trinity's Science Gallery offers an intriguing look at science in all its aspects. Even nonscientific visitors find plenty to fascinate them here. There's no permanent collection—instead you can sample up-to-the-minute exhibitions, open meetings, debates, and workshops. ■

Trinity College
- 🅰 Map p. 51
- ✉ College St., Dublin 2
- ☎ 01/896-1000 (central switchboard)
- 🚌 All cross-city buses

tcd.ie

Book of Kells
- ✉ Trinity College, College St., Dublin 2
- ☎ 01/896-2320
- 💲 $$

tcd.ie/visitors/book-of-kells

Trinity College dorms
- ☎ 01/896-1177
- 💲 $$$$$

tcd.ie/accommodations

Science Gallery
- ✉ Pearse St. entrance of Trinity College
- ☎ 01/896-4091
- 🚌 Bus: 44, 61; LUAS Green Line: Trinity stop; Rail: Pearse Station

dublin.sciencegallery.com

BOOK OF KELLS

This glorious 680-page book of the four Gospels was crafted by monks at Kells Monastery (see p. 260) in County Meath around A.D. 800, at the height of Ireland's golden age of monastic talent and influence. It is Ireland's finest example of an illuminated manuscript—a handwritten text beautified with hand-colored illustrations.

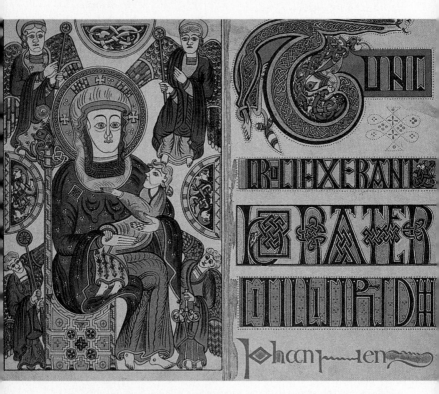

■ The monks who created the Book of Kells used dozens of natural sources of color to complement their exquisite artistry.

Viewing the Book of Kells

The Book of Kells lies under glass in its own special display area at the heart of the Turning Darkness into Light exhibition in the Old Library at Trinity College (see p. 53). In 1953, it was rebound in four volumes, of which two are always on display—one open at a sumptuously illuminated page, the other at a page of text. The pages chosen for display are changed every few months to prevent the illuminated script from fading from overexposure to light. But in fact the egg-white fixative employed by the monks 1,200 years ago has proved remarkably effective in keeping details sharp. On summer holiday weekends it's a good idea to plan your visit as early in the day as possible to avoid a tedious half-hour's wait in line.

Unmatched Artistry

Whichever page is displayed when you visit, you can't fail to be dumbstruck by the beauty, humor, and force of imagination that come shining through the patina of the centuries. The Kells illustrators must have been strongly influenced by the artistic brilliance of the monks of Iona (a monastery established off the west coast of Scotland in about 563), because the freedom of line and intricacy of detail so characteristic of Iona work of that era are all present here.

Each of the illuminated capital letters looks at first sight like an inextricable riot of circles, rectangles, and curlicued bits of foliage in gold, red, and blue. But as you stare you begin to see more—beasts with open mouths, misshapen devils, little domestic cameos, men passionately embracing, huge-eyed angels, heavenly flowers and fruit, all cunningly sneaked into uprights or packed into round spaces. The single page becomes an admonitory or encouraging sermon on the pitfalls and pleasures of life in the real world. What infinite pains the monks of Kells took in making their wonderful masterpiece—and what evident delight, too.

For colors, they used what they had on hand or could get by barter, purchase, or gift—gold leaf, chalk for white, copper verdigris for green. Red came from lead, black from charcoal, blue from either ground-up lapis lazuli or woad, a European plant. How much eyesight the Book of Kells consumed, and how many monkish migraines the crafting of its minuscule details provoked, one can only guess.

Other Books on Display

After admiring the unmatched artistry of the Book of Kells, take some time to admire the other superbly beautiful ancient

INSIDER TIP:

The reward at the end of the manuscript exhibit at Trinity College's Old Library is undoubtedly the Book of Kells, but be sure to also see the smaller and earlier Book of Mulling displayed nearby.

—ROZ HOAGLAND
Private guide,
Hoagland Art Travel

Gospel books on display. The eighth-century pocket-size **Book of Mulling** was intended for an unknown missionary monk. Another Gospel on display was made by Dimma the Scribe around the same time, while the **Book of Armagh** was made in 807 for Torbach, Bishop of Armagh. And the oldest decorated Gospel book in existence, the **Book of Durrow,** was created around 675.

Illustrations in the Book of Kells reveal both allegorical tableaux as well as a variety of scenes from life in eighth-century Ireland.

NATIONAL MUSEUM OF IRELAND–ARCHAEOLOGY

Inside Dublin's splendid National Museum is gathered the majority of the nation's most significant archaeological finds, brought here from the peat bogs, fields, and hillsides where they have been dug up or stumbled across over the years by turf cutters, plowboys, and amateur archaeologists. The best of Ireland's treasure trove of religious art is here, too. The museum itself was built in 1890, its grand entrance hall floored with a giant mosaic of the zodiac.

The Ardagh Chalice, an early eighth-century masterwork of silver gilding, enamel, brass, and bronze

National Museum of Ireland–Archaeology

🅰 Map p. 51

✉ Kildare St., Merrion Row, Dublin 2

☎ 01/677-7444

🕐 Closed morning on Sun. and Mon.

🚌 All cross-city buses; LUAS Green Line: Trinity stop; Rail: Pearse Station

museum.ie

The Exhibitions

The National Museum's exhibitions are arranged over two levels; the Treasury (the museum's chief attraction), Prehistoric Ireland, Ór–Ireland's Gold, and Kingship & Sacrifice are all on the ground floor, while upstairs on the first floor you will find the exhibition on Viking Ireland and the ancient Egyptian collection, as well as the Medieval Ireland, Life & Death in the Roman World, and Ceramics & Glass from Ancient Cyprus exhibitions.

Ground Floor

Treasury: Perhaps the most famous exhibits in the Treasury are the Tara Brooch and the Ardagh Chalice. These two works of Dark Ages and medieval art would in themselves justify a trip to the National Museum. The shape of the bejeweled eighth-century **Tara Brooch** with its circular gold clasp and long pin is familiar as the inspiration for countless pieces of modern Celtic jewelry. The brooch was found by chance in 1850 on the

Sharp Eyes & Illicit Liquor

The priceless eighth-century **Faddan More Psalter,** a most beautiful and intricately illustrated book of psalms, was discovered by sharp-eyed digger-driver Eddie Fogarty on July 20, 2006, as he excavated a trench in Faddan More bog near Birr on the Offaly-Tipperary border. By great good fortune Fogarty saw the ancient book drop from the bucket of his digger into a ditch. The landowners, Padraig and Kevin Leonard, had experience of other archaeological finds on their bogland, and so they knew what to do when summoned by Fogarty–they covered the pieces of the book with wet peat and called the National Museum. Years of painstaking restoration ensued. The psalter was scanned and photographed in the condition in which it was found; then it was slowly dried out. Experimentation showed that minimum shrinkage of the vellum would be achieved by soaking it in ethanol (rather charmingly the main component of *poitín,* Ireland's native home-brewed liquor!) and vacuum-packing in blotting paper. The Faddan More Psalter was finally put on display in June 2011.

seashore at Bettystown near Drogheda, just south of the mouth of the River Boyne. The National Museum has it beautifully displayed above a mirror so that you can see the exquisite interlacing patterns and gold filigree work on both sides of the clasp.

The **Ardagh Chalice**–a wide-bowled, two-handled cup of softly glowing silver-copper alloy banded with finely chased gold and set with crystal, enamel, and amber–was made in the eighth century, Ireland's golden age. It was discovered along with other treasures by a laborer digging potatoes in Reerasta ring fort near Ardagh, County Limerick, in 1868.

Another breathtaking collection of treasures is the **Broighter Hoard,** discovered in the 1890s near Limavady in County Derry. This is pre-Christian goldwork at its finest–leaf-thin hollow necklace balls, discs with hammered indentations, crescent-shaped lunulae to wear around the neck, and a model boat of sheet gold so thin it looks as if a touch would break it. You can enjoy more craftsmanship in precious metals in the form of the silver chalice, paten, and other treasures of the eighth and ninth centuries found as recently as 1980 by casual treasure seekers wielding a metal detector at Derrynaflan in County Tipperary.

Ór–Ireland's Gold: Ór is an astonishing collection of early gold work from rings and bracelets to collars and the breast ornaments know as gorgets–in particular the breathtaking **Gleninsheen Gorget,** a heavy, many-stranded gold collar with circular shoulder pads found near the 4,000-year-old Gleninsheen wedge tomb in the Burren, County Clare.

Prehistoric Ireland: Among the exhibits that really catch the imagination are the **Lurgan log-boat,** 52 feet (16 m) long, fashioned from a tree trunk nearly 5,000 years ago; the tiny and extremely beautiful **Knowth mace head** crafted of flint with whorls shaped like an astonished human expression, that came from Knowth burial chamber at Brú na Bóinne (see pp. 264–267); and the wood and leather **shields** with which Stone and Bronze Age Irishmen protected themselves during raids and battles.

Kingship & Sacrifice: This exhibition examines the "bog bodies," or human sacrifices interred in peat bogs, that have recently come to light. With its horned headdresses, leather

■ The shrine that housed St. Patrick's bell for centuries

INSIDER TIP:

Look for the design on the underside of the Ardagh Chalice. The intricate interlace would only be seen by worshippers when the priest drank from the chalice.

—ROZ HOAGLAND
Private guide,
Hoagland Art Travel

capes, horse gear, wooden bowls, and butter vessels, it shines a light on a dark but fascinating corner of rituals associated with the death and coronation of Iron Age kings.

First Floor
Viking Ireland: Giving the lie to the Vikings' enduring image as bone-headed philistines intent only on plunder and slaughter, this fine exhibition reveals them as sensitively skilled artists in metal—particularly the decorative pins and brooches swirling with interlacing patterns. Evidence of their artistry in practical matters comes in the form of a remarkable yew longbow of the late tenth century, a perfect curve of slim dark wood.

Medieval Ireland 1150–1550:
The exhibition examines power (life among the nobility), prayer (church furnishings and religious objects such as saints' bells and shrines, superbly jeweled reliquaries and statues), and work (life in medieval towns and cities).

Other Exhibitions:
The **Ancient Egypt** exhibition contains everything you'd expect from painted mummy cases to dog-headed gods, all beautifully displayed; while **Ceramics and Glass from Ancient Cyprus** and **Life & Death in the Roman World** highlight seldom-seen items from the museum's collections.

National Museum of Decorative Arts & History

The National Museum has an annex out at Collins Barracks (named after Michael Collins, the Free State hero) on Benburb Street, just north of Wolfe Tone Quay on the River Liffey, 1.7 miles (2.8 km) east of the parent museum. After the 1798 rebellion ended in defeat for the insurgents, the revolutionary Wolfe Tone was imprisoned here before his grisly death, self-inflicted with his own pocketknife. The building itself is impressive in its unadorned simplicity, a flat-faced gray stone barracks block with a pedimented central section, built in 1704 (when it was known as Royal Barracks) to house 3,000 men and 1,000 horses. Today, the museum is divided into two sections. One is dedicated to the decorative arts with a beautiful collection of Irish ceramics, silver objects, costumes from numerous periods, various types of furniture, and a collection of Asian art left to the museum by Albert Bender. The other is built around the country's military history and includes exhibits that address the various aspects of the infinite wars that have involved Ireland. The iconic yacht *Asgard,* in which nationalist Erskine Childers landed guns and ammunition for Home Rule rebels at Howth Harbour in 1914, has been beautifully restored for public display. **Soldiers and Chiefs** traces the history of the Irish soldier fighting at home, as an exile in Europe, in the American Civil War, and in the service of the British Empire; and **The Easter Rising: Understanding 1916** examines the War of Independence and Ireland's Civil War that followed soon after. ∎

National Museum of Natural History

Another branch of the museum, the National Museum of Natural History is a great place to take children. They'll love the hands-on workshops and Discovery Zone with drawers full of insects and other surprises. The ground floor has Irish wildlife, including a huge Irish elk skeleton with giant antlers and old taxidermic tableaux of animals and birds. Upstairs the story of evolution is illustrated with specimens from around the world—pangolin, anteater, tiger, and monkeys. Many are housed in "old-fashioned" glass cases.

National Museum of Decorative Arts & History

🗺 Map p. 51

✉ Collins Barracks, Benburb St., Dublin 7

☎ 01/677-7444

🕐 Closed morning on Sun. and Mon.

🚌 Bus: 25, 25A, 66, 67, 90; LUAS Red Line: Museum stop; Rail: Heuston Station

museum.ie

National Museum of Natural History

🗺 Map p. 51

✉ Merrion St., Dublin 2

☎ 01/677-7444

🕐 Closed morning on Sun. and Mon.

🚌 Bus: 7, 7A, 8; LUAS Green Line: St. Stephen's Green stop

WALK: THROUGH CENTRAL DUBLIN

This stroll through the heart of Dublin leads from the bustling riverfront to the leaf-green oasis of St. Stephen's Green and on through the trendy quarter of Temple Bar. From there it runs along the characterful quays of the Liffey to reach the city's grandest and most handsome Georgian building, the Custom House.

Boo! Don't be surprised by the "living sculptures" that you'll encounter around Grafton Street.

Starting on **O'Connell Bridge,** walk south to cross the River Liffey. Keep straight to pass **Trinity College ❶** (see pp. 52–53). Bear east along Nassau Street, then turn right on Kildare Street to pass the **National Museum of Ireland–Archaeology ❷** (see pp. 56–59). Go right at the end of Kildare Street and cross **St. Stephen's Green ❸** (see p. 63), then turn right into **Grafton Street,** which is famous for its elegant boutiques and talented street musicians. Stop and have a cup of coffee at **Bewley's Oriental Café ❹** *(78/79 Grafton St., tel 01/564-0900, bewleys.com)* while you admire Harry Clarke's six magnificent stained-glass windows. An old church at the beginning of Grafton Street is home to the **Visitor Center** and in front of it, you can see the statue of **Molly Malone,** the legendary fishmonger

NOT TO BE MISSED:

Trinity College and the Book of Kells
• National Museum of Archaeology and History • Chester Beatty Library and Gallery of Oriental Art
• General Post Office

that inspired a famous folk song by the same name. Turn left again along Dame Street to reach **Dublin Castle** and the **Chester Beatty Library ❺** (see pp. 64–67). From here, steer northeast through **Temple Bar** (see p. 62) until you hit the river. Bear left along the water to the end of Merchant's Quay. Cross the Liffey on **Father Mathew Bridge** to find the Georgian dome and facade of the **Four Courts** facing you to the right. The building still houses Dublin's High Court and Supreme Court.

Turn right to make your way back to the south end of O'Connell Street, heading for the great colonnaded portico of the **General Post Office** or **GPO** ❻ *(O'Connell St., tel 01/705-7000)*, where the Proclamation of the Republic was read during the Easter Rising of 1916. Nearby soars the **The Spire,** a 390-foot (120 m) stainless-steel needle built in 2003.

Return down O'Connell Street and turn left along Abbey Street Lower to find the **Abbey Theatre** ❼ *(tel 01/878-7222, abbeytheatre.ie, box office closed Sun., theater open for performances*

only—guided tours on Mon., Wed., Fri. at 4 pm and on Sat. at 11 am), Ireland's national theater, founded by poet W. B. Yeats and his patron, Lady Gregory.

Head back to the water and walk a block downriver to see the **Custom House** ❽ *(Custom House Quay, tel 01/888-2000)*, built between 1781 and 1791, one of Dublin's grandest buildings.

▲ See also area map p. 49 C3 & p. 51
▶ O'Connell Bridge
⟷ 4 miles (6 km)
⌚ From 2 hours to a whole day, depending on which attractions you decide to explore
▶ Custom House

Dublin Walking Tour

The **Dublin Discovery Trails** self-guided walking tours *(visitdublin.com/see-do/dublin-discovery-trails)* are a series of thematic walking itineraries that visitors can do on their own. They include **The Dubline,** which crosses the antique heart of the city, and **The Rebellion,** which touches on the historical sites of the Easter Rising. An app with multimedia content is also available.

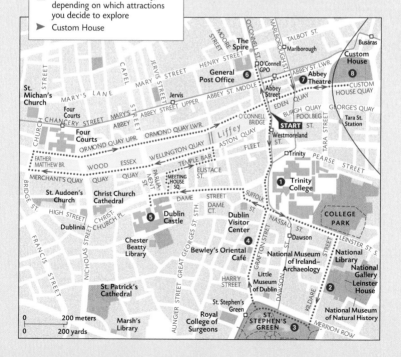

TEMPLE BAR

If you had mentioned to a group of Dubliners 20 years ago that you were going to hang out in the neighborhood of Temple Bar, a lot of funny looks would have come your way. These days all you'll get is advice as to where to shop, which street has this great little restaurant, and the nearest pub to hear some traditional live music . . .

Temple Bar

- Map p. 51

Visitor Information

- Dublin Tourism Centre, 25 Suffolk St., Dublin 2
- 01/850-230330
- Bus: All city-center buses; LUAS Green Line: Westmoreland stop; Rail: Tara St. station

templebar.ie

Not so long ago, Temple Bar (named after a local landowner, Sir William Temple, whose property included a sandbank, or bar, on the south side of the river) was due to be flattened to make way for a bus depot. The area just west of Trinity College had become so run-down and seedy that no one wanted to live or work there, much less visit for pleasure. Then Group 91, a group of young architects, came up with some radical plans for the district. They designed a compact mix of galleries, theaters, and an arts center around a market square. Rooflines became fun, sprouting twisted rods like punk hair; balconies curved and snaked; buildings lost their drab brick and whitewash in favor of hot orange or Mediterranean blue.

Temple Bar suddenly became the trendiest place in Dublin. New boutique and lifestyle shops proliferated. Artists, photographers, and filmmakers began to frequent the area and to exhibit their works. And at night a tide of young people spilled into dance clubs and pubs.

This is the place to come during the day for a good cup of coffee or a meal in an ethnic restaurant, shopping, or people-watching. Noisy, rowdy crowds descend at night.

Meeting House Square

The heart of Temple Bar is Meeting House Square, a big square with four retractable canopies that make it an all-weather venue. It's home to an open-air market on Saturday mornings. Nearby, there's a children's acting school and arts and recreation center, **The Ark,** as well as the **National Photographic Archive,** the **Gallery of Photography,** the **Temple Bar Gallery and Studios,** and the **Irish Film Centre and Archive.** ∎

Flashy decor in Temple Bar

ST. STEPHEN'S GREEN

At the far end of Grafton Street from Trinity College lies St. Stephen's Green, 22 acres (9 ha) of gardens at the heart of southside Dublin. Generations of Dubliners have come here to sunbathe, stroll, and flirt among the flower beds and under the trees.

The fountains and lawns of St. Stephen's Green exhibit the timeless elegance of Georgian Dublin.

You'll find monuments here to heroes of Ireland's long struggle for Home Rule—notably the 1798 leader Wolfe Tone, Constance Gore-Booth, Countess Markiewicz (see pp. 212–213), who was imprisoned during the 1916 Easter Rising, Nobel Prize–winning poet W. B. Yeats, and *Ulysses* author James Joyce.

Georgian buildings surround the Green, including the pedimented **Royal College of Surgeons** on the west side, where, in 1922, the constitution of the new Irish Free State was drafted under the chairmanship of Michael Collins.

The big hotel on the north side, with its sculptures of princesses lording it over bond maids, is the **Shelbourne,** a landmark mid-Victorian extravaganza.

More of Dublin's handsome Georgian architecture graces **Upper Merrion Street** and **Merrion Square** just northeast of St. Stephen's Green, and **Harcourt Street** to the south. Take a camera or camera-phone on your stroll—it's impossible to resist the famous double doorways, side-by-side entrances to neighboring houses, flanked by columns, with elaborate semicircular fanlights above. ■

St. Stephen's Green

Map p. 51

DUBLIN CASTLE

For seven centuries the prime symbol of English dominance over Ireland, Dublin Castle has long had its medieval grimness dressed up in mellow Georgian brick. There are the elaborate 18th-century State Rooms, an undercroft, and various towers to explore. The castle's Clock Tower is home to one of the world's great collections of Middle Eastern and Oriental manuscripts and art.

For centuries, Dublin Castle was a symbol of British power at the heart of the Irish capital.

Dublin Castle

- Map p. 51
- Dame St., Dublin 2
- 01/645-8813
- Bus: 13, 27, 40, 49, 59A, 77A, 123, 150, 151, 156; LUAS Green Line: St. Stephen's Green stop; Rail: Tara St., DART
- $$

dublincastle.ie

The castle was built in the early 13th century as the seat of power for the English rulers of Ireland, a function it served for the next 700 years right up until the establishment of an independent Irish Free State in 1922.

There were at least two sieges of Dublin Castle. "Silken Thomas" Fitzgerald made an attempt in 1534, but his forces were driven off when the garrison made a gallant sortie. The other attempt was made in 1916, a hopelessly brave attack by the republican rebels of the Easter Rising, who briefly succeeded in penning up the British Army soldiers.

Not much remains of the original castle, which was redesigned internally in Georgian style with a range of buildings added at the elegant height of the 18th century. Down in the **Undercroft,** you can inspect the ancient footings of the Norman castle's Powder Tower, bedded on walls that the Vikings raised around a fortress of their own three centuries before, along with ancient segments of city wall and moat—there's a real sense of a hidden past under your feet

The main focus of a tour around the castle, though, is a circuit of the opulent 18th-century **State Rooms,** still sometimes used to entertain foreign dignitaries. A complete tour of the castle follows a fixed itinerary and requires the company of a guide. The only exceptions are the State Apartments and the temporary exhibits, which guests are free to visit on their own. It includes **St. Patrick's Hall,** almost 100 feet (30 m) long and festooned with banners of the long-disbanded Knights of St. Patrick under a fine painted and paneled ceiling, the gorgeous powder-blue **Wedgwood Room,** the great **Drawing Room** entered between gilt Corinthian columns and barred with light from tall windows, and a **Throne Room** stiff with gold and lit by golden chandeliers. Other highlights to see are the Gothic revival–style **Chapel Royal** and the **Viking Excavations** that uncovered defenses dating back to the Viking era.

Chester Beatty Library

The real treasure of Dublin Castle, however, resides in the gardens at the back of the castle beyond the State Apartments *(enter by the Ship Street gate),* home to the incomparable Chester Beatty Library. Dublin is lucky to have this fabulous collection, bequeathed by the Canadian mining magnate, Sir Alfred Chester Beatty (1875 – 1968), who moved to Dublin in 1950. In 1954, he built a museum to house his collection,

which he later donated to Ireland.

Beatty was primarily interested in Oriental art and in religious manuscripts—he owned more than 300 copies of the Koran—and eventually amassed some 22,000 manuscripts as well as thousands of paintings, printed books, maps, and carved objects.

The exhibition housed in the **Clock Tower** is distributed on two floors of the building and is divided into two permanent displays in addition to other temporary exhibits. It showcases some of the best pieces chosen from an enormous wealth of fascinating materials and definitely deserves the half a day (at least) that it takes to see it well. Take advantage of the opportunity to stop for some refreshment at the characteristic **Silk Road Café** (see p. 354) on the ground floor.

INSIDER TIP:

Experience the life of a Viking warrior or housewife, and the street fairs, sounds, and stinks of medieval Dublin, at the Dublinia exhibit *(dublinia.ie)*, next to Christchurch Cathedral.

—JUSTIN KAVANAGH
*National Geographic
Travel Books editor*

Gallery Floor 1: The permanent exhibition, **Arts of the Book,** is simple but impressive. It's divided into three sections dedicated to Oriental art, Islamic art, and Western art and displays

Chester Beatty Library

✉ Dublin Castle, Dublin 2

☎ 01/407-0750

🕓 Closed Mon. Oct.–April

🚌 Bus: 50, 51B, 54A, 56A, 77, 77A, 78A, 123; Rail: Tara St. station

cbl.ie

objects from various countries in Asia, the Middle East, North Africa, and Europe that have been chosen from Chester Beatty's vast collection. The central theme of the exhibition is the making of books and manuscripts in a variety of cultures. The many objects on display on this floor include manuscripts, printed volumes, book bindings, calligraphy tools, printing instruments, miniatures, prints, and drawings.

On the right, you will discover treasures from India, the Orient, and Southeast Asia, particularly **works of art from China and Japan.** The works on display are periodically rotated in order to preserve them. Objects from China include cups made of sculpted rhinoceros tusks, lacquered boxes, finches painted on silk, and a series of small perfume bottles made of jade, enamel, porcelain and mother-of-pearl. One article that stands out among all the rest is an elegant silk robe embroidered with the imperial emblem: a dragon with five claws. The Japanese objets d'art represent one of the most precious collections. They include several **netsuke,** small sculptures in ivory, wood, or jade that portray people, animals, or plants. Their purpose, besides being ornamental, was to attach pouches and small containers to the kimono belt.

But it's the array of Japanese paintings that visitors will find most fascinating and inspiring. Many *emakimono*, hand-painted picture scrolls, and xylography engravings dating from the beginning of the 17th century to the end of the 19th century narrate history and military endeavors. Some are as much as 95 feet long and every scene is minutely detailed. Among the

■ A detail from "Snow at Night," one of the Chester Beatty Library's exquisite Oriental paintings

prints from the collection that are displayed on rotation, there are the works of celebrated artists such as Utamaro, Kuniyoshi, and Hokusai. These works constitute a bridge that connects eras and cultures and to have the opportunity to cross that bridge is a truly exciting privilege. Examples of Islamic, Arab, Persian, and Turkish art are displayed at the center of the gallery. Here, visitors can see a rare treatise about engineering, the use of arms, astronomy, and geometry written by a medieval Iraqi expert. On the left is an exhibit dedicated to **Western and European traditions.** The most invaluable pieces include the Book of the Dead from ancient Egypt, love poems in hieratic that have somehow survived since 1160 B.C., and the Book of Hours, an illuminated manuscript dating to the 1400s.

Gallery Floor 2: Upstairs, the permanent display **Sacred Traditions** explores the great religious traditions of the world. The layout is the same as on the floor below. To the left are items illustrating the **Western and Christian traditions**—pre-Christian texts, Judaic scrolls, and early Old and New Testament manuscripts. Here Christian treasures include a double papyrus page of St. Luke's Gospel, copied early in the third century, and a segment of the Book of Revelation of around the same date, the oldest fragment of the final New Testament chapter yet discovered. Even more astonishing is the version

Islamic Treasures

In the Islamic section on the second floor of the Chester Beatty Gallery are illustrated manuscripts of the Koran, miniature paintings of the life of the Prophet, and Islamic history and traditions within the Arab, Persian, Mughal Indian, and Turkish worlds. The Arabic calligraphy of the richly gilded Koran texts is of stunning beauty as an art form, as are the ancient jeweled Koran stands and the tiny gold cases inlaid with enamel that were made to hold miniature copies.

of St. Paul's Epistles written around 200 and a copy of St. Augustine's *City of God,* dated from around 1100.

The second floor also houses art of the **Eastern religions**—Buddhist, Hindu, Jain, Sikh, Daoist, and Shinto. In Southeast Asia, Sir Alfred Chester Beatty collected Thai paintings of the life of Buddha and gilded lacquer statues from Burma. Tibet yielded elaborate prayer wheels as well as a Thanka painting on cotton cloth of the four-armed Avalokitesvara.

A good tip to help ensure maximum enjoyment of this unique and remarkable collection: Don't try to see it all in one day. Set aside two half days and give your senses time to recover in between. ∎

LITERARY DUBLIN

If there's one art above all others for which Dublin is celebrated, it is the city's astonishingly rich literary heritage. The old saying that there's the making of a great novel on the backseat of every Dublin cab has some truth to it. Dubliners seem to be born with a feel for rhythm. Conversations in the bars and on the street corners of the city are rich in imagery and imagination to the eavesdropping outsider. On such fertile ground, it would have been impossible not to cultivate the great writers that have contributed to make Dublin one of UNESCO's Cities of Literature.

This Grand Canal bank statue of poet Patrick Kavanagh gets a bad review from a young Dubliner.

The Writers

James Joyce (1882–1941) towers over literary Dublin. His shadow has hardly diminished in over 90 years since his 1922 masterpiece and love-letter-in-exile to the city, *Ulysses,* was first published.

These days, Joyce fanatics from all over the world descend in fancy dress on Dublin each "Bloomsday"—June 16, the date on which all the action in *Ulysses* takes place—and embark on a James Joyce Trail that follows the perambulations of the novel's hero, Leopold Bloom, around the city's streets and pubs. You can take part in the wide program of events *(bloomsdayfestival.*

ie); along with the *Ulysses* readings, one ritual is immutable—the reenactment of Bloom's lunch of a Gorgonzola sandwich and a glass of burgundy in **Davy Byrne's pub** on Duke Street. Alternatively, enjoy the trail at any time of year by following the bronze plaques set into the sidewalks of central Dublin.

Dublin carries the mark of a host of literary giants besides Joyce. Dean Jonathan Swift (1667–1745), author of *Gulliver's Travels, Tale of a Tub,* and other furiously indignant polemic and political satire, lies buried next to his platonic lover, Esther Johnson, "Stella" (1681–1728), in the nave of St. Patrick's Cathedral.

The Abbey Theatre on Abbey Street Lower saw historic opening nights of plays by Nobel Prize winners W. B. Yeats (1865–1939) and Samuel Beckett (1906–1989). Near Baggot Street Bridge, a sculpture of Monaghan-born poet Patrick Kavanagh (1904–1967) contemplates the turbid water of the Grand Canal, as Kavanagh himself loved to do while recuperating from lung cancer operations in the 1950s.

The Pubs

So much of Dublin's literary life, high and low, has been conducted in the city's pubs. Patrick Kavanagh frequented **McDaid's,** a pedestrian-only lane off Grafton Street, as did also acid-witted columnist and novelist Brian O'Nolan (1911–1966) and the rambunctious playwright Brendan Behan (1923–1964).

Nearby, on Lower Baggot Street, is **Toner's,** where W. B. Yeats, who wasn't a fan of pubs, supposedly stopped for just one glass of sherry. **Kennedy's,** near Merrion Square in Lincoln Place, claims to be the bar where Oscar Wilde, who lived in the area, earned his first schillings.

North of the River Liffey are the working-class estates whose life and speech have been brilliantly captured by Roddy Doyle (born 1958) in his novels—*The Commitments, The Snapper, The Van,* and *The Guts.*

The Museums

One of the many literary museums worth visiting is certainly the **James Joyce Centre** *(35 N. Great George's St., tel 01/878-8547, closed Mon., jamesjoyce.ie, $).* It displays some of the author's possessions and offers a number of documentaries that illustrate the life and literary works of this extremely complex artist.

The dreamlike atmosphere of a large hall in the **National Library** *(Kildare St., tel 01/603-0200, nli.ie, closed Sun. mornings)* is home to the exhibit, **The Life and the Works of W. B. Yeats.** Videos and objects help guests revisit the life and works of the poet.

You can wrap up your immersion into Dublin's literary history with the exhibition and the mementos kept at the **Dublin Writers' Museum** *(18 Parnell Sq. North, tel 01/872-2077, writersmuseum.com, $)* or you can opt to participate in a **Literary Pub Crawl,** a tour of pubs with readings and actors that bring the writers back to life *(details available at the Dublin Tourist Office, $$$).*

Lastly, the **Museum of Literature Ireland** or MoLI *(86 St. Stephen's Green, tel 01/477-9811, moli.ie)* which recently opened in the elegant Newman House is a modern, interactive exhibition dedicated to Ireland's literature, both past and present.

EXPERIENCE: Attend Literary Festivals & Events

Dublin is justly famous for Bloomsday, its annual celebration of James Joyce's novel *Ulysses* (see p. 44). But the city plays host to so many other literary festivals and events that you are bound to find something that interests you no matter when you visit.

The **Dublin Book Festival** *(dublinbookfestival.com),* which celebrates the best of modern Irish literature, takes place in the middle of November. The festival's busy schedule includes book signings, children's workshops, literary tours, and book presentations.

The **International Literature Festival** *(ilfdublin.com),* which takes place at the end of May, has been the most important international literature event since 1998. For an entire week, esteemed poets and writers from all over the world gather in the city for performances, book signings, and workshops.

With its vibrant cultural panorama and its rich literary heritage, Dublin clearly deserves its status as a UNESCO City of Literature, which it received in July 2010.

DUBLIN CITY GALLERY THE HUGH LANE

Located in the elegant Charlemont House, the Hugh Lane Gallery is home to a number of impressionist masterpieces and to a conspectus of modern Irish art. The star of the collection is the reconstruction of Francis Bacon's studio, reassembled in all of its vibrant chaos.

Dublin City Gallery The Hugh Lane

Map p. 51

Parnell Sq., Dublin 1

01/222-5550

Closed Mon.

Bus: 7, 11, 13, 16, 38, 40, 46A, 123A; LUAS Green Line: O'Connell Upper; Rail: Tara St. station

hughlane.ie

It was Ireland's first modern art gallery, founded in 1908 by the expert art collector, **Sir Hugh Lane** (1875–1915). It was initially located in Clonmell House in Harcourt Street and in 1933, it was moved to its current location in the Charlemont House, a neoclassic mansion designed in 1765 by Sir William Chambers for James Caulfield, Count of Charlemont.

The heart of the collection comprises a bequest from Sir Hugh Lane—39 works by French artists including Manet, Monet, Degas, and Renoir that are shared with the National Gallery in London.

The addition of new display spaces in 2006 made it possible to highlight Irish works of art, particularly those of the painters **Jack B. Yeats** and **Roderic O'Conor,** the abstract canvases of the Irish-American painter **Sean Scully,** and **Harry Clarke**'s spectacular stained-glass panels including his famous masterpiece, *The Eve of St. Agnes.* The gallery is also home to **Francis Bacon**'s chaotic studio, a reflection of his eclectic personality, which was dismantled in London and reassembled here in 1998.

Its calendar includes a wealth of temporary exhibitions that showcase modern artists. ■

■ The neoclassical facade of the Charlemont House, house of the Hugh Lane Gallery

ST. PATRICK'S CATHEDRAL

St. Patrick's Cathedral is a beautiful, uncomplicated building, much of it dating back to the 12th century, with a west tower and spire that soar to 225 feet (69 m). It was built on the site of a well where St. Patrick is said to have baptized converts, and there was probably a church on the site from the fifth century onward.

Inside, you'll find the graves of Dean Jonathan Swift and his companion, "Stella."

They lie under the nave just beyond the entrance. On the south wall opposite hangs Swift's self-penned Latin epitaph, "laid . . . where fierce indignation can no longer rend the heart. Go traveller, and imitate, if you can, this earnest and dedicated Champion of Liberty." In the north transept is a Swift exhibition. Also in the north transept, don't miss the poignant memorial to Lt. Col. Tomlinson, killed in May 1842 fighting the Chinese in the Great Opium War of 1840–1842.

The cathedral's splendid tombs include the enormous 17th-century **Boyle Monument,** with its three tiers of Westons, Fentons, and Boyles. There are

■ The spire of St. Patrick's Cathedral soars into the Dublin sky, a landmark and symbol to the city's Roman Catholics.

revered musician, the blind harpist Turlough O'Carolan (1670–1738). Arrange in advance if you wish to make brass rubbings ($$$). Don't miss the wooden door with its central panels missing. In 1492, this was the door of the cathedral's chapter house, behind which the Earl of Ormond barricaded himself against his enemy, the Earl of Kildare. Ormond refused to come out, even though promised safe passage, so Kildare hacked a hole in the door with his spear and stuck his unprotected arm through in a gesture of trust. Ormond took the hand, the feud was ended, and the term "chancing one's arm," meaning taking a risk, entered the language. ■

INSIDER TIP:

For an atmospheric musical experience, visit St. Patrick's Cathedral during a choral service. Check the website for times.

—MARGARET ROBERTS
Irish dancer & musicologist

fine 16th-century brasses in the aisle south of the choir, as well as a feeble likeness of Ireland's most

St. Patrick's Cathedral

- 🅰 Map p. 51
- ✉ Patrick's Cl., Dublin 8
- ☎ 01/453-9472
- 🚌 Bus: 49, 49A, 49B, 50, 54A, 56A, 65, 65B, 77, 77A; LUAS Green Line: St. Stephen's Green stop; Rail: Pearse Station
- 💲 $$

stpatricks cathedral.ie

CHRIST CHURCH CATHEDRAL

Founded by the first bishop of Dublin, this impressive cathedral is one of the city's oldest places of worship and a symbolic site. The precious relics kept here make it a place of pilgrimage that attracts religious tourism from all over the world. Breathe in the medieval atmosphere of the 12th-century crypt. It's one of the largest in Ireland and is rich with treasures and unusual objects.

■ In Christ Church Cathedral, visitors can attend a performance by one of Ireland's oldest and most prestigious choirs, founded in 1493.

Christ Church Cathedral

🏛 Map p. 51

✉ Christ Church Sq., Dublin 1

☎ 01/677-8099

🚌 Bus: 13, 27, 40, 49, 77; LUAS Red Line: Four Courts; Rail: Tara St. station

christchurch dublin.ie

In the 11th century, a small wooden church founded by Dùnàn, the first bishop of Dublin, and by the Norse sovereign, Sitriuc, stood on this spot. In the 12th century, it was rebuilt in stone by the Norman **Strongbow,** who was later buried in the cathedral and although his original tomb was destroyed, is commemorated by an austere statue in the southern nave.

The cathedral fell into a state of abandonment and acquired its present-day aspect only after a massive restoration project carried out in the 19th century. The ruins

of the Chapter House, built in the 13th century are a must-see, as is the enormous crypt that runs the entire length of the church.

Visitors can admire the cathedral's treasure as well as some curious objects such as the mummified cat and mouse that were found in one of the organ pipes, immortalized in one last fatal chase.

A discounted combined ticket gives you access to **Dublinia,** an interactive museum that recreates the Viking history of Dublin. It's located on the other side of the bridge outside the cathedral. ■

GUINNESS STOREHOUSE

Half of all the beer drunk in Ireland is brewed in the sprawling Guinness Brewery at St. James's Gate on the Liffey's north bank and thousands of pints are drunk daily in 120 countries in all parts of the world—not bad for the little family brewery that Arthur Guinness established on the site in 1759.

The brewery itself is not open to the public, but the company's Guinness Storehouse attraction nearby will tell you all you want to know and then—fulfilling Guinness's proud boast—serve you the best pint and one of the best views in Dublin.

Inside one of Guinness's former fermentation and storage plants—a handsome 1904 building in cast iron and brick—the company has developed a six-story exhibition based around a giant atrium shaped like a pint glass. Here you'll find out exactly how the black nectar is made—ingredients, techniques, plant, malting process, and hop growing. One section is dedicated to the iconic Guinness ads that have gone down in advertising history. On the top floor, in the **Gravity Bar,** you can shop, relish a taste of "Black Gold," and enjoy the splendid view of the city. ■

Guinness Storehouse

- Map p. 51
- St. James's Gate, Dublin 8
- 01/408-4800
- Bus: 123; LUAS Red Line: James's; Rail: Heuston station
- $$

guinness-storehouse.com

EXPERIENCE: Discover the Great Pubs of Dublin

Dublin and pubs . . . now why would they come to mind together? Ireland is justly famous for its pubs—not as drinkers' dens, but as centers of social life, conversation, information, music, and fun. Here's a handful of suggestions to get you started.

At 8 Poolbeg Street, between Trinity College and the River Liffey, you'll find **Mulligan's;** the Guinness is superb. East of Grafton Street are **Davy Byrne's** at 21 Duke Street (see p. 68), **McDaid's** (see p. 69) at 3 Harry Street, and the traditional **Kehoe's** at 9 Anne Street South.

West of St. Stephen's Green lie three contrasting pubs. On Lower Baggot Street you'll find **Doheny & Nesbitt,** a popular spot-the-politician pub at No. 5, and the plain-fronted **Toner's** (see p. 69) at No. 139, the only pub, reputedly, that W. B. Yeats ever brought himself to enter, considering himself

too refined for such places; and at 15 Merrion Row is a traditional music pub, **O'Donoghue's.**

In Temple Bar you'll get tourist tunes in **Oliver St. John Gogarty** at 58–59 Fleet Street. The modern **Porter House** at 16 Parliament Street brews its own delicious beer, while the **Stag's Head** in Dame Court off Dame Street has a cozy backstreet atmosphere.

At 3 Great George Street South, the **Long Hall** is another pub full of character. Eastward, two great traditional music pubs face each other across Bridge Street Lower, **O'Shea's Merchant** and the **Brazen Head.**

North of the river is a splendid trio of pubs with music: the **Cobblestone Bar** on King Street North and **Hughes** at 19 Chancery Street for traditional sessions, and **Slattery's** at 129 Capel Street for rock and ballads.

PHOENIX PARK

Phoenix Park—the green lung of Dublin—is a vast oasis of trees and grassland with nature trails, bike paths, polo fields, and other attractions for Dubliners looking to enjoy a bit of fresh air. The park has been open to the public since the 18th century.

Dublin's Phoenix Park is the largest urban green space in Europe.

Phoenix Park

- Map p. 50
- Main entrance on Parkgate St.
- Bus: 25, 26, 46A, 66, 67, 69, 69X from city center; LUAS Red Line: Heuston; Rail: Heuston Station

phoenixpark.ie

Phoenix Park Visitor Centre

- 01/677-0095
- Bus: 37 from Abbey St. to Ashtown Gate, 38, 39, 70

Surprisingly few visitors to Dublin get out to Phoenix Park, although it lies only just over a mile (1.6 km) upriver of the city center and conveniently close to the national monument of Kilmainham Gaol. The park never feels crowded—this is the largest walled city park in Europe, with 1,750 acres (700 ha) of open space enclosed by 7 miles (11 km) of wall.

Displays in the **visitor center,** near the northern edge, trace the park's history. Toward the eastern end is **Dublin Zoo** (dublinzoo.ie). Visit primates on the Monkey islands, go on safari (sort of) in the African Savanna section, and don't miss feeding time for the sea lions.

Attractions

The president of Ireland lives in the park in a mansion called **Áras an Uachtaráin;** the residence of the U.S. ambassador is here, too. The park is also the site of **St. Mary's Hospital.**

By far the best thing to do in Phoenix Park is to bring a picnic and wander through woods and over grassland, watching for fallow deer and stopping to enjoy the spectacle of Gaelic sports such as hurling and Gaelic football that are played on weekends. ∎

KILMAINHAM GAOL

For anyone who wants to understand what has shaped modern Ireland, anyone with an interest in Irish history, a tour of the country's most famous jail is a must. Once you have walked its echoing corridors and stood silently in one of the tiny, chilly cells, you will appreciate why this national monument was a keystone in the building of independent Ireland.

Certain dates resonate around Kilmainham—1798, 1803, 1848, 1867, 1881, 1883. These were the years of abortive uprisings and rebellions in an Ireland ruled from mainland Britain.

But 1916 is the most poignant date in Kilmainham's history because, in May of that year, 15 leaders of the Easter Rising were shot for treason in the prison yard. The General Post Office on O'Connell Street, scene of the first proclamation of the Irish Republic and the subsequent weeklong siege of the Easter rebels, is one icon of the Irish struggle for independence.

Kilmainham is an even more potent symbol; its story goes back more than two centuries and represents the continuing struggle.

Building of the prison started in 1786, on open fields to the west of the city center. It was designed to look as grimly forbidding as possible: Above the door are carved the Five Devils of Kilmainham, five hissing snakes chained by the neck to represent evil under strict control.

The prison was closed definitively in 1924. After a period of abandonment, it was made into a museum and reopened to the public in 1966.

Kilmainham Gaol

- Map p. 50
- Inchicore Rd., Kilmainham, Dublin 8
- 01/453-5984
- Guided tours only; booking is recommended
- Bus: 69, 79; LUAS Red Line: Suir Road; Rail: Heuston Station
- $

kilmainhamgaol museum.ie

The claustrophobic facade of Kilmainham Gaol was designed to kill the hope of every prisoner.

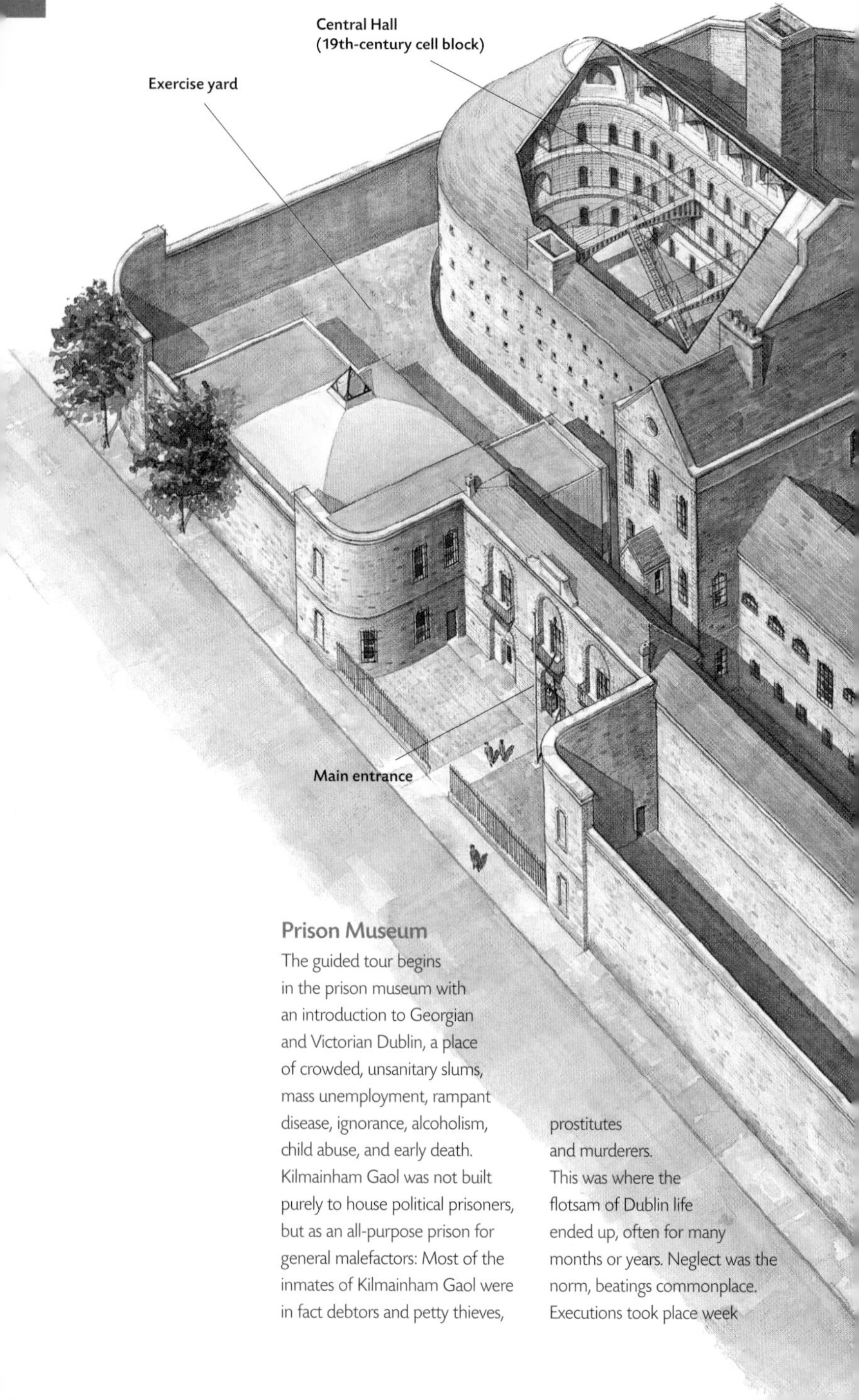

Central Hall
(19th-century cell block)

Exercise yard

Main entrance

Prison Museum

The guided tour begins
in the prison museum with
an introduction to Georgian
and Victorian Dublin, a place
of crowded, unsanitary slums,
mass unemployment, rampant
disease, ignorance, alcoholism,
child abuse, and early death.
Kilmainham Gaol was not built
purely to house political prisoners,
but as an all-purpose prison for
general malefactors: Most of the
inmates of Kilmainham Gaol were
in fact debtors and petty thieves,
prostitutes
and murderers.
This was where the
flotsam of Dublin life
ended up, often for many
months or years. Neglect was the
norm, beatings commonplace.
Executions took place week

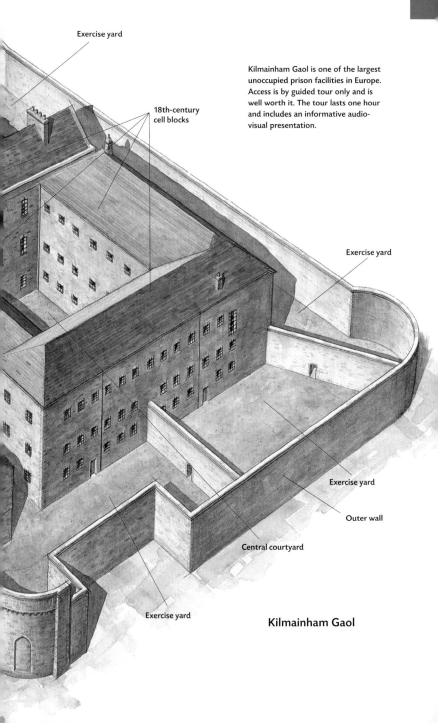

Exercise yard

18th-century
cell blocks

Kilmainham Gaol is one of the largest
unoccupied prison facilities in Europe.
Access is by guided tour only and is
well worth it. The tour lasts one hour
and includes an informative audio-
visual presentation.

Exercise yard

Exercise yard

Outer wall

Central courtyard

Exercise yard

Kilmainham Gaol

in, week out, in the prison or before large public crowds out at Blackrock on the southern arm of Dublin Bay.

With such scenes in mind, you move off from the museum, along the east wing's gloomy corridors to emerge into the frigid light of the huge Central Hall, a horseshoe-shaped structure built in 1862. With 100 cells stacked in four tiers and looking inward to a cats' cradle of iron walkways and stairs, it is the embodiment of control. Wardens muffled the walkways with carpet so prison-

Famine Refugees

Kilmainham Gaol in mid-Victorian times was as grim a place as could be imagined. Even so, to many desperate and starving men and women during the Great Famine (see pp. 28–29) it seemed a refuge. They would break windows or steal fruit in order to be sent to Kilmainham and qualify for a straw bed in a cold cell and a spoonful of the prison's anemic gruel.

ers never knew when they were being observed.

Here you find a cell decorated with a mural, the *Madonna and Child*. It was painted in 1923 by Grace Plunkett while she was held here as a republican prisoner during the Irish Civil War. Seven years earlier, as Grace Gifford, she had married Joseph Plunkett in the chapel of Kilmainham Gaol

at 1:30 a.m. on May 4, 1916, with 20 British soldiers as witnesses.

Two hours later her bridegroom was dead, shot for treason as one of the leaders of the Easter Rising. Thinking of this, you can't help but be moved as you inspect the chapel. A carpenter who was serving a seven-year sentence crafted the altar: His crime was the theft of a cart wheel.

Easter Rising Rebels

The cells where the Easter Rising rebels were held are in the older part of the prison. You can have yourself shut into one of these stark, claustrophobic boxes where the insurgents were held while the authorities decided their fate.

The cells had their final use during and just after the Civil War of 1922–1923, when Sinn Féin leader Eamon de Valera—later in life to become Taoiseach (prime minister) and president of Ireland—was incarcerated here. The prison then lay derelict until its restoration in the 1960s.

Outside, you walk through a grim, gray enclosure walled with stone—the **"Invincibles' Yard,"** named after members of a secret organization who were hanged in the yard in 1883.

And so you move on to the most resonant, most chilling place on the whole tour—the high-walled prison yard, once used as a place for convicts to break stones in hard labor, where 15 of the Easter Rising leaders were executed by firing squad for treason. The signatories

Thanks to the defining drama that the Easter Rising prisoners played out within its walls, Kilmainham Gaol has become a symbol of Irish independence and national pride.

of the original Proclamation of the Republic—Padraic Pearse, James Connolly, Joseph Plunkett, Sean MacDermott, Thomas MacDonagh, Eamonn Ceannt, and Thomas Clarke—were shot, along with eight others, in ones and twos over the week between May 3 and 12, 1916. Connolly could not stand, his ankle shattered, so he was shot sitting tied to a chair.

When details of these long-drawn-out executions began to emerge, the public mood in Ireland swung behind the rebels.

The British had succeeded only in creating martyrs out of men whose actions most ordinary Irish men and women had been inclined to view with bafflement or contempt.

The Poorest Prisoners

In among all the reverberations of Ireland's turbulent history, one still small voice is heard above all—the voice of the poor. Under the tide of great events, it is the stories of Dublin's poor and dispossessed that stay with you the longest—the young boy hanged for stealing some bread and the starving girl who had herself sentenced to Kilmainham Gaol to have at least a watery prison gruel to eat. ■

WALK: HILL OF HOWTH

Feel like taking a break from the city and getting a lungful of fresh sea air? This half-day stroll around a beautiful coastline is a favorite with Dubliners and easily reached by suburban DART train in less than half an hour from the city center.

Sea and coast views under huge skies enhance the bracing walk around Howth Head.

Disembark the DART *(tel 01/836-6222)* at Howth Station. Turn left out of the station along **Howth Harbour ❶**. In a third of a mile (0.5 km), turn right up Abbey Street. The **Abbey Tavern ❷**, on the right, serves good lunches. Take the steps beside the pub to reach the ruined shell of **St. Mary's Abbey ❸**, famous throughout medieval Europe for the brilliance of its monks. The view from here over Howth Harbour is excellent.

Spies from Paris University once landed at Howth, intending to entice away the abbey's students. But the abbot, forewarned, posted monks disguised as dock laborers on the harbor. The spies returned to France empty-handed, saying that it was useless to bring offers of education to a place where even the dockers conversed in Latin!

Return to Abbey Street and continue uphill, then turn right along St. Lawrence's Road. In about 100 yards (90 m), continue along Grace O'Malley Road, then turn left up Grace

> **NOT TO BE MISSED:**
>
> **Howth Harbour • Abbey Tavern • View from Howth Abbey ruins • Shielmartin summit • View of Baily Lighthouse**

O'Malley Drive. Where the road bends to the left, keep walking straight up the path for about 380 yards (350 m), and then follow the road to the top. Turn right at the top. A ramp next to house No. 53 leads to a grassy slope; climb it to go through trees and on up a steep bank to a golf course. At the top, bear right along the top edge of the course and follow the path under craggy Dun Hill. Cross the golf course and climb the slope ahead to the top of **Shielmartin ❹**.

Offering the best view of the walk, this summit takes in Dublin Bay, the city, and the Wicklow Mountains. Follow the path seaward off the hill,

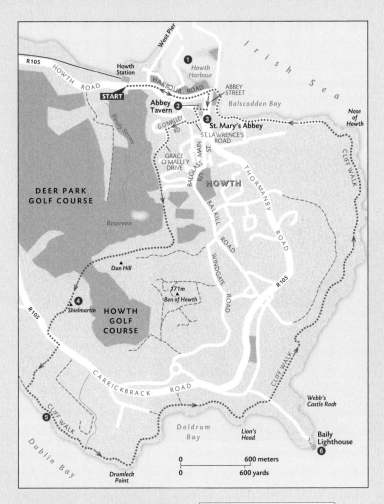

descending to turn left on Carrickbrack Road. In about 300 yards (250 m), cross the road and go through a gate, ignoring the ominous "Dangerous Cliffs" sign as the cliffs are perfectly safe. Take the footpath down to the shore. Turn left here and follow the **cliff walk** ❺ ("Howth Cliff Path"). Narrow in places, it runs for about 5 miles (8 km) around the bulbous nose of the Howth Peninsula.

You will pass by **Baily Lighthouse** ❻, built in 1814. Continue walking along the coast path

🗺 See also area map p. 49 D3

▶ Howth DART railway station, a 25-minute run from Connolly Station, central Dublin

↔ 7 miles (11 km)

🕐 3–4 hours

▶ Howth Harbour

among seabirds and wonderful sea views until the path deposits you safely back at the lovely Howth Harbour.

ATTRACTIONS OUT OF TOWN

By far the best way for visitors to get a feel for what lies beyond O'Connell Street and St. Stephen's Green is the DART—Dublin Area Rapid Transit. These little green trains are not just cattle trucks for commuters; they bring the pleasures of outer Dublin within easy reach of the city center. The DART is punctual, quick, and handy, with city-center stations north of the River Liffey at Connolly and south at Tara Street and Pearse Street.

Bathers launch themselves into the sea at Sandycove.

North of Dublin

Ride the DART north of the city center to reach **St. Anne's Park** (*Killester or Harmonstown Station*). On the west side of the park, a footpath dips through a wooded valley, past a number of eccentric architectural follies, before reaching the coast and some fine views across North Bull Island to the rounded peninsular hump of Howth Head.

North Bull Island, often known as Dollymount Strand, has an east-facing coast of fine sandy beaches where you can swim in a bracingly fresh sea. It is also a great favorite with bird-watchers. Its location is a good spot for migrating birds to descend and rest mid-journey, and many species of northern ducks, geese, and waders come to spend the winter here. Bring your binoculars for a stroll along the beach, and if you want to find out more about the wildlife, visit the interpretive center.

The terminus of the DART lies farther along the coast at **Howth—** the start point for a superb 7-mile (11 km) walk (see pp. 80–81).

South of Dublin

Southward from the city center, the DART reaches **Booters-town Station** on the shores of St. George's Channel. Here at low tide you can hop over the seawall and enjoy a superb bird-watching beach stroll on a great scimitar of sand. Farther along is **Dún Laoghaire** (pronounced "Dun Leary").

Next comes **Sandycove,** where the granite-built Martello tower now known as the **James Joyce Tower & Museum** is an object of pilgrimage for fans of *Ulysses*. For one week in August 1904, when Joyce was at the beginning of

INSIDER TIP:

The picturesque
seaside town of Howth
is best visited on a Sunday,
when the bustling local
farmer's market is in
full swing.

—CHIARA CECCHINI
National Geographic
contributor

his career, he stayed in this tower
(built in 1804 under the threat of
an invasion by Napoleon) with his
friend, Oliver St. John Gogarty.
He later used the setting for the
opening scene of *Ulysses*, in which
Mulligan, a character inspired by
Gogarty, goes about his morning
shave at the top of the tower.
The view from here is
spectacular. The museum
was opened in 1962 by the
courageous bookseller Sylvia
Beach, who put *Ulysses* into
print. It holds enough Joyce
memorabilia to make a visit here
truly worthwhile.

Beyond Sandycove, the DART
reaches the nicely preserved old
seaside town of **Dalkey,** with
its stubby fortified house called
Archbold's Castle. Flann O'Brien
made merry with Dalkey's genteel
atmosphere in his bitingly funny
book *The Dalkey Archive.* Dalkey lies
around the foot of **Killiney Hill**
(Killiney Station), worth climbing
for its stunning views around the
giant curve of Dublin Bay to far-off
Howth Head.

In the well-heeled village of
Killiney there's always the sport
of celebrity spotting; enough rock
stars, writers, and actors have
migrated here for locals to dub it
"Paddywood." Farther along the
coast, you can take a pleasant 4.3-
mile (7 km) walk from the DART
station in **Bray** to **Greystones.**
It takes approximately two hours
to reach the top of Bray Head,
where you can experience the
splendid views over the sea before
walking back down to Greystones
where you can eat in one of the
picturesque pubs or restaurants. ∎

**DART
information**
☎ 01/836-6222

**James Joyce
Tower & Museum**
🅰 49 D2
✉ Sandycove
Point, Dublin
☎ 01/280-9265
🚍 Bus: 59 from
Dún Laoghaire,
7 from Eden
Quay (Dublin)
Rail: Sandycove
and Glasthule
Station

joycetower.ie

EXPERIENCE: Swimming at Sandycove

For generations, Dubliners have learned
to swim at the **Forty Foot.** Located out at
Sandycove on the southern curve of Dublin Bay, the Forty Foot is a fortified headland whose name commemorates the
40th Regiment of Foot, which was sta-
tioned here around the turn of the 19th
century to resist any invasion attempt by
Napoleon Bonaparte.

With its stone-cut steps and slippery
rocks, the Forty Foot was, by tradition,
reserved exclusively for men, while its
relatively secluded position meant that

skinny-dipping was the rule rather than
the exception. However, these days,
things have changed at the Forty Foot;
both sexes now swim here, both suitably
attired.

To reach the Forty Foot at Sandycove,
take the N11 from Dublin city center to
Dún Laoghaire. From there, follow the
coast road past the East Pier. Turn left at
Sandycove. Be sure to bring with you a
bathing suit, sunscreen, and a good towel.
Be aware that the water around the Forty
Foot is notoriously chilly.

More Places to Visit in & Around Dublin

14 Henrietta Street

Henrietta Street was developed in the 1720s by architect Luke Gardiner and still conserves a number of authentic Georgian townhouses. A museum at 14 Henrietta Street (accessible only by guided tour) tells the story of one such townhouse, initially an aristocratic residence that in the beginning of the 19th century, during a period of economic decline, became a tenement used to house numerous working class families. *14henriettastreet.ie*  Map p. 51 ✉ 14 Henrietta St., Dublin 1 ☎ 01/524-0383 🚌 Bus: 1, 4, 9, 11, 13, 16, 38, 38A, 40, 46A, 83, 122, 140; LUAS Green Line: Dominick; Rail: Connolly Station 💲 $

EPIC The Irish Emigration Museum

The museum was inaugurated in 2016 in a building from 1820 that was once a customs warehouse. It uses high-tech, interactive installations to tell the story of the 70 million Irish people who left their homeland. Its 20 galleries explain the causes and consequences of emigration and tell the stories of people, both famous and unknown, who have never let go of the strong connection they feel with their native land. *epicchq.com* Map p. 51 ✉ CHQ, Custom House Quay, Dublin 1 ☎ 01/906-0861 🚌 Bus: 14, 15, 27; LUAS Red Line: George's Dock; Rail: Connolly Station 💲 $$

Farmleigh House & Estate

Farmleigh House lies in its 78-acre (31.5 ha) estate on the western edge of Phoenix Park. It was one of the Guinness family's private residences. The interior features Connemara marble columns, a magnificent wrought-iron staircase, the domed and stuccoed Nobel Room, and a superb ballroom with an oak floor—made out of superannuated Guinness barrels, according to Dublin legend! Outside are sunken and walled gardens, a café in a former boathouse, and plenty of leafy walks. *farm leigh.ie* 🏞 49 B3 ✉ Castleknock, Dublin 15 ☎ 01/815-5900 or 01/815-5981 🚌 Bus: 37 🕐 House tours: Wed., Sun., & bank holidays; grounds open year-round

The Marsh's Library collection includes fine manuscripts and books from the 15th to 20th centuries.

Chilling Churches

Dublin has several churches with more or less macabre items on display. The vaults of **St. Michan's Church** (Church St., Dublin 7, tel 01/872-4154, closed Sun., $ tour), on the north side of the Liffey, contains two remarkable curios—a gloriously carved organ case and, in the vaults, a collection of "mummified" bodies, including those of crusaders dating from the 12th century. They have been preserved by the water-absorbing qualities of the magnesian limestone foundations.

St. Valentine's remains are contained in a handsome black-and-gold chest under an altar in the **Whitefriar Street Carmelite Church** (56 Aungier St., tel 01/475-8821). They were given to Father John Spratt by Pope Gregory XVI as a reward for Spratt's preaching when the Dublin priest visited Rome in 1835.

In **St. Patrick's Cathedral** (see p. 71), the Jonathan Swift display in the north transept features a plaster cast of the writer's skull. The original skull was removed from Swift's grave in the 1830s and started a bizarre 100-year circuit of the drawing rooms of Dublin as a conversation piece. It was reburied in the 1920s.

Glasnevin Cemetery

A visit to Dublin's monumental cemetery is a plunge into the history of the country. Famous Irishmen like Charles Stewart Parnell, Michael Collins, Brendan Behan, and Jim Larkin are buried here, as is Daniel O'Connell, whose grave is marked by a 168-foot **tower**. The tower was damaged by a bomb attributed to the Loyalists in the 1970s and was later restored. You can take one of the guided tours of the cemetery or you can visit the **museum** ($) that narrates the history of the people who are buried here. glasnevinmuseum.ie 🗺 49 B3 ✉ Finglas Rd., Glasnevin, Dublin 11 ☎ 01/882-6500 🚌 Bus: 40, 140

Irish Museum of Modern Art

The museum is located in a beautiful building from 1860 that was originally designed to be the Royal Hospital. Since 1991, it has been home to a collection of over 3,500 works of modern art, both Irish and not. The temporary retrospectives of international modern artists are particularly interesting. imma.ie 🗺 Map p. 50 ✉ Royal Hospital, Military Rd., Kilmainham, Dublin 8 ☎ 01/612-9900 🕐 Closed Mon. 🚌 Bus: 51B, 78A, 123; LUAS Red Line: Heuston; Rail: Heuston Station

Little Museum of Dublin

In an elegant Georgian building, two halls are chock-full of unusual, nostalgic objects that tell the history of Dublin in 20th century. On guided tours, guests discover an array of anecdotes about the city that extend from Queen Victoria's visit to the U2's climb to fame. littlemuseum.ie 🗺 Map p. 50 ✉ 15 St. Stephen's Green, Dublin 2 ☎ 01/661-1000 🚌 Bus: All cross-city buses; LUAS Green Line: St. Stephen's Green; Rail: Tara St. Station

Marsh's Library

This little jewel in the heart of Dublin was founded in 1707 and still conserves the atmosphere of the era. The massive oak shelves hold antique manuscripts and books published between the 15th and 18th centuries. marshlibrary.ie 🗺 Map p. 50 ✉ St. Patrick's Close, Dublin 8 ☎ 01/454-3511 🕐 Closed Tue. and Sun. 🚌 Bus: 27, 56A, 77A, 150, 151; LUAS Green Line: St. Stephen's Green; Rail: Pearse Station

National Botanic Gardens

These gardens have more than 20,000 plant species. The impressive greenhouses contain ferns, alpine and tropical water plants, and much more. botanicgardens.ie

■ Dubliners take to the water of the Grand Canal basin aboard a Viking Splash tour boat.

INSIDER TIP:

Explore Dublin by land and water on a Viking Splash tour *(vikingsplash. com)*. The amphibious World War II craft is the best way to see the city.

—ALLY THOMPSON
National Geographic contributor

🗻 49 C3 ✉ Botanic Ave., Glasnevin, Dublin 9 ☎ 01/804-0300 🕐 Closed at 6 p.m. (winter at 4:30 p.m.) 🚍 Bus: 4, 9, 83

National Gallery of Ireland

The collection focuses on European art from the Middle Ages to the 20th century. Its masterpieces include J.M.W. Turner's watercolors, Caravaggio's *The Taking of Christ*, Picasso's *Still Life with a Mandolin*, works by a variety of Flemish artists, and French and English impressionists. One hall is dedicated to the "hallucinatory" works of Jack Yeats (see pp. 208–209). *nationalgallery.ie*

🗻 Map p. 51 ✉ Merrion Sq. West, Dublin 2 ☎ 01/661-5133 🚍 Bus: 5, 7, 7A, 10, 44, 48A; LUAS Green Line: St. Stephen's Green; Rail: Pearse Station

St. Audoen's Church

Two churches of the same name, one a Protestant church from the 12th century and the other a Catholic church built in the 19th century, sit adjacent to one another. Both are dedicated to Saint Audoen, the patron saint of Normandy. Follow the museum itinerary in St. Anne's Chapel for a full immersion into medieval Dublin. *heritageireland.ie*

🗻 Map p. 51 ✉ Corn Market High, Dublin 3 ☎ 01/667-0088 🕐 Closed at 5.30 p.m. 🚍 Bus: 13, 27, 40, 49, 77; LUAS Red Line: Four Courts

The Bridges of Dublin

Like an arrow shot through the heart of Dublin, the Liffey River divides the city's northern and southern areas. The two banks are connected by over 20 bridges. Some of the more famous ones are the **James Joyce Bridge,** designed by star architect Santiago Calatrava in 2003; the **O'Connell Bridge,** the widest bridge, open to both pedestrians and vehicles; and the romantic **Ha'Penny Bridge,** a narrow, winding cast-iron structure named for the price of what was once the bridge's toll, a half penny. But the most spectacular is the **Samuel Beckett Bridge,** inaugurated in 2009 and shaped like a harp, the symbol of Ireland.

From green Tipperary farmlands and the horse-racing plains of
Kildare to the Wicklow Mountains and the sandy coast of Wexford

EASTERN IRELAND

■ The beloved Irish horse

EASTERN IRELAND

Eastern Ireland takes in the mountains, grassy plains, sandy coasts, and rich green farm-land that make up the southeast of the island. It is instantly likeable, its pleasures easily accessible. All you'll need is plenty of time to take the narrow back roads, explore the little country towns, and bask in the good weather of Ireland's driest, sunniest region.

Kildare is the most celebrated county for horse racing and breeding in Ireland. If you are a horse fanatic, the county town of Kildare will entrance you with its National Stud and Horse Museum and its world-famous racing and training ground of the Curragh. But even if you do not care for horses, these characterful places will fascinate you.

To the east is County Wicklow, where the rugged, heather-clad mountains—crossed by a fine network of footpaths—hide the beautiful old monastic settlement of Glendalough in their heart. Yet most visitors content themselves with Glendalough and never get out of the hills and down to the uncrowded coast.

Two rivers cross the rolling farmland of little County Carlow—the Barrow in the west and the Slaney in the east. To the west, County Kilkenny has the finest medieval town in Ireland as its capital. South is County Wexford, with its fine sandy coast and superb winter bird-watching on the marshes, as well as the old-style county town of Wexford, full of music, from traditional to opera,

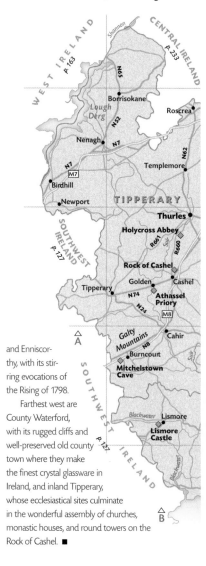

and Enniscor-thy, with its stirring evocations of the Rising of 1798.

Farthest west are County Waterford, with its rugged cliffs and well-preserved old county town where they make the finest crystal glassware in Ireland, and inland Tipperary, whose ecclesiastical sites culminate in the wonderful assembly of churches, monastic houses, and round towers on the Rock of Cashel. ∎

Area of map detail

Belfast

Dublin

CENTRAL IRELAND p.233

M4

Maynooth
M4 Lexlip
Carbury
Castletown House Celbridge
Clane
R403
Grand Canal
Bog of Allen
Liffey

DUBLIN
p.47

Irish National Stud
Russborough House
Enniskerry
Naas
Powerscourt
Bray
Kilmacanoge
Kildare
M7 **Newbridge** Blessington
Powerscourt Waterfall
Grey-stones
Monasterevin
M7
The Curragh
Kilcullen
Pollaphuca Res.
Sally Gap
Great Sugar Loaf
501m
Dan Donnelly obelisk
R413
R758
WICKLOW MTS. N.P.
R759
R761
Roundwood
Newtown Mt. Kennedy
M11
N78
Hollywood
N81
Wicklow Gap
R755
R756
KILDARE
Athy
N9
Wicklow Gap
R715
Glendalough
Devil's Glen
Ashford
Rathnew
R418
M9
Sloney
Laragh
Vartry
R752
Wicklow
Wicklow Head
Baltinglass
Wicklow Mountains
▲925m
Lugnaquilla
Rathdrum
R758
Brittas Bay
M7
CENTRAL IRELAND p.233
Castledermot high crosses
R418
WICKLOW
Meeting of the Waters
Mizen Head
Hackestown
Ow
Avoca
Carlow
Graiguecullen
Brownhill's dolmen
R747
Vale of Avoca
Avoca Handweavers'
Castlecomer
Tullow
Arklow
Ballyragget
CARLOW
Deel
R747
M11
Kilmichael Point
M8 Freshford
Black Castle
Leighlinbridge
Dunmore Cave
Ballyfogle
M9
Ballymoon Castle
Urlingford
Nore
Bagenalstown
Bunclody
N11
Gorey
N8
Kilkenny
N10
Slaney
Bann
Courtown
R741
Cahore Point
KILKENNY
Borris
Blackstairs Mts.
793m ▲Mount Leinster
Kells
Nicolas Mosse Pottery
Borris House
R742
Callan
King's
Thomastown
Graiguenamanagh
National 1798 Visitor Centre
Fethard
N75
Knocktopher
N10
Jerpoint Abbey
St. Mullin's
Enniscorthy
Vinegar Hill
WEXFORD
Ahenny Church
R697
M9
N9
Nore
N30
Clonmel
Ormond Castle
New Ross
Irish National Heritage Park
Carrick-on-Suir
Mullinavat
N25
Wexford Wildfowl Reserve
WATERFORD
N11
Wexford
Wellingtonbridge
Irish Agricultural Museum
Rosslare
Kilmacthomas
Waterford
Ballyhack
N25
Waterford Crystal
R734
Guillamene Cove
Waterford
R733
N72 Dungarvan
Tramore
Dunmore East
Fethard
Slade
Kilmore Quay
Carnsore Point
N25
Hook Head
SALTEE ISLANDS
Celtic Sea
Ardmore monastic site
Ardmore
Ram Head

St. George's Channel

Rosslare Harbour
Fishguard, Pembroke
Roscoff, Cherbourg

0   20 kilometers
0   10 miles

6

5

4

3

2

1

C   D   E   F

COUNTY KILDARE

County Kildare holds a splendid variety of treasures: a fine cathedral in a friendly town, the Irish National Stud with its flawless Japanese garden and Horse Museum, and the Curragh—hundreds of acres of grassland to run wild. You'll see horses everywhere, because the Curragh is the home of Irish horse racing and a world-renowned bloodstock breeding center.

Market Day in the shadow of St. Brigid's Cathedral in the town of Kildare

Kildare Town

Kildare is a little town with a storied history. Christianity—courtesy of St. Patrick—had been in Ireland for less than 60 years when, in 490, St. Brigid founded a mixed-sex monastery here on the wide plains of the Curragh (see p. 94), 30 miles (50 km) from Ireland's east coast.

St. Brigid's Cathedral: You can get an idea of what the Curragh must have looked like from the **scale model** of the walled settlement that stands in the present-day St. Brigid's Cathedral—thatched round wattle-and-daub huts for the monks and nuns, dining and kitchen buildings, and a big wooden church in the middle.

INSIDER TIP:

Try getting a bird's-eye view from one of Ireland's ecclesiastical landmarks: the round towers. St. Brigid's in Kildare and St. Canice's in Kilkenny (see p. 111) are open for the public to climb.

—TOM JACKSON
National Geographic Society

A handsome gray stone cathedral stands on the monastery site today. It dates from the 13th century, although it was heavily restored in 1875. Some amusing modern gargoyles adorn the corbel table—they include two bespectacled men, one with a cow across his shoulders, the other clutching a pair of moneybags.

Along with the monastery model in the south transept is the fragmented but beautiful **tomb of Bishop Walter Wellesley** (died 1539), with stone carvings that include a very poignant figure of Christ stripped for scourging, sitting with hands bound, his head bowed in sorrow and exhaustion. Under the eaves of the tomb, sharp-eyed explorers will spot a *sheela-na-gig* dancing with her legs lasciviously astraddle—and maybe a similarly unabashed sister, too.

The guard/guide will show you a so-called **pardon stone** with a penitential prayer carved on it. The carving also features a rare depiction of two angels holding jars to catch streams of the crucified Christ's blood.

The cathedral **font** is a tremendous piece of work, a crude and plain upright stone rectangle with a recessed top that might have been created anytime over the history of Christianity—and possibly long before that.

Round Tower: Beside the cathedral rears Kildare's impressive round tower (*tel 045/441-654*), 108 feet (33 m) tall, an orange-gray finger of stone now shaggy with innumerable clumps of grass. Some date it to the 10th century, some to the 12th. The fine recessed **Romanesque doorway**—unusually ornate for a round tower—was set into the tower 15 feet (5 m) above

Kildare Town

◬ 89 D5

Visitor Information

✉ Heritage Centre, Market Sq., Kildare, Co. Kildare

☎ 045/530-672

EXPERIENCE:
Riding Horses

Fancy a trot after a day at the races? The Curragh may be the nerve center of Irish racing and riding, but if you want to spend a day in the saddle, there are stables open to the public throughout Ireland.

Stables around the Curragh include: **Leinster Lodge Equestrian Centre** *(Old Carton, Maynooth, Co. Kildare, tel 086/813-7773);* **Jag Equestrian** *(Winterdown Farm, Rathmore West, Naas, Co. Kildare, tel 045/834-277, jagequestrian. com);* **Ballyteague Stables** *(Ballyteague, Kilmeague, Naas, Co. Kildare, tel 085/736-8783);* **Dunbyrne Equestrian Centre** *(8 miles west of Naas, Kilmeage, Co. Kildare, tel 085/805-9529);* and **Clonfert Maynooth Equestrian Centre** *(Clonfert, Maynooth, Co. Kildare, tel 087/932-2909).*

The **Association of Irish Riding Establishments** *(tel 045/854-518, aire. ie)* maintains a list of hundreds of other registered riding stables across the country.

Castletown House & the Guest from Hell

Castletown House (at Celbridge off R403, closed Dec.–mid-March, *castletownhouse.ie*) was built between 1722 and 1732 for William Conolly, Speaker of the Irish House of Commons, as a piece of Palladian splendor. The huge colonnaded facade and the follies in the park are breathtaking. Much of the interior—the hand-blown Venetian chandeliers in the Long Gallery, the elaborate stucco on the staircase walls—reflect the exuberant 18th-century taste of Lady Louisa Lennox, only 15 years old when she married into the house.

According to legend, in the days when Lord and Lady Conolly entertained in the great house, a mysterious stranger, invited to dinner, fell asleep with his feet on a chair. When the stranger's boots were pulled off, cloven hooves were revealed. A priest threw his breviary at the demon, but it went clean through him and smashed a mirror. Shrieking with laughter, the stranger burst into flames and vanished through a crack in the floor—a fissure still visible today!

Irish National Stud

🏛 89 D5

✉ Tully, 1.2 miles (2 km) S of Kildare, Co. Kildare

☎ 045/521-617

💲 $$

irishnationalstud.ie

ground level to secure it against Danish attack. Inside, you ascend wooden ladders (103 steep steps, so not for the unfit) to reach the tower's **original cap,** a shallow ribbed cone inside inauthentic 19th-century battlements. The view is tremendous, 30 miles (48 km) across the plain of the Curragh and north over the vast Bog of Allen.

If you find the cathedral and the round tower closed during the lunch hour *(1–2 p.m.),* a great place to sit it out is **Top Nolan's** *(tel 045/521-528),* a pub established in 1870 near the churchyard gates. Ancient wooden shelves behind the bar sag under their freight of vintage Guinness bottles and rolls of long-deleted brands of toilet paper, as if some past landlord had stocked up against nuclear war—a peculiarly Irish view of how to survive the apocalypse.

Irish National Stud

In 1900, Col. William Hall-Walker selected the village of Tully, 1.2

miles (2 km) south of Kildare, as the ideal place to start a stud farm—mainly because of the high levels of calcium carbonate (good for bone strength) in the waters of the River Tully and in the Curragh grass. Colonel Hall-Walker was phenomenally successful, so much so that when he gave the stud to the British Crown in 1915, he was created Lord Wavertree for his generosity with such a valuable asset.

A guided tour around the Irish National Stud (state property since 1943) makes for a fascinating hour, even for non-horse-lovers. Among the attractions are the **Foaling Yard,** with its intensive care stable, and the **Stallion Boxes,** with ten roomy boxes for the stallions whose fertility is the real business of the National Stud (covering fees can top $500,000 for a single impregnation). Mating takes place in the **Covering Shed.** The **Oak and Tully Walks** pass the railed paddocks where the beautiful creatures graze contentedly—mares and foals in small groups, the naturally aggressive stallions with a private paddock each.

Along the way, you learn plenty: that the Irish National Stud offers its breeding service to small-scale breeders at special cut-rate prices; that 90 percent of foals are born at night; that stallions work hard during the January to June breeding season, covering four mares a day (and being photographed while in action to prove paternity), six days a week. You'll also become acquainted with Colonel Hall-Walker's notions about astrology—he designed the stallions' stalls with special skylight roofs so that the moon and stars

could infiltrate with their beneficial influences, and he ordered all foals with inauspicious birth horoscopes to be sold, no matter how successful their bloodline.

The Gardens: Between 1906 and 1910, Colonel Hall-Walker engaged one of Japan's top gardeners, Tassa Eida, to lay out a **Japanese Garden** to reflect a "journey through life." From the Stallion Yard, you enter the garden by way of the Gate of Oblivion and make your way along the narrow Path of Life through gorgeous flower banks and trees, both dwarf and full size.

Bog of Allen
🔺 89 D5

EXPERIENCE: Visit the Bog of Allen Nature Centre

The peat bogs of Ireland are unique, both in their iconic status within Ireland and in the way they have been industrially exploited. You can learn all about these treasured natural resources at the **Bog of Allen Nature Centre** in Lullymore (Lullymore, Rathangan, Co. Kildare, tel 045/860-133, ipcc.ie), about 10.5 miles (17 km) north of Kildare.

The Bog of Allen, Ireland's largest expanse of raised bog, spills over the borders of nine midland counties and covers an area of about 235,000 acres (115,000 ha).

Like many boglands across the country, harvesting and development have wreaked havoc on its fragile ecosystem. The most devastating effects were felt in the last 50 years, when mechanized harvesting allowed for the swift destruction of mile after mile of bogland in order to feed power stations, agribusinesses, and urban consumers. Today, less than 10 percent of the bog remains unspoiled.

With the aim of returning the bog to wetland wilderness and preserving it for the enjoyment of future generations,

the Irish Peatland Conservation Council (IPCC)—a national charity that campaigns for the conservation of the country's peat bogs—established the Bog of Allen Nature Centre in 2003.

Visitors to the center learn all about the delicately balanced ecosystems of these fascinating and fragile places.

The insects that feed on the bog plants, for example, are themselves fed on by insectivorous plants, other insects, and small songbirds that in turn provide nourishment for larger birds, namely raptors. Frogs, otters, badgers, and red deer, wallowing away their parasites, also live in the bog, as have centuries of humans. Remarkable archaeological finds include ancient tools, wooden boats, leather shoes, and even preserved human bodies.

The IPCC—which conducts nature surveys of the area—runs bog trips, family nature days, and conservation work camps so that you can experience the bog in a hands-on way and contribute personally to its preservation.

HORSES & THE CURRAGH

What is it with the Irish and horses? Set up a horse race anywhere in the world and there'll be an Irish interest, and presence, more knowledgeable and intense than that of any other nation.

Horses thunder down the final stretch—another exciting day at the races!

Sales of Irish thoroughbred horses in Ireland alone approach 300 million dollars annually, and hundreds of millions more change hands each year in covering fees at Irish studs. Attendance at classic horse races swells year by year, while down at the other end of the scale you'll find ragged men with rusty old trotting rigs competing on country roads while onlookers bet as if money and common sense were going out of style.

The origins of good relations between the Irish and horses go back into pre-Christian times, with evidence that horses had been domesticated—perhaps for the table as much as for transport—as far back as 2000 B.C.

Steeplechasing had its origins in north County Cork in 1752, when Lord Doneraile staged a 4.5-mile (7 km) race between the two church steeples of Buttevant and St. Leger.

By the mid-19th century, there were nearly 30 flourishing racetracks in this small and poor country. Today, Irish men and women from all walks of life are as bound up as ever with the fortunes of horses, and Ireland still has the same number of racetracks.

Little of the elitism generally associated with racing obtains in Ireland—top hats mingle with cloth caps, morning coats with greasy anoraks, at meetings as prestigious as the Irish Derby or the 1,000 and 2,000 Guineas. These three premier races all take place at Ireland's best known racetrack, the Curragh (*cuirrech*, in Gaelic, means "racecourse"), just outside Kildare. The track is iconic among racegoers, and the broader expanse of the Curragh proper—6,000 acres (2,400 ha) of unfenced, gently rolling grassland around Kildare town—is the very heartland of Irish racing.

There are childhood's Tunnel of Ignorance, the Bridge of Engagement (broken in the middle!) and Bridge of Marriage, the mazelike Hill of Ambition, and the scarlet Bridge of Life to negotiate before you walk the smooth lawns of the Garden of Peace and Contentment in old age.

A recent addition to the attractions at the Irish National Stud is **St. Fiachra's Garden,** opened in 1999 by President Mary McAleese. In its way, this is as artificial as the Japanese Garden, with mock-ups of hermit huts and a "drowned forest" of imported bog oak. It lacks the subtlety of its senior cousin, but it still makes a pleasant stroll under silver birch and conifers.

INSIDER TIP:

On a sunny day, the Japanese Garden outside Kildare town is a beautiful setting for a stroll. For horse lovers, the National Stud is on the same grounds.

—SUSAN JOHNSTON
National Geographic field researcher

The Irish Horse Museum:

There is also the Irish Horse Museum to enjoy—the prize attraction here is the large but fragile preserved skeleton of Arkle, Ireland's great steeple-chaser of the 1960s, a rather bizarre but impressive item. Other exhibits include ancient

Dan Donnelly, the Curragh Bruiser

In a hollow on the south side of the R413 road, 3 miles (5 km) west of Kilcullen, stands a railed obelisk. It commemorates a bare-knuckle fight that took place in 1815 between Curragh-trained Dan Donnelly and the "famous English pugilist" George Cooper. Donnelly won, after a tremendous battle. In 1818, after another victory, he was dubbed "Sir Dan" by the Prince Regent. Less than two years later, Donnelly died, penniless. His body was exhumed and sold to a surgeon, who preserved the fighter's phenomenally long right arm.

pieces of horse equipment, a portrait of Colonel Hall-Walker with stiffly upswept moustache alongside one of his horse horoscope books for 1914, an enjoyable gallop through the history of the horse, and an entertaining account of the "pounding matches" of the 18th and 19th centuries. These challenges between country gentlemen—proxy dueling, in fact—involved each man in turn choosing a difficult or dangerous obstacle to jump, the other contestant being obliged to follow on behind. Needless to say, much money was wagered and many necks broken in pursuit of such macho honor and glory. ∎

COUNTY WICKLOW

If you have been exploring Dublin, you will almost certainly have seen the Wicklow Mountains already, rising enticingly in tall blue humps right on the southern doorstep of the capital. Inevitably, the mountains attract a lot of visitors; they are Dublin's country playground, after all, being less than half an hour's drive from the south of the city.

Early morning mists on the lakes at Glendalough are among many delights awaiting hikers in Wicklow.

Wicklow Mountains
🏔 89 E4

Wicklow Mountains

Most day-trippers make for only a handful of Wicklow destinations, the "must-see" sites: either the beautifully located monastic site of Glendalough, the picturesque village of Avoca with its photogenic handloom weavers, or the two great Anglo-Irish houses of Russborough and Powerscourt with their stunning gardens.

Once clear of them, however, you will find great tracts of upland and hillside, valley and coast, where you'll have only the birds—and maybe the occasional hiker or two—for company.

Getting There: There are several ways to drive into the Wicklow Mountains from Dublin, all of them increasingly beautiful the farther into the hills you go, all becoming steeper, slower, and more twisty. This is definitely not country for speed demons. The main coast road to Wexford, the N11, skirts the Wicklow Mountains on the east. Side roads from

INSIDER TIP:

The Wicklow Way's (see sidebar below) picture-perfect waterfalls and scenic views are perfect for both Sunday walkers as well as seasoned hikers venturing farther out.

—CHIARA CECCHINI
National Geographic
contributor

the N11 include the R755 from Kilmacanoge, under Great Sugar Loaf, and the R765 from Newtown Mount Kennedy—these both reach Roundwood on the shore of Vartry Reservoir.

Another beautiful way into the hills is via the R763 from Ashford near Wicklow town, which goes west to Laragh and Glendalough. Three miles (5 km) west of Ashford you can take a narrow side road on the right that leads to the entrance to the **Devil's Glen,** a spectacularly

rugged cleft threaded by a footpath from which you can see the Vartry River tumble 100 feet (30 m) into the agitated pool called the Devil's Punchbowl.

Alternatively, you could take the R115 from central Dublin through Rathfarnham and up over the wild **Sally Gap pass;** here the road divides, with the R759 swinging off to the left and down to Roundwood, while the R115 wriggles on down to Laragh and Glendalough. Or you could start out southwest from Dublin on the A81 Baltinglass road and follow it down to Hollywood, where the R756 cuts off eastward to Laragh over the **Wicklow Gap** in superb hill-country scenery of bare, heathery moorland rising to mountain ridges and peaks.

A lovely alternative to this last route is to leave the A81 at **Blessington,** 5 miles (8 km) north of Hollywood, and make your way on a minor road over narrow bridges and around the north

EXPERIENCE: Walking in the Wicklow Mountains

The Wicklow Mountains are wonderful country for hill walking. The usual precautions about keeping an eye on the weather and taking proper hiking gear and a good map need to be observed. They may look small in comparison with other mountain ranges—Lugnaquilla, the highest, reaches only 3,038 feet (927 m)—but the Wicklow Mountains and their notoriously changeable weather should be treated with proper respect. The **Wicklow Way** (wicklowway.com) is well marked, and any number of paths cross and climb the mountains.

Irish Ordnance Survey 1:50,000 sheets 56 and 62 (osi.ie) cover the mountains, as do the four more walker-friendly 1:30,000 Wicklow maps of EastWest Mapping (eastwestmapping.ie). The **Wicklow Mountains National Park** information point between Glendalough's Upper and Lower Lakes (open all year; Oct.–April, weekends only) has details of walks, or you can get books and maps from the visitor information offices at Glendalough (tel 0404/45-325; see p. 98), Wicklow town (tel 0404 /69-117), or Arklow (tel 0402/32-484).

St. Mary's Church

Glendalough

89 E5

Visitor Information

Entrance to
Glendalough,
Bray, Co.
Wicklow

0404/45-325

$ (site entry fee)

shore of the Pollaphuca Reservoir
to join the R758, then the R756.

Glendalough

Whichever route you choose, all
roads in the Wicklow Mountains
seem to lead inevitably to Glendalough. This remarkable monastic
site, tucked down in its lake valley
among steep mountainsides, well
repays half a day's exploration.
St. Kevin, its patron saint and
lodestar, was an awkward young
monk of the early sixth century,
so embarrassed at his unwanted
fame as a miracle worker that he
gave up monastic life to live in a
hollow tree in the utter seclusion
of Glendalough, the Valley of the
Two Lakes.

In 570, Kevin became abbot
of the slowly growing monastic

community in the valley, which
had consolidated into a sizable
fraternity by the time he died,
about 617. The lonely valley was
not immune from outside attack,
however; the community was
plundered by Danes in 922 and
again by Norman adventurers in
1176, but as a counterbalance there
was a great period of rebuilding
under Abbot Lorcan O'Tuathail
(St. Laurence O'Toole, 1128–1180).

In 1398, a party of English
soldiers razed the monastery,

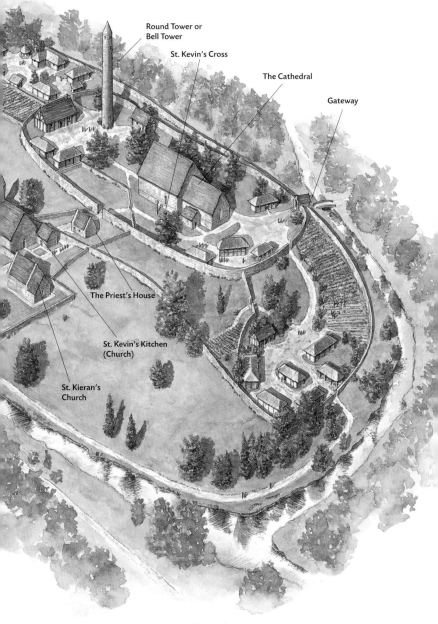

Round Tower or
Bell Tower

St. Kevin's Cross

The Cathedral

Gateway

The Priest's House

St. Kevin's Kitchen
(Church)

St. Kieran's
Church

**Glendalough monastic site,
reconstructed in the 12th century**

but the church continued in use. By then, holy pilgrimages to Glendalough, attracted by St. Kevin's piety, had become a fixture. Similar pilgrimages continue to this day.

It is not just the beautiful enclosed setting that makes Glendalough so special; equally remarkable are the number and density of the monastery's dozen or more 10th-, 11th-, and 12th-century buildings. A well-marked footpath leads through a sturdy granite double arch—the only surviving monastic gateway in Ireland, with a big sanctuary cross just inside—and runs around the riverside site. Here you will find **St. Kevin's Kitchen,** a cramped little oratory that might perhaps date as far back as the time of St.

INSIDER TIP:

Brittas Bay is a fantastic golden beach with impressive dunes (great for hide-and-seek!), but avoid visiting on the last weekend in August, when Dubliners descend on it in droves.

—ALLY THOMPSON
National Geographic contributor

Kevin, with a round 11th-century belfry. Nearby, among the remains of other buildings and a forest of graveslabs, are the shell of a ninth- or tenth-century cathedral, a 12th-century priest's house whose east wall contains a fine dogtooth arch, and a splendid tapering rocket of a tenth-century round tower, built 110 feet (33 m) high to give the Glendalough monks a good lookout, its stairless door some 12 feet (3.5 m) above the ground to keep besiegers at bay.

Toward the Coast

From Glendalough's neighboring village of Laragh, take the R755 to Rathdrum, the snaky road threading its way through the lovely tree-lined Vale of Clara. Then continue south on the R752, stopping 4 miles (6 km) south of Rathdrum to enjoy the spectacle of the confluence of the Avonbeg and Avonmore Rivers, an often crowded beauty spot known as the **Meeting of the Waters.**

From the town of Avoca (see sidebar left), the R752 and R747 lead southeast down the Vale of

Avoca Weavers

The village of Avoca, a scenic hamlet of whitewashed houses under slate roofs with wooded hills rising at its back, lies a mile (1.6 km) or so downstream from the Meeting of the Waters. Located on the banks of the River Avoca, the old mill here—the oldest still operating in Ireland—has been working since 1723. Inside, you can see weavers clacking and shuttling away at their rattly handlooms, though these days the mill also relies on power looms to keep up with demand. The mill shop *(The Mill, Avoca Village, Co. Wicklow, tel 0402/35105, avoca.com)* offers a good variety of rugs, blankets, and throws in natural fibers such as lamb's wool, cotton, mohair, and linen. You will also find a selection of gloves and scarves, as well as a line of tweed clothing for women.

EXPERIENCE: Staying on a Working Farm

If you want to experience the rhythms of life outside the city, consider spending a night or two on a working farm deep in the beautiful Irish countryside. Greet the dawn without an orchestra of cars, and breathe in the hay-scented air rather than traffic fumes and cigarette smoke.

Just across Dublin's southern doorstep sits the hilly county of Wicklow, temptingly near the capital but emphatically not spoiled by the close relationship. Leaving Dublin, travel south past the mountains of northern Wicklow to reach the region of south Wicklow around the village of Tinahely. There is great walking here, beautiful hilly country on the skyline, and best of all, **Kyle Farmhouse** *(Tinahely, Co. Wicklow, tel 059/647-1341, kylefarm.com)*, a working sheep and dairy outfit run by the

extremely hospitable Margaret and Hugh Coogan. Help milk the cattle or gather the sheep, go for a country walk under Hugh's guidance, or just relax with a nice cup of tea and a plate of Margaret's great home baking. Elsewhere, **Waterford Farm Accommodation** *(waterfordfarms.com)* lists a dozen working farms in County Waterford that offer a wide variety of experiences, from dairying to horses and sheep. Or try Northern Ireland's **Heathfield Farm** *(Coleraine, Co. Derry, tel 028/2955-8245, heathfieldfarm.com)*, an award-winning beef and sheep farm, very convenient for County Antrim's Causeway Coast.

Search for other farm opportunities online at *irishfarmhouses.com* and at *irishfarmholidays.com*.

Avoca to Arklow, a quiet little town situated on the Wicklow coast.

The coast of County Wicklow stretches north for 40 miles (64 km) from Kilmichael Point, a few miles below Arklow, to the rambunctious but enjoyable seaside resort of **Bray,** just south of Dublin. Generally overlooked in favor of the mountains, this is a coast for connoisseurs of moody, lonely shores and seascapes.

The old R750 road along the coast from Arklow to Wicklow town, followed by the R761 a mile or so (1.6 km) inland all the way up to Bray, has long been superseded by the fast N11, but offers a largely traffic-free saunter up the coast for those in no hurry.

Mizen Head and **Wicklow Head** are two fine promontories, and the harbor town of **Wicklow**

makes a good place to stop for a cup of tea. As for the beaches, they are mostly sandy as far as Wicklow, with **Brittas Bay** the pick of them, and mostly pebbly from there on up. Any side road to the right from the R761 will land you after a more or less potholed mile (1.6 km) on the low cliffs of the northern Wicklow coast, the perfect place to gaze at the sea and daydream with not another soul to bother you. St. Kevin himself could not have asked for more.

Russborough & Powerscourt

Two tremendous Palladian houses flank the northern Wicklow Mountains: Powerscourt near Bray to the east and Russborough near Blessington on

(continued on p. 104)

WALK: GLENDALOUGH & THE GLENEALO VALLEY

This is an easy, level walk among the remains of monastic and mining activity in Glendalough, with an upward climb into the upper Glenealo Valley. The first part of the walk is very popular. To avoid crowds, set off in early morning or wait until late afternoon.

St. Kevin's Kitchen could date back to the time of St. Kevin, in the early sixth century A.D.

Before you start, make sure that you look around the excellent display on St. Kevin and the Glendalough monastery in the **visitor center ❶** *(tel 0404/45-325)*. From the visitor center parking lot, cross the river by a footbridge and turn right along the track. In about 300 yards (300 m), recross the river to view **St. Kevin's Kitchen ❷**, the **round tower ❸**, and the other features of the main monastic site (see pp. 98–100).

Return across the river, where "Green Road to Upper Lake" signs guide you along the south side of the **Lower Lake ❹**. Walk for 1 mile (1.6 km), admiring the mountainside and white

> **NOT TO BE MISSED:**
>
> Visitor center display • St. Kevin's Kitchen • Round tower • Kevin's Bed View • View down Glenealo Valley from waterfall above the old mine workings

houses reflected in the lake, until you reach the ground between the Lower and Upper Lakes.

Just past the **Pollanass Waterfall ❺**, where the track swings right to cross between the

INSIDER TIP:

Lose yourself in the mists of time
with a stroll at dawn through
Glendalough—the "glen of the
two lakes"—site of a medieval
monastic settlement.

—JUSTIN KAVANAGH
*National Geographic
Travel Books editor*

lakes, continue to the **Reefert Church ⑥** ruins among weathered crosses and gravestones. Just beyond here, well signposted, is the semicircle of stones on a little promontory that marks the site of **St. Kevin's Cell ⑦**. Return to cross between the lakes and bear left on a path between tall pine and larch trees along the north shore of the **Upper Lake ⑧**. A sign, "Kevin's Bed View," leads to a viewpoint that looks across the lake to the tiny square black mouth of a partly man-made cave known as **St. Kevin's Bed ⑨**.

Continue beyond the lake end, through the ruined buildings and spoil heaps of 19th-century **lead-mine workings ⑩**.

You can retrace your steps from here back to the visitor center, but if you have waterproof footwear and sufficient energy, continue

Saintly Slayer

St. Kevin, good with wildlife, was hopeless with women. When an overzealous female follower came too close, the pious saint stung her cheeks with nettles to warn her off. Another story (probably a Victorian invention) tells how St. Kevin, meditating in the coffin-like cave (now called St. Kevin's Bed) above the Upper Lake, fell asleep and dreamed that one of his female acolytes, Kathleen, was standing between him and the Gates of Heaven. Waking to find Kathleen bending over him, and taking her to be a temptress sent by the devil, he plunged her in the lake and drowned her.

forward to reach the zigzag track up beside the **waterfalls ⑪** of the Glenealo River. The path leads to a memorable view back over the Upper Lake.

🏔 See also area map p. 89 E5
➤ Glendalough visitor center
🔄 6 miles (10 km)
🕐 Allow 3 hours
➤ Glendalough visitor center

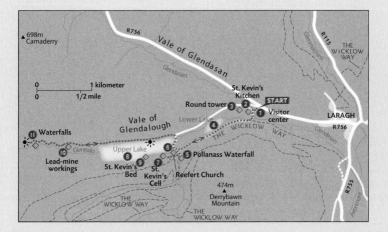

Russborough House

🗺 89 E5

✉ Blessington, Co. Wicklow

☎ 045/865-239

🕐 Open daily, May–Sept.; Sat. and Sun., April & Oct.

💲 $$

russborough.ie

the west. Built in the mid-18th century, they trumpet the wealth and power of the Anglo-Irish gentry of British origins who owned great tracts of Ireland. Some were absentee landowners who rarely set foot in Ireland. Others lived on their Irish estates and would move mountains—literally, in some cases—to get the land-scape effects they wanted. The interiors of the grandest Anglo-Irish houses, too, reflected what money, sophisticated taste, and influence could achieve.

Powerscourt House, never as grand as Russborough, was burned out in a fire in 1974, while Russborough's grounds were always intended to be wild and green rather than meticulously organized, so it is the house at

Russborough and the gardens and grounds at Powerscourt that are the main attractions today.

Russborough House:

Russborough was built in the 1740s for Joseph Leeson, Earl of Milltown and heir to a brewery fortune. He spent heavily creating one of the most impressive-looking houses in Ireland. Its immense **facade,** 900 feet (275 m) long, is topped with heraldic lions and features a twin sweep of curving colonnades.

Inside, all eyes turn to the richly unrestrained plasterwork. Italian brothers Philip and Paul Francini, the leading exponents of plaster ornamentation at the time, were commissioned to do the work and filled the house with

■ The upper terrace at Powerscourt House overlooks the formal gardens and the sunken Triton Lake.

intricate floral sprays, swags, fruit, faces, and foliage. Another artist, less delicate but more fantastical, created the hounds enmeshed in sprays and flowers who career up the main staircase.

The house contains an astonishing **art collection—** Vermeer, Rubens, Goya, Velazquez, Thomas Gainsborough, Hans Hals. Sir Alfred Beit, cofounder of the De Beers diamond mining empire, initially put it together. The Beit collection has suffered two high-profile robberies: In 1974, 16 paintings stolen to raise funds for the IRA were quickly recovered; in 1986, several pictures were removed and have not yet been retrieved. Recently, some paintings have been donated to the National Gallery for safekeeping.

Powerscourt: The glory of Powerscourt is its setting, best seen from the uppermost of the five terraces that drop away to **Triton Lake** and its 100-foot (30 m) fountain in the valley below. From here you look out over the lake, cradled in tall trees, to the peak of 1,643-foot (501 m) **Great Sugar Loaf,** 2.5 miles (4 km) away across a patchwork of farmland. The "wildness" of this prospect only enhances the artistry of the 50 acres (20 ha) of gardens.

The steeply sloping terraces were designed in the 1840s by Daniel Robertson, a martyr to gout who stimulated his genius with copious drafts of sherry while being trundled from one vantage point to the next in a wheelbarrow. Walking down the terraces between formal gardens, you pass a superb mosaic pavement featuring the planets, created with colored pebbles and enclosed by elaborate cast-iron screens. Beautiful Austrian cast-iron work appears beyond the upper terrace, too, in the 18th-century Bamberg Gate. The peaceful, terraced **Japanese Garden,** screened from the Triton Lake by bamboos and

Powerscourt

89 E5

Powerscourt Estate, Enniskerry, Co. Wicklow

01/204-6000

$$

powerscourt.com

INSIDER TIP:

The gardens at Powerscourt make a wonderful stop between Dublin and Glendalough. The Japanese Garden with its picturesque footbridge is a favorite.

—ROZ HOAGLAND
Private guide,
Hoagland Art Travel

shapely conifers, contains delicate temples and bridges.

After all this artifice, a visit to the **Powerscourt Waterfall,** a signposted 3.5-mile (6 km) walk or 3-mile (5 km) drive from the gardens, is refreshing. At 425 feet (130 m), this is the highest waterfall in Ireland— although "the longest" might be more accurate, as the River Dargle tumbles from one ferny rock face to the next. This is a great place to picnic, especially on a sunny afternoon, a day or so after heavy rain, when the fall is at its most spectacular. ■

COUNTY CARLOW

Tiny County Carlow is landlocked and surrounded on all sides by more glamorous counties—horse-mad Kildare, Kilkenny with the finest medieval town in Ireland, Wicklow and its mountains, and Wexford's sandy coast and superb bird-watching. Carlow tends to be overlooked. Yet there's plenty in this easygoing agricultural county to please you, if you are content to wander at a slow pace and listen to some fairly elastic local tales.

The capstone of Browne's Hill dolmen stands propped precariously on its supporting stones.

Carlow Town

89 D4

Visitor Information

College St.,
Carlow,
Co. Carlow

059/913-1554

carlowtourism.com

Carlow Town

The town of Carlow, up near the county's northwest border, was for centuries a frontier town between the Norman English of the Pale (the defended area of British influence around Dublin; see p. 26) and the troublesome Irish "beyond the Pale."

From certain viewpoints, Carlow's 13th-century stone castle still looks impregnable. However, closer inspection reveals a solitary castellated wall suspended between two towers, all that was left after a local doctor blew it up in 1814. He was trying to reduce the thickness of the walls, with the intention of turning the place into a refuge for psychiatric patients.

Carlow also boasts a handsome **courthouse** from 1828–1830. Small wonder if the Ionic columns of the portico look as if they should be gracing some Greek temple—they are modeled on the Parthenon.

On May 25, 1798, about 640 "Croppy," or Catholic, rebels supporting the United Irishmen's rebellion were massacred on Tullow Street. Their mass grave (the Croppies Grave), marked by a Celtic cross, lies across the River Barrow at **Graiguecullen.**

Father John Murphy, a priest who led a contingent of the rebels, was hanged in the market square at **Tullow,** 9 miles (14 km) east of Carlow; a memorial commemorates him there.

Located in an enormous glass and cement building, the **VISUAL Centre for Contemporary Art** *(Old Dublin Road, tel 059/917-2400, closed on Mon., visualcarlow.ie)* is a state-of-the-art facility that hosts exhibits and events dedicated to local and international artists.

Near Carlow

Two miles (3 km) east of Carlow, **Brownshill dolmen** is signed from the Hacketstown road. This is a wonderful site, the 4,500-year-old burial place of some leader important enough to have his tomb sealed with a capstone that weighs many tons. The weathered capstone lies propped on three of its original curbstones.

The threat of unrest and even insurrection in this frontier region led to the building of several castles in County Carlow. You can find the ruins of the 12th-century **Black Castle** at Leighlinbridge, in the lovely valley of the River Barrow, and, near Bagenalstown, the ruggedly massive ruins of **Ballymoon Castle.**

The Blackstairs Mountains

County Carlow tapers southward from Borris toward the rolling heights of the **Blackstairs Mountains.** These bleakly beautiful hills, straddling the border country between Carlow and Wexford, rise to the 2,600-foot (793 m) peak of Mount Leinster. A great way to enjoy the Blackstairs is to stroll along the well-marked **South Leinster Way,** a long-distance footpath

that skirts Mount Leinster on its way northeast to link up with the Wicklow Way.

The River Barrow forms all but a snippet of the western boundary of County Carlow. There is great coarse fishing (fishing for any freshwater fish other than salmon or trout) and good towpath walking along the **Barrow Way.**

Everything leads more or less southward to **St. Mullin's,** 3 miles (5 km) north of the Wexford/Kilkenny border, where remnants of a monastery founded in the late seventh century lie around the village's present-day church. ∎

Ballymoon Castle

[map] 89 D4

Borris House

[map] 89 D3

borrishouse weddings.ie

Borris House

Borris House, near the Blackstairs Mountains of County Carlow, is an impressive manor house dating from the late 18th century. Its owner in Victorian days, Arthur MacMurrough Kavanagh (1831–1889), was a determined and courageous man. Born with only stumps of arms and legs, he nevertheless succeeded in becoming not only an excellent shot and horseman but also a career politician—quite a feat for someone with such handicaps in mid-19th-century Ireland. The house is open to the public on specific dates throughout the year or tours can be arranged by appointment.

KILKENNY TOWN & AROUND

County Kilkenny lies to the west of County Carlow, with its county town, Kilkenny—by far the most complete medieval city in Ireland—at its heart. This is a small-scale town, a place with character stamped on its old buildings and narrow lanes.

Kilkenny Castle occupies a site that's both strategically superb and scenically outstanding.

Kilkenny Castle

The Parade,
Kilkenny,
Co. Kilkenny

056/770-4100

$$

kilkennycastle.ie

Kilkenny Castle

Set on the west bank of the River Nore, Kilkenny town lies between its two chief landmarks, the castle and the cathedral. Most visitors make straight for Kilkenny Castle, dominant on its bend of the river. This three-sided fortress (Oliver Cromwell's men knocked down the fourth in the 1650s) is built of local gray limestone, with castellated battlements and drum towers at the corners. Richard de Clare, the Norman baron better known as Strongbow, first built a wooden fort on this site in 1172 to guard the river crossing; his son-in-law, William Marshal, built the stone castle.

When the Butler family, Earls of Ormond, bought the castle and the lordship of Kilkenny in 1392, the city was already an important place, a fortified stronghold where parliaments were held. The parliament of 1366–1367 passed the famous Statutes of Kilkenny, aimed at keeping the Anglo-Norman heritage free from taint by the Irish. Their prohibitions on marrying Irish partners, speaking Irish, or playing Irish games or music were honored more in the breach than the observance.

The Butlers lived in Kilkenny Castle for nearly 600 years, suffering all the vicissitudes of fortune that flowed from being stubbornly loyal to the royal house of Stuart. They lost wealth and influence by backing the deposed king, James Stuart, in his defeat at the Battle of the Boyne in 1690, and when the second Duke of Ormond supported a Stuart-inspired plan in 1714 to invade England with Spanish troops, he was attainted for treason and lost his earldom. It took the rest of the 18th century for royal memories to fade sufficiently to allow the Butlers to resume their ancient title.

A tour around the castle takes in the Victorian library and drawing room, the bedrooms with their hand-painted wallpaper and beautiful Georgian furniture, and the showpiece **Long Gallery.** Here, Butler portraits frown down darkly below a delicately carved 19th-century hammerbeam roof (braced with arches), painted with trails of foliage in pre-Raphaelite style and furnished with a central skylight to admit the daylight. Outside there are terraces, gardens, and walks by the river and through woodland.

Across the road from the castle entrance are the handsome 18th-century stables that now house

the **Kilkenny Design Centre** *(tel 056/22-118, kilkennydesign.com),* a showcase for good modern design in textiles, jewelry, furniture, and fine ceramics.

INSIDER TIP:

Every summer, Kilkenny hosts the Sky Cat Laughs Comedy Festival *(thecat laughs.com),* featuring many of Ireland's top comics.

—STEPHANIE ROBICHAUX
National Geographic contributor

Kilkenny Town

From the castle, cross the top of The Parade and cross Rose Inn Street to enter **High Street,** the first part of a road that changes its name to Parliament Street and then Irishtown as it runs north through the heart of the city. On the right, you'll see the **Tholsel,** or toll stall, with its octagonal clock tower and round-arched arcade projecting into the roadway. It was built in 1761 as an office where traders and others could pay dues and tolls, and it is still in use as the offices of Kilkenny's city council. The Tholsel is only one of Kilkenny's many medieval buildings, rare survivals in Ireland.

The **Medieval Mile Museum** *(tel 056/781-7022, medievalmile museum.ie, $)* is located behind the Tholsel, in **St. Mary's Church**. The interactive exhibit reconstructs the history of medieval Kilkenny and its most important families, including the Rothe family, rich merchants

Kilkenny Town
🗺 89 C3
Visitor Information
✉ Shee Alms House,
Rose Inn St.,
Kilkenny,
Co. Kilkenny
☎ 056/772-2118
visitkilkenny.ie

Rothe House Museum

✉ Parliament St., Kilkenny, Co. Kilkenny

☎ 056/772-2893

💲 $

rothehouse.com

who built the Rothe Chapel where visitors can admire finely sculpted burial vaults.

Follow the narrow "slips" or alleyways, some of them so steep they require steps, to seek out these remnants of historic Kilkenny, from humble cottages to churches and merchants' houses. The one with the best story attached is the 13th-century **Kyteler's Inn** on St. Kieran's Street, which runs in from the right to join High Street at its juncture with Parliament Street. It was in this house that Alice Kyteler, the famed Witch of Kilkenny, was born. Alice was charged with being a witch in 1324 after she had been overheard offering peacocks' eyes and nine red cocks to her familiar, a sprite named Robin Artysson whom she would meet at the crossroads. She was also reported to have gone through the streets of the city at night with her broom, sweeping the dirt toward her son's house while chanting: "To the house of William, my son, Lie all the wealth of Kilkenny town." Dame Alice was convicted, but pardoned. Sentenced to death after reoffending, she escaped and left her unfortunate maidservant Petronella to be burned at the stake as a substitute. The Tholsel was later built on the place of execution on High Street.

Farther along Parliament Street are two notable medieval buildings. On the west side is **Rothe House Museum,** another arcaded building with a tall central gable, linked by tiny courtyards to two other houses. Built in the 1590s as a rich merchant's dwelling, the whole complex operates these days as a museum of Kilkenny history.

On the east stands **Grace's Castle,** built as a fortified tower in 1210, a prison since Tudor times and a courthouse from the late 18th century to the present day. Like every prosperous medieval city, Kilkenny had several monastic houses.

A bit farther ahead, in a building that rose from the ruins of the 12th-century St. Francis Abbey, guests can dive into the **Smithwick's Experience** (tel 056/778-6377, smithwicksexperience. com, $$), a sensorial, interactive itinerary that tells the story of Ireland's oldest beer, Smithwick's red ale, and includes a taste at the end. Along Abbey Street (running west from Parliament Street) you'll find the well-restored church of the 13th-century **Black Abbey,** with some beautiful medieval glass.

Toward its northern end,

Enjoy the Many Sides of Kilkenny Castle

Kilkenny Castle is not just a superb historic building, it's also the focus of dozens of events, exhibitions, concerts, and art displays throughout the year. No matter what your interests, there is bound to be something going on at the castle for you to enjoy.

Take a look at the castle's events calendar (kilkennycastle.ie), and plan your visit to take in a food market or a gourmet feast in the Great Hall. Lovers of veteran and classic cars will adore Kilkenny Motor Club's rallies; or you could slow things down with a horse and carriage ride around the grounds. Music fans are offered concerts ranging from music in the gardens to operas; there are family-friendly "Prams & Proms" events and family treasure hunts, too.

Parliament Street becomes Irishtown. In Norman times, the native Irish were confined to this ghetto outside the city walls, an area already sacred to them because of its holy well dedicated to St. Kenny or Canice, the founder of Kilkenny's first monastery in the sixth century.

St. Canice's Cathedral: On a rise of ground at the top of Irishtown you'll see the squat bulk of St. Canice's Cathedral *(tel 056/776-4971, stcanicescathedral. ie, $)*, built in the 1250s on the site of St. Canice's monastery. It's a massive building, its central tower pulled down low into the roofs like a square head tucked into hunched shoulders.

Beside the cathedral rises a slender 101-foot-high (31 m) **round tower,** built by the monks some time between 700 and 1000. You can climb its wooden ladders (weather permitting; $) to enjoy a stunning panorama over Kilkenny.

When Oliver Cromwell's troops captured the city in 1650, they used the cathedral as a stable, broke the font while letting their horses drink out of it, fired guns at the roof, and smashed stained-glass windows and other furnishings. Despite this, most of the church's glories survived, including its wonderful collection of carved memorial slabs and effigies in the shiny local limestone known as Kilkenny Marble.

The tombs of the ruling Butler family in the south transept are wonderful examples of the carver's art, particularly the smiling effigies of Piers Butler, Earl of Ormond and Ossory (died 1539), in his domed helmet and elaborate breastplate,

■ **The thick stone walls of Rothe House guard treasures of antique furniture and fine paintings.**

Nicholas Mosse Pottery

- 🗺 89 D3
- ✉ Bennettsbridge, Co. Kilkenny
- ☎ 056/772-7505
- 🕐 Tours on Tues. Wed., Thurs.
- 💲 $

nicholasmosse.com

Dunmore Cave

- 🗺 89 C4
- ✉ Ballyfoyle, Co. Kilkenny
- ☎ 056/776-7726
- 💲 $

heritageireland.ie

Jerpoint Abbey

- 🗺 89 D3
- ✉ Thomastown, Co. Kilkenny
- ☎ 056/772-4623
- 🕐 Closed Dec.– March, except pre-bookings
- 💲 $

and his wife, Margaret Fitzgerald, with billowing sleeves and horned headdress.

The dozens of humbler memorials, many of their images rubbed smooth and shiny by centuries of hands and feet, include the graveslab of Jose de Keteller (died 1280), probably the father of Dame Alice the Witch. Other slabs show the tools of trade of a cobbler, a weaver, and a carpenter.

When you have had enough of sightseeing, pop into a pub for a pint of Kilkenny ale. This fine beer, brewed in town, owes its reputation to its creamy texture.

INSIDER TIP:

Sculpture is the real high point at Jerpoint Abbey. Look for the tomb carved with images of the disciples, each identifiable by what they are carrying.

—ROZ HOAGLAND
Private guide,
Hoagland Art Travel

Bennettsbridge

Beside the old seven-arch bridge at Bennettsbridge, just south of Kilkenny, **Nicholas Mosse Pottery** makes beautiful hand-crafted pottery and offers workshop tours. From here a lovely 7-mile (11 km) waymarked trail beside the River Nore leads to Kilkenny town.

Dunmore Cave

A steep descent on foot takes you into this well-lit cavern, located 7 miles (11 km) north of Kilkenny

town and reached via the N77 and N78. It contains several rock formations—including the **Market Cross,** at 23 feet (7 m) reckoned to be one of the tallest stalagmites in Europe.

Dunmore Cave has a dark history. In 1973, spelunkers found the skeletons of 46 women and children who had taken refuge in the caves during a Viking raid in 928 in which their menfolk—more than a thousand of them—were slaughtered. There were no signs of violence on the bones, suggesting that the victims either starved to death or were suffocated with smoke from fires lit by the attackers.

Jerpoint Abbey

Ten miles (16 km) south of Kilkenny town via the N10 then the N9 eastward are the finest Cistercian abbey ruins in Ireland. Donal MacGiollaPhadruig, King of Ossory, founded the Jerpoint Abbey in 1158; its first abbot was Felix O'Dulany, founder of St. Canice's Cathedral in Kilkenny.

O'Dulany's tomb lies in the barrel-vaulted choir of the abbey, the carving showing his bishop's crosier being swallowed by a snake. More finely carved tombs of the 15th and 16th centuries can be seen in the transepts; one carries effigies of fiercely staring and heavily bearded Apostles.

Carving is also rich on the inner and outer faces of the double pillars in the cloister arches. Here you will find beasts and soldiers, a grinning knave, and St. Christopher with a long staff, his face as meditative as an Easter Island statue, raising one hand in blessing. ∎

WEXFORD TOWN & AROUND

Stretched out behind its long quays beside the Slaney Estuary, Wexford town has no glamour, but its lack of hurry and worry and the friendliness of its people draw visitors back time and again. Not that the town is uncrowded—narrow, undulating, and winding Main Street, parallel with the river, is usually thronged with customers of the old-fashioned stores. The sweet whiff of turf smoke from domestic fires hangs around the streets, and pubs such as Tim's Tavern, Kelly's, and Simon's Place make cozy, cheerful watering holes.

■ The quays of Wexford

Vikings founded Wexford town down in the southeast corner of County Wexford in the ninth century, and their street plan survives in the narrow covered alleyways, such as Keysers Lane, that run down from Main Street to the quays.

Wexford's history has been spectacularly bloody. When Oliver Cromwell captured the town in 1649, his men destroyed the 12th-century Selskar Abbey (its fine red stone ruins still stand off

Abbey Street) and slaughtered 1,500 citizens—three-quarters of Wexford's population. In the 1798 Rising (see p. 27), there were many brutalities on both sides. A heroic statue of a peasant pikeman in the Bullring commemorates the United Irishmen rebels. You can get more thorough information from the exhibit set up in the visitors' center next to the West Gate, a Norman tower and the only one to have survived medieval defense systems, or take your time over the small 1798

Wexford Town

🅰 89 E2

Visitor Information

✉ Crescent Quay, Wexford, Co. Wexford

☎ 053/912-3111

visitwexford.ie

EXPERIENCE: Enjoy Opera

Opera lovers in the tens of thousands come to Wexford town in the autumn for the two-week **Wexford Festival Opera** (*High St., tel 053/912-2144, wexfordopera.com*).

The first edition of this historical event dates back to 1951. It usually takes place between the end of October and the first week of November and offers three opera performances at the Theatre Royal. The festival has the honor of recuperating and rediscovering works that have been long forgotten as well as bringing lesser-known operas to the stage. It also organizes smaller events and other types of musical performances including blues, jazz, and folk music. Throughout the period of the festival, the city shows its support for the event: Shops decorate their windows and music can be heard inside and outside of the pubs.

Wexford Wildfowl Reserve

🗺 89 E2

✉ Visitor Center, North Slob, Ardcavan, Co. Wexford

☎ 076/100-2660

wexfordwildfowl reserve.ie

Irish National Heritage Park

🗺 89 E2

✉ Ferrycarrig, Co. Wexford

☎ 053/912-0733

💲 $

irishheritage.ie

Irish Agricultural Museum

🗺 89 E2

✉ Johnstown, Castle Estate, Co. Wexford

☎ 053/918-4671

💲 $

irishagrimuseum.ie

display in the beautiful and peaceful late 17th-century **Church of St. Iberius** on High Street.

Wexford Wildfowl Reserve

Tidal wetlands are known in Ireland as "slobs," and those along the estuary of the River Slaney northeast of Wexford town are internationally famous as breeding and wintering grounds for ducks, geese, and waders.

The North Slob, some 4,500 acres (1,800 ha) of marsh, is the site of the Wexford Wildfowl Reserve, where you can spot mallards, black swans, greenshanks, and redshanks, as well as reed warblers and reed buntings. Winter has the best bird-watching, when 10,000 Greenland white-fronted geese (about 45 percent of the world population) overwinter here.

Leave the visitor center at dusk and perch yourself on the seawall with a pair of binoculars; you'll never forget the extraordinary sight and sound as several thousand white-fronted geese rise into the air all at once with a mighty roar of wings.

Irish National Heritage Park

This 30-acre (12 ha) open-air park, created on the marshes of the Slaney Estuary just west of the Wexford Wildfowl Reserve, recounts Irish history up to medieval times by way of reproduced sites—a Stone Age encampment and stone circle, a *rath* (ring fort) and a *crannog* (lake island stronghold) from the native Celtic culture, a Viking shipyard (complete with longboat moored on the river), a Norman castle, and more. Trails and a guided tour are available.

Irish Agricultural Museum

This 4.2-acre (1.7 ha) museum is located about four miles south of Wexford, in the Village of Murntown. Housed in the old farm buildings of **Johnstown Castle** *(closed to the public)* it recreates the rural history of the country with a section dedicated to the Great Famine. Take a walk through the splendid gardens created by Daniel Robertson, famous for designing the gardens of the Powerscourt Estate.

Enniscorthy

Fifteen miles (24 km) north from Wexford along the N11, the lively small town of Enniscorthy holds the **National 1798 Visitor Centre,** an excellent and detailed exhibition about the United Irishmen's 1798 uprising. This attempt to win independence for Ireland by force of arms was fueled by widespread resentment of the oppressive penal laws (see pp. 26–27) and carried along on a wave of revolutionary fervor that was sweeping Europe.

The rising started in mid-May of 1798, when rebels and government forces set about slaughtering each other. Thousands were maimed, raped, and killed in Wexford, Carlow, and Kildare, as they were all over the country, before the insurrectionists in the southeast of Ireland were finally crushed on June 21 at the Battle of Vinegar Hill on the east bank of the River Slaney outside Enniscorthy. Five hundred people were killed there, many of them the wives and children of the fleeing rebels. The punitive measures that followed served only to stoke up more bitterness and resentment.

All this is told graphically with animated and static displays, light and laser effects, contemporary accounts, and cartoons. You can drive up to the battle site on **Vinegar Hill** (signposted from the town), where there is a round tower, a memorial plaque, and a fine prospect over Enniscorthy.

South of Wexford

The N25 leads south from Wexford to **Rosslare,** a busy harbor town with ferry connections to Fishguard and Pembroke in Wales. Beyond here, minor roads lead to the coast. The thatched cottages of **Kilmore Quay** look out to the **Saltee Islands.** From March to June, the islands are home to a quarter of a million puffins, kittiwakes, gannets, razorbills, and other seabirds. Boat trips are available from Kilmore Quay. ■

National 1798 Visitor Centre

🅰 89 E3

✉ Millpark Rd., Enniscorthy, Co. Wexford

☎ 053/923-7596

💲 $

1798centre.ie

Rosslare

🅰 89 E2

■ Glorious light and sound at a Wexford Festival Opera church concert featuring choir and orchestra

DRIVE: THE OLD COAST ROAD FROM DUBLIN TO WEXFORD

You can dash from Dublin to Wexford in an hour and a half by the fast N11, or you can saunter along the old coast road through quiet towns and villages, flirting with a coastline of low cliffs, lonely pebble strands, and splendid sandy beaches. This is real back-country travel—motoring just for the pleasure of it.

Courtown Bay and its sandy beach make a popular family resort.

Setting off from central Dublin, head east along the south bank of the River Liffey to Ringsend, where you pick up the R131 for Dun Laoghaire. This is the old coast road, easing south for 12 miles (19 km). Rediscover the pleasures of back-country driving by getting out of the car every so often and exploring the seaside towns along the way.

Pass through Sandymount to join the R118 at Merrion, continuing through Booterstown past the vast, low-tide sand and mudflats in Dublin Bay. Then join the N31 to head through Blackrock to the bustle of **Dun Laoghaire ❶**, with its Georgian terraces and busy ferry port.

NOT TO BE MISSED:

Great Sugar Loaf • Brittas Bay • Arklow • Courtown • Wexford Wildfowl Reserve

Continue on the R119 through Sandycove (see p. 83), past Dalkey and under the seaward flank of Killiney Hill, to reach Ballybrack and Bray. Stretch your legs with a walk along the cliff walk between Bray and Greystones, returning by DART railway.

Take the R761 south past the eastern outliers of the Wicklow Mountains. There's the first sight of sharp-peaked **Great Sugar Loaf ②**, with the rounded flanks of 2,380-foot (725 m) Djouce beyond. Past Greystones, a former fishing village whose charming harbor and old cottages are now surrounded by modern housing projects, the road enters flattish, well-wooded country. Just four side roads lead to the sea between here and Wicklow; each will land you on a strand of red, gray, and yellow pebbles. Turn left at Killoughter and get out for a peaceful stroll down to the shore.

At Rathnew, you join the R750 through Wicklow town and on along the lovely sandy curve of **Brittas Bay ③**, where duckboard trails through the dunes around Mizen Head may tempt you to stop for a breath of salt sea air.

Arklow ④ is a pleasant, slow-paced little town, just right for a sandwhich or a full Irish breakfast from the The Blue Cafè on Manifold Lane, close to Upper Main Street. From here, head south from the harbor on a minor road, aiming for Castletown and the fishing harbor of tiny **Courtown ⑤**. Here you pick up the R742 and follow it for 25 miles (40 km) to Wexford.

The pretty fishing village of **Curracloe ⑥** lies 5 miles (8 km) short of Wexford. If you're after seashore peace and quiet, take the side lanes to coastal hamlets such as Cahore Point, Morriscastle, or Blackwater Harbour. Or pack a picnic for a stroll along the half-mile duckboard walk that forms a nature trail through the Curracloe dunes.

Before plunging into Wexford town, follow signs from the R742 to the **Wexford Wildfowl Reserve ⑦** (see p. 114). The numbers of wildfowl are especially spectacular at dusk.

▲ See also area maps pp. 49 & 89
➤ Central Dublin
🕐 Half a day
🔁 85 miles (136 km)
➤ Wexford town

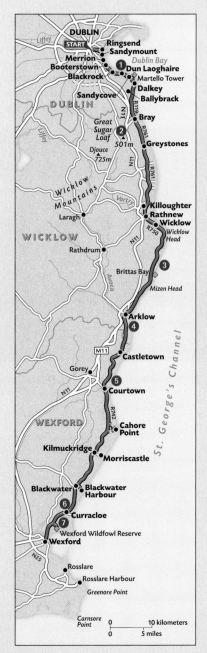

WATERFORD TOWN & AROUND

Looking at Waterford town from the quays that line both banks of the River Suir, many visitors feel a sense of disappointment. They don't expect a place with such a varied history to look so workaday. But that is part of the charm of the chief city of southeast Ireland—the gritty bustle of shipping along its river and the old streets and buildings of its historic heart hidden away just behind the southern quays.

Quayside pubs and houses are enticingly lit by night and reflected in the waters of the River Suir.

Waterford Town

89 D2

Visitor Information

✉ Waterford Discover Ireland Centre, Parade Quay, Waterford, Co. Waterford

☎ 051/875-823

Waterford Town

Waterford was founded in the 9th century by the Vikings. Some portions of the walls they erected around the city are still standing today. The part that's best preserved extends from the Watch Tower, where Castle Street meets Parnell Street, at the apex of the triangular layout of the ancient city known as the "Viking Triangle."

Three museums, Reginald's Tower, the Medieval Museum, and the Bishop's Palace make up the splendid **Waterford Treasures** museum complex where visitors can discover Waterford's eleven

centuries of history. **Reginald's Tower** (The Quay, $), focuses on the three centuries of Viking occupation and displays artifacts such as vases, jewelry, and weapons from the period. The cylindrical tower was erected by Ranguald the Viking in 1003. Its core, which dates back to the Norman period, was built by these new invaders shortly after they occupied the city in 1170. They also restructured the city's walls and added a series of watchtowers, many of which are still standing today.

The **Medieval Museum** (Cathedral Square, $) tells the story of the city in the Middle Ages. Among the

INSIDER TIP:

Join the chilly swimmers
at Guillamene Cove outside
of Waterford town. The
views are spectacular and
the locals friendly and
welcoming.

—ALEXANDRA BURGUIERES
National Geographic
contributor

many precious treasures on display there are the Great Charter Roll dating from 1372 (a 13-foot-long, illustrated roll that legitimized the power of England) and a sword and ceremonial cap belonging to King Henry VIII.

At the **Bishop's Palace** (*The Mall, $*), built in the mid-18th century, visitors can view a collection of objects from the Georgian and Victorian periods including silverware, furniture, paintings, and refined Waterford crystal.

During the Georgian period, stately homes were constructed along the Mall and O'Connell Street, as was the **Cathedral of the Most Holy Trinity,** on Barronstrand Street. East, on Bailey's New Street, another addition was the **Protestant Christ Church Cathedral,** with its rich stucco ceiling; the morbid effigy of James Rice, seven times Lord Mayor of Waterford in the 15th century, is shown as a sunken corpse being burrowed by toads and worms.

Today, the city of Waterford has a buzz about it, perhaps because of the student population, the commercial activity of the port, and the light industry around the outskirts.

Ardmore Monastic Site

Down in southwest County Waterford, the resort of Ardmore boasts a superb monastic site. On the hillside above the town, with wonderful coastal views, you'll find a 12th-century round tower standing 97 feet (29 m) tall next to ruined **St. Declan's Cathedral,** dating from the 10th to 14th centuries. The chief attraction is the stone tableaux, probably ninth century, on the outside of the cathedral's west wall. Framed in a double row of arcades, they include a winged Archangel Michael weighing souls in his scales, Adam and Eve being banished from Eden, and St. Declan converting the heathen Irish. The eighth-century oratory of the saint—he came from Wales sometime between 350 and 420—stands nearby. ∎

St. Declan's Holy Well & Stone

While at the Ardmore monastic site, follow the path toward the cliffs of Ram Head, where you'll find St. Declan's holy well guarded by rough-hewn crosses. Also down at this southern end of Ardmore beach is St. Declan's Stone, on which his bell and vestments are said to have floated to Ireland from Wales. It is said that rheumatics who manage to squeeze under the stone on the Feast of St. Declan, July 24, will gain a miraculous cure—even if they hurt their back in the process.

Waterford Treasures

✉ Cathedral Sq., Waterford, Co. Waterford

☎ 076/110-2501

$ $$ (combined ticket)

waterfordtreasures. com

Guillamene Cove

△ 89 D2

Ardmore

△ 89 B1

Visitor Information

✉ Seafront parking lot, Ardmore, Co. Waterford

☎ 024/94-444

WALKING IN IRELAND

Although Ireland has come to embrace recreational walking only recently, you will find ample opportunity to get out and about on foot.

■ The Dingle Peninsula in County Kerry offers excellent walking tracks.

Historically, people in Ireland had access to private land only with the permission of the landowners, many of whom were absentee landlords, who could withdraw permission at any time. A dependent peasant population and the lack of a confident, well-educated middle class able to stand up for its rights meant that, until recently, Ireland had few established public rights of way.

For the past couple of decades, interest in country walking and other outdoor pursuits has grown, fueled by greater mobility and prosperity, a desire to become fit, and the influence of enticing television and magazine images. Many visitors to Ireland expressed surprise and disappointment at the lack of opportunity to go walking on legally permitted routes. In response,

Ireland established a network of marked ways—long-distance routes of varying lengths, some of several days' duration.

In the last few years, serious efforts have been made on both sides of the border to cater to the needs of all walkers. The Republic's domestic tourist organization, Failte Ireland, and the Department of Rural and Community Development, working with the national forestry organization Coillte, have jointly developed a large number of signposted and maintained loop walks. These walks emanate out from designated trailheads and range from easy strolls of an hour's duration along flat terrain to rugged mountain hikes.

At the time of writing, there are more than 300 official Looped Walks across the country, with more in development. To find a walking route that suits you, along with lists of nearby accommodations and attractions, visit *discover ireland.ie*. Among the many things to do are the coastal walks such as the one that runs along the top of the Cliffs of Moher and the national park walks in the Cavan Burren and the Glenveagh National Park.

Northern Ireland has also begun to promote this kind of activity. Until recently it boasted only one long-distance path, a 600-mile (965 km) loop called the Ulster Way. The route was too long, primarily along roadways, badly maintained, and poorly waymarked. Today, the Ulster Way has been relaunched in 16 "Quality Sections"— which are primarily off road and well signposted— and 10 "Link Sections," unmarked trails along often busy roads. Read about the Ulster Way and many other walks in Northern Ireland by visiting *walkni.com*.

■ You never know who you'll meet around the next bend when walking the Irish countryside.

EXPERIENCE: Take Part in a Walking Festival

A marvelous way to enjoy walking on either side of the border is to take part in one of the numerous walking festivals held each year. Before the creation of today's popular walking routes, these festivals represented the best chance for many people to enjoy a new part of the country on foot and under the guidance of local experts. That is still their chief attraction, along with the chatter, fun, and partying that festivals of all kinds invariably generate.

Walking festivals typically last from one to three days and can draw thousands of participants of all ages. Many also feature multiple routes, with something suitable for every level of fitness and interest. Three grades of walk cater for most abilities. Gentle "C" Grade walks follow mostly level ground for a distance of about 7 miles (11 km), or 3–4 hours. "B" Grade routes usually take in ridges and peaks at a moderate pace. They are usually around 8 miles (13 km) in length, include a climb of about 3,000

feet (900 m), and last 4–5 hours. "A" Grade walks are strenuous, covering several peaks at a good pace (7–8 hours of walking). These routes can extend up to 13 miles (21 km) and climb 4,000 (1,200 m) feet or more. Family-friendly and educational routes are also usually offered.

Ireland's popular walking festivals include the brilliant **Glen of Aherlow Walking Festival** *(tel 062/56-331, aherlow .com)*, held every year in January and June; the **Ballyhoura International Walking Festival** *(tel 063/91-300, visitballyhoura. com)*, which explores the hills of North Cork, East Limerick, and West Tipperary; the **Slieve Bloom Walking Festival** *(tel 086/821-0056, slievebloom.ie)*, in April/ May, which shows off the hilly country of Tipperary and Laois; and the **Mourne International Walking Festival** *(tel 028/4372-2222, visitmournemountains. co.uk)*, a wonderful introduction to County Down's Mourne Mountains held each June.

COUNTY TIPPERARY

Tipperary is often glossed over by travelers racing through impatiently to get to the dramatic coasts and peninsulas of the southwest. But there are plenty of hidden delights hereabouts, just off the beaten path, for those who take the time to slow down.

Dark Age symbol of the power of Munster kings, the Rock of Cashel dominates the Tipperary plains.

Rock of Cashel

88 B3

Cashel,
Co. Tipperary

062/61-437

$

cashel.ie

Rock of Cashel

Your first sight of the Rock of Cashel rising out of the Golden Vale of Tipperary, its domed top tightly packed with towers, spires, and pointed gables, is unforgettable. During the first millennium, the Rock was indeed a kind of secular and spiritual capital, the seat of the Kings of Munster and a rival to the power of Tara, where the High Kings of Ireland held sway. Great and grim history clings to the Rock, and there's a resonance about the place that is enhanced at night when

floodlights throw it all into brilliant relief.

The limestone outcrop on which the walled citadel stands is 200 feet (60 m) high. Legend has it that the devil, who had just taken a bite out of the Slieve Bloom Mountains (they still call the place Devil's Bit), saw St. Patrick about to build a church in the Golden Vale. In disgust, he spat his mouthful out and it landed at Cashel. But this rock was already fortified in the fourth century, when it was known as "Cashel of the Kings." In the fifth century, it was the coronation place for the

Kings of Munster, and St. Patrick came here to baptize King Aengus in 450. During the ceremony he inadvertently jabbed his crosier through the king's foot, but stoical Aengus, thinking the saint was testing him, did not flinch.

By the 11th century, Cashel was held by Brian Boru, High King of Ireland, but in 1101, King Murtagh O'Brien gave it to the Church, after which the great buildings that now crowd the summit were erected.

You enter the complex through the **Hall of the Vicars Choral,** built in 1420 for the choristers of Cashel's cathedral. It houses an exhibition and the weathered 12th-century high cross of St. Patrick.

Cormac's Chapel: Outside, you pass a reproduction of the cross en route to Cormac's Chapel (1127–1134), built by King Cormac MacCarthy. This sturdy little building under a steeply pitched roof, its pinkish stone contrasting pleasantly with the dour gray of the great cathedral looming behind, is considered the earliest and finest surviving Romanesque church in Ireland.

Outside is a **corbel frieze** of the heads of men and beasts, and more of these look down from the pillar capitals of the arcade inside. The round Norman **chancel arch** is studded with heads, too, and there are highly colored fragments of the original **frescoes** in the chancel. At the west end stands a **sarcophagus,** probably that of King Cormac.

Even more impressive is the carving in the **tympanum** over the north doorway. It shows a wild scene of a grinning monster, its clawed feet trampling two unidentifiable animals, while a centaur in a Norman helmet (complete with noseguard) twists his upper body back to fire an arrow at it.

INSIDER TIP:

"Tipp" is famous for hurling. You can buy lovely hurleys hand-crafted out of ash wood at Jim O'Brien's workshop in Priestown, Drangan *(obrien hurleys.com).*

—JUSTIN KAVANAGH
*National Geographic
Travel Books editor*

St. Patrick's Cathedral: The cold, echoing shell of the 13th-century St. Patrick's Cathedral stands roofless and loud with jackdaw cries. Cobbled onto its west end is the fortified palace of the archbishops of Cashel.

The cathedral was burned in 1495 by the Earl of Kildare, who excused himself to King Henry VII by confessing with much honesty, "I thought the archbishop was in it." Cashel's prelates were as powerful and unpopular as any monarch. Archbishop Myler Magrath (1523–1622), whose tomb is in the choir, held one archbishopric, four bishoprics, and 77 other livings, making him extremely wealthy.

Tragedy came in 1647, when up to 3,000 people were sheltering from attack by Cromwell's

Athassel Priory

🏛 88 B3

✉ Golden,
Co. Tipperary

army under "Murrough of the Burnings," Lord Inchiquin. The attackers piled bricks of turf against the outside of the cathe-

canons in 1192, only a few years after the Normans had arrived in Ireland. His tomb lies inside. Irish marauders burned the

■ Oliver Cromwell's men walked into Cahir Castle unopposed in 1650—that's why its walls still stand.

Cahir

🏛 88 B2

Visitor Information

✉ Castle parking
lot, Cahir, Co.
Tipperary

☎ 052/744-1453

Cahir Castle

✉ Cahir,
Co. Tipperary

☎ 052/744-1011

💲 $

heritageireland.ie

dral and set them ablaze, killing everyone who had sought refuge inside. Beside the cathedral rises a round tower, 92 feet (28 m) high, of the 11th or 12th century.

Athassel Priory

The substantial ruins of what was once the largest priory in Ireland occupy a very peaceful location beside the River Suir. Rising above trees on the riverbank are the tall gray walls of the abbey church, pierced with lancet windows, and its shattered 15th-century tower. Other remains include the priory gatehouse, the cloister ruins, and the stump of the chapter house. William Burke founded the priory for Augustinian

priory in 1319 and again in 1329 and 1447.

Cahir

The main site to see in Cahir is **Cahir Castle**, one of Ireland's most impressive—and most complete battlements, having surrendered to Oliver Cromwell's forces in 1650 before they could set about battering it to pieces. It stands on a rock in the River Suir, a natural defensive site, first built on by Conor O'Brien in 1142. The fortified tower he erected is incorporated into the inner ward of the present castle, a two-stage rebuilding—first in the 13th century, when the Anglo-Norman keep was built, and second by the

Butler family, Earls of Ormond, once they had acquired the site in 1375. In the middle ward stands the keep, with its portcullis, and a chilling prison cell.

Swiss Cottage: A stroll along the river, 1.5 miles (2.5 km) south of Cahir's town center, will bring you to the Swiss Cottage, designed in 1810 by celebrated English Regency architect John Nash for Richard Butler, 12th Baron Cahir. Nash used the *cottage ornée* style, then extremely fashionable, to suggest that this crooked little hunting and fishing retreat, with its rustic timbering, artfully asymmetrical windows, and roses round the door, had somehow been engendered by the spirit of the surrounding countryside.

Carrick-on-Suir

One building distinguishes this quiet market town—the splendid ensemble of **Ormond Castle** and its satellite mansion, the finest Tudor domestic building in Ireland. The castle was built in 1309 and contains a brace of 15th-century fortified towers as proof of turbulent times in medieval Ireland. But when Black Tom Butler, tenth Earl of Ormond, built a new mansion onto his ancestral castle in 1568, he felt confident enough to dispense with any fortifications. The castle is lit by an almost continuous run of mullioned windows under the gables and is glorified inside by a tremendous carved fireplace and some

wonderful ornate plasterwork in the Long Gallery.

Mitchelstown Cave

This 2-mile-long (3 km) cave system, the longest in Ireland, is the one to visit if you abhor "touristification" of such natural attractions. Mitchelstown Cave is not overburdened with tourist developments or gimmicks—you simply walk through the three enormous caverns and admire the extraordinary mineral formations of stalactites, stalagmites, and calcite flows.

Although the cave complex lies in the Galtee Hills, the caves themselves are part of an intrusive band of limestone. Rain and stream water burrowing along cracks and fault lines in the rock has hollowed out the caves, and its chemical interaction with the limestone has formed their pinnacles and flows over countless million years. ■

Swiss Cottage
- ⊠ Kilcommon, Cahir, Co. Tipperary
- ☎ 052/744-1144
- 🕐 Closed Nov.– March
- 💲 $

Ormond Castle
- 🅐 89 C2
- ⊠ Castle Park, Carrick-on-Suir, Co. Tipperary
- ☎ 051/640-787
- 🕐 Closed Nov.– March

heritageireland.ie

Mitchelstown Cave
- 🅐 88 B2
- ⊠ Burncourt, Cahir, Co. Tipperary
- ☎ 052/746-7246
- 🕐 Closed Mon.–Fri., Nov.–March
- 💲 $

mitchelstowncave.com

Ahenny High Crosses

Two of the oldest ringed high crosses in Ireland stand in Ahenny churchyard, near Carrick-on-Suir. Dating from the eighth and ninth centuries, the sandstone crosses—each about 13 feet (4 m) tall—are covered with intricately carved decoration. Both feature beautiful geometric Celtic designs, and on the base of the northern cross, you will find an image from the biblical story of David and Goliath. The crosses came from the nearby monastic site of Kilclispeen.

To reach Ahenny Church (see map p. 89 C3), take the R697 north from Carrick-on-Suir for 3 miles (5 km). Turn left at Scrogh Bridge, then turn right. The church is located a little more than a mile (2 km) down the road on the right-hand side. Look for the crosses in the field to the right of the church.

More Places to Visit in Eastern Ireland

Castledermot High Crosses

These two tenth-century high crosses, near a lovely Romanesque arched doorway and a 67-foot (20 m) round tower, are carved with biblical scenes. *highcrosses.org*

🗺 89 D4 ✉ Off the M9, 10 miles (16 km) SE of Athy via the R418, Co. Kildare

Holycross Abbey

This Cistercian abbey was founded in 1168 by Donal Mor O'Briain, King of Munster, as a shrine for a splinter of the True Cross. The north range of the cloister and the abbey church have been carefully restored. The south transept contains two chapels, one with vaulting elaborate enough to suggest it was here that the sacred relic was venerated. The choir holds a beautiful 14th-century sedilia or priest's seat. *tipperary.com/holycross*

EXPERIENCE:
Behold the Beauty of Irish Crystal

The manufacture of Irish crystal—a very particular kind of heavy, lustrous glass—is a specialty pursued in several places in the Republic and Northern Ireland. You can visit several factory showrooms to admire the skill and craftsmanship. Buy pieces directly from the factories, at select retailers, or online.

Waterford Crystal (see entry, right), world leader in fine glassmaking, has opened a great new factory and visitor center at The Mall in Waterford city. Besides Waterford, several other crystal manufacturers have shops at their factories where you can purchase glassware, including **Galway Irish Crystal** (Merlin Park, Dublin Rd., Galway, tel 091/757-311, galwaycrystal.ie) and **Duiske Crystal** (High St., Graignamanagh, Co. Kilkenny, duiskeglasskilkenny.ie).

🗺 88 B3 ✉ Holycross, Co. Tipperary ☎ 086/166-5869 🚍 Bus: Thurles-Cashel service *(bernardkavanaghcoaches.com)* 🕐 Guided tours: Wed., Sun. 💲 Donation

Hook Head

The circular 30-mile (48 km) Ring of Hook Drive is reached via the Passage East to Ballyhack car ferry, 7 miles (11 km) east of Waterford. You'll find yourself driving down a lovely peninsula of green farmland and dark cliffs. Attractions include the gaunt gray shells of two 13th-century monasteries, Dunbrody Abbey and Tintern Abbey. You'll enjoy the vast sandbanks of Bannow Bay, the big star-shaped Tudor fort at Duncannon, and the craggy ruins of Slade Castle. All roads eventually lead south to the **lighthouse** *(tel 051/397-055 or 051/397-054, $)* on Hook Head's dusky red sandstone cliffs. The modern light sits atop a 100-foot (33 m) tower built in 1172, making it the oldest lighthouse in Ireland. Enjoy sensational views from the top. *hookheritage.ie* 🗺 89 D2 ✉ SE of Waterford via the R683, the R733, and minor roads, Co. Waterford 🕐 Seasonal **Waterford visitor information** ☎ 051/397-055

Waterford Crystal

Waterford sets the standard to which all other glassmakers aspire. Take a factory tour and view the fascinating process—litharge (lead monoxide), silica sand, and potash are blended in furnaces. The molten crystal is then blown into shape and smoothed. When the crystal has cooled, a master cutter engraves intricate designs: leaves, faces, a fox hunt, or a garden. *waterfordvisitorcentre.com* 🗺 89 D2 ✉ House of Waterford Crystal, The Mall, Waterford ☎ 051/317-000 🕐 Guided tours; Mon.–Fri., Nov.–Feb.; Mon.–Sat., March–Oct.; store closed on Sundays, Jan.–Feb. 💲 $$

Small-scale pastoral landscapes, the historic water-girdled city
of Cork, and the five stunning peninsulas of west Cork and Kerry

SOUTHWEST IRELAND

Southwest magic: kings in the wood

SOUTHWEST IRELAND

Three counties make up southwest Ireland: Cork, Kerry, and Limerick. Hereabouts, the landscape begins to break up and the edges of the land become ragged, splitting apart into five great peninsulas that push out into the Atlantic. These fracture further into headlands and islands, giving the map of this region the appearance of blobs of liquid streaking out from some central spillage.

The city of Cork has plenty of Dublin's zip and zing, and not too much of the capital's impatience and glitziness. Eastern County Cork is well wooded with wide farmlands, cut into on the south by the great lagoon of Cork Harbour with its historic town of Cobh.

The farther west you go, the more appealing County Cork becomes, its gorgeous south coast indented with bays and dotted with villages. The three southernmost peninsulas—Mizen, Sheep's Head, and Beara—break away and spear out to sea between their inlets of Roaringwater, Dunmanus, and Bantry Bays.

The southwest has one other big city, Limerick, a place with a vivid history that somehow can't quite match the warmth and intimacy of Cork. But the rest of County Limerick makes

NOT TO BE MISSED:

A stroll around Cork, Ireland's "second city"   130–135

Kissing the Blarney Stone   137

Following in the footsteps of Ireland's emigrants at Cobh   138–139

The slowed pace of life in the seaside villages of West Cork   141–143

The Ring of Kerry, Ireland's famous scenic driving route around the Iveragh Peninsula   150–153

The stark, deserted, and inspiring Blasket Islands   156

Visiting the ruins of Ireland's early Christian communities   158–159 up for what its capital lacks, with charming picture-book villages, fine houses, and a swath of underdiscovered country out west.

County Kerry shares the Beara Peninsula with County Cork and boasts two more of its own—Iveragh, whose mountainous spine is formed by Macgillycuddy's Reeks and whose beautiful coast is circled by the spectacular Ring of Kerry road, and rugged, otherworldly Dingle, with the remote Blasket Islands at its outermost tip. Kerrymen are the butt of jokes for their supposed backwoods gullibility. Don't let that fool you—the Kerrymen themselves make the same jokes about Corkmen.

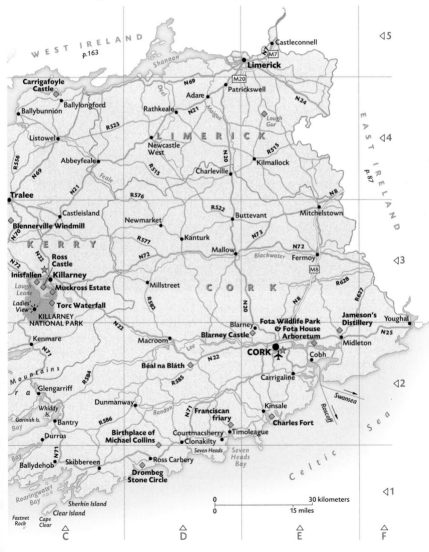

CORK CITY

Although the most important city in the southwest of Ireland, Cork wears a relaxed air. The best way by far to get the most out of this civilized place—and its "softly sharp" people with their distinctive roller-coaster intonation—is to take your time and stroll about, letting the city under your skin by slow degrees.

The bridges and fine old houses along the River Lee lend dignity and character to the city of Cork.

Cork City

129 E2

Visitor Information

125 St. Patrick St., Cork, Co. Cork

021/425-5100

purecork.ie

St. Peter's Cork Visitor Centre

North Main St., Cork, Co. Cork

021/427-8187

stpeterscork.ie

The physical shape of Cork is easy to grasp. The city center occupies a long island in the River Lee that is connected by numerous bridges to 19th-century suburbs on the steepish hills to north and south.

History of Cork City

The low-lying land in the Lee Valley was a good spot to settle. St. Fin Barre established a monastery at Corcaigh, the "marshy place," in 650, and once the Vikings had ceased plundering the monks,

they too settled and established a town during the ninth and tenth centuries.

With its fine river frontage and its great natural harbor just to the southeast, Cork prospered on trade in Norman and medieval times, and it developed an independent political spirit based on this mercantile confidence. Wisely, the city admitted Oliver Cromwell's forces in 1649; not so wisely, it backed the deposed King James II during his unsuccessful comeback bid against King William III in 1690 and had its town walls and many of its buildings flattened when the Protestant army broke in.

The 18th century brought prosperity to Cork—not least thanks to the industry of French Huguenot refugees, who settled here at a time when newly dug canals were bringing improved trade. In the 19th century, the city became a refuge for Home Rule activists, while in the 1919–1922 War of Independence, it was a hotbed of IRA plotting and action—a period brilliantly caught in *Guests of the Nation,* a selection of short stories by Cork's great writer, Frank O'Connor.

In 1920, the Black and Tans, a brutal paramilitary British regiment, murdered the mayor in front of his family and later burned and ransacked much of Cork. Some of what you see in the city center today is a rebuilding of what was burned in 1920, but many of the fine Georgian houses remain.

English Market & South

Cork's chief thoroughfare and shopping street is **St. Patrick's Street,** which curves south from the North Channel of the river and then westward through the center before resuming its southward course as Grand Parade to reach the South Channel.

As a base for a walk around Cork, off Grand Parade you'll find the **English Market** *(englishmarket.ie),* a handsome Georgian covered hall on the site of a 400-year-old market where people still go to meet, greet, and eat. Sounds and sights are on the vivid side around stalls such as the Real Olive Company, the Meat Centre, and On the Pig's Back (a

French deli stand), as well as at the vegetable stands, joke stores, and clothing booths, while smells are a rich jumble of bread, fish, apples, spices, leather, and earthy potatoes. Plunge in, then climb to the first-floor balcony and look down on the bustle below as you enjoy a meal at the outside tables of the Farmgate Restaurant.

INSIDER TIP:

For event guides and pretty much anything else you might want to know about Cork, visit the online phenomenon *peoplesrepublicofcork.com.*

—TOM JACKSON
National Geographic Society

Going south from English Market along Grand Parade, take a right turn down Tuckey Street and a left on South Main Street to pass a Cork institution on your way to the South Channel of the River Lee—**An Spailpín Fánac,** one of the best pubs in the city for sessions of traditional music (generally a 9:30 p.m. kickoff). Don't worry a bit if you can't play or sing—just sit back and enjoy the *craic* and the tunes. If you can play, ask to join in; the musicians will be delighted to welcome you. You are in for great atmosphere, great Guinness, and music you won't forget in a hurry.

Cross South Gate Bridge and turn right along the river to find the gray rocket tower of **St. Fin Barre's Cathedral,** its exterior walls carrying statues of saints, angels, and demons. The

St. Fin Barre's Cathedral

🗺 Map p. 135

✉ Dean St., Cork, Co. Cork

☎ 021/496-3387

💲 $

corkcathedral. webs.com

Crawford Art Gallery

🗺 Map p. 135

✉ Emmet Pl., Cork, Co. Cork

☎ 021/480-5042

crawfordartgallery.ie

■ St. Fin Barre's Cathedral shows off extravagant Victorian Gothic decor.

medieval cathedral was shattered during the siege of 1690, and this church, dating from 1878, is an exuberant example of high Gothic exterior and something more artsy-craftsy within. It has walls of bloodred Cork marble, a beautiful rose window on the theme of Creation, a finely colored mosaic floor in the choir, and glorious gold, blue, and red angels in the roof of the sanctuary. Lift the seats of the choir stalls to enjoy the carved grasshopper, butterfly, stag beetle, and dragonfly under the misericord ledges—on which choristers can recline while seeming to remain upright.

North of English Market

A walk north from English Market would start with a right turn along St. Patrick's Street, from which Carey Lane and French Church Street lead north into the old **Huguenot Quarter.** Now a chic part of the city, it's a peaceful area of high stone walls, small 18th-century houses, and brick-paved pedestrian alleys.

The heart is **Rory Gallagher Square,** honoring the Stratocaster-wielding blues man (who spent his young days in Cork) and featuring a sculpture of a twisted guitar with Gallagher's words and music streaming out of it.

Talk & Tipple at the Hi-B

South of English Market, down Grand Parade, a left turn on Oliver Plunkett Street will take you east all the way to the tip of the "island." If you are in search of a drink, there's no need to go farther than the General Post Office, for above the pharmacy opposite, you'll find the wonderful Hi-B bar up a flight of steps. The Hi-B is everything you look for in an Irish town pub—cheerful, friendly, comfortable, firelit, and a bit old-fashioned—a place where regular folk and connoisseurs can pass a pleasant hour trying to decide which is better, the talk or the ale. Both are among the very best in town.

A short walk west of the Huguenot Quarter you'll find art and photography exhibits at **Cork Vision Centre** in St Peter's Church off North Main Street.

North of the Huguenot Quarter, Paul Street runs east to pass the **Crawford Art Gallery.** Don't be surprised to find more people eating in the gallery's café than looking at the pictures—the fabulous food is provided by the Ballymaloe Cookery School (see sidebar right). Once you have had your fill, the paintings are definitely worth a look—among them an icy 1955 portrait of writer Elizabeth Bowen by Patrick Hennessy, a sentimental Victorian "Letter from America" by James Brenan, a thoughtful Barrie Cooke study of modern Irish poet John Montague, and a blazing yellow-and-blue "Rice Field" (1989) by William Crozier.

Shandon

Just north of the gallery, Christy Ring Bridge crosses the North Channel of the River Lee to reach the northern suburb of Shandon. From its perch high on the hillside, the tall tower of the **Church of St. Anne** calls you up twisty, steep old lanes. Here, for a small fee, you can ring the famous **Bells of Shandon.** Make up your own composition or "read" a tune off a crib card.

At the foot of the tower stands the **Butter Exchange,** built in 1770 to cope with the grading of hundreds of thousands of casks of prime Cork butter. Nearby are

the beautiful circular Firkin Crane dance center *(firkincrane.ie),* Cork Butter Museum *(thebuttermuseum. com),* and Shandon Sweets *(shandonsweets.com),* where father and son Dan and Tony Linehan produce old-fashioned, handmade boiled candies.

A half-hour walk west of Shandon leads to the former **Cork City Gaol.** The old prison houses a chilling exhibition about the harsh conditions in the jail and the even harsher social conditions in 19th-century Cork. The **Radio Museum** is located on the top floor of the building, in the exact rooms where some of RTÉ Radio's offices once were.

Located on the bank of the Lee River, east of the city center, the **Blackrock Castle Observatory** is the ideal place for stargazers and planet lovers. In addition to a walk through the castle and an interactive exhibit called "Cosmos at the Castle," the observatory offers a variety of activities and attractions for children. ∎

EXPERIENCE:
Cooking at Ballymaloe

With the country's culinary reputation on the rise, there's never been a better time to enjoy an Irish cooking class. Run by Ballymaloe House, one of Ireland's best known hotels, **Ballymaloe Cookery School** *(Shanagarry, Co. Cork, tel 021/464-6785, cookingisfun.ie)* offers one-day courses devoted to fabulous finger foods, Irish breakfasts, and even foie gras. No one will rap your knuckles if you make a mess or get it all wrong. This is how cooking is supposed to be—informative, lighthearted, and enjoyable.

Church of St. Anne & Bells of Shandon
- 🗺 Map p. 135
- ✉ Church St., Cork, Co. Cork
- ☎ 021/450-5906
- $ $ (bells)

shandonbells.ie

Butter Exchange
- 🗺 Map p. 135
- ✉ Shandon, Co. Cork

Cork City Gaol
- ✉ Convent Ave., Sunday's Well, Cork, Co. Cork
- ☎ 021/430-5022
- $ $$

corkcitygaol.com

Blackrock Castle Observatory
- ✉ Blackrock, Cork, Co. Cork
- ☎ 021/435-7924
- $ $

bco.ie

WALK: AROUND CORK CITY

Although Cork is Ireland's "second city," and by far the largest conurbation in the southwest of the country, it's an extremely manageable place to walk around. The center of Cork amounts to a spear-blade-shaped island between the North and South Channels of the River Lee. Everything that makes for an enjoyable city walk is contained within this island and on the river banks just north and south of it.

Cork's walkable city center lies between the North and South Channels of the River Lee.

NOT TO BE MISSED:

English Market • St. Fin Barre's Cathedral • Huguenot Quarter • Crawford Art Gallery • Quays along the River Lee

of **An Spailpin Fánac ❸** (see p. 131).

Halfway up South Main Street, turn right along Tuckey Street then left up Grand Parade. At the top of Grand Parade, turn right and make your way along St. Patrick's Street, crossing the road in 200 yards (180 m) to turn left along French Church Street into the quieter pedestrian lanes of the **Huguenot Quarter ❹** (see pp. 132–133).

After soaking up the atmosphere of the brick-paved lanes around **Rory Gallagher Square ❺** (see p. 132), continue north along French Church Street or Carey's Lane to reach Paul Street, where you turn right.

At the end of Paul Street, bear right for a

Start your walk in the **English Market ❶** (see p. 131) at Cork's center. Set off from the Prince's Street entrance. Turn right on Prince's Street and again on South Mall. At the foot of Grand Parade, turn left over the South Channel of the River Lee. Bear right along the south bank for 500 yards (450 m) to reach **St. Fin Barre's Cathedral ❷** (see p. 131), on the left side of Bishop Street.

After looking around the cathedral, retrace your steps along Bishop Street. Turn left at South Gate Bridge and walk up South Main Street. On your right is the great music pub

Cork City Tours

Compact and full of character, Cork is a great city for walking. **Cork City Walks** *(tel 085/700-4981)* offers 90-minute guided walks to the sites of Viking and Norman Cork—from the 7th century to the 17th—and tours of the modern city. For open-top bus tours of Cork, try **Bus Éireann** *(tel 021/450-8188, buseireann. ie)* or **Cronin's Coaches** *(tel 021/430-9090, croninscoaches.com).*

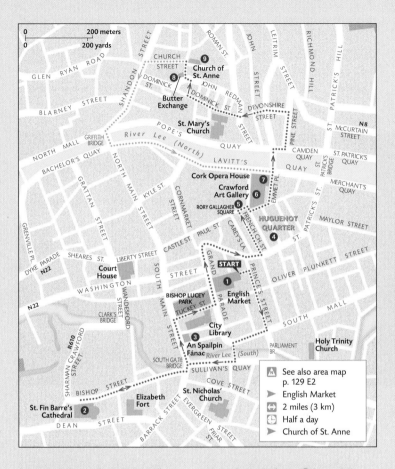

few yards, then turn left along Emmet Place. Soon you will see on your left the **Crawford Art Gallery 6** (see p. 133). This is a great place to stop and rest if you are feeling hungry or thirsty.

Just beyond the gallery, you pass **Cork Opera House 7** (*corkoperahouse.ie*). Cross the North Channel of the river, taking in the great views from the bridge along Lavitt's and Camden Quays. At the far bank, continue up Pine Street. Turn left along Devonshire Street and continue west on Dominick Street.

Take a right to climb Exchange Street and you will find yourself outside the handsome

Georgian **Butter Exchange 8** (see p. 133), with the circular Firkin Crane dance center opposite. Climb on another few yards to reach the tall tower of the **Church of St. Anne 9**. Announce your arrival by striking a tune on the famous **Bells of Shandon** (see p. 133).

From Shandon you could return the way you came. Or, walk west along Church Street opposite St. Anne's, turning left down Shandon Street to regain the North Channel of the River Lee at Griffith Bridge. Cross the bridge, then bear left along the quays to reach the Opera House and Emmet Place, from where you retrace your steps to the English Market.

COUNTY CORK

The largest county in Ireland, Cork is also one of the country's most diverse, with farms and forests, bays, inlets, and a wide variety of wildlife to suit everyone's tastes. Here you can relax along sunny beaches, delve into medieval Irish history, and relive the painful story of the Great Famine and Ireland's hopeful emigrants.

Bloody history and feisty legend cling to the 15th-century stronghold of Blarney Castle.

Blarney Castle

🗺 129 E2

✉ Blarney,
Co. Cork

☎ 021/438-5252

💲 $$

blarneycastle.ie

Blarney Castle

Everyone knows that those who kiss the Blarney Stone at Blarney Castle are magically endowed with the gift of the gab. In fact, the castle and its grounds are imbued with legends—so much so that a stroll about will introduce you to the Rock Close and its "druidical foundations," the Fairy Glade with its "sacrificial altar," and the Wishing Steps that will grant you your heart's desire if you can negotiate them backward with your eyes closed.

Blarney Castle itself is a battlemented keep standing on a rock outcrop overlooking the River Martin, 6 miles (10 km) northwest of Cork city. Dermot Laidhir (Strongman) McCarthy built it in 1446 on the site of a 13th-century fortified tower. Other towers rise as outposts, giving the whole ensemble a formidable look.

"Blarney" as a synonym for charming claptrap originated with an evasive McCarthy, Lord of Blarney, who was quizzed by the Earl of Leicester, Queen Elizabeth I's emissary. Either the queen had demanded the handing over of the castle or there was some dispute about land ownership, but whatever the disagreement, the loquacious McCarthy never got to the point. When Leicester reported the stalemate to Queen Elizabeth, she burst out: "But this is just more Blarney!"

The Queen's forces never did take Blarney Castle; it fell to Oliver Cromwell's commander Lord Broghill in 1646, but the garrison escaped during the siege by underground passage. There were reputed to be three of these, one running to the nearby lake, one to Cork, and one—not very feasibly—to County Kerry, 50 miles (80 km) to the west.

Blarney Stone: To find the Blarney Stone, climb to the top of the old keep, past the Great Hall with its enormous fireplace, the Earl's bedroom lit by big windows, and the Young Ladies' Room. Once out on the open top of the castle, you'll spot the stone's location easily enough—it's where the line ends amid much giggling and gasping. Kissing the Blarney Stone is one of Ireland's prime visitor activities. Come early in the morning to

INSIDER TIP:

Buses are a great way to travel around Ireland, but carry small change with you. There are no onboard bathrooms and the stations often require coins to access the facilities.

—KAREN MARTINEZ
National Geographic Society

avoid lines that can stretch down the castle stairs.

The stone is set into the outer face of a gap in the battlements. You'll have to lie on your back and wriggle your upper body outward and downward to kiss it. It's quite safe, as you perform the feat while gripping two safety bars, supported by a sturdy guard and shielded by a metal grille from the 83-foot (29 m) drop to the ground. Two words to the wise—take all your coins out of your pockets, or they'll shower through the grille, and don't wear a miniskirt if you value your modesty.

(continued on p. 140)

Legends of the Stone

Legends surround the Blarney Stone. One says that it was brought to Ireland by the prophet Jeremiah and claims it as the stone pillow on which Jacob slept in the desert when he had his dream of angels on a ladder—although that is also said of the Lialh Fail or Stone of Destiny at Tara (see pp. 262–263). Other tales tell of the stone being given to Cormac McCarthy, King of Munster, either by an old witch whom he had saved from

drowning or by Robert the Bruce of Scotland, as a thank-you present for sending 4,000 men to help Bruce defeat the English at the Battle of Bannockburn in 1314.

A (marginally) more credible account is that the stone was brought to Ireland by some crusader who had acquired it in the Holy Land as a curiosity, probably already the focus for legends—hence, perhaps, the Jacob's dream connection.

COBH & THE QUEENSTOWN STORY

East of the city of Cork, Great Island all but fills the northernmost portion of Cork Harbour, one of the world's finest natural sheltered havens. The port known as Queenstown, which developed during the 19th century along the seaward-facing side of Great Island, became Ireland's premier hub for commerce and communications with Britain's colonies and former colonies.

A monument in Casement Square remembers the passengers of the *Lusitania*, torpedoed in 1915.

Queenstown—or Cobh (Cove), as it was called before the visit of Queen Victoria in 1849—meant many things to many people. To sailors at the Admiralty station established here during the Napoleonic Wars, it was a strategic communications post in the North Atlantic. To the troops embarking for the Crimean War in the 1850s or the Boer War 40 years later, it was their last sight of home territory and the launch point to death or glory. For most of those who boarded the *Titanic* here in 1912, it was their last contact with earth. For prisoners, such as the rebel United Irishmen banished to a penal colony in Australia for their part in the 1798 Rising,

it meant the start of six months chained in the lightless, airless hold of a leaky convict ship. Above all, it was the point of embarkation for many millions of poor Irish emigrants seeking a new life in Canada, the United States, England, or Australia, away from the poverty or oppression that had dogged them in their native land.

In the beautifully refurbished former railway station at the old port—now once more named Cobh—the **Queenstown Story exhibition** *(Cobh Heritage Centre, Cobh, Co. Cork, tel 021/481-3591, cobhheritage.com, $)* tells the tale of those who left Ireland over the course of two centuries through this thronging gateway.

Here are ship models of every shape and size, tableaux, photographs, letters, and the poignant personal effects of emigrants—locks of loved ones' hair, rosaries, pocket watches. It is the stories of the men, women, and children, leaving Ireland because there was no other option, that strike home the hardest.

We see these mostly reluctant travelers, bold or frightened, optimistic or downcast, holding "American wakes" on the waterside before parting from relatives and lovers as they board the emigrant ships. These ranged from well-appointed vessels to the rotten old coffin ships, apt to founder in bad weather, that those fleeing the Great Famine of 1845–1849 were only too glad to scramble on board.

We learn of the bad water and food, the vomiting and cursing, the dances and *ceilidhs* in the steerage-class holds, and the daunting strangeness of the arrival on a foreign shore weeks or months later, weak and filthy from

INSIDER TIP:

If you're of Irish descent, chances are some of your relatives left Ireland from Cobh, making the Queenstown Story exhibition a must-see.

—CHRISTOPHER KLEIN
National Geographic Traveler
magazine writer

the voyage, with only the name of a relative or the vague promise of work to sustain them.

Between 1815 and 1970, some three million emigrants—three quarters of the population of Ireland today—left Cobh to seek a better life. This vast anonymous army, which enriched so many other countries while it drained the lifeblood of Ireland, is the real Queenstown story.

EXPERIENCE: Exploring *Titanic* & Irish Emigration

After visiting the Queenstown Story exhibition (see p. 138) in Cobh, you can dive into the **Titanic Experience** (*White Star Line Building, 20 Casement Sq., Cobh, tel 021/481-4412, titanicexperiencecobh.ie*), an interactive experience with audiovisuals and recreations of third- and first-class cabins, located in the original White Star Line Ticket Office.

You can learn more about the history of that fateful ship in the recently opened and beautifully laid-out **Titanic Belfast** exhibition (see pp. 291–293) in Belfast, where *Titanic* was built. Then delve further into the history of Irish emigration at the **Ulster American Folk Park** (*2 Mellon Rd., Castletown, Omagh, Co. Tyrone, nmni.com/uafp, $; see pp. 311–313*).

Follow in the footsteps of actual Irish emigrants on board the **Dunbrody Famine Ship** (*New Ross, Co. Wexford, tel 051/425-239, dunbrody.com, $$*), a reproduction

sailing vessel, and at the **Culkins Emigration Museum** (*Cannaghanally, Dromore West, Co. Sligo, tel 096/47-152, $*), located on the site of an emigration office that operated from the 19th century into the 1930s.

Poignant reminders of the cause of the early Irish emigration can be found at the **Famine Museum** (*Strokestown Park, Strokestown, Co. Roscommon, strokestownpark.ie, $; see p. 237*), which includes devastating written pleas from the starving tenants, while **Gáirdín an Ghorta** (*Garden of Remembrance; Newmarket, Co. Kilkenny, tel 086/839-4349*) offers a meditative view of Ireland's troubled past and promising future.

Lastly, in Dublin you can step into the **EPIC—The Irish Emigration Museum** (*Custom House Quay, Dublin 1, tel 01/906-0861, epicchq.com, $$; see p. 84*), where you can experience in 20 interactive galleries the story of Irish emigrants who left their homeland.

Kinsale

🏛 129 E2

Visitor Information

✉ Emmet Pl..
Kinsale, Co.
Cork

☎ 021/477-2234

kinsale.ie

Kinsale Regional Museum

✉ Market Sq.,
Kinsale, Co. Cork

☎ 021/477-7930

🕐 Closed Nov.–
March

Kinsale

The town of Kinsale, spread around a tight waterfront of green hills at a bend in the River Bandon's estuary, 15 miles (25 km) south of Cork city, is the perfect jumping-off point for the beautiful, unspoiled coastline of west Cork.

Reckoned the gourmet capital of the southwest, if not of all Ireland, Kinsale is made for wandering, its waterfront and snaking Main Street full of color-washed buildings. Lanes and narrow streets climb the hills behind the harbor, and the houses spread attractively above the water. The only eyesore is a development of close-packed green-and-pink apartments on the east bank of the estuary, brutally out of keeping with everything else in view.

EXPERIENCE:
Sailing & Water Sports

The strands and bays of west Cork offer some of the best water sports in Ireland. You can sign up for lessons at **Inchydoney Surf School** (*Inchydoney Beach, Clonakilty, Co. Cork , tel 086/869-5396, inchydoneysurf school.com*) or **Kite Sport Centre** (*tel 087/765-6317, kitesportcentre.com*) in Cork. A great place to learn to sail is the **Kinsale Outdoor Education Centre** (*St. John's Hill, Kinsale, Co. Cork, tel 021/477-2896, kinsaleoec.com*), or you can explore the coast with **Atlantic Sea Kayaking** (*The Abbey, Skibbereen, Co. Cork, tel 028/ 21-058, atlanticseakayaking.com*). **Baltimore Diving Centre** (*Harbour Drive, Baltimore, Co. Cork, tel 086/241-2855, baltimorediving.com*) offers a range of scuba diving packages.

St. Multose's Church:
St. Multose's Church (*tel 021/477-2220*) stands in from the harbor, where Higher O'Connell Street meets Cork Street—a squat church dating from the 12th century, whose sturdy Irish Romanesque tower has a curious top, smaller than the lower stories, awkwardly fitted on.

Desmond Castle: Desmond Castle (*tel 021/477-4855*), halfway up hilly Cork Street, is a fine late medieval fortified tower with craggy crenellations and stone mullioned windows. It has served as a customs house and a jail for French prisoners of war.

The castle was also used as a powder magazine during the Siege of Kinsale in 1601, when 4,000 Spanish troops under Don Juan del Águila landed at Kinsale to support a rebellion by Hugh O'Neill, Earl of Tyrone. The rebels held the town for three months, but when the Spanish failed to back the Irish during the decisive battle, the rebellion quickly crumbled. It was the last roll of the dice for the Gaelic chiefs of Ireland: In 1607, O'Neill and his fellow rebel the Earl of Tyrconnell fled to the Continent—the famous "Flight of the Earls"—and the English Crown took full control of Ireland.

Kinsale Regional Museum:
Much Kinsale history is expounded in endearingly ramshackle style at the Kinsale Regional Museum in the old Court House on Market Square. Here are ice picks and fish

■ **Enjoy the magnificent panorama from Charles Fort over the town of Kinsale.**

boxing hammers, boatbuilder's tools and Easter Rising rifles, ships' guns and Kinsale lace, all packed into the museum's few rooms. Most affecting are the mementoes of the British passenger liner *Lusitania,* torpedoed by the German submarine *U-20* on May 7, 1915, off the Old Head of Kinsale promontory. Of 1,951 passengers, 1,198 died, many of them women and children. A striped mail bag, a German commemorative medal, a cane deck chair, and a facsimile of the log of the *U-20,* translated into English, bring the tragedy up close.

For light relief there are the vast knee boot and the unnecessarily massive knife and fork of Patrick Cotter O'Brien (1760–1806), the celebrated "Kinsale Giant." At 8 feet 7 inches (262 cm), O'Brien

was certainly phenomenally tall. He was also a sad figure, unable to walk properly or even rise from his chair without pain, obliged to exhibit himself as a freak to earn a living.

West Cork Coast

Explore this area when you have adjusted to the slow tempo of the southwest. It's no good hurrying over the 100-mile (160 km), in-and-out coast of west Cork because the twisty roads won't let you speed along, and the seaside villages and windy headlands will do their darndest to detain you. It is good to take two days rather than one—better still to take three, or a week.

Charles Fort: Any exploration of the west Cork coast from

Charles Fort

🅰 129 E2

✉ Summer Cove, Kinsale, Co. Cork

☎ 021/477-2263

⑤ $

heritageireland.ie

Kinsale ought to start with the short trip along the east side of the estuary to Charles Fort, an eerie and striking star-shaped fort built in the 1670s to be impregnable from the sea. Designed on the principles of French military engineer Vauban, the fort fell in three days when actually put to the test by King William III's army in 1690—they attacked it from the land.

The extensive interior of Charles Fort is filled with ruined barracks, magazines, officers' quarters, an armory, and a cooper-age—all massively constructed, but all now roofless and blank-eyed. Strolling around these lifeless monuments to defense is a surreal, gripping experience. The view from the headland over Kinsale of the boats on the river and the estuary mouth is sensational.

The Coast Road: From Kinsale, the scenic Coast Road wriggles and snakes for about 80 miles (128 km) westward to Skibbereen, making use of byways and lanes in which you are almost bound to lose yourself. Don't worry: There's always someone to ask when the signposts give out. In any case, this is one of the most beautiful corners of Ireland, a gentle coastal landscape that simply begs you to put the car in low gear and wander aimlessly.

■ Sea-bitten cliffs at the Old Head of Kinsale, south of Cork, typify the region's dramatic coastline.

A high-banked lane colorful with poppies, ragwort, fuchsia, and bindweed, will take you on to **Timoleague,** one of several attractive color-washed villages sited around the estuaries whose shining mudflats are haunted by seabirds and crossed by narrow causeways. Timoleague's 14th-century **Franciscan friary** is astonishing complete—Cromwell despoiled it in 1642, but the shell stands almost perfect in lichen-green stone. Lancet windows, tomb niches, a tall arched nave, and fragments of cloister echo to the cooing of nesting pigeons.

It is worth sidetracking through pretty Courtmacsherry and around the lanes that crisscross the **Seven Heads Peninsula.** The moondaisies, roses, and silver sand beaches around Dunworley are a delight. You can swim here, or pass through the lively town of **Clonakilty** and cross the causeway to Inchydoney Island with its broad strands. At Ballinascarthy near Clonakilty, a silver Model T honors Henry Ford, whose father was born here.

Three miles (5 km) west of Clonakilty, the **Four Alls pub** and Sam's Cross are signposted off the N71. The dark and cozy Four Alls is where the commander-in-chief of the Free State Army, Michael Collins, stopped on August 22, 1922, for his last drink before an IRA bullet felled him in an ambush. The pub walls are covered in photographs, drawings, and newspaper clippings relating to the hero.

The **Birthplace of Michael Collins** stands nearby at Woodfield (ask at the pub for directions) and is the object of many a pilgrimage. A bronze bust of Collins generally has a posy of fresh flowers on its plinth.

Across another estuary stands **Rosscarbery.** The cathedral here has a splendid heavy Victorian chancel roof and some excellent 19th- and 20th-century stained glass, notably the pre-Raphaelite young knight in the south transept

INSIDER TIP:

In rural Ireland, don't overplan the entertainment. Find a local pub that encourages local musicians, then get yourself a pint and enjoy the free show.

—ROBIN CURRIE
National Geographic author

who commemorates a dead soldier of World War I.

The **Drombeg Stone Circle** (ca 150 B.C.) is well signposted along the Glandore road.

This circle of 17 closely spaced, man-size stones slopes up toward the "Druid's Altar," a long recumbent stone that is set in line with the winter solstice sunset. Nearby, is the *fulacht fiadh,* an ancient cooking pit with a primitive oven. When you reach **Skibbereen,** a colorful little town on the River Ilen, stop to visit the **Heritage Center,** where an exhibition tells the story of the Great Famine of the 1840s that hit this area heavily, killing more than a third of the population.

Birthplace of Michael Collins

▲ 129 D2

✉ Woodfield, Clonakilty, Co. Cork

☎ 023/883-3226

Skibbereen

▲ 129 C1

Visitor Information

✉ Skibbereen Heritage Centre, Old Gasworks Building, Upper Bridge St., Skibbereen, Co. Cork

☎ 021/425-5100

🕐 Closed Nov.– Feb.

skibbereen.ie

Islands of South-west Cork

129 C1

Visitor Information

125 St. Patrick's St., Cork, Co. Cork

021/425-5100

Islands of Bantry Bay

128 B2–129 C2

Visitor Information

Old Courthouse, Bantry, Co. Cork

027/50-229

Seasonal

Lough Hyne: Located about 4.5 miles south of Skibbereen, this marine lake, linked to the ocean by a narrow canal, is Ireland's first natural marine reserve, established in 1981. The Skibbereen Heritage Center offers useful information about this habitat that is home to a variety of species including the triggerfish and the red-mouthed goby. It's also a popular place to kayak. The 4.3 mile Lough Hyne Loop Walk starts from the parking lot, travels along quiet roads, and climbs to the top of a small hill that offers a beautiful view of the lake.

Islands of Southwest Cork

Roaringwater Bay, poetically and aptly named, forms the underbelly of the Mizen Peninsula. There are said to be 127 islands scattered in the bay, and the two largest—Sherkin Island and Clear Island—are accessible by ferry.

Sherkin Island: Sherkin Island *(10-minute ferry ride from Baltimore or Schull, tel 087/911-7377, sherkin island.eu)* is some 3 miles (5 km) long, a great island for swimming with safe, sandy beaches. The 70 inhabitants run a couple of pubs: the Jolly Roger and Murphy's beside the ruins of an O'Driscoll castle. There's also the ruin of a 1460 **Franciscan friary** to explore, along with the enjoyable little island museum in the volunteer-run **Marine Station,** which monitors the marine environment around the island.

Clear Island: Irish-speaking Clear Island, or Cape Clear as

some call it *(ferry from Baltimore, capeclearisland.ie),* lies 6 miles (10 km) out from land at the mouth of Roaringwater Bay. It is roughly the same size as Sherkin but more mountainous and bulky. The island, which has a bird observatory with a worldwide reputation, is a landfall for millions of migrating birds and sees spectacular flypasts in summer of gannets, kittiwakes, shearwaters, guillemots, cormorants, and storm petrels.

North Harbour, where the boat docks, has a couple of pubs, and there's a third one on the potholed road to sheltered **South Harbour.** On the south side of the island—Ireland's southernmost point—are splendid cliffs from which to gaze out at the rugged hump of Fastnet Rock, 4 miles (6 km) out into the Atlantic.

Islands of Bantry Bay

In Bantry Bay, northward beyond the Mizen and Sheep's Head Peninsulas, lie four islands. **Whiddy Island** *(ferry from Bantry, tel 086/862-6734, whiddyferry.com)* is little visited, mostly because it holds the ugly remains of an oil storage depot abandoned in 1979, when the tanker *Betelgeuse* blew up, killing 51 people.

Garinish Island, also known as **Garnish** or **Ilnacullin** *(ferry from Glengarriff, tel 027/63-116 or 027/63-333, garnishisland.com),* is, at 37 acres (15 ha), a scrap of an island that was bare rock until transformed by English landscape gardener Harold Peto for owner Arran Bryce. Between 1910 and

A touch of Romanesque elegance in the Italian garden on Garinish Island in Bantry Bay

1913, Peto planted on imported topsoil a garden of plants and shrubs from all over the world. Among the lush growth is a formal Italian garden.

Farther down the bay lies **Bere Island** *(ferry from Castletownbere, tel 027/75-009, bereisland.net),* a former British naval base that has a sailing school and some fine hilly walking and scrambling based on a 13-mile (21 km) stretch of the circum-peninsular Beara Way.

Out at the tip of the Beara Peninsula, you can sway in a cable car over a furious tidal race to lonely **Dursey Island** *(durseyisland .ie),* a rugged finger of land where some 50 people live without shop, pub, or other mainland amenities.

Follow a 7-mile (11 km) loop of the **Beara Way** around the island, pausing at the seaward end to look out over the three sea islets: the Bull, the Cow, and the Calf.

Three Peninsulas

County Cork boasts three of the five great peninsulas of southwest Ireland—south to north: Mizen, Sheep's Head, and Beara. Each has a quite distinctive character and individual magic. Take a day, at least, on each peninsula; they hide

Mizen Peninsula

🗺 128 B1–129 C1

Skibbereen Visitor Information

✉ North St., Skibbereen, Co. Cork

☎ 028/21-489

their secrets from those who rush through.

Mizen: Traveling the Mizen Peninsula clockwise from pretty Ballydehob, you enter a sparse world of gorse-covered bog, rock outcrops, and high hills. Roses, purple flowering heather,

view, too, and maybe a sight of dolphins, whales, and any number of seabirds.

Sheep's Head: The village of Durrus is where you turn left for the Sheep's Head Peninsula, another clockwise circuit. There are no tourist attractions, which

■ Whorls and windings of the sea around the shores of the Beara Peninsula

Mizen Head Visitor Information

✉ Harbour Rd., Goleen, Co. Cork

☎ 028/35-115

🕐 Closed weekdays Nov.– March

mizenhead.net

Sheep's Head Peninsula

🗺 128 B1–129 C2

and brilliant orange monbretia grow in the roadside hedges.

Schull and Goleen are sleepy villages on coastal bays, while charming Crookhaven sits on an isolated mini-peninsula. Barleycove, just beyond, is a huge, fabulous beach system backed by huge grassy dunes and spreads of *machair* (shell-sand turf). Out at the end, **Mizen Head** is the southernmost point of mainland Ireland, with impressive vertical cliffs. You can walk beyond the visitor center and cross a bridge over a rocky sea chasm to see a display of charts, photographs, and signal flags in the old fog station. There's a fine

only adds to the magic of this slim and low-rolling promontory, with its scatter of tiny villages and well-ordered farmland that turns wild as you approach the lighthouse at the tip. The scenic drive back to Bantry along the north side is called the Goats Path, with good reason.

Beara: The Beara Peninsula is another matter altogether, a great ragged leg of land, 30 miles (50 km) long, divided between Cork and Kerry—though Cork has the lion's share. The purple slabs of the Caha Mountains march along the spine of the

INSIDER TIP:

The Beara Peninsula is a hidden gem. It has as much spectacular scenery as the Ring of Kerry to the north, but without the endless caravans of tour buses.

—CHRISTOPHER KLEIN
National Geographic Traveler
magazine writer

peninsula, rising to 2,251 feet (685 m), and the Slieve Miskish Mountains are in the west— lower, but no less impressive— rising above inhospitable bog and stony fields. The shoreline is heavily indented. Southward it looks to Bantry Bay and its islands (see pp. 144–145); on the north is the Kenmare River, with more, smaller islands and the backdrop of Kerry's mountainous Iveragh Peninsula (see pp. 150–153).

Tour the Beara in an open-ended figure eight route, starting at the pretty Victorian health resort of **Glengarriff.** In a beautiful location, backed by wooded mountains, the town is full of hydrangeas and palm trees, with 19th-century villas peeping out. You can also visit a small bamboo forest that has thirty different species. *(tel 027/63-007, bamboo-park. com, $).*

Going west along the southern coast road, you reach the right turn for the Healy Pass. Try to pick a clear day for the ascent of the narrow mountain road to the pass, at almost 1,100 feet (334 m): The

view from the Crucifixion shrine at the top is stupendous.

At the northern foot of the pass, you'll find beautiful **Derreen Garden,** with walks to the shore through flowering shrubs and giant feathery tree ferns from Australia. Continue west along a narrow, winding road over the end of Slieve Miskish to **Allihies,** on the black cliffs of west-facing Ballydonegan Bay. Allihies was a copper-mining center in the 19th century, and above the village you can explore the remains of mine buildings and a small museum.

At the end of Beara is the swaying cable car ride to Dursey Island (see p. 145). Back along the south coast, have a look at the extraordinary ruin of **Puxley Mansion,** west of Castletownbere. The IRA torched this mansion in 1921, leaving a Gothic horror of vaults, huge blank windows, and grand rooms open to the sky. ∎

Beara Peninsula
🗺 128 B2–129 C2
Visitor Information
✉ St. Peter's Church, Castletownbere, Co. Cork
☎ 027/70-054
bearatourism.com

Derreen Garden
✉ Lauragh, Co. Cork
☎ 083/166-2160
💲 $
derreengarden.com

Gougane Barra Forest Park

Coillte, the Irish state forestry service, owns and administers many forest parks across Ireland, and County Cork's Gougane Barra *(coillte.ie)* is one of the finest. Here, in a deep rocky bowl of cliffs surrounding peaceful and lovely Gougane Barra Lake in the headwaters of the River Lee, Coillte has laid out hiking trails of varying degrees of difficulty—a waterfall trail, an oakwood trail, the trail of the Red Hollow, and more. They introduce you to a beautiful wilderness of coniferous and broad-leaved trees, of rushing streams and falls, and of mountainside lookouts that will take your breath away.

COUNTY KERRY

County Kerry is home to the mountains, craggy coasts, and charming small towns and villages depicted in chocolate-box photographs, only close-up and for real. Best known perhaps for the Ring of Kerry, the spectacular coast road around the Iveragh Peninsula, Kerry also boasts the relaxed charm of the Dingle Peninsula, as well as the stark beauty of the Blasket Islands.

The grand beauty of the Lakes of Killarney has attracted visitors for more than 200 years.

Killarney National Park

129 C3 & 151

killarney
nationalpark.ie

Killarney National Park

Some of Ireland's most beautiful lake and mountain scenery falls within the boundary of Killarney National Park. The heart of the park is the 10,000 acres (4,000 ha) of the Muckross Estate, given to the Irish nation in 1932. Careful purchases by the Irish state and donations of land in subsequent decades have safeguarded a total of 25,000 acres (10,000 ha) of wonderful country from development.

Victorian and Edwardian holidaymakers eulogized the Killarney landscape as the "Mecca of every pilgrim in search of the sublime and beautiful in Nature—the mountain paradise of the west." Yet all were agreed that Killarney town itself was far too touristy. Located at the northeast corner of the park, it is still an all-out tourist town where the sales of leprechauns, shamrocks, and shillelaghs keep the gift shops ticking over nicely.

Muckross Estate: While Killarney is just the place to rent a horse-drawn jaunting car complete with a silver-tongued *jarvey,* or driver, to trot you out to the lakes, the town has no views of the lakes themselves. The best thing to do is to refuel and head straight for the Muckross Estate on the shores of Lough Leane.

Muckross is extremely popular and perhaps best avoided on public holidays in summer. At other times of the year, this carefree estate is a great place to stroll by the lake or through the beautifully kept rhododendron and azalea **gardens.**

Muckross House is a Victorian mansion with an appealingly cranky **museum** of folklore and rural life. To the north of the house, you'll find the largely 15th-century cloisters and ruined church of **Muckross Abbey.** Jarveys and their jaunting cars are thick on the ground here, too, if you feel like a horse-drawn tour.

Ross Castle: Head northward along the lakeshore to reach the restored 15th-century fortified *bawn,* or walled tower, of Ross Castle where you can take a tour to discover its history. Rent a rowboat here and pull out across the lake to **Inisfallen,** a lovely little island whose thick woods conceal a church and monastic ruins.

From Ross Castle, head south again along the N71 to reach the Middle and Upper Lakes, where willing boatmen will row you about.

Lakes of Killarney: The star attraction of Middle Lake (also known as Muckross Lake) is the **Meeting of the Waters,** set in a flowery and shrubby dell. Climb past the beautiful Upper Lake to reach **Ladies' View,** a famous viewpoint looking north over the spectacularly narrow Gap of Dunloe and the Killarney Lakes.

INSIDER TIP:

If you're thinking of proposing to that special someone while in Killarney National Park, Torc Waterfall is the local time-honored place to do it.

—WENDY YASCUR
*National Geographic
contributor*

Torc Waterfall, another classic Killarney sight, is signed off the N71 beside Middle Lake. Getting to the fall, a fine 60-foot (18 m) cascade down a staircase of rock overhung with sycamore and mountain ash, involves a short climb up a stepped path. If you feel like a moderate stretch of the legs, you can leave the crowds behind in a twinkling if you carry on up the path beyond the waterfall. Turn around when you've had enough. This is the old road over the mountains to Kenmare (12 miles/19 km away) by way of Esknamucky Glen and Windy Gap, now part of the long-distance **Kerry Way.** It will lead you up through mossy woods of dwarf

(continued on p. 154)

Muckross Estate

✉ Muckross, near Killarney, Co. Kerry

☎ 064/667-0144

🕐 Farms closed Nov.–Feb., & weekdays, March–April & Oct.; house & gardens open year-round

💲 House & farms: $$

muckross-house.ie

Ross Castle

✉ Ross Rd., Killarney, Co. Kerry

☎ 064/663-5851

🕐 Closed Nov.–Feb.,

💲 $

heritageireland.ie

DRIVE: RING OF KERRY

This looping route around the coast of the Iveragh Peninsula, known as the Ring of Kerry, is Ireland's best known scenic drive. Although you have to start early, especially in the summer, to avoid becoming stuck behind a crawling line of vehicles, this is one treat you must not miss. A few diversions along smaller roads are suggested here to give you the chance to explore and to escape any traffic jams on the main road.

Start your full day's drive by leaving **Killarney** for Killorglin along the N72, with great views to your left on the outskirts of town down the wide, mountain-framed expanse of **Lough Leane.** In 12 miles (19 km), you will reach **Killorglin ❶**, a characterful small town where each year in August a wild goat is enthroned as master of an extremely enjoyable three-day revel called Puck Fair.

Leave the main N70 Ring of Kerry route here and enter the town across its bridge, driving up the hill and taking the second street on the right (signed "Caragh Lake"), which soon becomes a bumpy road across forested boglands. At P. O'Shea's shop in **Caragh** village, fork left (signed "Hotel Ard Na Sidhe"), and in 1 mile (1.6 km), bear left up a forest track (wooden sign: "Loch Cárthaí; Caragh Lake") for

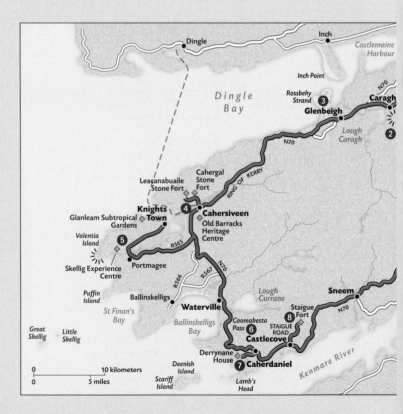

NOT TO BE MISSED:

Cahergeal & Leacanabuaile stone forts • Valentia Island • Views over the Skelligs and Kenmare River • Derrynane House

half a mile (0.75 km) to a **viewpoint ②**. The view here sweeps over Lough Caragh to the mountains—making it a great place for a picnic.

Return to Caragh and turn left to reach the N70, bearing left through Glenbeigh village. A right turn just before you reach the end of the village leads to **Rossbehy (Rossbeigh)**

Strand ③, with a wonderful view of a giant spit of shaggy dunes stretching 3 miles (5 km) north across Dingle Bay toward the mountainous spine of the Dingle Peninsula. The narrow road continues in a loop back to the N70.

Continue on the N70 down the northern coast of the Iveragh Peninsula through glorious hilly scenery. Just before crossing the bridge into the village of **Cahersiveen ④**, glance to your left to see the ruins of the birthplace of Daniel O'Connell (1775–1847), champion of Ireland's poor and the first Irish Catholic to be elected to Parliament in London.

INSIDER TIP:

If you're in Kerry August 10–12, don't miss Puck Fair (puckfair.ie), one of the oldest fairs in Ireland. Mass revelry ensues when a wild mountain goat is crowned "King Puck" and placed on a platform in the middle of Killorglin town for three days.

—TOM JACKSON
National Geographic Society

Turn right in the village to pass the **Old Barracks Heritage Centre** (*theoldbarrackscaher siveen.com, $*), with exhibitions and displays of local interest, then cross a bridge and go left, following brown "Stone Houses" signs, to find **Cahergal** and **Leacanabuaile stone forts.** Leacanabuaile—certainly inhabited during the Bronze Age, and maybe dating back more than 4,000 years—is especially impressive. Perched on a rock outcrop, it is a great stone-built enclosure, 80 feet (25 m) across, with a square

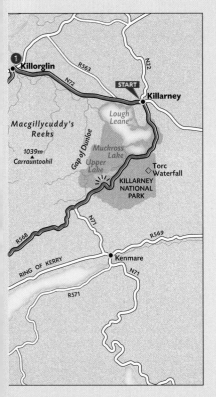

	See also area map pp. 128 A2–129 C3
►	Killarney
⏱	1 day
⬌	150 miles (240 km)
►	Killarney

Cahersiveen's old police barracks resembles a Bavarian castle.

building in the center and the remains of three beehive huts, all inside a circular 6-foot (2 m) wall.

Three miles (5 km) beyond Cahersiveen, a side road (R565) leaves the N70 and makes for Portmagee, where you cross the causeway onto **Valentia Island** ⑤ *(valentiaisland.ie)*. This is a most delightful island of tiny patchwork fields, with fine high cliffs on the west and north, and the small but beautiful **Glanleam subtropical gardens** *(tel 066/947-6176, closed Nov.–March, $)*. From the western tip of the island the view looks down to the remote, jagged-edged profiles of **Great Skellig** and **Little Skellig.** These towering rocks in the Atlantic are seabird

sanctuaries, but until the 12th century, hardy monks inhabited Great Skellig. Inquiry about boats in Portmagee or Ballinskelligs may yield a fisherman willing to run you out to Great Skellig, where you climb thousand-year-old steps to the sixth-century beehive huts and tiny oratory chapels of the monks, 700 feet (215 m) above the waves. You can take a boat tour organized by **Casey's Tours** *(skelligislands. com, tours from April to September, $$$$)*, or by the **Skellig Experience Centre** *(tel 066/947-6306, skelligexperience.com, $)*, which also has an exhibition center that is particularly interesting when the water is too rough to reach the islands.

Return from Valentia Island to the N70, where you turn right to continue your Ring of Kerry circuit. The seaside resort of **Waterville** stands on the beautiful sandy Ballinskelligs Bay, from where the road climbs (more very fine

---

INSIDER TIP:

On Kerry's Valentia Island, visit Telegraph Field, the site of the first permanent communications link between Europe and North America, established in 1857.

—JUSTIN KAVANAGH
*National Geographic
Travel Books editor*

---

views of the Skelligs from here) to the classic viewpoint from **Coomakesta Pass** ⑥—back to the Skelligs, then forward to Scariff and Deenish Islands, with the prospect improving all the time as you come in sight of the mighty, islet-fringed Kenmare River, far more like a great bay than an estuary as it opens in front of you. Turn right at **Caherdaniel,** signposted "Derrynane House," stopping if you wish at the Blind Piper, an excellent pub.

Derrynane House ⑦ *(tel 066/947-5113, derrynanehouse.ie, closed Mon.–Fri. in Nov.–Dec., Mon.–Tues. in April & Oct., $)* was the home of Daniel O'Connell from 1825 onward and is now a museum to Swaggering Dan, or "The Liberator," as his fans preferred to call him. O'Connell was a great Irishman, passionate and persevering, and inside the slate-hung house you get a good idea of the Kerry lawyer who inspired such devotion and raised such expectations among the poorest of the poor.

In the dining room a table is set with silverware presented to O'Connell by grateful supporters; upstairs in a display case is a silver cup voted to him in December 1813 by the "Catholics of Ireland." Also here are portraits,

contemporary cartoons, the dueling pistols with which he killed an opponent named D'Esterre, in 1815, and, most poignantly, the bowl he was baptized in and the bed he died in.

Outside, the wooded grounds of Derrynane House are threaded by walking trails that will lead you to a ring fort and to a Mass rock. It was here, during the 18th century when practicing the Roman Catholic religion was outlawed, that local faithful would gather clandestinely to hear Mass.

Return to the N70 and in 4 miles (6 km) bear left in Castlecove to find the magnificent **Staigue Fort** ⑧ Set in a beautiful lonely valley, this wonderfully preserved ring fort of 1500 B.C. is well over 100 feet (30 m) in diameter, with great thick walls in which steps lead to some fine sea and mountain views.

Back at the N70, turn left and continue as far as **Sneem** village, where you fork left on the R568 for a wild and lonely 30-mile (50 km) mountain run, later passing the lakes of Killarney National Park (see pp. 148–149) and back to Killarney.

Off the Beaten Path

If you find yourself stuck behind a caravan or just fancy taking things slow, there are several worthwhile diversions to make the most of the Ring of Kerry. For example, you could go for a stroll or swim along Rossbeigh Strand, working up an appetite for the fabulous fish at **Jack's Bar and Seafood Restaurant** *(Cromane Lower, Killorglin, tel 066/976-9102, jackscromane.com)*. Or enjoy a picnic lunch at Bray Head, on the southern tip of Valentia Island, in full view of the Skelligs. If you want to walk part of the Kerry Way, detour to the left from the N70, between Aghatubrid and Waterville, and follow one of the twisty roads through the Iveragh Peninsula to find where the trail crosses the road.

The atmospheric Dingle Peninsula

Dingle Peninsula

🗺 128 A3–B3

dingle-peninsula.ie

Dingle Visitor Information

✉ Strand St., Dingle, Co. Kerry

☎ 066/915-1188

Tralee Visitor Information

✉ Ashe Memorial Hall, Denny St., Dingle, Co. Kerry

☎ 066/712-1288

Kerry County Museum

✉ Ashe Memorial Hall, Denny St., Dingle, Co. Kerry

☎ 066/712-7777

💲 $$$

kerrymuseum.ie

oaks and ancient holly trees to an exciting fording of a mountain torrent by way of stepping-stones.

Dingle Peninsula

The Dingle Peninsula is the connoisseur's choice among the five peninsulas of southwest Ireland. Here are beautiful sandspits, beaches, and mountains, and Ireland's greatest concentration of early Christian sites—not to mention the laid-back charm of Dingle town and the extraordinary literary hothouse of the remote and rugged Blasket Islands. The 110-mile (179 km) Dingle Way footpath circumnavigates the peninsula.

Tralee to Inch: The gateway to the Dingle Peninsula is Tralee, a sizable country town with a bloody history, having been sacked and destroyed in 1583, and again in the 1640s and '50s during the Cromwellian

repressions. These dark deeds are recalled in the excellent **Kerry County Museum** on Denny Street, a fine street of handsome Georgian buildings that leads to Tralee's trademark rose gardens. The annual **Rose of Tralee International Festival** (tel 066/712-1322, roseoftralee. ie), held in August, to the delight of the media, pits lovely girls from all over the world (they are supposed to be of Irish extraction) against each other in what is essentially an old-fashioned beauty contest. Tralee is a town of narrow streets, usually crowded, with good traditional music sessions in several pubs—try Paddy Mac's or Baily's Corner.

Until 1953, the Dingle Peninsula had its own eccentrically delightful railway, which connected Tralee with Dingle town (see sidebar p. 157). A short section of track has been reopened (Tralee & Blennerville

Steam Railway, traleesteamrailway. webs.com), and you can rattle behind a steam locomotive as far as the restored **Blennerville Windmill**, 60 feet (20 m) tall, a landmark visible for miles around.

From Tralee, the N86 follows the northern flank of the Slieve Mish Mountains. The western end of this ridge is dominated by the stone-walled promontory fort of **Caherconree,** perhaps built around 500 B.C. You can scramble up to the fort from a minor road, signed to the left off the R559 at the eastern edge of Camp village.

According to legend, Caherconree was the stronghold of King Cu Roi MacDaire, a warrior who made the fatal misjudgment of stealing and "marrying" beautiful Blathnaid, girlfriend of the Ulster hero Cúchulainn. Shut up in Caherconree, Blathnaid waited until an auspicious moment arrived for her lover to attack the fort, then summoned him by pouring milk into the springs of the Finglas River. Cúchulainn saw the sign, stormed

the fort, slew the king, and was reunited with his beloved.

From the south coast of the peninsula, the superb 4-mile (6 km) sand-dune spit of **Inch** curves out into Dingle Bay—a wonderful sight at low tide with the whorls and channels of sand and water backed by the spectacular Macgillycuddy's Reeks across the bay. West of here is Dingle.

Dingle Town: Dingle has a reputation as a hippyish sort of place. However, this is still a working fishing town and a shopping and socializing center for the wide Gaeltacht area toward the end of the peninsula. It's also a tourist town, often crowded in summer—especially around August, with the Dingle Races, Dingle Show, and Dingle Regatta all happening.

Each St. Stephen's Day, December 26, the town is given over to the Dingle Wren (see sidebar), when the so-called "Wren Boys" dress up and play tricks on

Blennerville Windmill

- West edge of Tralee
- 066/712-1064
- Closed Nov.– March

Dingle Town

- 128 A3

EXPERIENCE: Watching the Dingle Wrenboys

If it is true, as legend tells, that the wren betrayed St. Stephen, then the folk of the Dingle Peninsula in west Kerry have certainly done their best to punish the little bird over the years. In years past, they hunted wrens and nailed them to a pole before parading them through the streets every year on December 26, St. Stephen's Day.

These days, wrens go unharmed come St. Stephen's Day. Instead, "Wren Boys," men dressed in suits and hats of straw, celebrate with music, dancing, and the wild gyrations of the hobby horse—half

steed, half devil—through the streets of Dingle town.

Approach this festival with caution! The **Dingle Wren** (dingle-peninsula.ie) can get a bit wild, and as a stranger on this day of misrule, you may find yourself the target of some . . . well, let's call it "teasing," especially in the pubs during the later stages of the festivities. It's best to take a backseat and enjoy the craziness from a discrete distance. If you do get involved, don't forget to keep close at hand that most effective of all weapons— a sense of humor.

Dunquin

🗺 128 A3

Blasket Centre

✉ Dunquin,
   Co. Kerry

☎ 066/915-6444
   or 066/915-
   6371

🕐 Closed Nov.–
   March

💲 $

heritageireland.ie

each other, with plenty of alcohol thrown in.

Boat rides run around the sheltered harbor, enlivened if you are lucky by a sighting of Dingle's fabled resident dolphin, Fungie. Try the Small Bridge pub for traditional music and don't forget to sample a Dingle pie, a delicious mutton pie served with a jug of mutton broth to pour over it.

Farther west on the R599, into Irish-speaking territory, you'll come to **Ventry** on its glorious curve of sand, and then to the rich archaeo-logical treasury of the hillsides under **Mount Eagle.** Here, a few steps off the road to either side, are standing stones and cross-inscribed slabs, beehive huts, and *souterrains* (underground storehouses) built

on these slopes by early Christian hermits.

Blasket Islands: As you near Slea Head at the peninsula's end, the four Blasket Islands swim into view—Inishvickillaun, Inishnabro, the big green hump of Great Blasket, and Inishtooskert, with its sleeping-man shape. Life was simple for the hundred or so islanders who once lived on Great Blasket; yet in the 1930s they produced three of Ireland's most respected writers: Tomás O'Crohan, Maurice O'Sullivan, and Peig Sayers. The island was evacuated in 1953 because the disparity between island poverty and mainland prosperity had become too stark.

In **Dunquin** village on the mainland, you can learn something of what Blasket life was like at the modern **Blasket Centre.** Better yet, cross the sometimes lively Blas-ket Sound on one of the regular boats from Dunquin and wander over the island for yourself.

Dunquin to Brandon Bay:
From Dunquin, the R559 takes you northeast to the **Gallarus Oratory,** a boat-shaped chapel some 1,500 years old. Nearby is **Kilmalkedar Church.** They say that if you can squeeze yourself through the narrow east window, you'll never suffer from a bad back (see sidebar, left).

Soon you come to a signpost pointing right for **Brandon Creek,** 5 miles (8 km) north. This is a wonderfully peaceful spot, under the slope of 3,127-foot (953 m) **Mount Brandon,** second highest

---

EXPERIENCE:
Taking Traditional Cures

Early Christian missionaries may have appropriated the springs, rocks, and trees sacred to the ancient Celts, but a strong belief in the efficacy of cures beyond medi-cal or scientific proof has survived. Take, for example, **Kilmalkedar Church.** According to tradition, if you can squeeze through the church's tiny east window, not more than nine inches (23 cm) wide, you will never suffer from a bad back. Other similar cures abound: For homesickness, lie on the **Flagstone of Loneliness** by Gartan Lough (*Co. Donegal; see p. 223*); for baldness, rinse your head at **St. Kevin's Well** (*Glendalough, Co. Wicklow*); for headaches, put your neck through the stone arch at **St. Colman's Well** (*Kilmoon, Co. Clare*); for bad eyes, bathe them in the **Eye Well at Fairy Hill** (*Dromore, Co. Tyrone*); and for lameness, bathe and drink at **Doon Well** (*Kilmacrennan, Co. Donegal*).

Tralee & Dingle Light Railway

The Tralee & Dingle Light Railway (T&DLR), opened in 1891, was one of the world's great eccentric railways, fulfilling every stereotype of an Irish—and more specifically a Kerry—backcountry branch line. The T&DLR was seldom on time, never worked to capacity or made a profit, and operated with increasingly antiquated locomotives and carriages. It was a friendly, informal line, whose engineers were known to emerge from Fitzgerald's Bar at Castlegregory Junction wiping porter froth from their moustaches as they prepared to drive their trains—a railway whose firemen were valued just as much for the accuracy with which they could throw lumps of coal from the footplate at sheep grazing on the tracks as for their skill in firing the locomotives. The 20-odd-mile (30 km) line incorporated steep gradients and sharp curves, which added to the delays, as did the grass that often smothered the rails. When the T&DLR closed in 1953, it was widely mourned by steam lovers and connoisseurs of curiosities.

mountain in Ireland after Carrantuohill (3,414 feet/1,039 m) in Killarney National Park. A ruined oratory at the summit (reachable from nearby Ballyhack via a stiff 3.5-mile/5 km climb up the waymarked Saint's Road—but only in clear weather) is said to be the one St. Brendan prayed in before his epic sixth-century transatlantic voyage in a leather *curragh*. It was from Brandon Creek that the adventurer Tim Severin set sail for Newfoundland in 1976 in his replica boat, following the wake of Brendan (see p. 167).

There are wonderful views from the steep road over the Conor Pass and a warm welcome to be had in O'Connor's pub in Cloghane on the north side of the peninsula before you set course eastward for Tralee. First, though, stretch your legs around the tip of the beautiful **Magharees sandspit** (see pp. 158–159). ■

Dog meets dolphin, an everyday Dingle Bay delight

WALK: THE MAGHAREES

This is an easy stroll, all on the level, in the flat but remarkable landscape of the Magharees sandspit that divides Tralee Bay from Brandon Bay on the north side of the Dingle Peninsula.

Early Christian hermits lived and prayed in the wildflower fields of the Dingle Peninsula.

Start your walk in the tiny village of **Fahamore,** and follow the road north to **Scraggane Bay** ❶ at the tip of the scimitar-shaped spit. Local men paid by the Congested Districts Board, a body set up to aid poverty-stricken and overpopulated rural Ireland, built **Scraggane pier** in 1887. At that time, the United States was taking as many barrels of salted mackerel as Ireland could supply.

In the bay, you'll see moored the black fishing canoes, tough and responsive in lively seas, that are so characteristic of the west

of Ireland; they are built here at Fahamore. Elsewhere this kind of craft is known as a *curragh,* but hereabouts it is called a *namhog* (pronounced na-vogue).

NOT TO BE MISSED:

Scraggane Bay with its *namhogs* *&* **pier • View of the Magharee Islands • St. Senach's Church, Kilshannig • Brandon Bay**

Clustered offshore you will see the **Magharee Islands,** also called the **Seven Hogs.** On the largest, **Illauntannig,** a wall encloses two tiny oratories and three *clochans,* or stone huts, the remnants of an early Christian monastery. You may be able to persuade a local boatman to take you out there at a price. Farther out is **Inishtooskert,** off which the German vessel *Aud* idled for a day and a night during Easter Week of 1916. She was waiting for an all's-well signal from accomplices on Inishtooskert, when they were to bring ashore weapons to support the planned Easter Rising, but the signal never came. At last *Aud* departed, and a day later the crew scuttled her off Cobh Haven in County Cork (see pp. 138–139) when they were accosted by the Royal Navy.

Follow the shore to your left around the curve of Scraggane Bay for 1 mile (1.6 km). Halfway around the bay, turn briefly inland where the road makes a right angle to see a fine, tall **standing stone ❷,** a pagan monument carved with a rough cross by some early hermit in an attempt to appropriate its power.

Continue along the shore, then turn inland through the hamlet of **Kilshannig** to reach the ruin of **St. Senach's Church ❸.** Look inside the 16th-century building to see an incised slab marked with a chi-rho crucifix symbol, dating from the seventh century.

After exploring the church ruins in Kilshannig, head east. Turn right for 1.5 miles (2.5 km) along the beach until you come opposite **Lough Naparka ❹.** Cross the spit here (looking out for sea holly and pyramidal orchids in the splendid dunes), and return to Fahamore up the glorious wide **beach ❺.**

If you wish to double the length of the walk, continue for another 1.5 miles (2.5 km) from Lough Naparka to the outflow from **Lough Gill ❻,** and follow it inland to reach the lough—a famous place for bird-watching, especially when black swans come from Siberia to overwinter.

From Lough Gill, continue to the west side of the spit for a 2-mile (3 km) beach walk back to Fahamore.

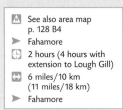

- See also area map
  p. 128 B4
- Fahamore
- 2 hours (4 hours with extension to Lough Gill)
- 6 miles/10 km (11 miles/18 km)
- Fahamore

LIMERICK

The capital of County Limerick, this little medieval city located at the mouth of the Shannon River is famous for its dedication to sports, particularly rugby. Although it's often overshadowed by other, more frequently visited Irish cities, its museums and other attractions are of great interest and are certainly worth a visit.

Limerick

🗺 129 E5

Visitor Information

✉ 20 O'Connell St., Limerick, Co. Limerick

☎ 061/317-522

limerick.ie

King John's Castle

✉ King Island, Limerick, Co. Limerick

☎ 061/360-788

💲 $$

shannonheritage. com

The city's main attraction is **King John's Castle,** a gigantic fortress from the 13th century that overlooks the River Shannon. It's home to exhibits, movies, and reconstructions that narrate the fascinating medieval history of the city. Climb to the top of one of its towers to enjoy the splendid view.

To the south is another interesting site, **St. Mary's Cathedral** with its extraordinary collection of 15th-century misericords carved with medieval emblems and demonic beasts. The **Hunt Museum** *(Rutland St., tel 061/312-833, huntmuseum.com,*

$) is also located to the south. It boasts an exceptional collection of religious and medieval artifacts as well as the works of such artists as Pablo Picasso and Jack B. Yeats. Continuing on to the **Limerick City Gallery of Art** *(Pery Sq., tel 061/310-633, gallery.limerick.ie),* visitors can admire a collection of Irish art from the 18th to the 21st century. Another option is a visit to the **Frank McCourt Museum** *(Lower Hartstonge St., frankmccourt museum.wixsite.com, $, closed Sat.– Sun. Nov.–March),* located in what was once the school of this author whose celebrated novel, *Angela's Ashes,* is set in Limerick. ∎

▪ St. Mary's Cathedral and the colorful houses of Limerick that overlook the River Shannon

LOUGH GUR

Scattered in a loose ring around the small, C-shaped Lough Gur is a multitude of stone structures, evidence of occupation of this site for the past 5,000 years. An interpretive center helps pull the known facts together around the sites.

■ The Grange Stone Circle at Lough Gur is the largest prehistoric stone circle in Ireland.

The importance of this archaeological site going back to 3000 B.C. was first noticed in the 19th century, when the lake level was lowered and thousands of artifacts came to light. They included the Lough Gur shield, dating from about 700 B.C.. The original is now in the National Museum in Dublin (see pp. 56–59), and many other Lough Gur finds can be seen in Limerick's Hunt Museum (see p. 160). The interpretive center has copies and genuine items— axes, tools, weapons, pottery, arrowheads, and a metalworker's furnace. Once outside, you are within 100 yards (100 m) or so of The Spectacles, the foundations of a farmstead of about 900, where neolithic or late Stone Age artifacts have been found on site.

Down on the lake shore, it's a five-minute clockwise walk to the reed bed where you can stare across at **Bolin Island crannog.** Just 100 feet (30 m) in diameter, the crannog can only have held one family at a time during its occupation between A.D. 500 and 1000. Two castles stand nearby— the 15th-century **Bourchier's Castle,** and the **Black Castle,** which the Earls of Desmond used periodically from the 13th century onward.

A short car ride away is the huge **Giant's Grave** megalithic wedge tomb, 1 mile (1.6 km) toward the Limerick–Bruff road from Lough Gur Cross. The tomb was constructed about 2500 B.C. with a curb of upright stones around a central grave of massive boulders, topped by four huge side-by-side capstones. ■

Lough Gur
🅰 129 E4

Lough Gur Heritage Centre
✉ Bruff Rd., Holycross, Co. Limerick
☎ 061/385-386
💲 $

loughgur.com

More Places to Visit in Southwest Ireland

Adare

County Limerick's most delightful little town exudes charm from every one of its thatched-roof cottages and colorful flower gardens. The Earl of Dunraven created the village in the Victorian era as a small town at his service. On the edges of the hamlet, overlooking the River Maigue, are the ruins of **Desmond Castle** (guided tours June–Sept., $). It was built in the 13th century and was home to the Earls of Kildare for 300 years before being granted to the Earls of Desmond, whose name it bears. adareheritagecentre.ie ⚠ 129 D4 ✉ Adare Heritage Centre, Main St., Adare, Co. Limerick ☎ 061/396-666 🕐 Closed Jan.

Ardfert Cathedral, Ardfert Franciscan Friary, & Banna Strand

Beautiful lancet windows grace the 13th-century cathedral at Ardfert. Next door are the shells of two chapels, one with lovely south window carvings, the other with two intertwined wyverns (heraldic winged dragons) on the northeast window. The **Ardfert Friary**, about one third of a mile from the village of Ardfert, was founded in 1253 by the Anglo-Norman Fitzmaurice family. The building, much of which is without a roof, has a tower that was built in the 15th century. The friary is an open site, freely accessible to visitors all year. Nearby, **Banna Strand** offers a 5-mile (8 km) stretch of beach that looks over Tralee Bay. ardfert.ie ⚠ 128 B4 ✉ On the R551, Ballyheige Rd., 6 miles (10 km) NW of Tralee, Co. Kerry ☎ 066/713-4711 🕐 Closed Oct.–March ⑤ $

Béal na Bláth (The Hollow of the Flowers)

A Celtic cross marks the spot where the commander of the Irish Free State Army, Michael Collins—still a hero to many in Ireland—was ambushed and shot dead by anti-Treaty gunmen on August 22, 1922, during the Irish Civil War. ⚠ 129 D2 ✉ On the R585, 3 miles (5 km) SW of Crookstown, Co. Cork

Carrigafoyle Castle

This 15th-century stronghold has a wonderful location on the banks of the Shannon. Climb the 95-foot (29 m) tower for memorable views along the estuary. ⚠ 129 C4 ✉ On the Shannon Estuary; signed (2.5 miles/4 km) off the R551 at Ballylongford, 8 miles (13 km) N of Listowel by the R552, Co. Kerry

Fota Wildlife Park & Fota House Arboretum

Fota Wildlife Park has free-running zebras, giraffes, antelopes, kangaroos, and oryx, as well as caged cheetahs, its breeding specialty. The arboretum possesses rare and beautiful trees from South America, Australasia, the Himalaya, China, and Japan. fotawildlife.ie, fotahouse.com ⚠ 129 E2 ✉ Carrigtwohill, Co. Cork, signed on the R624, off the N25, 7 miles (11 km) E of Cork city ☎ 021/481-2678 ⑤ $$

Jameson's Old Midleton Distillery

See the world's biggest copper still and a huge old waterwheel—then sample Jameson's nectarous whiskey. jamesonwhiskey.com ⚠ 129 E2 ✉ Midleton, off the N25, 10 miles (16 km) E of Cork, Co. Cork ☎ 021/461-3594 🕐 1-hour guided tours 9 a.m.–6 p.m., last tour 4:30 p.m. ⑤ $$

Listowel

The main attractions in this vibrant little city on the banks of the River Feale are the ruins of a 15th-century castle (closed Oct.–April) and the nearby **Kerry Writers' Museum** (kerrywriters-museum.com, $), which focuses on local writers and the history of the castle. listowel.ie ⚠ 129 C4 ✉ 16.7 miles (27 km) N of Tralee, Co. Kerry

From the Connemara Mountains and the flowery Burren hills
to the ancient mystery of Mayo—a region that breathes romance

THE WEST
OF IRELAND

■ Malachy Kearns, Connemara's master maker of traditional bodhrans (goatskin drums)

THE WEST OF IRELAND

Of those visitors to Ireland who intend to get any farther than Dublin, the majority head out west. Anyone who has heard anything about the character of the different regions of Ireland will have been told that west is best, whether you want wild traditional music, spectacular coast and small island scenery, vast open tracts of ruggedly beautiful landscape, or the most laid-back approach to life in this admirably relaxed country.

The west of Ireland presents an Atlantic-facing seaboard, but its peninsulas and bays are not as elongated or clearly defined as those of Kerry and Cork. Here the coast is fractured and battered by the sea into ragged lumps and gashes, all dotted with fragments ranging from well-populated islands to tiny scraps of offshore rock.

Three great inlets shape the coastline: the mouth of the Shannon running in under the avocet's bill of southwest Clare, the squarish indentation of Galway Bay with the three Aran Islands at the entrance, and islet-spattered

Clew Bay in southern Mayo. With the domed hills of Clare, the all-but-uninhabited mountains, and the lakes and boglands of Galway and Mayo, it adds up to a memorably untamed mingling of land and sea.

County Clare is the greenest, mildest, and gentlest of the west's three counties. Down in the southwest are old seaside towns such as Kilrush and Kilkee, while farther north you come into the strange, haunting landscape of the Burren region—naked gray limestone hills where an incredibly rich flora flourishes.

Galway has a lively county capital in Galway city. It also boasts the rugged beauty of the mountains and boglands of Connemara, the westernmost part of the county, as well as the great fishing lakes based around mighty Lough Corrib, and a cluster of Irish-speaking islands.

As for County Mayo, discerning explorers are beginning to wake up to the wild beauty of this boggy and mountainous northern corner of the west, with its holy mountain of Croagh Patrick, its buzzing music town of Westport, and its empty, glorious beaches.

NOT TO BE MISSED:

SOUTHERN CLARE

The southwest corner of County Clare is gentle, easygoing, and essentially rural—a long green peninsula where countryside or seaside are yours for the asking. Hereabouts, you'll grow accustomed to the slow tempo of daily life, livened with a splash of nighttime gaiety.

■ The great arches of Bunratty Castle lead to medieval feasts of meat and mead.

Southern Clare

🗺 165 B1–D2

Visitor Information

✉ Frances St., Kilrush, Co. Clare

☎ 065/905-1577

🕑 Closed mid-Sept.–late May

Bunratty Castle & Folk Park

Bunratty Castle & Folk Park, off the N18 Ennis–Limerick road, is worthwhile if you don't mind sharing your enjoyment with a few thousand others.

The well-restored castle, built around 1460, has a splendid keep where nightly "medieval banquets" are held. You can quaff mead and eat with your fingers, while minstrels serenade you and serving wenches bustle around with platters and jugs.

To those who have already traveled among and appreciated real, living Irish villages, the folk park—a reconstructed 19th-century village set on 25 acres (10 ha)—can seem a theme park travesty; however, if you come out of season to enjoy the cottages, shops, small businesses, and pub without the holiday crowds, you can catch an appealing atmosphere enhanced by the blacksmith, weavers, spinners, and butter makers who bring a touch of life to the place.

Craggaunowen Project

Ten miles (16 km) north, off the road from Kilmurry to Moymore, you'll find the Craggaunowen Project. Centered around a fortified tower house of 1550, Craggaunowen tells the story, via costumed guides, of the Irish Celts, their domestic lives, their warfare and religious practices, and the way they hunted and farmed. Specially constructed features include a walled ring fort enclosing typical fifth- or sixth-century huts under conical thatched roofs; a causeway to a lake-bound *crannog*, or artificial fortified island, sheltering a wattle-and-daub house; burial sites; and a *fulacht fiadh* (hunter's cooking pit).

Also on display is the leather-hulled *curragh, Brendan,* in which explorer Tim Severin sailed to Newfoundland in 1976–1977.

Other Attractions

County Clare sweeps away southwest in a narrowing spike of a peninsula. The south coast of this 40-mile (65 km) promontory forms the northern shore of the widening Shannon Estuary, while the cliff-bound north coast, far more indented and battered, faces out into the Atlantic. The hinterland is gentle and green, while the coast is lined with long, sandy swimming beaches. There are a handful of old-style seaside resorts and some nice quiet country towns.

North coast resorts with plenty of accommodations and sandy beaches are **Lehinch** (Lahinch) and **Kilkee,** the former with a beautiful golf course, the latter with some exciting natural rock-pool swimming in the Duggerna Reef at the western end of the beach. Between them is **Milltown Malbay,** a quiet town, where Willie Clancy Week *(tel 065/708-4281, scoilsamhraidhwillieclancy.com),* a music festival each July, celebrates the life and skill of local piper Willie Clancy.

Loop Head, at the southwestern point of the peninsula, has fine cliff walks, while farther around into the mouth of the Shannon is the handsome riverside town of **Kilrush.** Ask at the **Scattery Island Centre** *(tel 087/995-8427)* on Merchant's Quay about boats to **Scattery Island,** a mile (1.6 km) offshore. Here you'll find several ruined medieval churches and a 110-foot-high (33 m) round tower. ∎

Bunratty Castle & Folk Park

Ⓜ 165 D1
✉ Bunratty, Co. Clare
☎ 061/360-788
💲 $$ (tour) $$$$$ (medieval banquet)

shannonheritage.com

Craggaunowen Project

Ⓜ 165 D2
✉ 4 miles (6 km) SE of Quin
☎ 061/360-788
🕐 Closed mid-Sept.–March
💲 $

shannonheritage.com

EXPERIENCE:
Going to the Horse Fair

Held in late June every year for the past 300 years, the **Spancilhill Fair** *(just outside Ennis, Co. Clare, spancilhillfair.com)* is one of Ireland's most characterful horse fairs, a genuine slice of old Ireland. Crowds are big and loud, with a tremendous amount of knowledgeable horse talk flung about. And, of course, there is a multitude of equines of every kind; you can even buy one if you have the money—and the cheek. Fiercely contested prizes include best cob, best pony, best donkey, and more.

Other Irish horse fairs include the well-known **Ballinasloe Horse Fair** *(Co. Galway, ballinasloeoctoberfair.com),* a week of fun and frolics in early October, only some of it horse related; and the lively **Cahirmee Horse Fair** *(at Buttevant, Co. Cork, on July, 12).*

BURREN NATIONAL PARK

Mysterious and concealing, yet lying wholly open to view, the Burren region of north County Clare is a remarkable and haunting place. Among its bare gray hills lie hidden ancient tombs, churches, dwellings, and ring forts in a bleak setting jeweled with Ireland's richest flora. At the outer edge of the hills are villages that seem to run entirely on wonderful music. And the flanks of the hills themselves, solid though they look, conceal a heart of rock riddled with caves, passages, and seldom-seen underground rivers.

Mighty dolmens, burial places of pre-Christian chieftains, stand on the limestone of the Burren.

Burren National Park

🄰 165 C2

Visitor Information

✉ Clare Heritage Centre, Corofin, Co. Clare

☎ 065/682-7693

🕐 Closed Oct.– March

burrennational park.ie

The Burren forms the whole of northwest Clare, some 97 square miles (250 sq km) bounded on the north and west by the sea and on the south and east by typical Clare grazing country, mild and green. But there is nothing green, mild, or typical about the Burren. *Boireann*, its Gaelic name, means "rocky land." The region rises from a sharp-cut sea coast through a collar of meadows into a cluster of dome-shaped hills with rounded tops and stepped flanks, their pale gray limestone seemingly naked of vegetation. It looks like a dry, harsh landscape, drained of life—one in which nothing can have flourished for a very long time. It is not until you get into the heart of the Burren, abandon your car, and walk out into this barren-looking world that you begin to appreciate just how much life and interest there is. And the fascination is not all above ground: The **Aillwee Cave,** south of Ballyvaghan, offers a glimpse of the stalactites and stalagmites, cavernous spaces, waterfalls, and passages at the heart of the hills.

Limestone & Flowers

The Burren region is formed of rough, cracked limestone known as karst. The surface of the limestone is fractured into deep, narrow channels *(grykes)* a few inches wide but several feet long, with oblongs of rock (known as clints) of varying sizes islanded among them. To the untuned eye, it looks like rubbly, useless land. Gen. Edmund Ludlow reported to Oliver Cromwell in 1651 that the Burren region "had not any tree to hang a man, nor enough water to drown him, nor enough earth to bury him"—a telling remark, considering the Puritan leader's intentions for the Irish at that time. But Ludlow was observant: "Their cattle are very fat, for the grass growing in tufts of earth of two or three foot square that lie between the rocks, which are of limestone, is very nourishing."

It is the space "between the rocks," and the soil and rainwater trapped in the grykes, that allow such an extraordinarily varied range of plants to flourish in the Burren. These limestone crevices are sheltered from the salt wind, watered by the frequent rainfall of the area, and warmed by the

Gulf Stream that moves just off the Clare coast and by sunlight reflected into their depths off the pale limestone. Plants that would not normally be found on the same continent, let alone on the same hillside, find the Burren conditions right for them. Some botanists think that certain Arctic alpine plants are descendants of those that arrived in the Burren as seeds moving south in melting Ice Age glaciers 10,000 years ago.

Here you'll see plants of the north, such as the large creamy

Aillwee Cave

🅰 165 C3
✉ Ballyvaughan
☎ 065/707-7036
💲 $$

aillweecave.ie

INSIDER TIP:

Standing on the cliffs of the Burren gives you the sense that you're overlooking the entire Atlantic—that you're on the bow of a mighty ship that is Europe, heading west.

—ALEX DI SUVERO
National Geographic photographer

---

cups of mountain avens, coexisting with plants of the south like the yellow hoary rock-rose. In certain places, streams bring acid bog peat to lodge in hollows of the alkaline limestone so that acid-loving plants such as heather and saxifrage thrive side by side with lime-loving plants like spring gentian and bloody cranesbill.

What this means in practical terms is a glorious flood of color across the gray hills and coastal shelves, and endless fascination hopping across the rocks with a

EXPERIENCE: Enjoy the Wildflowers of the Burren

The violet throats of self-heal open along the grassy verges of the Caher River, overlooked by the parrot beak–shaped seedheads of the yellow rattle. Sulfur-colored lady's bedstraw peeps out from a gryke, a shadowed slit in the limestone pavement, while acid-loving Irish saxifrage—rarer than hens' teeth—thrives in the hollow of a clint, or natural cobble, of pure limestone. Everywhere you look are the diminutive white peepers of eyebright. Where else in the world could you be but the Burren? This unique region of northwest County Clare, with its pale gray domes of limestone hills, is home to the richest

plant life in Ireland (see pp. 172–173).

You could rummage around on your own in such a botanical jewel case for the simple pleasure of bedazzlement by color, shape, and scent.

But those who walk with Mary Howard's **Burren Guided Walks and Hikes** *(tel 065/707-6100 or 087/244-6807, burrenguidedwalks.com)* enjoy an experience they will never forget. Mary is a Burren resident and a passionate devotee of the Burren landscape. She also really knows her plants and has a knack for bringing the apparently dry and barren terrain to life.

Newtown Castle

- 165 C3
- SW of Ballyvaghan
- 065/707-7200
- Closed Nov.– March

flower book. You don't have to be an expert to appreciate the delicately marked orchids, the brilliant blue trumpets of spring gentians, or the extraordinary flush of magenta that stains the hills overnight to announce proudly the dramatic June flowering of the bloody cranesbill.

Past Inhabitants

The Burren interior is completely devoid of settlements today, thanks to its shortage of water—the thirsty karst draws the rivers underground—and to what amounted to an ethnic cleansing policy by Cromwell, but there is plenty of evidence of a vigorous population in times gone past. The splendid portal dolmen of **Poulnabrone** and the nearby **Gleninsheen** wedge tomb show with what pomp and ceremony the prehistoric Burren-dwellers buried their chiefs. Stone-walled Celtic ring forts abound— **Cahermacnaghten** and

Caherballykinvarga lie close to roads and can be explored. The law school run in medieval times by the O'Davorens at Cahermacnaghten was so well regarded that pupils came from all over Ireland to learn the tenets of ancient Brehon law (see p. 24). Nowadays it stands empty, a magnificent circular enclosure where cattle shelter.

Graveyards, crosses, and ruined medieval churches dot the Burren. **Rathborney Church** was built inside a pre-Christian circular earthen rampart that must have been an object of superstitious awe, while the ruins of **Corcomroe Abbey** (fine stonework) in the northeast and of the church at **Dysert O'Dea** (magnificent high cross and a bizarre doorway of sculpted heads) in the south are notable examples.

Life in medieval Ireland being the risky business it was, there are also some fine fortified towers and houses in the Burren—**Newtown**

Castle, southwest of Ballyvaghan (Ballyvaughan), and **Leamaneh Castle** *(closed),* east of Kilfenora, are worth a look.

Hundreds of such sites lie tucked away across the Burren, and to help find them you can't do better than to buy Tony Kirby's *The Burren & the Aran Islands: A Walking Guide*—by far one of the most informative guides you could wish for and widely available locally. It also features the many holy wells and "old faith" cures for headaches, sore backs, tooth trouble, and weak eyes to which Burren people still resort.

INSIDER TIP:

Watch for Tina Mulrooney singing and playing her harp on the steps by the dramatic Cliffs of Moher. Her CDs make wonderful souvenirs.

—ROZ HOAGLAND
*Private guide,
Hoagland Art Travel*

Cliffs of Moher

The rocky coastline of the Burren is relieved by caravan-ridden dunes at **Fanore,** then trends southwest for another 15 miles (25 km) to culminate in the mighty Cliffs of Moher, at 665 feet (200 m) a magnificent piece of natural sculpture in layers of flagstone and shale. O'Brien's Tower, a Victorian viewpoint, tops them off. A "Visitor Experience" offers cliff-edge walkways and seating,

viewing platforms, and an inviting and educational subterranean visitor center. Seabirds abound, and the view on a good day from the top of O'Brien's Tower takes in a circle of more than

Cliffs of Moher

🅰 165 C2

✉ SW of Doolin

☎ 065/708-6141

💲 $

cliffsofmoher.ie

■ **O'Brien's Tower, built in 1835, looms at the summit of the Cliffs of Moher, which face out to the Atlantic Ocean.**

100 miles (160 km), from the Kerry hills to the Aran Islands and the Twelve Bens of Connemara—even to a far glimpse of Croaghaun on Achill Island up in County Mayo.

Villages of the Burren

Looped around the skirts of the uninhabited Burren hills is a string of villages that rely mainly on farming and tourism—all of them great places for conversation and music.

Ballyvaghan (Ballyvaughan) is the northernmost settlement, looking out to Galway Bay. Monk's Bar is the place for music here. **Doolin,** however, is the traditional music-lover's mecca (see pp. 174–175). Sleepy **Lisdoonvarna** comes alive each September

The Flora of the Burren

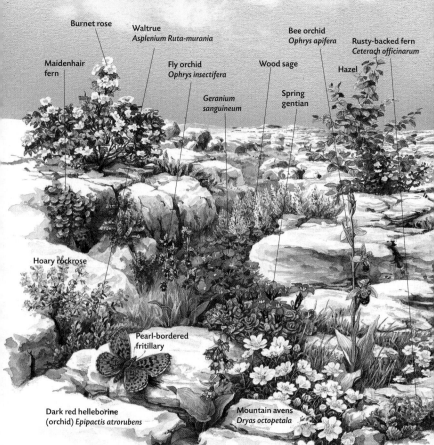

Burnet rose

Waltrue
Asplenium Ruta-murania

Bee orchid
Ophrys apifera

Rusty-backed fern
Ceterach officinarum

Maidenhair
fern

Fly orchid
Ophrys insectifera

Wood sage

Hazel

*Geranium
sanguineum*

Spring
gentian

Hoary rockrose

Pearl-bordered
fritillary

Dark red helleborine
(orchid) *Epipactis atrorubens*

Mountain avens
Dryas octopetala

for its Matchmaking Festival *(tel 065/707-4005, matchmakerireland. com, held late Aug.–early Sept.)*, when unmarried men and women of the west converge on the village for a week of taking the spa waters, dancing, and making acquaintance. Part media circus, part revival of an old tradition, this is a good-time week that anyone can enjoy.

At **Kilfenora,** there's a 12th-century cathedral without a roof and four carved high crosses of the same date; the **Burren Centre** *(tel 065/708-8030, theburrencentre. ie, closed Nov.–mid March, $$),* with its excellent displays on the wildlife, geology, and archaeology of the Burren; and two great music pubs in Vaughan's and Linnane's. ■

Ajuga pyramidalis

Pyramid orchid
Anacamptis pyramidalis

Cat's foot mountain everlasting
Antneria dioica

Hart's tongue fern
Phyllitis scolopodendrium

Twayblade (orchid)
Listera orata

Dense-flowered orchid
Neotina maculata

Spiranthes spiralis (orchid)

Harebell

Irish hare

Shrubby cinquefoil

Bearberry

Irish saxifrage

Fragrant orchid
Gymnadenia conopsea

PUBS & MUSIC OF THE WEST

Pub-going in the west of Ireland is an activity as natural as breathing. You'll find yourself gravitating naturally to the pub because it's there that you'll meet local people and other visitors, join in the *craic* (pronounced "crack"), and hear the best music in Ireland. Note that information about sessions is given over the bar on the day—don't be afraid to ask.

▪ Get out of the rain, into the bar, and up with the mood at an exhilarating traditional music session.

Whatever it is about the west of Ireland—the lifestyle or the land, the peculiarly magical atmosphere woven by mountains, boglands, and coasts, or something in the water—it's a well-attested fact that the traditional music here is something special.

Some connoisseurs claim to detect a correlation between the character of the music and the shape and nature of the landscape it springs from—a smooth gentleness to the compositions and performances of Clare, for instance, or a melancholy wildness to those of Mayo. You can judge for yourself, as either a participant or an onlooker, in the numberless great music pubs of the west.

In southwest Clare, try **O'Mara's** on O'Curry Street, Kilkee, where you'll get music of all sorts and great atmosphere, and **Clancy's** and **Lynch's** (Friels) in Milltown Malbay for wonderful traditional sessions.

Around the Burren—famous music territory—you'll enjoy **Linnane's** in Kilfenora and the

Roadside Tavern on the edge of Lisdoonvarna (great music here), while in the music-to-its-fingertips village of Doolin it's **McGann's** by the bridge for evening tune sessions, and **O'Connor's** nearer the sea for rollicking ballads and showmanship, day and night. Ennistymon, too, is a famous town for music, in the **Archway**—beautifully placed by the River Cullenagh—and a dozen other pubs.

Galway city offers good impromptu music in **Taaffe's** bar, on Shop Street, and more of the same in the wonderful old-fashioned **Ti Neachtain** on Cross Street, all cozy snugs and odd corners—there's a first-class restaurant here as well.

Out in Connemara, there's a great pub around every corner, but for real character you could try the Irish-speaking **Ost na nOilean** down at the foot of Gorumna Island or the even more remote and Gaelic pub on Inishmaan, the middle one of the three Aran Islands. The **Strand Bar,** out at Claddaghduff in the far west (always known as Sweeney's), does a great hot whiskey when the weather is biting back.

As for Mayo—head for Westport if you want music. Matt Molloy, flute player with celebrated traditional music band the Chieftains, owns a bar on Bridge Street named

INSIDER TIP:

Taaffe's bar has the best live music in Galway. They stop serving food after lunchtime, though, so have an early dinner at one of the many nearby restaurants before choosing your spot for the free show.

—KAREN MARTINEZ
National Geographic Society

Matt Molloy's, where the back bar sessions are regularly infiltrated by the great names of Irish music (including Molloy himself when he's around). **Hoban's** is another marvelous pub for music, where quiet-mannered whistle player and tour leader Olcan Masterson (see p. 190) leads blinding sessions with modesty and good humor.

In the country, westward, **Owen Campbell's** enormously friendly bar in Murrisk, the port of call for outward or incoming pilgrims walking up the holy mountain of Croagh Patrick (see pp. 192–195), is often still humming at midnight.

The *Craic*

Even if you would never normally set foot in a bar, you should do so—regularly—in Ireland. The Irish pub is far more than a boozing den, and it has become even more enjoyable since the smoking ban cleared the air in 2004. In the city, the pub is where that great Irish art, conversation, is practiced away from the roar and bright lights, while in small country towns and villages, it is the focus of community activity. You get advice, make friends, and hear charming nonsense; the pub is where you pick up local news, get a bite and a sip, and enjoy that wonderful tide of

live music—traditional tunes, ballads, country, and rock music.

All this mixture of talk, fun, music, leg-pulling, and drink goes under the generic name of the *craic* (pronounced "crack"). You'll hear the craic talked of wherever you go—"You should have been in McGing's, the craic was mighty"; "We'll call in on Joe and have a bit of craic"; "Marie? Ah, she's great craic." You might run across the craic in a pub, a back kitchen, a corner shop, or a country lane—you never know your luck. But you'll know it when you find it.

GALWAY CITY

Galway is a lively city, one of the liveliest in Ireland thanks to its university and colleges and to a great revival in its economy and optimism over the past years. At any time of year, but particularly in the summer, Galway's an exciting place to be.

The Galway Arts Festival turns the city into a crucible of creativity and *craic* every summer.

Galway City

🗺 165 C3

Visitor Information

✉ Áras Fáilte,
Forster St.,
Galway,
Co. Galway

☎ 091/537-700

The Anglo-Normans built Galway into an important castle town and port in the mid-13th century, and for 400 years it was an Anglicized enclave amid the Irish people and culture of Connemara. The "Fourteen Tribes of Galway" were the Anglo-Norman families who prospered on trade with Europe, notably with Spain. Oliver Cromwell put an end to this golden age when he sacked Galway in 1652, and King William III completed the job in 1691. It took 300 years, but Galway rose again, thanks to high-tech industries and the economic boom of the 1990s (see p. 14).

City Attractions

As it runs south from the gardens of **Eyre Square,** Galway's main street changes name, from Williamsgate to William Street, then Shop Street, High Street, and finally Quay Street as it reaches the River Corrib. Curious carved stones sit high on the walls of shops and houses—heraldic shields, beasts, foliage, and human faces, mostly dated to show when eminent persons married or took possession of the premises.

At the Four Corners, where William Street becomes Shop Street, stands **Lynch's Castle,** a very fine late 15th-century fortified stronghold tower with a bank on its ground level. On the walls are coats of arms, elaborate roundels, several lions with human faces, and a row of gargoyles supporting the top of the tower.

A sidestep up Church Lane leads to **St. Nicholas' Collegiate Church** (stnicholas.ie), rich in this vigorous, expressive Galway carving. A seductive mermaid clings to the west window. Inside are some fine tombs and more examples of the mason's art—they include graveslabs carved with the symbols of their incumbents' trades.

North of the church stands the rebuilt Lynch memorial window. On this spot in 1493 the chief magistrate of Galway, James Lynch Fitzstephen, hanged his own son Walter for murder. Across the way, at 8 Bowling Green is where Nora Barnacle lived before she ran off with James Joyce in 1904.

A very pleasant walk follows the River Corrib to the whitewater sluices beyond Salmon Weir Bridge and the enjoyable **Galway City Museum.** Here you'll find a collection of objects that date from ancient times to the 20th century and offer an overview of the city's history as well as a number of interesting temporary exhibits. The **Wild Atlantic Sea Science Gallery** with an interactive itinerary dedicated to the marine ecosystem is on the third floor.

Summer Festivals

A great time to be in Galway is around the end of July, when the **Galway International Arts Festival** (tel 091/509-700, giaf. ie) is followed by **Galway Races** week (tel 091/700-100, galwayraces.com) at Ballybrit Racecourse. For three hectic weeks, normal life is suspended as activities from classical music and literary lectures to street theater and music keep the place buzzing day and night.

When the Arts Festival ends the races begin, with a full card of racing daily, and the city puts on dances, pub music, and exhibitions for gamblers both lucky and unlucky. ■

Galway City Museum

✉ Spanish Arch, Galway, Co. Galway

☎ 091/532-460

🕐 Closed Mondays

galwaycitymuseum.ie

EXPERIENCE: Learn Irish Dancing

Traditional Irish dancing can seem pretty staid. Dancers clip their arms to their sides, their expressions immobile as only their twinkling feet seem to convey any emotion. However, you don't need to be a real connoisseur to enjoy Irish dancing, and it's fun to have a go yourself.

Classes in Irish dancing of all kinds are available in Galway city. **Conradh na Gaeilge** (tel 091/567-824, cnag.ie) runs popular classes in Sean-Nos, a solo style of dancing perfect for beginners.

Spontaneous dancing often occurs in pubs, drawing an enthusiastic audience. In Galway, you are most likely to find dancing at the **Crane Bar** (Sea Road, tel 091/587-419, thecranebar.com), on the west bank of the River Corrib, and **Quays Bar** (Quay St., tel 091/568-347).

Around Dublin, try the **Merry Ploughboy** (Edmonstown Rd., Rathfarnham, Dublin, tel 01/493-1495, mpbpub.com), where you can watch an Irish dancing show, or take a class at the **Glenside** pub (Landscape Rd., Churchtown, Dublin, tel 01/298-5932). Consult ceili.ie for listings.

ARAN ISLANDS

The Aran Islands are a byword for harsh, unforgiving landscape, and their Irish-speaking people have always epitomized hardy self-reliance. Things are changing fast under the influence of tourism and modern amenities, yet there's a strong thread of a way of life long passed into history elsewhere in Ireland.

The 2,000-year-old sea forts of Inishmore stand dramatically at the very brink of the cliffs.

Aran Islands

165 B3–C2

Visitor Information

Kilronan tourist information, Inishmore, Aran Islands, Co. Galway

099/61-263

aranislands.ie

The three islands (not to be confused with County Donegal's Aran Island) resemble a family of sea beasts swimming north-west out of Galway Bay. Inishmore, the largest island at 8.5 miles long (14.4 km), is followed by Inishmaan, which is 3 miles (5 km) long. Round-bodied Inisheer—the smallest island, at less than 2 miles (3 km) across—brings up the rear.

Wind-scoured, sea-bitten limestone gives the Aran Islands their extraordinary atmosphere,

more out-of-this-world than any other landscape in Ireland. The dark gray limestone is scored with thousands of north–south fractures, giving each of the three islands the appearance of having been raked by a giant comb.

These are virtually treeless islands, where soil has been built up laboriously by hand out of sand, seaweed, compost, and manure, and shielded from blowing away in stone-walled fields. The stone walls— the islands' best known feature—are built of thousands of loosely stacked blades of unmortared limestone through which pours the light, so that on a sunny day they form a lacy mosaic of gray stone and blue sky. The walls are repositories for unwanted stone cleared off the fields as much as they are windbreaks or property boundaries.

Inishmore

As the capital island, Inishmore has a defined port village, Kilronan, and gets almost all the visitors, many of whom leave with one of the trademark fishermen's sweaters still made on the islands. Minibuses offer whistle-stop tours of the island; pony traps do the same thing at a more leisurely pace. It's best to rent a bicycle or set out on foot, however, if you want to catch the spirit of the place.

The chief attraction is undoubtedly **Dun Aengus** ($), the Fort of King Aengus, which stands two-thirds of the way up the south coast—a mighty semicircular stronghold some 2,000 years old, breathtakingly sited on the brink of a 300-foot (91 m) cliff. A cunning *cheval-de-frise* (belt of upright stone blades) was set up to guard it from onrushing enemies.

Dún Dúchathair, the Black Fort, located a couple of miles (3 km) down the cliffs from Dun Aengus, is less well preserved than its better known neighbor. But here you are more likely to have elbow room in which to admire the crumbling stairs and walkways in its 20-foot (6 m) walls of dark stone and the enigmatic little labyrinth at its heart.

For other Inishmore sites

well worth seeking out, you can use the help of Tony Kirby's *The Burren & the Aran Islands: A Walking Guide*, available in most bookstores around the country.

Emigration of youngsters and the influence of incomers and holidaymakers have brought Inishmore further into line with mainland thinking and attitudes than the two smaller Aran Islands.

Inisheer & Inishmaan

Inisheer, cheerful and relaxed in atmosphere, makes a memorable day trip from Doolin on the Clare coast. But it is on the middle island, Inishmaan, that you are most likely to hear Irish spoken and see old folk still wearing homespun clothes. The south end of Inishmaan, with its spouting blowholes and stony coast, is as wildly bleak and beautiful a spot as any you'll find in Ireland. ■

EXPERIENCE:
Walk the Aran Islands

Walking on the Aran Islands is one of the most popular activities. The extraordinary landscape of stark flat limestone should be experienced at a slow pace to enjoy its wilderness, with a rare flora and fauna.

To get the most out of your walks in the Arans, Tony Kirby's The Burren & the Aran Islands: A Walking Guide, **published by Collins Press, is an excellent book. You will be amazed at what they bring to light, including standing stones, ancient churches, forgotten tombs, and a whole tumble of holy wells.**

Alternatively, the Ordnance Survey (osi.ie) **covers the Arans on a detailed 1:25,000 map.**

CONNEMARA

Few place-names in Ireland are more evocative than Connemara, and no region is more steeped in the romance of harshly beautiful, remote, and alluring country. Irish city-dwellers in search of their roots find inspiration and a confirmation of their Irishness in this wild western half of County Galway, and you can expect the same magic as you wander among Connemara's mountains, bogs, and lakes and along its ragged coasts.

A line of craggy mountains forms the horizon between wide waters and vast cloudscape skies.

Connemara

165 B4

Visitor Information

Clifden tourist office, Station House Complex, Clifden, Co. Galway

095/21-163

Closed Sundays & Nov.–Feb.

connemara.ie

Lay of the Land

Connemara is the region of west Galway bounded on the north by the narrow fjord of Killary Harbour, on the east by Lough Corrib, on the south by Galway Bay, and on the west by the Atlantic. In the center rise the mountain ranges of the Twelve Bens and the Maumturks. From the feet of the mountains, untamed boglands riddled with lakes and spattered with granite boulders stretch to a coast cut by the sea into rags and tatters

of inlets, coves, headlands, and hundreds of islands.

This uncompromising landscape has always demanded backbreaking labor from its small-time farmers and fishermen in return for a meager living. Sour land of rock and bog, geographical isolation, and poor communications spelled hardship and poverty for Connemara inhabitants until very recently. Even today plenty still eke out a thin livelihood from the soil and sea.

"You can't eat scenery" is an

INSIDER TIP:

A horseback beach trek should be on everyone's itinerary in Connemara. The area is famed for both its horses and its fabulous stretches of sand.

—ALLY THOMPSON
National Geographic contributor

oft-heard local reaction to a compliment on Connemara's untamed landscape. But tourism, the bread and butter of the region these days, is turning the truism on its head—not packaged, bus-borne tourism for the most part, but a stream of independent visitors enjoying the lonely white-sand beaches, tiny towns with their musical pubs, offshore islands, and mountain paths.

The long upper coast of Galway Bay, the southern edge of Connemara, runs due west from Galway city past the resort of Spiddal. After some 20 miles (30 km), this straight westward line shatters into an explosion of islands linked by causeways—Lettermore, Lettermullan, Gorumna, Furnace, Dinish, and their offshoot islets and rocks. If you enjoy strange, hard-edged country, windswept and weather-beaten, turn south at Casla. Hungry locals built the causeways that link these Irish-speaking islands at a time late in the 19th century when this area was the poorest and most overpopulated in Ireland. Life is still hard here. The stone walls separating the tiny fields carry on

over granite boulders and through rushy bogs to mark out exactly which morsel of poor land belongs to whom. Rainstorms off Galway Bay are fierce and frequent here, double rainbows commonplace, sunsets magnificent, visitors few and far between. If you hit Ost na nOilean, the Hotel of the Isles at the toe-tip of Gorumna, on the right Saturday night, you might take part in a *ceilidh* (communal Irish dance) that you'll never forget.

Inland of the islands, there is a vast apron of granite-studded bogland, terraced and crenellated with turf beds cut by hand for domestic fuel, that stretches north to the Maumturk Mountains.

EXPERIENCE:
Learn to Speak Irish

If you spend any time in the west of Ireland, particularly in the Gaeltacht or Irish-speaking areas, you'll long to know more of the complex, beautiful Irish language—even if it's only to say "Good morning—*Dia duit ar maidin*," or "Thank you—*Go raibh maith agat.*"

The **National University of Ireland, Galway** *(nuigalway.ie)* offers Irish Language classes at many levels each summer. Courses are located at the University's Irish-Language Centre in the heart of Connemara. Opportunity also beckons at the **Ennis Trad Festival** *(Ennis, Co. Clare, early Nov., ennistradfest. com)*, where amid the music there's a chance to learn a little beginner's Irish.

There are also many Irish-learning resources online. Find toasts, jokes, stories, songs, sayings, greetings, teachers, and courses at *irishpage.com* and *gaelchultur.com.*

**Padraic Pearse's
Cottage**

🗺 165 B3

✉ Rosmuc, near
Gortmore,
Co. Galway

☎ 091/574-292

🕐 Closed mid-
Sept.–late May

💲 $

heritageireland.ie

Padraic Pearse's Cottage

On the shores of Lough
Oiriúlach near Gortmore stands
Padraic Pearse's Cottage, white-
washed under a thatched roof
and plainly furnished with hard
beds and simple furniture. It
was to this peasant house and
landscape that Padraic Pearse
brought groups of students in
the early 20th century to learn
their native language and culture.
The cottage and its Connemara
backdrop were a source of
refreshment and inspiration for
the dreamy Dublin schoolmaster
and poet who would become
the symbol of Ireland's struggle
for independence, proclaimer of
the fledgling republic from the
steps of Dublin's General Post
Office on Easter Monday 1916,
and patriotic martyr a few days
later when he was shot for treason in the yard of Kilmainham
Gaol (see pp. 30–32 & 75–79).

Roundstone

The coast road twists on from
Costelloe (Casla in this Irish-
speaking area) and the islands
to skirt the wildly indented
shores of Bertraghboy Bay. At
Roundstone on the west side—a
beautifully placed village with
the easily climbable 1,000-foot
(300 m) mountain of Errisbeg
at its back—lives and works
Malachy Kearns of **Roundstone
Musical Instruments**

▪ Traditional ways are still widespread in the Gaeltacht (Irish-speaking) areas of Connemara.

(tel 095/35-808, bodhran.com).
He has gained his nickname,
Malachy Bodhrán, through
nearly 30 years of hard labor
over his handcrafted bodhrans.
These goatskin drums provide
the *rum-a-dum, rum-a-dum* beat
behind Irish jigs and reels,
and the great names of Irish
traditional music trust Malachy
to choose the right skin to
stretch and pin over an oiled
circle of beech or birch wood.

Continue by the white shell
sands of Gorteen Bay and Dog's
Bay and the strands of Ballyconneely and Mannin Bay with their
"coral" made of the calcareous
seaweed Lithothamnion. You
will pass the hillside memorial to
Sir John Alcock and Sir Arthur
Whitten Brown, who completed
the first nonstop transatlantic
flight in June 1919 by landing their
Vickers Vimy bomber plane nose-
down in Derrygimlagh bog.

Clifden

And so to Clifden, Conne-
mara's one and only town, a
handsome and lively bayside
resort planned in the early 19th
century in the classic layout:
oval in shape, with three main
streets, a market square, and
a jail, courthouse, and harbor.
Its two 19th-century churches
are worth visiting: **St. Joseph's
RC Church,** built in 1879 with
emigrant money in post-famine
times; and **Christ Church,** built
in 1853 and offering superior
views over town. Nowadays,
Clifden is mostly known for
its summertime Connemara
Pony Show *(cpbs.ie).* Sturdy

EXPERIENCE: Take Archaeological Walks

Visible archaeology is a fact of life in
Ireland. Everywhere you look, standing
stones, ring forts, ruined churches, stone
crosses, and castles dot the landscape.
Michael Gibbons, who runs **Michael Gibbons Archaeology Travel** *(tel 095/21-379,
walkingireland.com)* in Clifden, can help you
make sense of what you see. Gibbons—an
expert practical archaeologist, local histo-
rian, and dry humorist—conducts expeditions of discovery and enlightenment
through the wilds of Connemara, drawing
participants into the region's great 8,000-
year saga. Walk in his company and soon
you, too, will begin to see the tombs, holy
wells, hut circles, and lazybed strips shap-
ing themselves as if by magic out of the
grass and heather.

Other organizations that cater to visitors in search of Ireland's archaeological
riches include **Setanta Tours** *(tel 086/340-
994, setantachauffeurtours.com),* which specializes in the history of northwest Ireland.
Tours explore the Cooley Peninsula of
County Louth, the Mourne Mountains of
County Down, and County Armagh's Ring
of Gullion hills. **Cultural Tourism Ireland**
(tel 01/202-0521, culturaltourismireland.ie)
is an upmarket company offering expert
guidance all over Ireland.

---

little Connemara ponies, bred
for hard work in the boglands,
are gathered for judging and
sale in an atmosphere of fun
and celebration. This mid-
August show brings together
many of the best attributes
of Connemara—west Galway
people in festive mood in a
beautiful setting backed by the
Twelve Bens, with a touch of
sharp reality in the deals struck
and judgments delivered.

Kylemore Abbey

🅐 165 B4

✉ Kylemore,
Connemara,
Co. Galway

☎ 095/52-001

💲 Abbey: $$,
garden: $$; joint
ticket available

kylemoreabbey.com

**Connemara
National Park**

🅐 165 B4

✉ Letterfrack,
Co. Galway

☎ 076/100-2528
or 095/41-054

🕐 Visitor center
closed Dec.–
Feb.; park
grounds open
year-round

**connemaranational
park.ie**

Claddaghduff & Omey Island

In Clifden, the scenic Sky Road forks off to encircle the Kingstown Peninsula, while another narrow road continues along the north shore of Streamstown Bay to Claddaghduff at the western tip of Connemara.

At low tide, cross the sand causeway to visit the ancient **graveyard** and **St. Fechin's Well** on **Omey Island.** If you get caught on the island by an incoming tide, you'll have an enforced stay of six hours before the causeway is dry again, but this will give you plenty of time to explore. The low cliffs of Omey Island hold remnants of medieval cooking sites (look for the burned red stones), and locals in search of a cure or help from St. Fechin still leave offerings all around the holy well on the reverse slope of the island.

Kylemore Abbey

From Claddaghduff, it's only a few miles to the harbor of Cleggan for the ferry to Inishbofin (see sidebar below). Head east along the N59, and just before reaching Letterfrack turn right to **Connemara National Park Visitor Centre.** From here a footpath leads up the flank of **Diamond Mountain** to a superb view from the top over the Twelve Bens, Kylemore Lough, and the wild Connemara coast. Beyond Letterfrack stands the mock-Tudor Kylemore Abbey on Pollacappul Lough, deservedly one of Ireland's most photographed buildings.

A mile (1.6 km) or so farther east, the view across Kylemore Lough to the Twelve Bens mountain group is stunning.

Through the Mountains

The N59 is the main highway through Connemara, the choice of those who want to avoid the tortuous coast road. Travel west from Galway city to Clifden via Maam Cross and Recess, with superb views en route of the mountains at the heart of Connemara—the **Twelve Bens** (often marked on maps as the Twelve Pins) and the **Maumturks.**

Just west of Recess, the R344 leaves the N59 to follow the spectacular Inagh

Inishbofin

One of the most enjoyable of Connemara expeditions is the short ferry cruise from Cleggan out to Inishbofin. The island, 4 by 3 miles (6 by 5 km), has a small and friendly population and a landscape that is low-lying, boggy, and wildly beautiful.

You can find the ruins of the 13th-century St. Colman's Abbey on the site of the seventh-century monastery founded by Colman (there are two very early Christian slabs inscribed with crosses, too), a star-shaped fort built by Cromwellian soldiers who imprisoned and killed Catholic priests on the island, and the outlines of Stone Age and Bronze Age field systems, huts, and cooking pits.

A glorious view: The great pile of Kylemore Abbey, dwarfed by the wooded mountain slope behind

Valley northward as it squeezes between the two ranges.

Driving through this landscape, the traveler is aware that these are real mountains, although the Twelve Bens rise to only 2,395 feet (730 m) and the Maumturks to 2,300 feet (701 m). The Twelve Bens cluster close around their summit peak of Benbaun, while across the Inagh Valley, the Maumturks swing southeast in a long curved ridge. Capped with quartzite that glitters white in sunlight, they look majestic.

The **Western Way** offers a low-level walk along the flanks of the Maumturks to the east of the Inagh Valley. If you're after something more physically challenging, seek advice at Ben Lettery hostel on the N59, 5 miles (8 km) west of Recess.

A great but demanding circuit of six of the Twelve Bens can be made from the north end of the side road that leaves the N59, a mile (1.6 km) back toward Recess. But you don't have to hike—the road also offers stunning, close-up views of the rugged mountains. ■

DRIVE: SHORES OF LOUGH CORRIB

Sprawling for some 27 miles (44 km) northwest of Galway city, Lough Corrib is a vast sheet of water that hides itself cunningly in a low-lying landscape. This drive seeks out its hidden delights.

Cong Abbey is a picturesque ruin amid wooded hillsides on the north shore of Lough Corrib.

Start out of Galway on the N59 Clifden road. In Moycullen, turn right ("Tullokyne, Knockferry" sign) between stone-walled fields and thick hedges for a few miles to **Carrowmoreknock ❶** (or is it Collinamuck, or even Callownamuck? The signs seem unsure!), where there is a peaceful jetty with boats and a view over Lough Corrib to the mountains.

At the next T-junction, turn left to the N59, then right to resume your drive. In 2 miles (3 km), a sign on the right leads to **Aughnanure Castle ❷** *(Oughterard, tel 091/552-214, closed Nov.–Feb., $),* a fine six-story O'Flaherty castle bristling with murder holes, secret rooms, and bartizan side turrets, enclosed in a walled ward with its own picturesque lookout tower. The floral carvings on

> ### NOT TO BE MISSED:
>
> **Aughnanure Castle • Lake-shore detour in Oughterard • Cong Abbey • Annagh-down Priory**

the window of the old banqueting hall are best seen from the external walkway.

Back on the N59, continue to the little town of Oughterard. Keep an eye out for the sign on the right that points to the **Lakeshore Road ❸**, a beautiful, meandering 5-mile (8 km) drive through intensely green and lush backcountry of rhododendrons and woodland to the shores of the lake at Currain with fine hilly scenery all around.

Return to Oughterard by the same route and follow the N59 northwest to **Maam Cross** ❹, which lies bleak and exposed in the bogland. Here a signed turning on the right leads over wild moors to Maam (aka Maum), where you turn right on the R345 for Cong. Soon **Lough Corrib** ❺ appears on your right, offering superb lake views and opportunities for bird-watching.

Continue on the R345 to **Cong** ❻ (visitor information in Old Courthouse, closed mid-Nov.– mid-March), a beautifully kept village. At the far end, you'll come to **Cong Abbey,** a handsome gray-stone monastery founded in 1128. Carved flowers, leaves, and tendrils decorate the pillar capitals, and tiny staring heads peep out among the leaves.

From Cong, follow the R346 to Cross, then the R334 southeast to Headford, where

you'll see signs to the glorious monastic ensemble of **Ross Errilly** ❼ out in the fields by the sullen Black River. Under the slim church tower, the 14th- and 15th-century buildings stand simple and perfect—the best preserved Franciscan friary in Ireland. Elaborate tombs abound, such as that of Hugh O'Flaherty under the east window; there are huge fireplaces, spouts, chutes, and bread ovens, giving an eerie feeling of monkish presence.

Five miles (8 km) south of Headford, another detour from the N84 brings you to Annaghdown. Turn right immediately past the graveyard ("Annaghdown Pier" sign) to find the blunt and undecorated ruins of **Annaghdown Priory** ❽, a complete contrast to the elegance of Ross Errilly. St. Brendan died here in 577, nursed by his sister Brigid, in the nunnery he had founded.

Return to the N84 and turn right for your journey back to Galway.

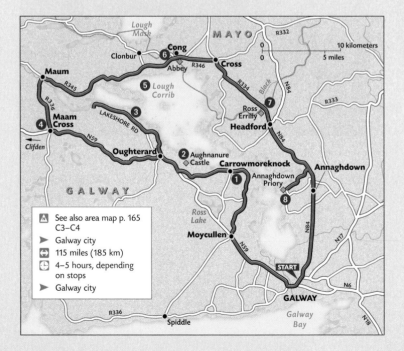

EAST GALWAY

Most visitors traveling west ignore the eastern region of County Galway, intent as they are on immersing themselves in the dramatic beauty of Connemara as quickly as possible. But the quiet, low-lying landscape of east Galway—an area larger than Connemara—holds some enjoyable places, too.

St. Brendan's Cathedral at Loughrea houses a unique collection of Celtic Revival art treasures.

Tuam

165 D4

Visitor Information

093/25-486
or 093/24-463

Seasonal

Tuam

The city of Tuam, 20 miles (30 km) northeast of Galway city, has two cathedrals. The Protestant **Cathedral of St. Mary,** with a 200-foot (61 m) spire, is mostly Victorian neo-Gothic work, but the red sandstone chancel is a relic of the 12th-century cathedral founded here and has a splendid Romanesque arch. The Roman Catholic **Cathedral of the Assumption** has some notable windows by one of Ireland's best known exponents of stained-glass work, the symbolist artist Harry Clarke (1889–1931).

More memorable church art is on show at 12th-century **Knockmoyle Abbey,** 8 miles (13 km) southeast of Tuam on the River Abbert. A rare early 15th-century fresco shows three kings out hawking, while three other dead kings admonish them: "We have been as you are; you will be as we are." Knockmoyle is a beautiful building with some fine carving in the chancel. It was founded by Cathal "Red Hand" O'Connor in 1189 to celebrate a great victory over the invading Normans and takes its ominous name from the battlefield—Cnoc Muaidhe, the Hill of the Slaughter.

Athenry & Loughrea

Athenry (pronounced a-then-RYE), 14 miles (22 km) east of Galway city, preserves its Norman castle keep, the ruins of a 13th-century Dominican friary, and the North Gate and other sections of the defensive walls built around the town in 1211.

From here, the R348/R349 will take you 12 miles (19 km) southeast to Loughrea, where **St. Brendan's Cathedral,** built between 1897 and 1903, is a treasure-house of Celtic Revival craftsmanship—textiles, wood, stone carving, metalwork, and wonderful windows by Michael Healy, Sarah Purser, and Evie Hone, leading lights of the hugely influential 20th-century collective of stained-glass artists An Túr Gloine, the Glass Tower.

Monastic Sites

Near the eastern border where the counties of Galway, Offaly, and Longford meet, two notable monastic sites lie not far apart. The diminutive **Clonfert Cathedral,** built around 1160 on the site of a monastery founded in 563, possesses a masterpiece

---

Turoe Stone

Take the R350 north from Loughrea for a couple of miles (3 km) to Bullaun. Just outside the village, off the left turn signed Kiltullagh, you'll find the extraordinary Turoe Stone standing 3 feet (1 m) tall in a field. This granite pillar—heavily carved with swirling and zigzag patterns, the outline of a bird's head, and a four-pointed St. Brigid's Cross—dates from the late Iron Age period, 300 B.C.–A.D. 100, and was brought here from a nearby earth-banked hill fort known as the Rath of Fearmore, the Big Man's Fort.

Athenry

⚑ 165 D3

Visitor Information

✉ Heritage Centre, The Square, Athenry, Co. Galway

☎ 091/844-661

$ $

athenryheritage centre.com

---

of Irish Romanesque art in its wonderful west doorway of red sandstone. Six recessed orders of round arches frame the door, each carved with animal heads and flowers, while above rises a tall triangular tympanum filled with alternating triangular darts and human heads, some grinning, others simply gazing.

Off the R355 Portumna–Ballinasloe road, 10 miles (16 km) northwest of Clonfert, stand the ruins of the Augustinian **Clontuskert Abbey,** founded during the 12th century in the flat meadows by the River Suck. Most of what you see is 15th-century work. Saints Michael, Katherine, and John—along with a pelican, a curly-haired mermaid, and others—flank the west doorway of 1471. ∎

WESTPORT & CLEW BAY

Westport is the most agreeable town in County Mayo, a lively place full of music and talk. To the west of the town opens one of the most beautiful bays in Ireland, Clew Bay, spattered with over 300 islands and dominated on the south by the cone of Croagh Patrick (see pp. 192–195).

The River Carrowbeg tumbles under a series of old stone bridges through the heart of Westport.

Westport

165 C5

Visitor Information

James St., Westport, Co. Mayo

098/26-711

westporttourism. com

Westport

Laid out in 1780 by English architect James Wyatt (1746–1813), Westport has an air of elegance, especially strong along the tree-shaded mall that flanks the River Carrowbeg that flows through the middle of town. From here, Westport's two parallel main streets run uphill—Bridge Street to the **Clock Tower** and James Street to the **Octagon,** its tall column crowned by a statue of St. Patrick.

Shops in Westport are friendly, chatty places—so are the pubs, many of which boast fine

traditional music in the evenings (see p. 175). A prime mover on the scene is whistle player Olcan Masterson (*olcanmasterson@gmail. com*), one of the guiding hands behind the fabulous sessions of traditional music in Hoban's and other bars in town. Masterson is also a knowledgeable and sensitive guide for photographic and other tours in the area.

Settlers from all over the world have come to this trim town for its agreeable atmosphere, its glorious scenery, and the energetic friendliness of its locals. Their presence has given the town an arty, liberal-minded flavor, best seen during the **Westport Arts Festival** *(westival. ie)* in October.

On **Westport Quay,** west of town, stand handsome 18th-century stone warehouses. From here look out across Westport Bay, itself only a corner of the great opening of Clew Bay.

Clew Bay

Eight miles (13 km) across from north to south, 13 miles (21 km) from its inner eastern shore to its mouth in the west, Clew Bay is a mighty chunk carved out of the Mayo coast. Scattered across the eastern half of the bay are 365 or so green humpbacked islands; they originated as drumlins or hillocks of glacial rubble. Their seaward sides have been eaten by western winds into low cliffs of pebbly clay so that they resemble a shoal of green sea creatures baring their yellow teeth as they set off into the Atlantic.

Spectacularly beautiful when the setting sun lays their black shadows on silvered water, the islands once supported a population of thousands. These days, just a few hardy folk live and work on the islands—fishermen on **Inishlyre,** a sailing school on **Collan More,** multimillionaires refurbishing tiny **Inish Turk Beg** to the peak of luxury and selling it on when times turn tough. John Lennon bought **Dorinish,** one of the Clew Bay islands. Lennon hardly set foot on the island, but for a few years Dorinish was a miserably uncomfortable hippie hangout, to the bemusement of locals.

You'll find wonderful sandy beaches between **Louisburgh** and **Murrisk,** on the south shore of Clew Bay, and at **Mallaranny** on the north side.

Sporty souls can sail (Mayo Sailing Club, Rosmoney Quay; *contact Westport visitor information)* or fish in Clew Bay, while lovers of wild local history should seek out Burrishoole Abbey and Rockfleet Castle near Newport, on the north shore of the bay. The 15th-century tower and arches of **Burrishoole Abbey,** founded by sea raider Grace

Westport House & Country Park

✉ Westport Estate, Westport, Co. Mayo

☎ 098/27-766 or 098/25-430

🕐 House: closed Jan.; open Sat. & Sun. only, Dec.–Feb.; attractions: open summer only, call for times

💲 House and garden: $$; attractions: $$$

westporthouse.ie

Westport House & Country Park

Westport House & Country Park, on the western edge of town, is a Georgian country house whose construction started about 1730; celebrated architect James Wyatt completed the job half a century later. Inside you can admire family portraits (and a beautiful "Holy Family" by Rubens), Georgian silver and glassware, and fine mahogany furniture. The wood was brought to Westport from the Jamaican sugar plantations owned by the wife of the second Marquess of Sligo, who lived here during the early 19th century. Dungeons from an earlier castle that stood on the site, horse-drawn caravan rides, a zoo, and slot machines cheer and cheapen the tone.

O'Malley's second husband, "Iron Dick," stand at the edge of the bay. **Rockfleet Castle,** just along the coast, is also right on the water, a wonderfully grim late medieval tower house, where Grace got the better of "Iron Dick" in 1567 (see sidebar p. 202). ∎

CROAGH PATRICK

Tall, graceful, and impressive, Croagh Patrick ("the Reek" to locals) rises on the southern shore of Clew Bay. Around its cone-shaped head, legends have gathered over millennia. An object of reverence to all manner of religious believers, it is the destination of one of the world's great Christian pilgrimages—and a stunningly beautiful mountain in its own right.

Croagh Patrick

🅐 165 B4

Visitor Information

✉ Croagh Patrick Visitor Centre, Teach na Miasa, Murrisk, Co. Mayo

☎ 098/64-114

croagh-patrick.com

The Legend of St. Patrick

Traveling through Ireland on his great missionary expedition, St. Patrick reached County Mayo in 441. There he climbed the 2,510-foot (764 m) peak of Cruachan Aigil, a mountain feared and venerated by the pagan Irish of the region. A canny operator with an excellent understanding of his fellow man, Patrick was not about to turn his back on a place with such spiritual resonance for thousands of potential converts.

Instead, he fasted 40 days and 40 nights at the summit, a feat that must have seemed tremendously brave to minds that had peopled the peak with demons, and made them more receptive to his message of baptism and salvation.

What happened at the peak quickly became the stuff of stories. Patrick secured assurances from God that the Irish would never lose their faith and that they would be saved on Judgment Day—in fact, that Patrick himself would be their judge. Patrick also cleared Ireland of all its poisonous and offensive beasts by repeatedly ringing his Cloigin Dubh or Black Bell and then hurling it over the precipice of Lugnanarrib, sweeping masses of snakes, toads, and other nasties to their doom with every throw. Helpful angels retrieved the bell and returned it to the saint after each consignment. The Cloigin Dubh also came in handy for dealing with a cloud of evil spirits in the form of black birds, which dispersed when Patrick slung his bell through their ranks.

The Holy Mountain

Within a short time, the mountain peak had become a holy site for Christian pilgrims that neither storms, lightning strikes, nor legal prohibitions could halt.

■ Croagh Patrick, Ireland's holy mountain

EXPERIENCE: Join an Irish Pilgrimage

Few group activities are more friendly and sociable than an Irish pilgrimage, and there is no better way of understanding the unique mix of Christian and "older" faith that underpins so much of Ireland's social fabric than to take part in one. You are not expected to share the faith of your fellow pilgrims, merely to respect it. These communal expeditions, with an earthy spirituality and sense of grounded-ness, are a wonderful way to get to know the "real" Ireland.

The famous annual pilgrimage up Croagh Patrick (see pp. 194–195) is only one of hundreds of pilgrimages in Ireland waiting to be discovered. A tougher prospect is the **Lough Derg** pilgrimage *(Station Island, Lough Derg, Co. Donegal, loughderg.org)*, a spiritual journey centered around a 24-hour vigil during which the penitent stays awake, walking barefoot and repeating a prayer cycle. Pilgrimage participants are restricted to one meal a day, and the whole experience acts as a serious unburdening of body and spirit and serves as a tremendous bonding exercise between those who take part. The three-day pilgrimage takes place from late May to mid-August; one-day retreats are also held from early May to late September.

The monastic site of **Clonmacnoise** in County Offaly (see pp. 250–251) marks St. Ciarán's Day (Sept. 9) with a pilgrimage, while the town of **Máméan** in County Galway holds one-day pilgrimages on St. Patrick's Day (March 17), Good Friday, and the first Sunday in August. At **Glendalough** in County Wicklow (see pp. 98–100), you can navigate your own pilgrimage around St. Kevin's holy valley and monastic site with Fr. Michael Rodgers's superb guidebook, *Glendalough: A Celtic Pilgrimage*.

A 23-mile (37 km) pilgrim path, **Tóchar Phádraig** (see p. 195), was established from Ballintober Abbey along an ancient pagan route to the sacred mountain. Garland Sunday, the last Sunday in July, became the "official" day to climb Croagh Patrick—maybe because of its proximity to August 1, the date of a wild festival of fire and dancing that celebrated the Celtic harvest feast of Lughnasa.

In the late 20th century, a spate of accidents put a stop to the traditional night climb—an unforgettable spectacle as thousands of flashlights wrapped a glowing chain of light around the mountain. But the pilgrimage itself remains as popular as ever, with up to 50,000 people climbing the mountain on Garland Sunday, many of them barefoot, to attend Mass on the summit. Nonbelievers can climb, too—it is one of the world's classic "anyone-can-do-it" ascents (see pp. 194–195).

In 1988, gold was discovered on Croagh Patrick and a license applied for. But so numerous and passionate were the protests—from all over the world—that the scheme to mine the mountain was rejected, no matter how much County Mayo might need the jobs and money. The Reek still carries the scar of the road cut by the mining company, a slowly fading mirror image of the pilgrim path kept fresh by countless feet each year. ∎

WALK: TO THE TOP OF CROAGH PATRICK

A hike up the holy mountain of Croagh Patrick is one of the classic activities in the west of Ireland. It's demanding and tiring, but good for body and spirit, and when you finally reach the summit, you will be rewarded with a stunning view. Whether you opt for the short but challenging route from Murrisk or the 23-mile (37 km) pilgrimage route from Ballintober Abbey, go prepared and do not attempt the trip in thick mist or heavy rain.

St. Patrick stands in statue form at the foot of the Pilgrim Path, overlooking Clew Bay.

To tackle Croagh Patrick you will need a very strong and comfortable pair of walking boots, a stick, and plenty of determination. The route is clear and you need little skill, but you will find it impossible to get all the way to the top if you are out of condition. Don't be put off if you see the summit wrapped in clouds; they may just part when you reach the top.

Short Climb

Set off west from **Murrisk ❶**, beside **Campbell's pub**—where you can admire the vintage collection of pilgrimage photographs and memorabilia—and then head due south along the signposted lane. In about 200 yards (200 m), you will pass the **statue of St. Patrick,** there to give you his blessing at the beginning of your climb.

NOT TO BE MISSED:

Campbell's pub • Statue of St. Patrick • Leacht Mionnain cairn or "station" at the foot of the summit cone • St. Patrick's Church at the summit

Follow the path southward, ascending to a **saddle of ground ❷** at 1,650 feet (500 m). At this point, the pilgrimage route from Ballintober Abbey (see p. 195) joins the path. You might want to take a rest here because your next task is arduous. The summit awaits at the end of a very steep and boulder-strewn ascent of 860 feet (265 m), and you will need to gather all your strength for the climb ahead.

EXPERIENCE: Take the Pilgrimage Route

Following the pilgrimage route to the summit is long and tiring, and unless you are very fit, you will need two days. Anyone taking this walk must register with **Ballintober (Ballintubber) Abbey** *(tel 094/903-0934, ballintubberabbey.ie)* before setting out. Start at the abbey and take the route westward, guided by marker stones incised with crosses and numbered stiles. A useful guidebook, *Tóchar Phádraig, A Pilgrim's Progress*, is available at the abbey. It points out holy wells, standing stones, inscribed rocks, enchanted woods, and fairy hillocks along the way. It also contains details of flora and fauna, and local history and stories. Break your journey at **Aghagower,** where there is an ancient church and a round tower. From here, take a cab to Westport (a ten-minute ride) for a good meal and a bed for the night. On day two, return to Aghagower and continue west, following the track up the south flank of Croagh Patrick to the saddle (see ➋ opposite), where the path from Murrisk merges. Follow the directions for the Short Climb to reach the summit.

At the top, you'll spot **St. Patrick's Church ➌**. The magnificent view from here, at 2,510 feet (764 m), encompasses the sweep of the Connemara Mountains, the Nephin Beg range, the whole of Clew Bay and its islands, Achill Island, and Clare Island. You can even glimpse the Slieve League cliffs some 80 miles (128 km) to the northeast on the coast of County Donegal.

From the summit, return back down to the pub the way you came**.**

▲ See also area map p. 165 B4
► Campbell's pub, Murrisk. Pilgrimage route: Ballintober Abbey, signed off the N84 Castlebar–Ballinrobe road, 7 miles (11 km) S of Castlebar
🕑 Depending on fitness, allow 4–5 hours. For the pilgrimage route, allow 2 days.
↔ 5 miles (8 km) up and down. Pilgrimage route: 23 miles (37 km)
► Campbell's pub

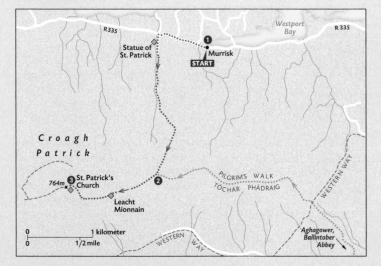

NORTHWEST MAYO

One of the least visited parts of Ireland, northwest Mayo is about as rugged, lonely, and beautiful as you can get. Islands, peninsulas, cliffs, and bays indent the coastline, while the interior is mountain and bog . . . interspersed with bog and mountain. If you love wild places, this is the region for you.

The dark, dramatic ramparts of the Minaun Cliffs loom beyond Keel Bay on Achill Island.

Northwest Mayo

165 A5–B6

Visitor Information

Bridge St., Westport, Co. Mayo

098/26-711

Achill Island

165 A5–B5

Visitor Information

Davitt Quarter, Achill Sound

098/20-705 or 098/20-400

Seasonal

achilltourism.com

Achill Island

From Westport, it's a leisurely hour's drive via Mallaranny (aka Mulrany) to Achill Sound, with the mountainous profile of **Achill Island** growing ever more prominent ahead. At roughly 14 by 12 miles (22 by 19 km), Achill is Ireland's largest offshore island. **Knockmore** (1,119 feet/340 m) and **Minaun** (1,320 feet/403 m) command the view as you cross the bridge over Achill Sound. Their loftier sister mountains, **Croaghaun** (2,195 feet/668 m) and **Slievemore** (2,204 feet/672 m), rise in the north of the island. Achill is very rarely crowded, though tourism has begun to

infiltrate—welcomed by most of the islanders, who until only a few years ago were generally eking out hard lives.

Drop into Sweeney's super-market at the island end of the bridge to catch the current buzz of the island before heading south on the narrow and winding coastal road labeled "Atlantic Drive."

Atlantic Drive: Many island-ers still farm in traditional ways, and in season you'll see ricks of cut turf and hay weatherproofed with vividly colored canvas "head scarves." Monbretia and fuchsia brighten the roadsides; silver sand and orange seaweed fill the rocky bays.

At the southern tip of the island, the tall, grim 15th-century **Kildavnet Castle**—once a base for the famed Mayo "pirate queen" Grace O'Malley (see sidebar p. 202)—stands near the ruined **Kildavnet church.** There are many poignant graves in the cemetery here and a brackish holy well on the shore.

The character of Achill changes as soon as you swing north up the west side of the island, with a tremendous coastline of wave-battered rocks and cliffs. There's a beautiful view down over **Ashleam Bay.**

At **Keel** you will find a fine Blue Flag beach (conforming to EU standards of cleanliness and safety; there are others at Keem and Doogort) and a spectacular prospect of the **Minaun Cliffs.**

Dooagh has attractive white-washed cottages under thatch or tiles, and the Pub, where you can look through a book of photographs recording the arrival of Don Allum. He reached the shore here on September 4, 1987, after 77 days at sea—having just completed the first there-and-back rowing of the Atlantic.

Keem Strand, a couple of miles (3 km) beyond Dooagh, is a perfect beach in a pincer-shaped bay under the slopes of Croaghaun. Amethysts are found on this southern part of the mountain.

Back in Keel, continue straight at Minaun View, and in a mile (1.6 km) steer straight ahead again where Atlantic Drive bends to the right. Just in front, on the slope of **Slievemore,** you'll see an abandoned village of roofless houses—"booley houses," or summer pasture dwellings, depopulated when famine struck Achill in the mid-19th century. You can walk the streets, peer at cold fireplaces and empty stone cupboards, and ponder on the harshness and simplicity of island life back then. Then it's back across the bridge to the Mayo mainland.

The country between Achill Island and the Mullet Peninsula is harsh, rolling brown bogland patched with somber green forests. Just inland rise the **Nephin Beg Mountains,** Ireland's loneliest and most remote range. One footpath threads them: the **Bangor Trail,** a demanding and boggy but extremely rewarding 22-mile (35 km) hike—for the fit and determined only!

Horse Races on the Beach

Because it's on the beach, **Lacken Strand** *(betw. Killala & Ballycastle, Co. Mayo)* spends part of its life underwater. But come late May, this 5-furlong racetrack is the annual home to exciting horse races that draw passionate crowds and mighty *craic*. In days gone by, the family-friendly Lacken Strand Races were a far more rustic affair, with anyone who fancied his chances turning up to have a go aboard every kind of steed, from racehorses and prime Connemara ponies to knock-kneed old nags from the local stables and farms. The modern event is a lot more professional, and you have the chance of seeing some excellent racing by top jockeys and horses. Whatever you do, don't pass up this chance to enjoy a very Irish bit of fun. The **Laytown Races** *(Laytown Strand, Co. Meath, laytownstrandraces.ie)* is another well-known beach racing event in Ireland held in September.

Children of Lir

Inishglora, a scrap of an island off Cross Strand just west of Binghamstown, is the setting for the poignant conclusion of one of Ireland's best known legends, the story of the Children of Lir.

Turned into swans (but retaining their beautiful voices) at the hand of their jealous stepmother's magical powers, the four children of the powerful chief Lir are condemned to spend 900 years in exile from their home. The final 300 years are spent on Inishglora, and it is here that the coming of Christianity finally releases them from their enchantment. But the shapes they resume are those of 900-year-old human beings.

A holy man (Could it have been St. Brendan? He built a church on Inishglora in the sixth century.) baptizes the Children of Lir before they crumble into death and buries them on the island as they have directed—standing upright, with their arms supportively around each other in death as in life.

The Mullet Peninsula

Bangor is a village isolated in the bog, and **Belmullet,** 12 miles (19 km) to the northwest, is equally easy-paced. Belmullet is the gateway to the Mullet Peninsula, a little-visited but beautiful finger of land that runs south for some 20 miles (32 km).

INSIDER TIP:

A self-guided bike tour of western Ireland is a wonderful experience. Don't be afraid to strike out on your own: The locals are especially welcoming and friendly to the single biker.

—KATE RENNER
National Geographic Television

Deeply indented, the peninsula shelters Blacksod Bay on its east and looks out west from a treeless and weathered coast to a scatter of Atlantic islands offshore. Like Achill Island, the Mullet is a Gaeltacht or Irish-speaking area, where locals receive grants to preserve traditional speech, culture, and ways of life.

Belmullet stands on an isthmus connecting the peninsula to the mainland. North and northwest of the isthmus, the Mullet Peninsula coast fractures into innumerable rocky headlands—**Doonamo (Doonamore) Point,** segregated beyond an ancient wall, contains house foundations and fortifications of pre-Christian date.

Reedy, shallow **Termoncarragh Lake** supports rare red-necked phalarope and several other bird species. Houses are widely scattered down the peninsula, with only Binghamstown calling itself a village.

Of the superb beaches, the west-facing ones such as Belderra, Portacarn, and Carricklahan are wilder and more weed-strewn. Cattle walk the strands and feed on the flowery shell-sand meadows or *machair*.

The offshore **Inishkea** and **Duvillaun islands,** and little **Inishglora** (see sidebar above), are uninhabited these days. Their low green curves enhance already sublime Atlantic views.

The country and coast northeast of Belmullet are as wild as can be. This is quintessential Mayo bogland, across which switchback roads lead to pretty little **Pollatomish,** tiny **Portacloy** on its slip of sandy beach, and the equally small fishing harbor of **Porturlin.**

A little farther east, you will find the astonishing archaeological site of **Céide Fields.** In the 1930s, local schoolteacher Patrick Caulfield began to investigate the ancient stone walls being

in to smother the Stone Age farmers' green fields with up to 15 feet (5 m) of turf. The climate certainly became wetter around 3000 B.C., and the early farmers probably contributed to the growth of the wet bog by felling trees so that rain soaked the ground instead of evaporating off the forest leaves. This smothering of the fields and settlements by the creeping bog kept the ancient landscape intact; almost all other such sites were destroyed by the later generations who took over the land. Guided tours show you

Céide Fields

🗺 165 C6

✉ Ballycastle, Co. Mayo

☎ 096/43-325

🕐 Closed Nov.– mid-March, except by appointment

💲 $

heritageireland.ie

▪ **Hand-raked haycocks stand in the village fields at Dooagh, Achill Island.**

unearthed by turf-cutters in the boglands between Belderrig and Ballycastle. In the 1970s, his son, Dr. Séamus Caulfield, put archaeological students to work, and they traced the patterns of a 5,000-year-old farming landscape hidden in the bog.

At the modern visitor center, learn how blanket bog crept

what there is to be seen on the ground—mostly lengths of crude stone walling, which don't look too exciting to the nonexpert.

Just east of Céide Fields, the promontory of **Downpatrick Head** makes a stimulating walk. There's a giant rock stack just off the head and a couple of blowholes that can drench you. ▪

More Places to Visit in the West of Ireland

Clare Island

Out beyond the mouth of Clew Bay lies Clare Island (population about 145), accessible by ferry from **Roonah Quay** *(tel 098/23-737, clareislandferry.com)*. Its castle was the home of Grace O'Malley (see sidebar p. 202). It has a sandy beach near the harbor, fantastic music in the pub (island work rhythms of fishing and farming mean it can open at midnight and close the following noon, if then), and the shapely and steep hill of Knockmore (1,529 feet/461 m) for a literally breathtaking climb and view. *clareisland.ie* 165 B5 Mouth of Clew Bay, Co. Mayo

Coole Park

The home of Lady Augusta Gregory, friend and patron of W. B. Yeats no longer exists. In its place is an interesting visitor center that recreates the daily life of the house when it was in its prime, giving particular attention to the famous guests who stayed there. In the beautiful gardens that surround it, visitors can admire the Autograph Tree where literary geniuses such as W. B. Yeats, George Bernard Shaw, Sean O'Casey, J. M. Synge and many others carved their names into the bark. The path through the woods leads to Coole Lake, the inspiration for one of Yeats's famous poems (see pp. 208–209). *coolepark.ie* 165 D2 Signed off the M18 Galway–Ennis road, 2 miles (3 km) N of Gort, Co. Galway 091/631-804 Park: open all year round. Visitor center: closed winter $

Ennis

The county town of Clare, Ennis is a characterful place of long, narrow streets packed with little pubs. There's a tall column with a statue of "Swaggering" Dan O'Connell, elected in 1828 to represent Ennis in the British Parliament as the first Catholic MP. *visit ennis.com* 165 C2 Arthur's Row, Ennis, Co. Clare 065/682-8366

The calm surface of Killary Harbour conceals Ireland's deepest sea inlet.

Iar Connacht

The loneliest, wildest, most extensive bogland in County Galway, crossed by a single winding road, is sheer bliss for solitude seekers and lovers of bleak landscapes. 🗺 165 C3 ✉ Bounded by the road triangle of the R336 Galway–Ballynahown–Maam Cross and the N59 Maam Cross–Galway, Co. Galway

Killary Harbour

The splendid fjord of Killary Harbour forms the western Galway-Mayo border. It runs in from the west for 10 miles (16 km) in an upward-curving saber shape and in places is more than 150 feet (45 m) deep.

Tremendous mountains sweep up from its shores—the **Maumturks** on the south, the massive **Mweelrea** (2,699 feet/819 m) near the western entrance, and **Ben Gorm** (2,303 feet/750 m) toward the eastern head of the inlet. Their flanks are scarred with the corduroy stripes of lazybeds, the potato ridges tended by peasants of not so long ago.

From **Leenane,** the impossibly photogenic one-street village at the inland end of Killary Harbour, the R335 passes north through the narrow, dramatic defile of Doolough. **Doo Lough** itself, the Black Lake, is a moody stretch of water 2 miles (3 km) long, hugged by the road that weaves through **Doolough Pass** between Mweelrea and the 2,500 feet (750 m) bulk of the Sheeffry Hills. This pass, like the Pass of Glencoe in Scotland, seems darkened as much by its own history as by the crowding mountain slopes, for it was along here that 600 men, women, and children struggled to Delphi Lodge to beg for food during the Great Famine of 1845–1849. Having been turned away empty-handed, 400 died on the return journey through the pass. 🗺 165 B4 ✉ 20 miles (30 km) SW of Westport (N59), Co. Mayo

Kilmacduagh Monastic Site

Backed by the Burren, here are ruins of four

EXPERIENCE:
Drive the Wild Atlantic Way

The 1,500-mile (2,500 km) drive along the **Wild Atlantic Way** (wildatlanticway.com) winds all the way down Ireland's rugged and sea-sculpted west coast. It takes in the island's most northerly point, Malin Head, the wild west coasts of Donegal (huge surfing waves and the highest cliffs in Europe at Slieve League), W. B. Yeats's Sligo and remote Mayo, the dramatically beautiful coasts of Connemara and the flower-spattered Burren of Clare, the mighty Shannon's estuary, and the five mountainous and beautiful peninsulas of West Kerry and Cork that lead to Ireland's southernmost point, Mizen Head.

If you'd prefer two wheels to four, the **Ballyhoura Mountain Bike Trails** (visitballyhoura.com) form a superb 60-mile (100 km) network up, down, and across the Ballyhoura Mountains on the Limerick-Cork border. Map boards, surfaced trails, parking lot, bike wash, and local bike rental are all on offer.

churches (tenth century or earlier), a roofless cathedral, a medieval tower house, and a 115-foot (34 m) tower leaning off-kilter. 🗺 165 D2 ✉ On the R460 Gort–Corofin road, 3 miles (5 km) SW of Gort (N18 Galway–Ennis road), Co. Galway **Galway Visitor Information** Forster St., Galway ☎ 091/537-700

Lough Derg

This long, ragged-edged lake, a great favorite with boaters and fishermen, is handsomely backed by mountains and dotted with pretty villages. **Killaloe,** the main town at the south end, has the 12th-century **St. Flannan's Cathedral and Oratory.** From Mountshannon, a boat will land you on **Holy**

■ Dunguaire Castle on Kinvarra Bay was built by 16th-century descendants of a seventh-century king of Connaught.

Island *(holyisland.ie)* to explore the remains of four churches, an 80-foot (24 m) round tower, elaborately carved medieval tomb slabs, and the holed Bargaining Stone of the monks. *loughderg.org* ⚠ 165 D2–E2 ✉ From Killaloe, Co. Clare, NE for 20 miles (30 km) to Portumna, Co. Clare **Killaloe Visitor Information** The Bridge, Killaloe ☎ 061/376-866 (seasonal)

National Museum of Ireland—Country Life

A modern building houses the National Folklife Collection. The exhibits illustrate elements of country life in Ireland between the Great Famine of the 1840s and the "rural idyll" of Eamon de Valera's Eire of the 1950s: traditional trades, farming and home life; tools, implements and clothing; leisure and beliefs, dancing and story-telling. *museum.ie/Country-Life* ✉ Turlough Park, Castlebar, Co. Mayo ☎ 094/903-1755 🕐 Closed Mon. morning & bank holidays

Thoor Ballylee

In 1916, for the modest sum of 35 pounds, W. B. Yeats bought Thoor Ballylee, a Norman tower built in the 14th century that was in ruins at the time. It underwent a simple but elegant restoration and became his favorite country dwelling. It inspired his poetry collections *The Tower* (1928) and *The Winding Stair* (1933). Inside, an exhibit and a number of objects show the connection that the poet felt to the place. A climb to the fourth and last floor offers a view of the surrounding area, and a small café on the ground floor is a good place to stop for refreshments. ⚠ 165 D3 ✉ Signed off the N66 Gort–Loughrea road, 3 miles (5 km) NE of Gort, Co. Galway ☎ 091/631-436 🕐 Closed Nov.–April 💲 $

Grace O'Malley

With dashing skill, Grace O'Malley (ca 1530–1603), the daughter of a Connacht chief, ran her own army and fleet of privateers from Clare Island (see p. 200) and strongholds along the coast. Stories say that she had the mooring ropes of her fleet run through her bedroom in the castle on the island and tied to her big toe so that she would wake if anyone tried to steal her ships while she slept. She and her privateers exacted pilotage charges and cargo levies from passing shipping until she controlled the entire sea trade from the west of Ireland to the Continent.

Grace was 16 when she married her first husband, Donal O'Flaherty. In 1566, two years after he was murdered, she married Anglo-Irish lord "Iron Dick" Burke on the understanding that, after a year, either could divorce the other. This she duly did, slamming the door of Rockfleet Castle (see p. 191) against him—having first secured all of Iron Dick's castles by putting her own people in charge.

The mountains and coasts immortalized by the Yeats brothers, and the wild hills and peninsulas of Donegal

NORTHWEST IRELAND

■ A Carrowmore dolmen in northwest Ireland, stronghold of the Stone Age

NORTHWEST IRELAND

The three counties that make up northwest Ireland differ greatly. Sligo, to the south-west, has a sandy coastline based around the inlets of Sligo Bay and a lake-filled southern border, while Donegal, to the north, bursts out westward into a vast number of peninsulas and islets. Little Leitrim, squeezed in between, has a coastline only 3 miles (5 km) long and a wooded, hilly interior with Lough Allen as its main water feature.

■ The landscape around Gortahork is typical of the wide wilderness that forms so much of County Donegal.

William's poetry, while the settings for many of Jack's paintings can easily be identified.

Some of Ireland's most impressive prehistoric monuments lie in County Sligo—examples range from dozens of megalithic tombs in the cemeteries of Carrowmore and Carrowkeel to great prehistoric tombs such as the Labby Rock portal dolmen near Lough Arrow and the court tomb at Creevykeel.

Leitrim, sandwiched between the literary and artistic resonance of Sligo and the grand wildness of Donegal, lacks the glamour of these neighboring counties. For spectacles, Leitrim claims the Glencar Waterfall and Parke's Castle on Lough Gill, but this is mostly

Sligo is forever associated with the Yeats brothers, poet William and painter Jack, who spent much of their childhood around Sligo town. The town itself is one of Ireland's most enjoyable, a lively but relaxed place of nar-row streets and musical pubs. Weathering and glacial scraping on the limestone of the surrounding hills has produced striking table mountains with flat tops and shiplike prows. This is Yeats Country—there is a signposted drive around many sites connected with

NOT TO BE MISSED:

Jack Yeats's paintings at Sligo's Model Arts Gallery 206

Queen Medb's Cairn at the summit of Knocknaree 210–211

Picnicking at the Far Point of the Low Rosses 212

Paying your respects at the grave of poet W. B. Yeats at Drumcliff's Church of St. Columba 213–214

Slieve League's stunning cliffs 220

Standing on Malin Head, Ireland's northernmost point 227

Admiring (and maybe buying) a Tory Island painting 229

The gardens and deer of Glenveagh National Park 232

6 ▷

0   30 kilometers
0   15 miles

Tau Cross   Tory Island   **James Dixon Gallery**

Malin Head   Inishtrahull

Ballymacstocker Bay   White Strand Bay   Pollan Bay   **Carnickabraghy Castle**

Fanad Head   Trawbreaga Bay   Carndonagh

Dunfanaghy   Horn Head   Rosguill   **Fanad**   Inishowen Moville

Bloody Foreland

5 ▷   Gweedore   431m   Tievealehid   751m Errigal

Bunbeg   Rathmullan   **Doon Well**   Buncrana   Lough Foyle

Cruit Is.   **The Rosses** Crolly   Inch I.   **Inch Wildfowl Reserve**

Aran Island   Dunlewy   Lough Beagh   Gartan Lough

Leabgarrow   Burtonport   Derryveagh Mountains   **Flagstone of Loneliness**   **GLEN VEAGH N.P.**   **Glebe House**   **Grianan of Aileach**   E

Green I.   Dungloe   Owenmore   **Letterkenny**

Crohy Head   Doocharry   D O N E G A L

Gweebarra Bay   Dooey Point

Lough Doon   Narin   Finn   Lifford

Dawros Head   Rossbeg   Stranorlar

4 ▷   Loughros More Bay   Glenties   Blue Stack Mountains   Ballybofey

Port   Ardara   Lough Eske

Glencolmcille   Rossan Point   Slieve League   Carrick   Killybegs   Donegal   Lough Derg

Cliffs of Slieve League   **One Man's Pass**   St. John's Point   Doorin Point   Ballintra   The Pullans

Donegal Bay   Ballyshannon

3 ▷   Mullaghmore Head   Bundoran   Lough Melvin   **NORTHERN IRELAND** p. 275

Creevykeel   Dartry Mts.

Yeats Country   **Gleniff**   **Horseshoe**

Lissadell House   Benbulben   **Glencar Lough**   Manorhamilton

Lenadoon Point   Sligo Bay   Drumcliff   Rosses Point   Coney I.   **Sligo**   **Deerpark**   **Parke's Castle**

2 ▷   Inishcrone   N59   Knocknarea   **Carrowmore**   **Innisfree**   Dromahair   CENTRAL IRELAND p.233

Queen Medb's Cairn   Ballysadare   SLISH WOOD   **Dooney Rock**   LEITRIM

Slieve Gamph (Ox Mountains)   Collooney

S L I G O   **Heapstown Cairn**

Ballymote   **Labby Rock**   Lough Allen   Ballinamore

1 ▷ p.163   Tobercurry   **Carrowkeel**   Drumshanbo

Lough Arrow   Leitrim   Shannon-Erne Waterway

Lough Gara   Carrick-on-Shannon   **Costello Chapel**

WEST IRELAND   CENTRAL IRELAND p.233   Mohill

A   B   C   D

Area of map detail   **Belfast**   **Dublin**

a county for watery pleasures: boating on the Shannon–Erne Waterway around Carrick-on-Shannon or fishing in Lough Allen and dozens of smaller lakes.

"It's different up here" is the Donegal tourism slogan—a fair summing-up. Donegal feels remote; the county is all but detached from the Irish Republic, with only a 5-mile (8 km) border connecting it to Leitrim. Much of the west of the county is Gaeltacht (Irish-speaking); in the south rise the spectacular cliffs of the Slieve League, while up in the diamond-shaped Inishowen Peninsula, at the top of Donegal, you reach the wild, northernmost tip of Ireland. ∎

SLIGO TOWN

Although it can seem a staid and sleepy place, laid-back Sligo is the social and commercial center of northwest Ireland. At night, there's great music in the pubs; by day, shoppers pack its narrow Georgian and Victorian streets, appealingly lined with old-fashioned shop fronts. There is a May arts festival, the town's main jamboree in August, and autumn music festivals.

■ Warm sunny days attract many a diner to a riverside restaurant in Sligo town.

Sligo Town

🅰 205 C2

Visitor Information

✉ Old Bank Bldg., O'Connell St.

☎ 071/916-1201

sligotourism.ie

Model Arts Gallery

✉ The Mall

☎ 071/914-1405

🕒 Closed Mondays

themodel.ie

The Yeats Brothers

It was the Yeats brothers (see pp. 208-209) who put Sligo on the tourist map. The poet, William Butler (1865-1939), better known as W. B., and the painter, Jack (1871-1957), spent their childhood vacations here and the city still conserves many sites that are connected to them. The Niland Collection, housed in the **Model Arts Gallery,** boasts 50 of Jack's paintings but also works of other Irish painters such as George Russell and Sean

Keating. At the **Sligo County Museum** on Stephen Street visitors can admire a collection of mementos that belonged to W. B. Yeats but a more detailed exhibit, "Yeats in the West," is housed in the **Yeats Memorial Building,** which commemorates the poet with manuscripts and other memorabilia. The building is also home to the **Hyde Bridge Gallery** and to the headquarters of the Yeats Society (*yeatssociety.com*), which organizes the Yeats Summer School every year (see sidebar p. 208). Finally, in front of the bank on Stephen Street, a bronze impressionist-style statue created by Rowan Gillespie in 1989 depicts the poet with his long, thin legs wrapped in a cape that has his poetry written all over it.

History of Sligo

Sligo is not all Yeats, by any means. A poignant sculpture on Quay Street of a ragged, skinny man, woman, and child is a reminder of how badly the town suffered during the Great Famine of 1845–1849, when about a third of Sligo's population died or emigrated. Bad times had hit the town before: Vikings raided it in the ninth century, local clans fought over possession of Sligo Castle (later completely destroyed) in medieval times, and in 1641, Sir Frederick Hamilton took and burned the 13th-century Dominican friary, killing many of the monks.

Exploring the Town

Follow the broad, shallow Garavogue River through town, passing colorwashed houses old and new. Fishermen brave the slippery rocks in hopes of a catch. Or you can wander around Abbey Street, where you'll find the majestic ruins of **Sligo Abbey,** a Dominican abbey founded by Maurice Fitzgerald in the mid-13th century. Although it was destroyed by fire in 1641, it still holds a treasure of headstones, and gothic and renaissance tombs, in addition to a well-conserved cloister and an altar sculpted in the 15th century.

Continue along Castle Street and Grattan Street (Cosgrove's Delicatessen, where Market Street cuts in, is the place to buy the makings of a picnic lunch), before turning right along O'Connell Street to find **Hargadon's pub.**

Hargadon's is a Sligo institution, one of the rare, genuine "talking pubs," where music does not transgress upon the pleasures of conversation. The front part of the pub remains unchanged, a dark den of partitioned snugs with sagging apothecary's drawers and shelves of old jars. Back rooms ramify into recently constructed bar and eating areas.

INSIDER TIP:

For many visitors, the name Yeats immediately draws to mind the poet W. B.—but his painter brother Jack's output is equally impressive. You'll see his work at Sligo's Model Arts Gallery.

—LARRY PORGES
National Geographic Travel Books editor

If you are after an evening of superb traditional music, head for **Furey's pub** on Bridge Street. It's owned by Sligo band Dervish, who have made their name playing breakneck traditional music on the concert stages of the world. Band members take part in the fast and furious sessions here whenever they are in town. ∎

Sligo County Museum

- ✉ Stephen St.
- ☎ 071/911-1679
- 🕑 Closed Sun. & Mon.

sligoarts.ie

Yeats Memorial Building

- ✉ Wine St.
- ☎ 071/911-1679

sligoarts.ie

Sligo Abbey

- ✉ Abbey St.
- ☎ 071/914-6406
- 🕑 Closed Mon.– Thur., mid-Oct.– March

heritageireland.ie

SLIGO & THE YEATS BROTHERS

In spite of the worldwide experience and fame they gained as, respectively, Nobel Laureate poet and celebrated Postimpressionist painter, William Butler Yeats and his younger brother, Jack, looked on this small corner of Ireland as the primary source of their inspiration.

Their mother, Susan Pollexfen, was a Sligo woman; their father, John Butler Yeats, was a lawyer turned not-too-successful artist. When money got tight, as it frequently did, Susan would take the boys and their sisters from their home in Dublin to stay for weeks and months at a time with her parents in Sligo. Both William and Jack responded passionately to the dramatic mountains and coasts, the swirling Atlantic skies, and the life of the harbor town and its countryside—horse races, market days, and country fairs; sailors, jockeys, and ballad singers.

■ **A 1907 etching of W. B. Yeats by Augustus John**

W. B. Yeats

The tales, legends, and other yarns that William heard in and around Sligo stirred his imagination. His beloved uncle George Pollexfen had a servant, Mary Battle, who would regale William with tales of fairies, goblins, and wee folk. Mary had the "second sight," a door of spiritual imagination that opened at times, fascinating the young boy. He learned tales of Queen Maeve, or Medb, whose "tomb" he could see from his grandparent's house in profile on top of the hill of Knocknaree (see pp. 210–211), and the story of Fionn MacCumhaill's final reckoning with

EXPERIENCE: Events dedicated to W. B. Yeats

William Butler Yeats—Ireland's master poet and playwright of the 19th and early 20th centuries, winner of the 1923 Nobel Prize in Literature, and author of such iconic poems as "The Lake Isle of Inisfree," "Byzantium," "Easter 1916," and "When You Are Old"—is without doubt the most famous figure in Sligo history. Born and bred in Dublin, Yeats himself frequently acknowledged that it was the time he spent in Sligo that made him a poet and shaped all his writing.

That's why every year, from late July to early August, hundreds of Yeats scholars and enthusiasts from all over the world gather in Sligo for the two-week

Yeats International Summer School (yeatssociety.com), run by the Yeats Society Sligo. Events include lectures and short seminars, dramatic readings and musical presentations by some of Ireland's renowned performers, and workshops with leading poets, actors, and theater directors. Performances and readings are held at the **Hawk's Well Theatre** (Temple St., Sligo, tel 071/916-1526, hawkswell.com). Check online for application and scholarship information.

For other events in Sligo related to W. B. Yeats, and Irish poetry and drama in general, check with the **Sligo Arts Service** (tel 071/911-1850, sligoarts.ie).

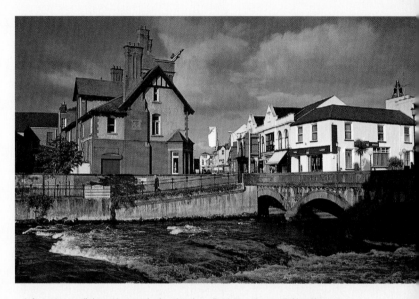

■ Information on all things Yeats can be found at the redbrick Yeats Society (left) in Sligo town.

his cuckolder Diarmuid on the slopes of Ben-bulben mountain (see pp. 214–215).

These stories from Ireland's deep mythi-cal past were generally regarded in the 1870s and '80s as superstitious nonsense fit only for peasant nursemaids and children. But the Yeats brothers continued to holiday regularly around Sligo later in life, steeping themselves in this highly distinctive and seductive landscape and culture. It was at the root of William's passionate championing of a specifically Irish literature enriched by tradition—what would become the Gaelic Revival, from the 1890s onward, intertwining with republican politics in the years leading up to the Easter Rising and the War of Independence. And Sligo drew the poet back at the end of his life to lie under a self-penned epitaph taken from the poem "Under Ben Bulben" in the graveyard at Drumcliff, where his great-grandfather had been rector.

Jack Yeats

Susan Pollexfen's father, William, was a grim, solid businessman, disapproving of his feckless son-in-law and silently stern with his Yeats grandchildren. Grandmother Elizabeth was warm and loving to the Yeats children, but grandfather William was forbidding with all—except young Jack, with whom he struck up a very close relationship. Between the ages of 8 and 16, Jack lived with his grand-parents, an immersion in the Sligo scene that influenced him all his life. In adulthood, he continued to visit whenever possible, staying in his uncle George's seaside house out at Rosses Point (see pp. 211–212) and sketching local scenes. "Sligo was my school, and the sky above it," he wrote later. From 1910 on, Jack was painting in oils, increasingly blurry and mystical in style and subject matter.

Sligo town has finally paid its adoptive art-ist son the honor he deserves with a gallery dedicated to his work (see p. 206). Donating his painting of Uncle George, himself, and his wife, "Leaving the Far Point," to the Sligo Corporation in 1954, Jack wrote, "From the beginning of my painting life every painting which I have made has somewhere in it a thought of Sligo." ■

YEATS COUNTRY

The lonely, sandy coasts of Sligo Bay, Drumcliff Bay, and Ballysadare Bay, the flat-topped mountains of the Benbulben range north and east of Sligo town, and the deeply indented shores of Lough Gill to the southeast—these contain the haunts of William and Jack Yeats and the landscape that influenced them from childhood onward. An established Yeats Country Drive, marked with brown-and-white quill-and-inkstand signs, runs a meandering course for about 100 miles (160 km) around the area.

■ The mighty wrinkled table of Benbulben, W. B. Yeats's favorite among the Sligo mountains

Yeats Country

🗺 205 B2–C3

Visitor Information

✉ Old Bank Bldg., O'Connell St., Sligo, Co. Sligo

☎ 071/916-1201

sligotourism.ie

Queen Medb's Cairn

A good place to start the Yeats circular route *(details from Sligo visitor information)* is at the 1,074-foot (328 m) summit of **Knocknaree** (Knocknarea). Shaped like an upturned dish with a round button on top, it towers over the landscape west of Sligo town. You can reach it by leaving the town along Castle Street—passing en route the

house of Thornhill, where the Yeats boys often visited their uncle, George Pollexfen (see pp. 208–209).

In 3 miles (5 km), a turn on the left *(signed "Meascán Meadhbha")* leads to a parking lot. From there, it's a 45-minute hike to the summit. The "button" is in fact the huge Stone Age monument of Queen Medb's Cairn, a mini-hill of boulders (estimated at 40,000

INSIDER TIP:

Climb Benbulben for fantastic views of Sligo. The south face is the easier side to scale, as winds from the Atlantic make the north slope dangerous.

—STEPHANIE ROBICHAUX
National Geographic
contributor

tons/36,000 tonnes of stone) that covers a passage grave. It was Queen Medb ("Maeve" to W. B. Yeats), the mythical (probably) first-century warrior queen of Connacht, who initiated the famous Cattle Raid of Cooley (see p. 334). Her tomb reflects the size of her reputation: It stands 80 feet (24 m) high and measures 630 feet (192 m) around the base.

The extensive view from the summit is foregrounded by the tidal channels and sandbanks of Sligo Bay and Ballysadare Bay. Due west of the mountain lies the stony shore at **Strandhill**, backed by huge sand dunes. Ulster hero Cúchulainn fought the sea here.

Coney Island

Farther around the blunt-headed Strandhill Peninsula you reach the tidal causeway to Coney Island, much beloved of Jack Yeats in his day. He set his late painting "The Sea and the Lighthouse" (1947) here, with a wind-torn figure staring out into a dark blue sky lit by a piercing beam from the Oyster Island lighthouse. You can study the painting for yourself in the

Model Arts Gallery in Sligo town (see p. 206). The great swath of sand enclosed in the bay is Cummeen Strand, often whipped by storm winds out of the west.

Rosses Point

Across the bay is the shark-tooth peninsula of Rosses Point, scene of so much freedom for the Yeatses, as children and well into adulthood. Rosses Point is a neat, compact little place with fine sandy beach walks. Waiting on the shore is a heart-wrenching statue that faces out to Oyster Island. It represents a woman waiting in vain for the return of her loved one from the sea. Nearby, "The Metal Man," a statue of a sailor, emerges from the sea and marks

EXPERIENCE:
Take a Seaweed Bath

If you are in need of some downtime or are just up for a new and strange experience, you shouldn't leave Sligo without paying a call on **Kilcullen's Seaweed Baths** (*Enniscrone, Co. Sligo, tel 096/36-238, kilcullenseaweedbaths.net, $$$*). Here, in a rather grand Edwardian bathhouse—complete with huge period porcelain tubs and brass taps—you lie back in a bath full of hot, pure Atlantic seawater. The highly concentrated iodine released from the seaweed gives the water an amber tint and has natural therapeutic properties. As you soak, your aches and pains, worries and tensions, fade away. You leave (after a needle-sharp cold shower) with silky smooth skin and a fantastic sense of well-being. Kilcullen's also offers steam baths and massages.

Picnicking in Yeats Country

If you have any of the poet or painter in you, don't rush through Yeats Country. Get out of the car, spread a blanket, and do some daydreaming. As Maurteen metaphorically tells Shawn as he opens a bottle in *The Land of Heart's Desire*, "It's precious wine, so take your time about it." For stunning views, try **Queen Medb's Cairn** (see pp. 210–211) on Knocknarea.

For a shore picnic with connections to Jack Yeats, walk out from Rosses Point (see pp. 211–212) to the **Far Point** of the Low Rosses ("Leaving the Far Point"). Other tranquil, W. B. Yeats–inflected picnic spots are **Glencar Lough** (see p. 215) and the shore of **Lough Gill** (see p. 215), opposite Innisfree (*turn off the R287 bet. Slish Wood & Dromahair*).

Lissadell House & Gardens

📍 205 B2

✉ Ballinfull, signposted on the N15, 4.6 miles (7.5 km) NE of Drumcliffe, Co. Sligo

☎ 071/916-3150

🕐 Closed Nov.– March

💲 $$

lissadellhouse.com

the safe deep channel and the incoming tide. William loved the muted, often melancholic attractions of Rosses Point, from where he could see Knocknaree and Benbulben. A shore path leads to the tip of the sandspit known as the Low Rosses, where in summer intensely pink pyramidal orchids and sky blue harebells nod in the sea wind.

Rosses Point came to stand at the heart of Jack's art, and many of his best paintings were set here: "Shruna Meala, Rosses Point" of 1923, an early watercolor "The Metal Man," and "The Old Pilot House, Rosses Point," in which two capped figures stare seaward out of one of the pilot house's round windows.

Other pictures, such as "White Shower" (1928) and "The Grave-yard Wall" (1945), are clearly set on a sea-bound landscape such as this. Most ethereal and suffused with spirituality is "Leaving the Far Point." Jack in a dark hat and his wife Cottie—a young woman in the painting, with one hand steadying her hat against the sea wind—are walking the wet gray strand at Rosses Point under a wild, cloud-streaked sky. With

them is the otherworldly figure of Uncle George Pollexfen, faint to the point of transparency. He had died in 1910, so this painting is a study on past happiness and the presence of loved ones long gone. Cottie Yeats died soon after the painting was finished, adding poignancy to its effect.

Lissadell House

From the northerly tip of the Rosses Point sandspit, one looks across Drumcliff Bay to the estate of Lissadell, 2 miles (3 km) away. It was a clear view in Yeats's day, but now conifers and tangled woodland make it hard to see the Gore-Booth family mansion of Lissadell.

W. B. Yeats first visited it in 1894 as a sensitive poet of nearly 30, fully into his "Celtic Twilight" phase of romantic nostalgia and soft-focus nationalism. He became friends with the two Gore-Booth girls, Constance and Eva, who provided plenty of hard-edged realism as a counterbalance—especially Constance, who was to gain notoriety as Countess Markiewicz at the Easter Rising and during the run-up to the 1919–1922 War of Independence.

A fervent Irish nationalist and an active participant in the fighting, she was given a death sentence (immediately commuted) for her part in the Dublin fighting on Easter 1916. She was soon imprisoned again for making speeches in support of the outlawed Sinn Féin. W. B. Yeats wrote of her at that time, in "On a Political Prisoner," as "Blind and leader of the blind / Drinking the foul ditch where they lie."

William himself had gone through an intensely nationalistic phase. After the Easter Rising he became more conservative, but both he and Jack still supported nationalism—Jack expressing this sentiment in his 1924 painting "Communicating with Prisoners." In 1927, in "In Memory of Eva Gore-Booth and Con Markiewicz," William remembered: "The light of evening, Lissadell / Great windows open to the south / Two girls in silk kimonos both / Beautiful, one a gazelle."

Drumcliff & Benbulben

Back on the N15 Sligo–Bundoran road, at Drumcliff is the austere gray **Church of St. Columba,** the stump of a round tower, and an ancient cross carved with biblical scenes, including Cain axing Abel in the head and Adam and Eve shielding their private parts under the branches of the Tree of Knowledge. The church incorporates a visitor center offering guided tours and events.

Next to the northwest angle of the church tower is the grave of W. B. Yeats and his wife, George Hyde-Lees (1892–1968). The view from the graveside, through a thin screen of churchyard trees

Drumcliff

⬛ 205 B2

Church of St. Columba & Visitor Center

✉ Drumcliff, Co. Sligo

▪ "Under bare Ben Bulben's head / In Drumcliff churchyard Yeats is laid. . . . Horseman, pass by!"

■ The romantic lake isle of Innisfree in Lough Gill inspired Yeats's best loved poems.

Benbulben
 205 C3

to the great bareheaded bulk of Benbulben, is as simple as it is majestic.

Noble-looking **Benbulben** (Benbulbin) dominates the landscape for 50 miles (80 km). It is table-topped, with sheer, deeply furrowed cliffs dropping from the summit to the upper rim of a great skirt of green that slants down to the agricultural lands below. The Yeats boys roamed all over the mountain, fishing for trout in the pools and streams. In "The Tower" (1926), W. B. looked back nostalgically to "boyhood, when with rod and fly / Or the humbler worm, I / climbed Ben Bulben's back / And had the livelong

summer day to spend."

Jack slipped the distinctive dreadnought-prow shape of the mountain into his 1946 painting "The Mountain Window," as a silhouette seen in a cottage window, crowned with a cloud through which a gold sun is bursting.

Legends abound on Benbulben, the best known being the saga of Diarmuid and Gráinne, with the final face-off between the elderly Fionn MacCumhaill and Diarmuid, who had run off with Fionn's betrothed, the beautiful Gráinne. It was on the slopes of Benbulben that Fionn's warriors, the Fianna, drove a savage boar toward Diarmuid. In the act of killing it Diarmuid was gored. Twice Fionn went to the sacred spring for healing water, remembered Diarmuid's treachery, and let the water trickle through his fingers. The third time he relented and brought back the water, but it was too late—Diarmuid was dead. The bed where Diarmuid and Gráinne made love is suitably heroic in size, a huge rock arch 40 feet (12 m) high and 60 feet (18 m) wide, standing above the inner end of Gleniff, 3 miles (5 km) east of Benbulben summit. You can admire it during a circuit of the spectacular **Gleniff Horseshoe,** signposted from Ballintrillick Bridge *(reached via Cliffony on N15).*

The road at the foot of Benbulben curves southeast around the mountain's flank to reach beautiful **Glencar Lough** and its waterfall. Diarmuid built a *crannog* in the lake to hide Gráinne from the Fianna. The waterfall is signposted from the road—a paved path leads up through mossy trees to where the stream plunges over a sill into a pool. In "Towards Break of Day," W. B. Yeats described it as "a waterfall /Upon Ben Bulben side / That all my childhood counted dear."

Lough Gill

One of the Yeats brothers' favorite Sligo places was the large, beautiful Lough Gill, east of Sligo town, with a 24-mile (38 km) scenic drive around much of its deeply indented shoreline. The southern shore road (R287 Sligo–Dromahair) passes a parking place at **Dooney Rock,**

where marked paths lead up to the top of the rock—a well-known beauty spot and lookout point. W. B. had his "Fiddler of Dooney" rejoicing: "When I play on my fiddle at Dooney, / Folk dance like a wave of the sea."

Farther on around the lake, the road skirts **Slish Wood** ("Sleuth Wood" to Yeats), where the young poet once trespassed and spent a sleepless night in fear of the wood ranger—the subject of much saucy teasing by the servants. Close to the shore here lies **Innisfree,** the tiny wooded islet that W. B. made the subject of his best known poem. Here Yeats longed to live in dreamy seclusion. In one of his well-known

---

INSIDER TIP:

Two CDs to take on your rambles around Yeats Country: *An Appointment With Mr. Yeats* by The Waterboys and *Now and in Time to Be,* a selection of Yeats' poems interpreted by various musicians.

—MARGARET ROBERTS
Irish Dancer and Musicologist

---

poems, "The Lake Isle of Innisfree," he wrote: "I will arise and go now, and go to Innisfree, / And a small cabin build there, of clay and wattles made: / Nine bean-rows will I have there, a hive for the honey-bee, / And live alone in the bee-loud glade."

You can reach the "Lake Isle of Innisfree" by boat *(visitor information at Sligo Tourist Office)* from Parke's Castle (see p. 230). ∎

PREHISTORIC SLIGO

Sligo is a county rich in prehistoric monuments, and its various ancient burial sites—from cairns and portal dolmens to court tombs and whole cemeteries—are atmospheric places to visit. Most have far-ranging views. Wandering the hilltops and field slopes puts one's imagination to work on the nature and motivation of the people who labored so hard to build these monuments to the dead.

Stone Age mourners constructed the remarkable tombs at Carrowmore, just outside Sligo town.

Carrowmore

205 B2

West of Sligo Town

In the north Sligo country around Sligo town, several sites are well worth exploring. To the west of the town *(brown sign)* lies **Carrowmore** megalithic cemetery *(tel 071/916-1534)*, the largest and oldest such site in Ireland. About 30 monuments remain, some mere scatters of stones, others complete with lintels and interior walling. Cremated bones, stone and bone ornaments, and flint arrowheads have been found here, the artifacts of burials covering some two or even three thousand years. The oldest passage tombs may date as far back as 5000 B.C.

A couple of miles (3 km) away is **Meascán Meadhbha** or **Queen Medb's Cairn,** the giant mound of stones on the top of Knocknarea (see pp. 210–211). The cairn is still unexcavated (it is bad luck to remove any stone), but it probably covers a 5,000-year-old passage tomb.

Deerpark & Creevykeel

East of the N15 Sligo–Bundoran road lie two remarkable court tombs, each built between 4000 and 3000 B.C. There are many examples in Ireland of this style of tomb, in which a ceremonial open-air court (presumably for rituals) gives access to a number of burial chambers arranged in galleries inside the covered part of the tomb. But Deerpark and Creevykeel are two of the finest.

Deerpark court tomb is reached by turning right *("Giant's Grave" sign)* off the road to the north of Colgagh Lough *(via the R287 Sligo–Dromahair road)*, then walking uphill for 30 minutes from the parking lot. The whole structure, on an open ridgetop above woods, is about 100 feet (30 m) long, with a central court, twin galleries on the east, and a simple gallery on the west.

Creevykeel court tomb *(signed off the N15 just N of Cliffony)* is trapezoidal, with a pincer-shaped court, its rectangular chambers placed centrally and let into the sides of the huge pebbly monument. Massive jambs still support one of the lintels.

South Sligo

A cluster of three monuments lies around Lough Arrow in south Sligo. Among the hilltops of the Bricklieve Mountains, to the west of the lake, are the scattered passage tombs of **Carrowkeel** neolithic cemetery, signposted from Castlebaldwin on the N4 Collooney–Boyle road. Superbly sited to catch all the best views (and to be seen from far off), they vary in type—some have corbeled roofs like beehives and three central chambers, others fall between court and passage tombs. All date from circa 3800–3300 B.C.

Directly to the north of Lough Arrow is **Heapstown Cairn** *(from Castlebaldwin, follow the signs for Highwood, after approximately 2 miles, at the intersection of Heapstown, curve left and you'll find it a bit farther ahead on your right).* This huge mound of stones is over 5,000 years old and is still unexplored.

INSIDER TIP:

Survey the grand panorama from Carrowkeel Neolithic cemetery with binoculars and you'll be able to spot many more cairns on the neighboring hilltops.

—CHRISTOPHER SOMERVILLE
National Geographic author

The megalith, **Labby Rock**, looms 2 miles to the southeast *(from Castlebaldwin, head toward Ballindoon then follow the road to Carrickglass).* Built between 4000 and 2500 B.C., both burial chambers have a capstone and entrance jambs. Labby Rock's capstone, a single block of limestone 14.5 feet (4 m) long and up to 6 feet (2 m) thick, weighs an estimated 70 tons (64 tonnes).

To find out more about the archaeology of Sligo, contact the Sligo visitor information office *(tel 071/916-1201, sligotourism.ie).* ∎

Deerpark
🅼 205 C2

Creevykeel
🅼 205 C3

Carrowkeel
🅼 205 C1

Heapstown Cairn
🅼 205 C2

Labby Rock
🅼 205 C2

SOUTHWEST DONEGAL

County Donegal, northernmost and remotest of the Irish Republic's counties, throws dozens of peninsulas west and north into the Atlantic. The southwest corner of this ragged coastline bulges out the farthest, leading at its tip to Europe's highest sea cliffs and the beautifully enfolded sacred site of Glencolmcille.

■ Tiny Station Island, otherwise known as St. Patrick's Purgatory, Lough Derg

Bundoran

🗺 205 C3

Visitor Information

✉ The Bridge,
   Bundoran,
   Co. Donegal

☎ 071/984-1350

**discoverbundoran.
com**

Donegal Town &
Points South

Donegal makes its tenuous
connection with the rest of
the Republic south of Donegal
town, a 5-mile (8 km) border
shared with County Leitrim.
Bundoran, a first-class little
seaside resort, has a Blue Flag
beach (conforming to EU standards of cleanliness and safety)

and all the holiday trimmings.
   Farther north lies

Ballyshannon, a vibrant little
city that is proud to be the oldest
in Ireland. It comes to life at the
beginning of August with the Folk
Festival *(ballyshannonfolkfestival.
com),* an event that draws Irish
and international artists alike. You
can look out on Inis Sainer, and
the winding sandbanks and grassy

dunes of the River Erne's estuary, from Ballyshannon Harbour, where a beautiful memorial commemorates three drowned fishermen, showing the men transformed into gamboling dolphins.

On the way north to Donegal town, it is worth turning east to **Lough Derg,** where **Station Island,** long a place of retreat to restore the soul, is smothered in early 20th-century buildings of functional design. They cater to the many thousands of Roman Catholics who make a pilgrimage to the island each May *(tel 071/986-1518, loughderg.org),* enduring three days and nights of barefoot perambulation and prayer while fasting.

Donegal town is an enjoyable place to idle for a day. The central square is known as the Diamond, as are the squares of plantation towns all across the ancient province of Ulster. County Donegal was one of the disputed "three counties" where Catholics were in the majority—the others were Cavan and Monaghan—arbitrarily separated from Ulster by the 1920 act that created Northern Ireland.

The accents you'll hear in County Donegal seem harder and more rapid than those in the rest of the Republic—closer, in fact, to the speech of Northern Ireland. The celebrated Donegal style of playing traditional music is noticeably quick and staccato, too. Catch the brisk style for yourself in one of the many excellent music pubs in Donegal town.

Donegal Castle, built in the 15th century by Hugh Roe O'Donnell, stands on a cliff overlooking the River Eske. Guided tours tell you the story of the castle and its owner, Sir Basil Brooke, who restored and extended the old castle in the 17th century.

It is worth taking a whole day over the 75-mile (120 km) clockwise drive from Donegal town around the roundish bulge of County Donegal's most southwesterly peninsula. There are so many places to stop, stare, and explore, and the roads are twisty and humpbacked. Glencolmcille (see pp. 220–221) in particular is not a place to hurry through.

INSIDER TIP:

If you're traveling by car, don't hesitate to venture down any of the numerous tiny side roads, especially if you see a sign with "trá" on it— it's Irish for "beach."

—ALEXANDRA BURGUIERES
National Geographic contributor

West of Donegal Town

A few miles west of Donegal town, a thin 8-mile (13 km) peninsula runs southwest from the village of Dunkineely to **St. John's Point.** Out toward the tip of the peninsula, you pass through a wild landscape of limestone pavement rich in flowers, with fine views from the lighthouse at the tip that extend—with the help of binoculars—on a clear day from

Donegal Town

▲ 205 C4

Visitor Information

✉ The Quay, Donegal, Co. Donegal

☎ 074/972-1148

govisitdonegal.com

Donegal Castle

✉ Castle St., Donegal, Co. Donegal

☎ 074/972-2405

$ $

discoverireland.ie

Ardara
🏔 205 C4

Cliffs of Slieve League
🏔 205 B3

One Man's Pass
🏔 205 B3

Glencolmcille
🏔 205 B4

Glencolmcille Folk Village Museum
☎ 074/973-0017
🕐 Closed Oct.–Easter Sunday
💲 $

glenfolkvillage.com

the north Mayo coast through Sligo and Leitrim to the cliffs just east of Slieve League.

The Glencolmcille Peninsula

Northwest of Donegal town, on the Glencolmcille Peninsula, the mountains begin to rise around **Killybegs,** Donegal's premier fishing town. The harbor is lined with tough-looking, salt-rusted trawlers painted red and blue, and a fishy aroma wafts from the big fish-processing factory. West of Killybegs the coastal landscape becomes wild, a broken region of heathery headlands and small green fields sloping up to the feet of the mountains. The Coast Road detour *(marked with brown*

Ardara

Ardara (pronounced ar-da-ra) is a friendly little town east of Port on the Glencolmcille Peninsula that grew prosperous in times past through the tweed-weaving industry. Visitors can see demonstrations of hand-loom-weaving at the **Ardara Heritage Centre** *(ardara.ie)* located beside the bridge in the town center, and half of the shops in town seem to sell Aran sweaters and Donegal tweed garments. **Nancy's,** halfway up the hill, and **The Corner House,** on Main Street, are great music pubs.

signs off the R263) shows you the best of this wild landscape, where trees are windblown and farmhouses are built of rough stone under slate roofs. You are into the Gaeltacht now, Irish-speaking country.

At Carrick, a left turn

(marked *"Teelin Pier")* leads off the main road. Soon, signs to **Bunglass: The Cliffs** point up a steeply winding road that climbs through gates and around rocky shoulders to a windy parking place and viewpoint above a ruined Napoleonic watchtower in a most precarious position. A few steps from the car bring you to a stunning view of the **cliffs of Slieve League,** reputedly the tallest in Europe, towering some 2,000 feet (600 m) out of the sea in a wall of black, yellow, orange, and brown. Brave scramblers with a head for heights can attempt the **One Man's Pass** (or Path), a skywalk 2 feet (0.6 m) wide in places that teeters between the sheer cliff top and the sloping rock above to reach the summit. Do not attempt this path in wet or gusty weather.

An expanse of wild bogland, ramparted by the workings of many generations of turf-cutters, leads from Slieve League to the beautiful green valley of **Glencolmcille** (Glencolumbkille), one of Ireland's "special places" whose magical atmosphere far transcends the merely picturesque. Glencolmcille runs due west, a long, sheltered valley that reaches the sea between rugged headlands.

The **Glencolmcille Folk Village Museum,** founded in the 1960s by Father James McDyer, attracts a fair number of tourists with its six, accurately reconstructed, thatch-roofed cottages that portray rural life of the past. One of the cottages is dedicated to the museum's

Trawlers lie up in the fishing harbor at Killybegs, a Donegal town with a friendly, fishy atmosphere.

founder. If you fancy a bottle of seaweed or fuchsia wine, the Shebeen shop is the place to buy one.

But the real magic of Glencolmcille has most to do with its connections with St. Columba, the Donegal-born saint from whom the valley takes its name. Born in 521 at Gartan Lough, Columba established monasteries and places of retreat in several Donegal locations and was drawn by the loneliness of Glencolmcille as well as by its reputation among pagan locals as a center of spirituality—witness the many standing stones and pre-Christian burial sites in the valley.

Columba's Journey

An Turas Cholmcille, Columba's Journey, is a 3-mile (5 km) circuit of 15 stations or sacred sites, followed barefoot at midnight by pilgrims every year on Columba's feast day, June 9. You can seek out these sites and follow the Turas at your own pace from station 1,

a court tomb in the churchyard, via standing stones and slabs incised with crosses, and a cluster of stations around **St. Columba's Chapel, Bed, and Well** on the north slope of the glen. The chapel is a sturdy box of chest-high walls on a knoll among incised cross slabs, and his highly uncomfortable bed in one corner of the chapel is a low-lying arrangement of two stone slabs boxed in by stones.

From Glencolmcille, the road ribbons on eastward across stark bogland toward Ardara (see sidebar opposite). A detour that's worth taking leaves the main route at a turning on the left in 2 miles (3 km). The narrow road becomes progressively bumpier after 5 miles (8 km) as it forks left and runs down to the abandoned fishing village of **Port,** a great spot for lazing on the hillside above the ruins of old houses, looking over a white pebbly beach to blue sea and sky. Only occasionally do fishermen come down to Port, so it's perfect for seekers of solitude. ∎

Port
🗺 205 B4

WEST & NORTHWEST DONEGAL

Dozens of granite-scabbed, lake-strewn peninsulas, great and small, make up the spectacular coastline of west and northwest Donegal. Together with the mountainous interior, they form a landscape wild, harsh, and extraordinarily compelling. Hereabouts, you'll find spoken Irish, tall tales, and breakneck music.

West & Northwest Donegal

🗺 205 B4–D5

Visitor Information

✉ Blaney Rd., Letterkenny, Co. Donegal

☎ 074/912-1160

Dawros Peninsula

The Dawros Peninsula sticks out across the bay of Loughros More, with views across to the mountains around Glencolmcille. Low hills hide numerous lakes. In **Lough Doon,** between Kilclooney and Rossbeg, you'll find a fine island ring fort perhaps 2,000 years old, with walls standing up to 15 feet (5 m) tall. Row yourself to the island in a rented boat *(signposted)*.

The peninsula has flat coasts of sand dunes and sandy beaches—especially around sheltered **Narin,** looking north into Gweebarra Bay. Sandbanks and shining mudflats in the tidal creeks attract large numbers of overwintering geese.

Dooey Point & Crohy Head

North of Dawros juts **Dooey Point Peninsula,** with more fine beaches and dunes. The **Crohy Head Peninsula,** north again, is rougher country with a meandering coast road good for walking or driving on the seaward slopes of a more mountainous interior. Try the 40-mile (64 km) drive from Lettermacaward northeast up the Owenwee Valley into the skirts of the Derryveagh Mountains, then down the Owenbeg and back by Fintown and Lough Finn.

The Rosses

Donegal has more Irish speakers than any other county in Ireland, and the indigenous Irish language and culture are maintained most strongly in the Rosses, north of Crohy. The population is growing

■ The majestic simplicity of the Donegal coast near Gweedore

and new houses are being built, but the landscape here is harsh—pieces of granite pushing through bog, uncountable loughs and lakelets, and a deeply cut and broken coastline.

Donegal's little airport (donegal airport.ie) is at **Carrickfinn,** on the flat grassy coast north of Annagry.

INSIDER TIP:

Tune your radio to Raidió na Gaeltachta (RnaG; 92–94 FM) to hear the beauty of spoken Irish and the wonderful traditional Irish music and song.

—CHRISTOPHER SOMERVILLE
National Geographic author

Burtonport has trawlers in its harbor and some salty fishermen's pubs, though the fishing the town relies on is going through hard times. From here you can catch the ferry to Aran (Arranmore) Island (see p. 228).

A more visitor-oriented village is **Dungloe,** on the south side of the Rosses, with its annual "Mary from Dungloe" charm and beauty contest (maryfromdungloe.com)—an excuse for a few weeks of money-making and drinking in late July/ early August.

Two further enjoyable Rosses venues are **Cruit Island,** a spit of land a couple of miles (3 km) north of Burtonport with fine beaches and bird-haunted reed beds, and far-famed **Leo's Tavern** (leostavern.com), at Meenaleck

near Crolly in the north of the region. The owners' children are fine musicians—most perform under the name of Clannad. Their famous sister, Enya, is queen of ambient Celtic lullabies.

North again from the Rosses is **Gweedore,** where sandy coasts harden to the red cliffs of **Bloody Foreland.** Inland stands bulky **Tievealehid,** 1,413 feet (430 m) tall. This is lonely country of twisty lanes on hillsides yellow with gorse (purple with heather in season), with marvelous sea views from Bloody Foreland—notably the low block of **Tory Island** (see p. 229), some 7 miles (11 km) to the north. **Meenlaragh,** 5 miles (8 km) east of the Foreland, is the port of embarkation for the island.

Derryveagh Mountains

Southeast of these peninsulas rise the Derryveagh Mountains, whose highest peak, **Errigal** (see pp. 224–225), is the highest mountain in Donegal, at 2,466 feet (751 m). A series of glens runs through the mountains, some with beautiful long lakes such as **Lough Beagh** and **Gartan Lough.** Overlooking the west shore of Gartan Lough, a cross marks the place of St. Columba's birth in 521 (signposted from the road).

A collapsed Bronze Age tomb lies nearby, its capstone covered in copper coins slipped into the cupmarks gouged into the stone. This is the **Flagstone of Loneliness,** where emigrants would come to lie in penance before setting out for America. ∎

Dungloe
🗺 205 C5
Visitor Information
✉ Ionaid Temple Crone, Chapel Rd., Dungloe, Co. Donegal
☎ 074/952-2198

Flagstone of Loneliness
🗺 205 D5

WALK: TO THE TOP OF ERRIGAL MOUNTAIN

At 2,466 feet (751 m), Errigal is the highest mountain in Donegal. It may look formidable from down below, but the hike presents no technical difficulty and the 150-mile (240 km) view from the top is reward enough for the long, upward slog.

The reward for your effort is the breathtaking view toward Lough Altan.

As you approach from the northwest, along the R251 (the Bunbeg direction), Errigal Mountain appears at its most formidable, its sharp-peaked cone apparently covered in snow. As you get closer, you see that its dazzling whiteness is not snow but quartzite. Corries (circular hollows) scoop shadowed chasms in its southern flanks, and whitened curtains of scree cover its shoulders. By the time you reach Dunlewy on the shore of Dunlewy Lough, directly under the mountain, you may be thinking that it all looks a bit much for an ordinary walker to tackle.

But take courage! You can get information at **Dunlewy Lakeside Centre** (tel

NOT TO BE MISSED:

Views of Errigal from the north-west • Dunlewy Lakeside Centre • Summit path • Glorious views from the "far" summit

074/953-1699, dunleweycentre.com, closed Nov.–March) or take part in a guided tour arranged by Walking Ireland (tel 086/605-9220, walking ireland.ie). The staff there will direct you the 3 miles (5 km) along the road to the start of the climb and tell you, "Sure, there's nothing to it."

You will find, however, that there is quite a lot of upward effort to it. This is not a hike to attempt if you are unfit, nor when low cloud, mist, or rain is obscuring the peak. Yet, in normal conditions, it's a climb that anyone who is reasonably fit and wearing a good pair of ankle-supporting boots can manage.

From the **pull-off and "walking man" sign** on the R251, the track is obvious, rising steadily up the long southeast shoulder of the mountain. In clear weather you cannot mistake the way.

At first you climb among grass and heather; then, as you get higher up the mountain, rough scree of slippery stone shards and boulders take over. Now you are into the quartzite zone—in sunshine you may see these upper slopes of the mountain sparkle with a million diamond winks of light. Near the top, the stones become more fractured and slablike, and the path weaves around and over shelves and outcrops of bare quartzite as it steepens and zigzags.

The ridge curves around to the right above and ahead of you, with antlike figures moving slowly along it. The first **summit** is reached, and then the trick of Errigal becomes clear—there is a second, narrower peak beyond,

connected to the first peak by a short ridge only 2 feet (0.6 m) wide in places. Vertigo sufferers could have difficulty here, since the slopes descend sharply on the right side.

It's worth attaining at least the second (lower) peak, though, for the 360-degree view. This is a stunning prospect, with a foreground of scree dropping 2,000 feet (608 m) to lakes (Altan to the right, Dunlewy and Nacung to the left) and a magnificent far-flung backdrop of mountains and coasts. These generally extend to about 50 miles (80 km) and, in exceptionally clear weather, might be three times that—150 miles (240 km) from the Connemara Mountains in the south-west to Antrim and even across to Scotland in the northwest.

Return to the pull-off by the same path.

▲ See also area map p. 205 C5

➤ "Walking man" sign in a pull-off on the R251, 3 miles (5 km) east of Dunlewy

🕒 Allow 2.5–3 hours round-trip, depending on fitness

↔ 1.5 miles (2.5 km) each way and about 1,750 feet (530 m) of ascent

➤ "Walking man" sign

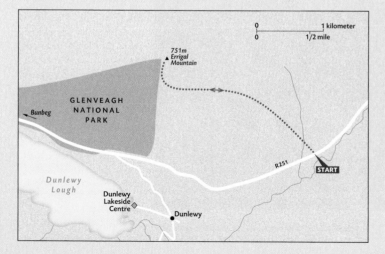

INISHOWEN & THE NORTHEAST PENINSULAS

The northeast of Donegal is a wonderfully wild region of bog, heather, and rocky slopes, cut into tatters by the sea. It's worth taking the time to skirt these coasts at leisure, savoring the loneliness, the seabirds, and the untamed scenery.

The Northeast Peninsulas

Three peninsulas of very different character lead east to Donegal's largest and least visited peninsula, Inishowen. The most westerly of these smaller three is the **Horn Head Peninsula.** At **Dunfanaghy,** a smart plantation

Rugged pinnacles of rock mark the northernmost point of Ireland—Malin Head—at the top of the Inishowen Peninsula.

village, the former workhouse, built in 1845 at the start of the famine, has been reopened as a museum. Called the **Dunfanaghy Workhouse Heritage Centre,** it tells the story of the famine and demonstrates the grimness of workhouse life. To the north, the peninsula bulges out to a mountainous tip where the 600-foot (180 m) cliffs of Horn Head plunge to the sea, their ledges lined with guillemots and puffins.

Eastward is **Rosguill,** less dramatic but even more beautiful, with an 8-mile (13 km) Atlantic Drive that corkscrews up steep lanes to superb coast views.

East again lies **Fanad,** a fractured mass of land split almost in two by the narrow and tortuous inlet of Mulroy Bay. This is a flatter peninsula of lovely beaches—the best at **Ballymacstocker Bay,** on the east or Lough Swilly side.

Rathmullan, farther south, has a Blue Flag beach. On September 14, 1607, this was the embarkation point for the Flight of the Earls, when Hugh O'Neill, Rory O'Donnell, and Cuchonnacht Maguire, Ulster chiefs who could not accept British crown rule, sailed into exile on the Continent.

Inishowen

Most easterly of all Donegal's peninsulas, and also the largest

Carrickabraghy Castle

The story of Carrickabraghy Castle could stand for so many of the ruined castles a visitor sees all over Ireland, strongholds built in the turbulent 15th and 16th centuries when local lordlings fought and feared each other and the invading English with almost equal intensity.

Such fortresses quickly became superfluous once the rule of English law had become established. When Phelemy Brasleigh O'Doherty built Carrickabraghy in Tudor times it boasted seven towers, a hugely strong *bawn* or fortified courtyard, and a sturdy keep. O'Doherty was pro-English and needed the stout castle to preserve himself and his followers. But once the dust had settled and the English and Scots settlers had the upper hand, the castle on the Inishowen headland became redundant. Within half a century it stood empty and abandoned, never to be reoccupied.

and most northerly, is the great diamond-shaped mass of **Inishowen.** From a southern neck near Londonderry city only 8 miles (13 km) wide, the head of Inishowen broadens to three times that width before narrowing again toward its tip at Malin Head.

Inland, Inishowen features barren uplands above fertile valleys and long seacoasts—especially to the southeast, where a string of resorts faces Lough Foyle. Few visitors trouble to explore the beautiful, if bleak, northern and western parts, but the peninsula is worth a day of back-road motoring.

Up at **Malin Head** there's not much to see except an old signaling tower and a fine vista. Most visitors come here to stand on Ireland's most northerly point and, strangely, look south into Northern Ireland.

Both coasts of Inishowen make enjoyable drives, detouring often onto the little country lanes that bring you near the sea. The western or Lough Swilly coast is the more dramatic, with three wonderful beaches in its northern section:

White Strand Bay, near Malin Head; **Pollan Bay** on the dune-covered Doagh Isle Peninsula; and the estuary of **Trawbreaga Bay** near Malin village. Doagh Isle also offers the multicolored stonework of 16th-century **Carrickabraghy Castle** (see sidebar), a dolefully beautiful ruin, on its northwest tip. A mountainous coast runs south down to **Inch Island** and its bird-haunted mudflats.

The greatest archaeological treasure of Inishowen is undoubtedly the cashel or circular stone fort of **Grianan of Aileach,** set commandingly on an 800-foot (245 m) hill northwest of Londonderry. Dr. Walter Bernard reconstructed it in the 1870s, restoring it to how it must have looked when built around 1700 B.C.—a mighty ring fortress, rising in three tiers to a narrow rampart 18 feet (5 m) tall. The O'Neill chiefs of Ulster made it their stronghold from the 5th to the 12th centuries, and St. Patrick preached here in 450. From the wall-top rampart, the views extend across Londonderry city and over Lough Foyle and Lough Swilly. ∎

Inishowen & the Northeast Peninsulas

🗺 205 C5–E6

Visitor Information

✉ Blaney Rd., Letterkenny, Co. Donegal

☎ 074/912-1160

Dunfanaghy Workhouse Heritage Centre

✉ Dunfanaghy, Co. Donegal

☎ 074/913-6540

🕐 Closed weekends, Dec.–April

💲 $$

ARAN ISLAND & TORY ISLAND

Donegal's two main inhabited islands, Aran and Tory, differ tremendously. Each has accommodations, or you can visit on day trips—although in the case of the more remote Tory, be prepared for an overnight stay due to a sudden worsening in the weather. You should not leave Donegal without experiencing one or other of these idiosyncratic outposts.

The hut circles, defence ditch, and rampart of Balor's Fort, Tory Island, are visible from the air.

Aran Island

🗺 205 B5

🚢 20 minutes from Burtonport by Arranmore Island Ferry Service (arranmoreferry.com)

☎ 074/954-2233

💲 $$

arainnmhor.com

Aran Island

Aran (locally called Arranmore to avoid confusion with the Aran Islands in County Galway; see pp. 178–179) lies a couple of miles (3 km) west of Burtonport in the Rosses area (see pp. 222–223). Close to 1,000 people live on this hilly island that rises to 750 feet (228 m) in the center and measures about 3 miles (5 km) wide by 4 miles (6 km) long. August is a good time to visit—the island's festival sees everyone letting their hair down.

But with half a dozen pubs, you are able to find music and conversation anytime in the island's village of **Leabgarrow.**

A long morning or afternoon would suffice for a walk around the rugged coast. Roads and *boreens* (narrow lanes) climb from the low-lying eastern shore into the wild, boggy interior, but with a good pair of boots you can strike across the heather, rock, and rough grass. There's tremendous bird activity around **Green Island,** off the southwest tip of the island.

Tory Island

Aran is conveniently close to the mainland and sees a fair number of visitors, but you have to be more adventurous—and a better sailor—for Tory Island, 7 miles (11 km) off the northern coast of Bloody Foreland. In contrast to Aran, Tory lies low, a slim bar measuring approximately 2.5 miles (4 km) long and less than a mile (1.6 km) wide. Wind is a constant factor, whipping up the intervening seas, often driving salt-laden spray across the island. Anything that is grown here has to be protected in little stone-walled fields. Fishing is good enough, but hazardous. For the tiny Irish-speaking community, times have always been tough—they were nearly evacuated during a particularly bad winter in the 1970s. It took a tremendous publicity campaign by the priest of Tory to gain a sheltered harbor and regular ferry service for the island, along with proper sanitation and electricity.

Tourism has supplied a lifeline for Tory Island, which has archaeological treasures such as the ancient **Tau Cross** (now displayed at the pier in West Town, Tory's main village), and visitors enjoy the strong flavor of the life of this proudly independent island that has been (and still is) ruled by its own king since St. Columba first appointed a Tory islander in the sixth century.

Craic can be mighty in the pubs, especially during the festival in July, but the islanders do not put on an act for the visitors—they are as frank and outspoken about the difficulties of island life as they are willing to pass on Tory Island legends and beliefs. The island was the lair of the ferocious Fomorian brigands, who attacked the mainland in the mythical era under their chief Balor of the Evil Eye, whose single eye was in the back of his head.

Painting for pleasure was almost unknown on Tory Island until 1968, when local fisherman James Dixon chanced upon English artist Derek Hill painting a Tory landscape and suggested that he could do a better job. He proved his point, and other islanders became interested, until a Tory Island school of naïve art was flourishing. Examples are on view (and for sale) in the **James Dixon Gallery,** in the late fisherman-painter's former home. ∎

Tory Island

- 📍 205 C6
- 🚢 1–2 hours from Bunbeg, depending on weather
- ☎ 074/913-5502
- 🚢 45 minutes– 1 hour from Magheroarty by Turasmara Teo (toryferry.com)
- ☎ 087/199-3710
- 💲 $$$

oileanthorai.com

James Dixon Gallery

- ✉ Near the school, Tory Island
- 🕐 Closed mid-Sept.–May

Tory Islanders

Two factors allow the population of Tory Island to stay put in such a tough, windy, salt-sprayed, and bare environment: the commitment of successive Irish governments, and hence Irish taxpayers, to underwrite the island economy, and the grit and determination of the islanders themselves. Rather than their ways of livelihood or dress, it is their warmth and hospitality in the face of adverse circumstances that make the Tory Islanders an iconic example of a traditional, Irish-speaking, rural community.

COUNTY LEITRIM

Leitrim is certainly the most overlooked and undervisited county in the west of Ireland. It has no glamour, but an understated charm well repays a day or two, especially if you are fond of fishing, boating, or hill walking.

County Leitrim

🗺 205 C2

Visitor Information

✉ Old Barrel Store, Carrick-on-Shannon, Co. Leitrim

☎ 071/962-0170

🕐 Seasonal

leitrimtourism.com

Leitrim lies squeezed by Donegal and Fermanagh on the northeast, Cavan on the east, Longford to the south, and Roscommon and Sligo to the west. Its coastline is a strip only 3 miles (5 km) wide, which explains why it is not more popular with visitors. But only a few miles inland rise the beautiful heartlands of the **Dartry Mountains,** book-ended by beautiful lakes. **Lough Melvin,** on the Fermanagh border, has a spatter of islands

and some fine hill slopes on the south.

County Sligo to the southwest has the lion's share of **Lough Gill,** but Leitrim's eastern quarter of the lake boasts **Parke's Castle,** a handsome fortified house with a turreted *bawn* (tower) built in 1609 for Capt. Robert Parke on a lakeside knoll. The castle was abandoned by the Parke Family in 1691 and stood in ruins until the mid-20th century. Now it has been restored using Irish oak for the roofs—held together with wooden dowels in the traditional manner.

Dromahair

Just to the south of the lake head is the village of Dromahair, scene of an abduction (or perhaps seduction and elopement) that dramatically changed Irish history. The 17th-century **Old Hall** stands on the site of Breffni Castle, a 12th-century stronghold of Tiernan O'Rourke, whose wife, Dervorgilla, made off with O'Rourke's bitter rival, Dermot MacMurrough, King of Leinster. In 1166, O'Rourke and his ally, King Rory O'Connor, drove MacMurrough out of Ireland. But it was a Pyrrhic victory. MacMurrough rallied support from Richard "Strongbow" de Clare, Earl of Pembroke, with the backing of King Henry II

■ Parke's Castle stands sentinel on the shores of Lough Gill.

INSIDER TIP:

For a unique Lough Allen experience, Lough Allen Adventure (tel 087/275-6495) offers kayaking, windsurfing, and more.

—STEPHANIE ROBICHAUX
*National Geographic
contributor*

of England. Strongbow landed in Ireland in 1169, obtaining a foothold for the Anglo-Normans that eventually became an islandwide conquest.

The Leitrim Way

Northeast of Dromahair is **Manorhamilton.** A well-marked long-distance footpath, the **Leitrim Way,** reaches Manorhamilton at the end of a 30-mile (48 km) northward course from Drumshanbo. Walking the path *(Irish Ordnance Survey 1:50,000 sheet No. 26)* is the best way to get a feeling for this rolling countryside, especially as the first section runs up the east bank of **Lough Allen.**

On emerging at the foot of the lough some 8 miles (13 km) south, the Leitrim Way winds past the neat village of **Drumshanbo** to reach modest **Leitrim town** at the start of the **Shannon-Erne Waterway.** Reopened in 1994 after 125 years of dereliction, this meandering 40-mile (65 km) waterway provides the final link in a chain of lakes and rivers that can be navigated from Belleek (see pp. 318–319), on Lough Erne in County Fermanagh, all

the way south to Limerick and the Shannon Estuary, a total distance of 239 miles (382 km).

The canal began life as the Ballyconnell and Ballinamore Canal in 1860, but it soon fell victim to competition by the Sligo, Leitrim, & Northern Counties Railway (SLNCR, known locally as the Slow, Late, and Never Completely Reliable). It winds eastward to Upper Lough Erne through attractive green countryside of rounded drumlin hills, lakes, and small farms—the setting for many novels and short stories by Leitrim's master storyteller, John McGahern.

This is prime fishing country, with plenty of well-stocked rivers and lakes. It's boating country, too, especially downriver at **Carrick-on-Shannon.** Here you can rent boats for cruising or angling, or sit back and enjoy a river cruise with humorous local commentary. ∎

Parke's Castle

✉ Dromahair, Lough Gill, near Sligo, Co. Leitrim

☎ 071/916-4149

🕐 Closed Nov.–mid-April

💲 $

heritageireland.ie

EXPERIENCE:
Take to Leitrim's Waters

Leitrim's pride is its waterways—lakes, rivers, and the mighty Shannon-Erne Waterway. For cruising, **Ballinamore** is a good center—it's a sizable place with all the facilities you'll need *(locaboat.com, cruiseireland.com).* The same goes for **Carrick-on-Shannon,** the acknowledged Shannon-Erne cruising center *(cruise-ireland.com/routes/carrick-on-shannon).* Information on fishing can be found at *fishinginireland.info*—here you'll find details of locations from rivers to lakes, which species you can expect, fishing-friendly accommodations, permits, and more.

More Places to Visit in Northwest Ireland

Ballysadare

At Ballysadare (Baile Easa Daire, the "town of the waterfall of the oak tree"), the Ballysadare River runs through town over a series of weirs, with the remains of mills standing along its banks. A jungly graveyard surrounds the shell of a medieval church on the site of a seventh-century monastery. W. B. Yeats rode and rambled in the fields around here during his boyhood holidays: His Pollexfen relations owned the Ballysadare mills.
🗺 205 B2 ✉ Junction of the N59 (Ballina) & N4 (Boyle) roads, 5 miles (8 km) S of Sligo town, Co. Sligo **Sligo Visitor Information** ☎ 071/916-1201

Doon Well & Rock of Doon

Bushes at the approach to Doon Well are laden with rags, pairs of spectacles, and tiny holy statues, a clear message that the purported healing water of this famous well still draws large numbers of pilgrims. Steps lead from the parking lot to Carraig a' Duin, the Rock of Doon, its summit imprinted with the shape of a human foot. From the 13th century to the Flight of the Earls in 1607, each O'Donnell King of Tyrconnell was crowned here. 🗺 205 D5 ✉ Signposted off the N56 bet. Kilmacrenan & Termon, 9 miles (14 km) N of Letterkenny, Co. Donegal **Letterkenny Visitor Information** ☎ 074/912-1160

Glebe House & Gallery

Built as a Regency-style rectory in 1828 and bought by English artist Derek Hill in 1953, Glebe House has an Arts and Crafts feel, decorated with William Morris wallpaper and the colorful naïve paintings of Tory Islanders, including James Dixon (see p. 229). The **Gallery,** opened in 1982, displays work by Picasso and Augustus John, as well as Irish artists such as Jack Yeats (see pp. 208–209). *glebegallery.ie* 🗺 205 D5 ✉ Churchill, Gartan Lough, on the R251, 10 miles (16 km) NW of Letterkenny (R250, R251), Co. Donegal ☎ 074/913-7071 🕐 Closed Nov.–late May & Fri. in June, Sept. & Oct. 💲 House: $ *(gallery: free admission)*

Glenveagh National Park

Based around Lough Beagh, Glenveagh National Park covers 23,887 acres (9,650 ha) of hilly country. At the heart of the park is **Glenveagh Castle,** built of granite in Scottish baronial style by John George Adair, who notoriously evicted 244 tenants in the harsh winter of 1861 so that he could incorporate their land. His wife, Cornelia, laid out the rhododendron gardens and introduced the red deer that have become Ireland's largest herd. *glenveaghnationalpark.ie* 🗺 205 C5–D5 ✉ Entrance on the R251, 10 miles (16 km) E of Dunlewy & Errigal Mountain, Co. Donegal **Glenveagh Visitor Information** ☎ 076/100-2537 🕐 Open year-round

Inch Wildfowl Reserve

Inch Wildfowl Reserve is one of Ireland's premier bird-watching sites. When the Londonderry & Lough Swilly Railway Company built twin embankments from the mainland out to tiny Inch Island in the 1850s, they enclosed an area of lagoon, marsh, wetlands, and grasslands that has become a wildfowl reserve of international importance. Walk the paths with a pair of binoculars and enjoy the sight and sound of Greenland whitefront and greylag geese, whooper swans and nesting gulls, ducks and grebes, wading birds, huge rafts of scaup and coot—not to mention brilliant blue-and-orange kingfishers, and a good population of otters. *inchwildfowlreserve.ie* 🗺 205 E5 ✉ Inch, Burt, Co. Donegal ☎ 074/937-4218, 🕐 Open year-round

The least well known part of Ireland, with farms, lakes and bogs, and medieval abbeys—a secret waiting to be discovered

CENTRAL IRELAND

 Faith and art at Monasterboice

CENTRAL IRELAND

The Midlands inspire little of the heightened expectation that travelers feel when they see the grand mountains and coasts of the west. But given the chance, the round drumlin hills, secretive lakes, and great sullen boglands of the Irish heartland—where the pace of life is easy and unruffled—will work their magic on you.

From the air, central Ireland appears a vast green flatland, patched brown with bogs and winking with lakes. On the ground, it gives the impression of endless miles of farm country, its lakes well hidden, its bogs sterile and barren. This uncrowded land, owing as much to water as to earth, is just the place for country pursuits—canoeing along the River Shannon, angling for pike in the Cavan lakes, tramping the Slieve Bloom Mountains, riding a horse along byways and green lanes, cruising up the Grand Canal in a narrow boat.

The nine counties of the central region fall loosely into three groups. Monaghan and Cavan are neighbors on the borders with Northern Ireland. Like Donegal, they were part of ancient Ulster and still have a plantation feel to their neat, well-laid-out towns. They are drumlin counties, pimpled with small hills and trenched with hundreds of valleys.

The five most central counties— Roscommon, Longford, Westmeath, Offaly, and Laois—are dairying regions with old-fashioned market towns and hedged, gently rolling landscapes. The River Shannon flows on the borders of all but Laois, draining immense boglands that have recently begun to be conserved after decades of exploitation. Clonmacnoise, Fore and Boyle Abbeys, Strokestown Park House, and Birr Castle are prime attractions.

Meath and Louth, coastal counties north of Dublin, are rich in historical sites, from the remarkable Stone Age necropolis at Brú na Bóinne to Monasterboice and the abbeys at Bective and Mellifont. ∎

NOT TO BE MISSED:

0 — 30 kilometers
0 — 15 miles

NORTHERN IRELAND
p. 275

◁6

NORTHERN IRELAND
p. 275

Cuilcagh
Mountains

N87

Monaghan

N54

Clones

M O N A G H A N

Ballyconnell

Belturbet

Ballybay

Castleblayney

Slieve
Foye Carlingford
R173 Cooley
Peninsula

Shannon-Erne
Waterway

N3

Redhills
Equestrian Centre

Butlers Bridge

R180

Inishkeen

N53

Lough
Oughter

KILLYKEEN
FOREST PARK

Cavan

Carrickmacross

N2

Dundalk

Dundalk
Bay

Crossdoney

R165

Kingscourt

C A V A N

L O U T H

Irish

R198

Erne

N55

Ballyjamesduff

Virginia

Lough
Sheelin

Lough
Ramor

Ardee

R166

Dunleer

M1

Sea

N4

Granard

R154

N3

N52

Monasterboice

Drogheda

Longford

N63

Oldcastle

Seven
Wonders
of Fore

Loughcrew
Passage Graves

Kells

Blackwater

Mellifont Abbey

Knowth

Slane
Castle

Newgrange

Dowth

Drogheda

Brú na Bóinne
Visitor Centre

N4

Fore

Fore
Abbey

Lough
Lene

Lough
Derravaragh

Inny

R57

Navan

M E A T H

N2

N G F O R D

Lough
Owel

N52

Boyne

Trim

Hill of Tara

DUBLIN
p. 47

◁3

Royal Canal

R392

N55

R390

Lough
Ennell

Mullingar

N6

N4

R125

N3

W E S T M E A T H

M6

N6

Kilbeggan

M6

R400

M4

M6

N80

Brosna

Grand Canal

Edenderry

R402

◁E ◁F

Tullamore

O F F A L Y

EAST IRELAND
p. 87

N62

Lough Boora
Parklands

N52

Rosenallis

R420

R422

Mountmellick

Barrow

N7

◁2

Birr
Castle

R423

Emo
Court

N80

R421

Slieve Bloom Mountains

Portlaoise

M7

Rock of
Dunamase

N62

Nore

L A O I S

N7

Abbeyleix

N78

N80

N8

◁1

△C △D

Area of map detail

Belfast

Dublin

STROKESTOWN PARK HOUSE & THE IRISH NATIONAL FAMINE MUSEUM

Unlike almost every other Ascendancy house in Ireland, Strokestown Park House retains the effects accumulated by one family over 300 years. The Irish National Famine Museum explores the disaster that befell rural Ireland in the 1840s. After seeing the style in which a Big House family lived, the high-handed attitudes of so many landlords in the time of the Great Famine fall into perspective.

When they extended Strokestown Park House in the 1730s, the Mahon family chose severely classical architecture.

Strokestown Park House & the Irish National Famine Museum

🗺 234 B4

✉ Strokestown, Co. Roscommon

☎ 071/963-3013

💲 $$ (house), $$ (garden), $$ (museum)

strokestownpark.ie

Strokestown Park House

The last of the Pakenham-Mahon family to live at Strokestown was Olive, born here in 1894—she sold it in 1978 to local garage owner Jim Callery, whose company still owns and runs the estate. Looking to buy 5 acres (2 ha) of land to park his fleet of trucks, Callery actually purchased the entire estate!

The **drawing room** where Olive and her husband ended up living, eating, and sleeping in the 1970s, selling pictures off the walls in order to keep solvent, contains family photos that include one of Olive's mother, her waist corseted to an incredible 16 inches (40 cm).

The **library** has more photos, including a poignant one of Olive's first husband, Edward Stafford-King-Harman—he was killed during World War I only four months after their marriage, while Olive was carrying their child. To lighten the mood, the guide sets the windup gramophone to play a 78-rpm record of Margaret Burke-Sheridan singing "Galway Bay" in the fruitiest of operatic voices.

Upstairs you view the **Lady's and Gentleman's bedrooms,** with their four-poster beds; the children's **schoolroom,** where 1930s copybooks lie on their desks; and a wonderful **playroom** full of evocative old toys, dress-up clothes, and a dolls' tea party.

The **kitchen** downstairs lay forgotten behind false walls until Callery rediscovered it after he had bought the house, complete with a huge black range and an 18th-century gallery from which the lady of the house could inspect the domestics at work without having to come into contact with them.

INSIDER TIP:

Set aside time to explore Strokestown's beautiful gardens, complete with a lily pond, rose garden, croquet lawn, and amazing perennial border.

—LARRY PORGES
National Geographic
Travel Books editor

Irish National Famine Museum

How the families of the domestic servants suffered during the Great Famine of 1845–1849 (see pp. 28–29) is vividly told in the Irish National Famine Museum, housed in the old stable block. Original Strokestown documents and well-mounted reproductions of cartoons and lithographs lead you through the story of what happened after a fungus reduced the Irish potato crop to black slime.

The English government—and the English in general—thought of the Irish poor as "indolent, idle, inclined to do evil, and beyond the pale of civilization." Relief was ineffective, insufficient, and callously withdrawn when it was most needed. Dependent entirely on the potato, the peasants starved. Responsibility for helping the destitute people was thrown on landlords and rentpayers who were unwilling or unable to play their part. Evictions for nonpayment of rent were widespread, enforced emigration commonplace.

At Strokestown, Maj. Denis Mahon, in the process of evicting two-thirds of his tenants (about 5,000 people), was shot dead in 1847, one of seven landlords or agents murdered that year. Anguish and resentment followed the poor and rode with them on the disease-ridden emigration ships.

Blaming the landlords alone is too simplistic. Major Mahon received little government help, had no resources to help those dependent on him, and had to either watch them starve or pay for them to emigrate. More culpable were English politicians, who made such statements as: "The great evil with which we have to contend is not the physical evil of famine, but the moral evil of the selfish, perverse and turbulent character of the people." ■

Potato Fungus

Phytophthora infestans is a fungus that attacks both leaves and tubers of the potato. White growths seen around infected leaves are the tubes that carry the fungus spores, which spread most readily in typically Irish conditions of gentle wind and warm misty rain. In such conditions, one diseased plant can produce several million spores, attacking neighboring plants. The leaves wither; the potatoes blacken and rot. The fungus can be controlled with copper sulfate, but this fact was unknown in the 1840s.

BOYLE ABBEY

Boyle Abbey, near County Roscommon's border with County Sligo, is a rare survival in Ireland—a remarkably complete, very early Cistercian monastery. Equally remarkable is the fact that Boyle owes its survival to the military. Instead of following its usual pattern of destroying what it found, the military took over the buildings in the 17th century and converted them into a barracks.

■ Few monastic sites survived Ireland's bloody wars and repressions as unscathed as Boyle Abbey.

Boyle Abbey

🗺 234 B5

✉ Boyle,
   Co. Roscommon

☎ 071/966-2604

🕐 Closed mid-
   Sept.–Easter

💲 $

heritageireland.ie

History of Boyle Abbey

Monks from Mellifont Abbey (see p. 274) came to Boyle in 1148 looking for a place to build a new abbey and fired with enthusiasm for a spartan but charitable way of life. Six years earlier, a group of them had returned to Ireland fresh from a visit to France, where they had been inspired by the discipline and self-denial of the monks at St. Bernard's monastery. After founding the Cistercian abbey of Mellifont, the monks were keen to spread their influence.

The MacDermot clan, sensing an opportunity to gain prestige, gave the monks 1,000 acres (400 ha) of land on which to build

their abbey and community at Boyle.

At the height of its prosperity, from the 13th to 15th centuries, Boyle Abbey ruled vast tracts of land and supported a community of more than 400, but, by the time of its dissolution in the mid-16th century, there was only a handful of monks in a range of decayed buildings. Queen Elizabeth I granted the monastic lands to the Cusack family, and they allowed the monks to linger on in the abbey. Then, in 1603, the new Stuart king of England, James I, gave the estate to a Staffordshire adventurer, John King. He turned the abbey into a garrisoned fortress known as Boyle Castle, and it remained in use as a military barracks for a century and a half. In 1788, the Connaught Rangers—a rough lot—moved on, and the old buildings began a period of decay that was not arrested until the 20th century.

Touring the Abbey

Imagination and a sense of history are kindled from the outset as you walk into the site through the arch of the **gate-house,** notched by the sword cuts of the idle soldiery. The inner gate jambs are incised with graffiti cut by bored guards. In the gatehouse, an exhibit sets the scene around a scale model of the abbey in its heyday. In monastic times, the gatehouse would have contained a 24-hour guard and quarters for unexpected guests.

Cloister Garth: Stepping through the archway, you come into the wide, grassy cloister garth, or garden, with low walls. Around these rises the outer wall of the abbey complex, patched roughly where it was broken through to create military gateways.

Daily Life in the Abbey: You will find **kitchens** with enormous fireplaces to the south. The cooking, cleaning, and general spadework of the abbey was done by a large community of laypersons—St. Benedict's original decree that monks attend eight services of prayer a day while remaining self-sufficient through their own hard work proved impossible to obey.

INSIDER TIP:

Taking a guided tour around the extensive ruins of Boyle Abbey is an atmospheric experience that shouldn't be missed.

—CHRISTOPHER SOMERVILLE
National Geographic author

In the big **refectory** to the southeast, the monks ate in silence (a custom common to most Cistercian abbeys) while edified by readings of scripture from a wall lectern. Between mid-September and Easter, they ate only once a day—and since they rose at 2:30 a.m., those days must have seemed long indeed.

Farther along the east wall were **reading rooms, dormitories** with a calefactory (hot room) to warm them, a **parlor** for occasional conversation, the **chapter house,** and the **abbot's house.**

Abbey Church: A low arch leads into the splendid abbey church—austere Romanesque at the eastern end, more decorative Gothic toward the west.

Capitals become floral and the pillars more elaborate. The westernmost capital of the north wall (which slopes alarmingly outward) has 14 little grimacing men peeping out of foliage—the master mason's team, suggests the guide, caricatured by him as a signing-off gesture on completion of the church's construction. ■

COUNTY CAVAN

If you like lakes, you'll love County Cavan. The little border country is spattered with them so thickly that a Cavan view without a slip of water in it soon feels strange. Bring your fishing rods, and you could do worse than to pack your walking boots, too. Out to the west sticks a long thin panhandle separating Leitrim from Fermanagh, where the Iron Mountains meld into the Cuilcagh range and the land rises and becomes beautifully wild, ideal for hill tramping.

Retreating glaciers formed the hillocks and lakebeds so characteristic of County Cavan.

Cavan Town

🗺 235 D5

Visitor Information

✉ 1 Farnham St., Cavan, Co. Cavan

☎ 049/433-1942

🕐 Seasonal

thisiscavan.ie

Cavan County Museum

✉ Virginia Rd., Ballyjamesduff, Co. Cavan

☎ 049/433-1942

🕐 Closed Sun.-Mon.

cavanmuseum.ie

The trim little county town of **Cavan** is not particularly visitor-oriented but is pleasant enough as a base for exploring the lakes. Or you could try the villages of **Butlers Bridge** and **Belturbet,** a little nearer to the lakes.

Upper Lough Erne wriggles down from Fermanagh and breaks up into hundreds of thin, winding watercourses. These lakes, lakelets, and threads of river make islands and peninsulas of the green, well-wooded land between Belturbet, near the border, and the point near Crossdoney where the River Erne emerges to flow on south.

Ballyjamesduff

You can make a stop in the village of Ballyjamesduff to visit the **Cavan County Museum,** which holds artifacts dating from the Stone Age on, a collection of period costumes, and farming implements and has a section dedicated to Gaelic sports.

Killykeen Forest Park

Driving and walking here is puzzling at first, with innumerable signs pointing to different lakes. Look for brown signs to **Lough Oughter—** leading to a meandering circuit through brackeny back lanes with Killykeen Forest Park at its hub. The Cavan tourist office has information about the park and to the best fishing locations (excellent at Belturbet and Butlers Bridge). Or follow one of the marked trails through the woods of the park. The country lanes hereabouts are mainly *boreens*—grassy tracks that make for fine strolling.

Ballyconnell

Farther west, at Ballyconnell, you reach the Ballyconnell and Ballinamore Canal, also called the **Shannon-Erne Waterway.** It starts at Leitrim town and runs to the south shore of Upper Lough Erne at Foalies Bridge. The 1994 reopening of this 36-mile (60 km) link between the Erne and Shannon river and lake systems made the village of Ballyconnell into a lively boating hub. Rent a

---

INSIDER TIP:

Cavan is a fisherman's heaven. But you'll need a license. (See margin note at right.)

—JUSTIN KAVANAGH
National Geographic Travel Books editor

---

boat in Ballyconnell to cruise the waterway to Ballinamore in County Leitrim.

The Cuilcagh Mountains

West of Ballyconnell, the Cuilcagh Mountains dominate the bleak, wild landscape. They climb in a series of flattish peaks to the summit of the range on Cuilcagh itself at 2,180 feet (663 m). The summit is best climbed along the Ulster Way from Florence Court Forest Park in Fermanagh—about 10 miles (16 km) round-trip with a climb of about 1,350 feet (410 m). ∎

FISHING PERMITS:
Licenses are available from local visitor information offices and fishing shops. For more information contact North West Tourism *(tel 071/916-1201, irelandnorthwest.ie)* or the Northern Regional Fisheries Board *(tel 071/985-1435 or 049/433-7174, fisheriesireland.ie)*.

EXPERIENCE: Walking the Cavan Way

The 14-mile-long (22.5 km) **Cavan Way** *(irishtrails.ie)* starts in Blacklion on the border with Northern Ireland and runs south through flowery limestone hills to finish in the village of Dowra.

You'll experience many wonderful vistas over the hills, valleys, and lakes of County Cavan. The wide tent shape of Cuilcagh Mountain lies ahead, with the ancient humps of the Ox Mountains far away in the west, while the view opens over Upper and Lower Lough Macnean. Soon you are walking on limestone pavements spattered with orchids and blue milkwort. This is Cavan's Burren region (not to be confused with that of County Clare; see pp. 168–173), partly

covered with a coniferous forest in which the Cavan Way passes several remarkable ancient burial and ritual sites—boulder graves, wedge tombs, ring-marked stones.

South of the forest you reach Legeelan crossroads with its beehive-shaped sweat house, a primitive kill-or-cure sauna for sufferers of agues and pains. The Way crosses marshy fields bright with fragrant orchids, bog myrtle, and rare greater butterfly orchids, to reach the **Shannon Pot,** where Ireland's mighty major river wells from a dimpling pool as dark as copper. It is here that the 230-mile (368 km) river—the longest in the British Isles—has its birth; from here the path follows the infant Shannon down to Dowra.

MONAGHAN TOWN & AROUND

County Monaghan and County Cavan complement each other topographically. Cavan (see pp. 240–241) is full of lakes, and Monaghan is full of hills—little ones, roundish drumlins of rubble and clay dumped by retreating glaciers 10,000 years ago. The hills give the sprawling border country of Monaghan an intimate, enclosed character very different from the open landscapes of the southern midlands or the west.

Monaghan Town

🗺 235 D6

Visitor Information

✉ The Market House, Monaghan, Co. Monaghan

☎ 047/81-122

monaghantourism. com

Monaghan lacemakers need keen eyes and quick fingers.

Monaghan Town

The county town of Monaghan, stone-built and solid, epitomizes the virtues of hard work and respectability. Though County Monaghan has lain in the Republic since 1921, it formed part of the ancient kingdom of Ulster and was planted or colonized by non-Catholic Scottish settlers in the early 17th century. Monaghan shared Ulster's rise to prosperity through the linen trade, reflected in the substantial architecture of the county town with its three squares, great Victorian drinking fountain, and huge **St. Macartan's Cathedral** (constructed 1861–1891), whose 250-foot (76 m) spire dominates the town.

The **Monaghan County Museum** is one of the best of its kind, with an archaeological overview covering 5,000 years. Chief prize is the 14th-century **Cross of Clogher,** a beautifully worked altar crucifix of bronze from the ancient bishopric of Clogher a few miles northwest.

Carrickmacross & Clones

South of Monaghan, the two lacemaking towns of Carrickmacross and Clones still ply their trade, though for the specialist collector market these days. You can see occasional demonstrations of the art in the **Carrickmacross Lace Gallery** on Market Square.

In Clones, it's also worth looking for the weathered but still striking tenth-century **high cross,** relocated on the Diamond from the ruins of St. Tiernach's Monastery on Abbey Street. Panels on the south side show Old

EXPERIENCE: Join in the Festival Fun

Hilton Park (hiltonpark.ie) is a grand country house turned splendid hotel. It's also the site of the **Flat Lake Literary & Arts Festival** (Hilton Park, Clones, Co. Monaghan, hiltonpark.ie/flat-lake-festival), a tremendously fun three-day event that draws tens of thousands of people each year.

Dreamed up by local author Patrick McCabe and Welsh filmmaker Kevin Allen, the relatively new festival mixes poetry readings and music performances with competitions, crazy games such as Catch the Hen and Toss the Sheaf, and art auctions. You'll also find stand-up comedians, poets celebrated and obscure, one-woman shows, history talks, films, and plenty for the kids. As for the music, you can expect everything from the tried and true to romantic lounge lizards and the latest young firebrands. If this is country-house culture, it's been a long strange road here from cucumber sandwiches in the Blue Drawing Room.

Testament scenes, while on the north, New Testament miracles are depicted.

Inishkeen

So to the eastern border of the county and the countryside around Inishkeen—poor farming land, where small farms make the best of the steep drumlin sides and reedy valley bottoms. Ireland's greatest poet of the mid-20th century, Patrick Kavanagh (1904–1967), celebrated, excoriated, and revealed this hedged-in landscape in his wonderful poems, colorful or black according to mood. Kavanagh was a small-time farmer around Inishkeen until he left in his early thirties to live as a writer in London and Dublin. Alcohol and cancer took hold of him before he died.

Inishkeen was always the spur to his talent, from lyrical works, such as the autobiographical *The Green Fool* (1938), to bitterly realistic poems such as "Stony Grey Soil" (1940), in which he writes of how peasant life and work sapped his joy and restricted his range.

In Inishkeen, **Kavanagh's birthplace** (not open to the public) is signed off the road—a dour gray house on a ridge. The old church in the village contains the excellent **Patrick Kavanagh Rural and Literary Resource Centre,** which features a fascinating exhibition about the poet and his work. Kavanagh's grave lies outside, marked with a simple wooden cross and the words: "And pray for him who walked apart on the hills, loving life's miracles."

Just past the modern church, on the road to Carrickmacross from Inishkeen, a brown sign marked "My Black Shanco" indicates a track that winds for a mile (1.6 km) toward Kavanagh's farm of **Shancoduff,** mentioned in many of his poems. "The sleety winds fondle the rushy beards of Shancoduff," he wrote in "Shancoduff," and here you can walk the lane and the rushy fields that the poet loathed and loved. ∎

Monaghan County Museum
⊠ Hill St., Monaghan
☎ 047/82-928
🕐 Closed Sun.

Carrickmacross
🅰 235 E5

Lace Gallery
⊠ Market Sq., Carrickmacross
☎ 042/966-4176
carrickmacrosslace.ie

Inishkeen
🅰 235 E5

Patrick Kavanagh Rural and Literary Resource Centre
⊠ Inishkeen
☎ 042/937-8560
🕐 Closed mid-Dec.– March; Mon., April–Dec.; Sun., Oct.–May

patrickkavanagh country.com

CRUISE: RIVER SHANNON & LOUGH REE FROM ATHLONE

The bustling if not exactly beautiful town of Athlone sits in the center of Ireland, more or less at the midpoint of the Shannon, Ireland's longest river. It makes a great base for exploring the Shannon—southward to the monastic site of Clonmacnoise or northward among the wooded islands of Lough Ree. You can rent your own cruiser or travel onboard one of the excursion boats.

The broad, majestic Shannon sweeps past Athlone on its 230-mile (368 km) journey to the Atlantic.

When you set off south from **Athlone** ❶ *(visitor information, Athlone Castle, St. Peter's Sq., Athlone, tel 090/644-2130, athlonecastle.ie)* for Clonmacnoise, you'll need to take account of Athlone's lock, through which you have to pass before reaching the Shannon. It's best to be first in line, early in the day—otherwise you may have to wait an hour or so for the lock to fill and empty several times. But it's a pleasant place, where freshwater admirals exchange yarns and boats bump companionably together. Once through, just remember to keep the black markers on your left and the red ones on your right.

NOT TO BE MISSED:

Athlone lock & waterfront
• **Clonmacnoise** • **Inchcleraun**
• **Fishing—bring a rod!**

The broad Shannon curves gently through grazing meadows; several of these are left uncut until late in the summer to give shelter to the now very rare corncrake. You probably won't see this unassuming brown bird, but if lucky, you may hear the male's loudly grating repetition

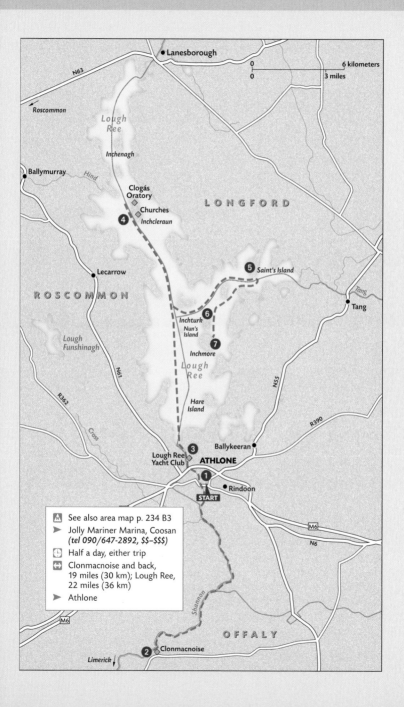

Lanesborough

N63

Roscommon

Lough Ree

Inchenagh

Ballymurray

Hind

Clogás Oratory

4 Churches

Inchcleraun

L O N G F O R D

Lecarrow

R O S C O M M O N

5 *Saint's Island*

Tang

Tang

6 *Inchturk*

Nun's Island

Lough Funshinagh

N61

7

Inchmore

N55

R390

Lough Ree

R362

Cross

Hare Island

Ballykeeran

Lough Ree Yacht Club **3**

ATHLONE

1

Rindoon

START

⛰ See also area map p. 234 B3

➤ Jolly Mariner Marina, Coosan (*tel 090/647-2892, $$–$$$*)

🕐 Half a day, either trip

↔ Clonmacnoise and back, 19 miles (30 km); Lough Ree, 22 miles (36 km)

➤ Athlone

M6

N6

M6

Shannon

O F F A L Y

2 Clonmacnoise

Limerick

6 kilometers

3 miles

of his Latin name, *crex crex*, before the towers of **Clonmacnoise ②** (see pp. 250–251) come in sight. A convenient jetty lies below the monastic site. Allow up to half an hour longer for the return journey to Athlone as you'll be sailing against the current.

Cruising upriver from Athlone, it's only a mile or so (1.6 km) before you pass the **Lough Ree Yacht Club** *(lryc.ie)* **③**, founded as far back as 1770, on your right. Don't forget that for upriver travelers, the black markers are now on

beyond, made to look taller by the flatness of the landscape.

If you wish to land on any of the islands, make sure that your boat has an anchor and a dinghy—complete with oars and oarlocks—attached. Ree is a great fishing lake, and you can take full advantage if you are in a rented craft.

Of the many islands and islets in Lough Ree, the most interesting in terms of its archaeological remains is **Inchcleraun ④**, sometimes known as the **Quaker's Island,** in the northern

One of the most enjoyable pastimes in central Ireland is to explore the many islands of Lough Ree.

your right and the red on your left.

Beyond the yacht club, the waterway broadens out into the great expanse of **Lough Ree** at the heart of the Shannon. It is wise to heed the navigation advice given you at the Jolly Mariner Marina, Coosan, as the lake is shallow and has plenty of rocks and barely submerged reefs. The lough is 16 miles (26 km) long, shaped like a pointy-headed leprechaun with one ragged sleeve extended to the east. Its shore lies flat and is mostly smothered with trees; low hills rise

part of the lake. If you want to explore, you'll need to anchor near the red lake-navigation marker No. 7 and row to the bouldery island waterline to scramble ashore. On haphazardly grazed grass in a smother of trees you'll find the tiny, ancient **Teampull Diarmuid Church,** the 13th-century **Teampull Mor** ("big church"), with its big gable and low door with a rugged lintel, and the little 12th-century **Chancel Church** and **Church of the Dead** near the shore. Toward the higher center of the island stands the dignified 12th-century **Clogás Oratory,** with its square bell tower.

Harder to find is the ruin of **Fairbrother's House**—Fairbrother was the Quaker who lived on Inchcleraun early in the 19th century. While he was building the cottage, so stories say, he took the cornerstones from the Clogás Oratory to use in his work. St. Diarmuid, sixth-century founder of the island's monastery, saw what was going on from his seat in heaven and was not amused. The saint "smote the Quaker's horse with the bolt of his holy revenge, which caused it to run furiously, untamedly, terribly, outrageously, irresistibly mad." Then all the beasts on the island ran crazy and were only restored to sanity when the Quaker vowed to touch no more of the holy stones.

It was only natural for reclusive early Christian hermits to choose the islands of Lough Ree as their prayerful refuges. There are remains of churches on **Saint's Island** ❺ (in fact the tip of a peninsula) and on **Nun's Island,** both now used as pasture.

Early in the 20th century, most of the islands supported resident families of eel fishermen, who would hitch their boats to the back of passing Guinness barges for a free ride down to Athlone. Now many of the islands have become holiday retreats.

Some incumbents have found the realities of

A Storybook in Stone

A storybook in stone—the medieval township of Rindoon (irishwalledtowns network.ie) has been thus described. It lies at the tip of a short peninsula near Lecarrow on the west side of Lough Ree. Rindoon consists of a church, castle, harbor, and turreted town wall. Some of it is restored, other parts are smothered under mats of ivy. One of the National Looped Walks, the 2-mile (3 km) Rinn Duin Castle Loop (discoverireland.ie/walking), encompasses stretches of the old town wall and gateways, Rinn Duin church with its sanctuary arch, and the old harbor. Rindoon Castle is an amazing fortress well worth a visit.

island life at odds with their fantasies, like the Dublin bookmaker who painstakingly built a beautiful retreat for his family on **Inchturk** ❻ with wood interior, thatched roof, and local stone. The wife and son came over, spent one night, and pronounced it too quiet: The place was abandoned forthwith.

On **Inchmore** ❼, the largest island in the lake (private property), St. Liobán's Monastery shows a few remains.

EXPERIENCE: Sailing & Cruising Central Ireland

Boating is the best way to explore the Irish midlands, in either a slick cruiser or a barge. To rent a cruiser, try **Locaboat** (The Marina, St. George's Terrace, Carrick-on-Shannon, Co. Leitrim, tel 071/962-0236, locaboat.com), **Carrickcraft** (The Marina, Carrick-on-Shannon, Co. Leitrim, tel 01/278-1666, cruise ireland.com), **Quigleys Marina** (Killinure Point, Glasson, Athlone, Co. Westmeath, tel 090/648-5711, quigleysmarina.com), or **Silver Line Cruisers** (The Marina, Banagher, Co. Offaly, tel 057/648-5866, silverlinecruisers .com). For barges, contact **Riversdale**

Barge Holidays (Riversdale, Ballinamore, Co. Leitrim, tel 071/964-4122, riversdaleholi-days.com), **Barge Trip** (Canal View, Sallins, just off the N7 main Dublin to Limerick/Cork road; tel 087/646-5465, bargetrip.ie), or **Canalways Ireland Barge Holidays** (Grand Canal, Barrow River Navigation; Spencer Bridge, Rathangan, Co. Kildare, tel 045/524-646, canalways.ie). The **Inland Waterways Association of Ireland** (tel 1890/924-991, iwai.ie) has a database of boat rental services, charts, and day-trip listings.

SEVEN WONDERS OF FORE

In a quiet Westmeath valley, 15 miles (24 km) northeast of Mullingar, a remarkable group of monuments—some man-made, some works of nature—lies on the outskirts of the tiny village of Fore. On a fine day, you will have an experience to savor as you explore these curiosities, known as the Seven Wonders of Fore.

Mullingar

🗺 235 D3

Visitor Information

✉ Market House, Mullingar, Co. Westmeath

☎ 044/964-8650

Monastery in the Quaking Scraw

A Quaking Scraw is a bog, on which nothing can normally be built. The Monastery in the Quaking Scraw, also known as Fore Abbey—a group of largely 15th-century Benedictine monastic ruins a couple fields away from the road—seems to be surrounded by bog but is in fact founded on an islet of solid ground within the marsh. The most extensive Benedictine ruins in Ireland, they have a full range of monastic buildings with huge fireplaces and solid walls abutting a plain but lovely church. Restored cloister arches have discreet carvings of long-stemmed flowers. East stands the gatehouse, in use as a farm building; northeast are the circular remains of a dovecote.

■ It's not unusual to see animals grazing around Fore Abbey.

St. Fechin's Bath

Walking back down the path toward the minor road, you'll find an ash tree standing over a tumble of mossy stones beside the wall on your right. This is St. Fechin's Bath (not in fact one of the seven wonders, but curious all the same); St. Fechin founded the first monastery at Fore in 630. The tree is usually hung with rags and the bark of its trunk crammed with coins—the traditional offerings to leave at holy wells. The mossy stones are the remnants of the basin where the saint kneeled praying in cold water all night. Ailing children were bathed here in expectation of a cure.

Other Wonders

The **Mill Without a Race**—a jumble of broken walls—and the **Water That Flows Uphill** are on your left as you reach the road. St. Fechin commissioned the original mill despite an absence of water, which he supplied by striking a hill at Lough Lene (south of Fore) with his staff. The water still flows.

Copper poisoning and the depredations of souvenir-hunters have reduced the **Tree That Won't Burn** to a stub. It stands near the road beside St. Fechin's Well, which contains the **Water That Won't Boil**—a muddy puddle these days. Bad luck attends anyone rash enough to make the experiment.

Across the road you'll find the **Stone Raised by St. Fechin's Prayers.** It forms the massive lintel of a church that mostly dates to

the 12th century. Look for the little seated monk carved on the chancel arch. The stone may be much older. On it is carved a Greek cross in a circle, a more Eastern than Western religious symbol.

Up the bank from the church dwelt the hermit Patrick Begley, the **Anchorite in a Stone,** in the early 17th century. His humble cell was later incorporated into the grand mausoleum of the Greville Nugent family. The cell is marked with a Latin inscription translated as: "I, Patrick Begley, hermit of the sacred retreat, hidden and buried in this hollow heap of stones." The key to the mausoleum is kept at the Seven Wonders pub in Fore, a friendly place for a drink. ∎

"Physician, Heal Thyself!"

St. Fechin of Fore seems to have been a Sligoman who came east to found Fore Abbey. The fact that the holy man was evidently a powerful healer makes the odd account of his demise in A.D. 665 even odder. The story says that two High Kings, perturbed by the rate at which the peasantry were breeding, asked Fechin if he could call down a plague from on high to curtail their numbers. The saint obliged, but somehow neglected his own precautions—and himself fell victim to the epidemic.

Fore

⬛ 235 D4

Visitor Information

✉ Fore Abbey Coffee Shop, Fore, Castlepollard, Co. Westmeath

☎ 044/966-1780

🕐 Closed Mon.– Sat., Oct.–May

Seven Wonders of Fore

⬛ 235 D4

✉ Head N from Mullingar on the R394 to Castlepollard, then NE on the R395 to Fore. The Stone Raised by St. Fechin's Prayers and the Anchorite in a Stone lie to the south of the minor road through the Fore Valley, the other five wonders to the north.

CLONMACNOISE

Beautifully situated among isolated meadows on a bend of the River Shannon, Clonmacnoise is the most complete and evocative monastic site in the central region. With its exquisitely carved high crosses, multitude of ancient churches, and splendid round tower, Clonmacnoise is claimed by many as the best such site in all Ireland.

Clonmacnoise
🗺 234 B3
✉ Shannonbridge, Co. Offaly
☎ 090/967-4195
💲 $
heritageireland.ie

Clonmacnoise is well signposted from Ballynahown on the N62, 7 miles (11 km) south of Athlone, and you can reach the site equally easily 5 miles (8 km) north of Shannonbridge, on the R357, 8 miles (13 km)

southeast of Ballinasloe. But the most memorable way to arrive is by water from Athlone (see pp. 244–247), with the tower and churches of the site outlined against the sky above their own reflections in the Shannon.

The grandeur of the site lies partly in its superb rural and river location, partly in the variety and splendor of its buildings. St. Ciarán founded the first monastery here circa 548, building it on Esker Riada, the Kings' Highway—a glacial ridge that ran west as a high road through the kingdoms of Leinster and Connacht. Between its foundation and the coming of the Normans in the 12th century, Clonmacnoise was Ireland's most important center of Christian faith, literature, and art.

The kings of Connacht and the High Kings of Tara were buried here. In spite of scores of assaults by Danes and ill-disposed Irish—it was attacked 27 times and burned 12 times by the native Irish between 720 and 1205—the influence of Clonmacnoise grew to extend over northern Europe. But after the Normans landed in Ireland, the monastery's power waned. In 1179, there were reported to be at least 100 houses and 13 churches in the monastery precincts; 300 years later, the place had declined in status to the seat of a minor bishop. In 1552, an English

▪ Don't whisper your secrets too close to the west doorway at MacDermot's Church—someone might hear them.

regiment marched down from Athlone, wrecked the buildings, and stole every treasure they could carry—even the books, stained glass, and church bells.

Castle & High Crosses

The ruins of a 13th-century Anglo-Norman **castle** totter on a hillock overlooking the Shannon. You enter the site through a visitor center with a must-see exhibition—it contains the monastery's three high crosses (replicas brave wind and rain in their original positions outside).

The tenth-century **Cross of the Scriptures** is richly covered with carved panels. Scenes include a flute player summoning the righteous to judgment; the devil lying on his back, his upraised feet providing a seat for St. Anthony; and a bird administering the kiss of life to Christ, who wears a beaded halo and lies in the tomb guarded by two Viking-looking warriors. Also exhibited is a collection of inscribed gravestones.

Inside the Walls

The walled site itself is roughly circular. A landmark for miles around, **O'Rourke's Tower,** some 65 feet (20 m) high, is named after Fergal O'Rourke (died 964), King of Connacht. The top was shattered by a lightning strike in 1135 and never properly reconstructed.

Scattered around the site are several smaller churches: **Teampull Doolin, Teampull Hurpan,** and **Teampull Finghin,** with a dogtooth chancel arch and round tower belfry. Some call Teampull

Finghin McCarthy's Church; built around 1160, this beautiful chapel contains fine Romanesque carvings. The door of the attached tower is at ground level; by the time the church was built, the Viking threat had faded, so the tower was probably constructed as a belfry rather than for defense.

The Lepers' Confessional

East of O'Rourke's Tower lies the cathedral, or **MacDermot's Church,** built in 904 and rebuilt during the 12th century. There is a side chapel full of carved stone fragments and a Gothic west door of many recessed courses, decorated with dragons and foliage, overseen by Saints Francis, Dominic, and Patrick in statue form. This doorway was erected, says the 15th-century Latin inscription, for the eternal glory of God. Press your ear to one side of the doorway and you can hear someone quietly whispering at the other side—priests used this to hear lepers' confessions in safety.

Around Clonmacnoise

Just up the slope stands tiny **St. Ciarán's Chapel,** burial place of the saint. The floor of the chapel lies below ground level—generations of local farmers have scooped up handfuls of soil mixed with saintly dust to scatter in their fields, thereby ensuring a good crop.

Most beautifully carved of all is the **Nun's Church,** 500 yards (450 m) east of the walled site, with heavy dogtooth arches, tiny faces, and, in the outer doorway, 11 beaked heads with bulging eyes. A penitent Dervorgilla, the Irish Helen of Troy (see sidebar p. 257), built the chapel in 1167. ■

BIRR TOWN & CASTLE

The fortunes of Birr have been bound up since 1620 with one talented and out-of-the-ordinary family—the Parsons clan, who became Earls of Rosse. They built a fine Georgian town in the farmlands of County Offaly, and at Birr Castle successive generations were at the cutting edge of scientific inquiry all through the 19th century, the great age of the amateur gentleman scientist.

■ The Earl and Countess of Rosse have long welcomed the public to the grounds of their home.

Birr Town

▲ 234 B2

Visitor Information

✉ Civic Offices &
Birr Library,
Wilmer Rd.,
Birr, Co. Offaly

☎ 057/912-0110

🕐 Closed mid-
Sept.–April

visitoffaly.ie

Birr Town Trail

The way to get the best out of Birr is to follow the Birr Town Trail *(leaflet guide available from the visitor information office).* You start in **John's Mall,** one of the fine strolling streets laid out by the Parsons family. Another, farther along the trail, is **Oxmantown Mall.** John's Mall is shaded by well-grown Jerusalem plane trees, its small Georgian houses with their wide front door fan-lights looking out on flower beds and neat white chain railings.

The trail takes you past the **Mercy Convent** behind its high wall (English architect Augustus

Pugin, 1812–1852, designed it), and along **O'Connell Street** and **Main Street** with their handsome old shop fronts. Many of these have carved wood surrounds. Keep an eye out for the druidic mistletoe-gatherers outside Mulholland's Pharmacy and more examples at Guinan's Footwear, Owen's Fruit and Veg, and Barber the Watchmaker.

Birr Castle & Estate

Birr Castle is still the residence of the Earl and Countess of Rosse. It is closed to the public except for special openings but the estate (gardens and parkland) is open to all. These are some of the finest grounds in Ireland, continually being refurbished and improved. Paths crisscross the entire demesne, giving access to parkland and river and lake walks.

Particular features are the immense box hedges, which are more than 200 years old and up to 60 feet (18 m) tall. Walking between the hedges is a creepy but enjoyable experience. So, too, is searching for **"Sweeney,"** the wickerwork figure of the legendary Irish half-king, half-bird. With knees drawn up to a pointed beard, he sits in the fork of a holly tree near Lovers' Walk. Other delights are the roses, magnolias, and intricate formal gardens.

INSIDER TIP:

Is it true that Guinness tastes better in Ireland? A fine spot to conduct some research is The Thatch (see Travelwise p. 372), a beautiful 200-year-old pub in Crinkill 2 miles (3 km) outside Birr town.

—KAREN MARTINEZ
National Geographic Society

Ireland's Historic Science Centre

To appreciate the extent of the achievements of the Parsons family in the fields of science, it is worth spending an hour looking around Ireland's Historic Science Centre, established in the castle stables. The absorbing exhibition has plenty of original material—plans, letters, photographs, models, and instruments. Charles Parsons (1859–1931) invented the steam turbine, spent $22,000 and 25 years trying to make diamonds, and got a steam-powered helicopter off the ground in 1897—six years before the Wright brothers' first official powered flight.

William Parsons (1800–1867), the 3rd Earl of Rosse and president of the British Association for the Advancement of Science, planned and built the **"Leviathan,"** a monstrous telescope with the largest cast-metal mirror ever made. It took four months to cool after casting and four years (1841–1844) to grind and polish it to a perfect parabolic curve.

By the mid-19th century, the sky had been mapped into 7,000 areas of light, and the great puzzle was what exactly they were. When William Parsons first looked through his telescope in April 1845, he saw what he named a "whirlpool nebula"—another galaxy 40 million light years away.

Thanks to William's wife, Mary, a pioneer of photography, we have remarkable images of the great telescope in action. Even better, the instrument itself—beautifully restored and still in its original position in the demesne—is housed between two mock castle walls, a giant black barrel almost 70 feet (21 m) long. On rare demonstrations, chains and weights raise the telescope along its immense curved rails. You don't have to be a scientist to appreciate this extraordinary feat. ∎

Birr Castle

🗺 235 C2

☎ 057/912-0336

💲 $$ (grounds only)

birrcastle.com

THE BEAUTY OF BOGS

Fifty years ago, anyone who found beauty in the bogs would have been dismissed as a fool. But eco-awareness has brought a new understanding and appreciation of these magnificent, if moody, landscapes.

Cutting turf from a bog in the Maumturk Mountains in Connemara, County Galway

About one-seventh of Ireland is bog—three million acres (1,200,000 ha) of the stuff, either in the form of blanket bog or raised bog. Blanket bog tends to occur in the west, generally above 1,000 feet (300 m). It is undulating grass, heather, and other plants, and can smother archaeological sites to a depth of 6 to 10 feet (2–3 m).

Ireland is an ideal location for the growth of bog. The retreating Ice Age glaciers scraped hollows in the rock and plastered them with impermeable clay. In the rainy climate that followed, lakes developed and filled with vegetation that died but did not rot because of the underlying acidity. Peat formed, piling up into thick mattresses of bog fed by plentiful water supplies—peat that can perfectly preserve bodies for thousands of years, as in the case of the Iron Age men, ritually murdered, who were excavated from bogs at Croghan Hill, in County Offaly, and Clonycavan, in County Meath, in 2003.

Decades of Exploitation

Peat—"turf" in Ireland—burns hot and slow when dried, and for thousands of years it was cut by hand for domestic use. But the exploitation increased in a quantum leap in 1946, when Bord na Móna (bordnamona.ie), the Peat Board, was set up to remove as much turf as possible for use in electricity-generating stations, as peat moss for gardeners, and as turf briquettes for domestic fireplaces. Bord na Móna owned more than 200,000 acres (80,000 ha) of land perceived as otherwise valueless, which could yield several million tons of milled peat every year. For half a century, the turf-cutting machines ripped up and devastated the bogs, with only the occasional pioneering conservationist voice raised to oppose them.

Changing Awareness

But opinion changed. The bogs came to resemble World War I battlefields, sodden black wastelands so ugly that people began to mourn the destruction. Awareness has grown of their unique interdependent wildlife—the plants that thrive in these inhospitable places, the insects that are attracted by the plants, and the birds that live off the insects.

Today, Bord na Móna no longer purchases bog, and it is committed to cease exploitation by 2030. There are grand plans to turn the ruined bogs into wildlife reserves and outdoor recreation areas with lakes, fens, and forests.

▥ A soon-to-be-bygone practice? Peat is harvested at a bog near Drumlish, County Longford.

Visiting the Bogs

If you want an absorbing experience of the bogs, either walking out across the quaking turf on a duckboard trail or actually rolling up your sleeves and helping with hands-on planting and conservation work, visit the **Bog of Allen Nature Centre** (see sidebar p. 93), 30 miles (50 km) west of Dublin. Also worth a visit are **An Creagan** in County Tyrone (see pp. 316–317) and the **Céide Fields** of County Mayo (see p. 199).

EXPERIENCE: Walking the Girley Bog

Inaugurated by the Meath County Council in 2009, the **Kells Girley Bog Eco Walk** follows a 3.5-mile (6 km) route around the bog and through the surrounding forest.

The trail begins and ends at the Drewstown parking lot, accessed on the N52, 3 miles (5 km) from Kells (see p. 260) toward Mullingar. The walk is not strenuous, but walking or hiking boots are essential due to the uneven terrain.

You will pass through woodlands (stunning in autumn when the foliage is multicolored), along trails flanked by conifers, and down an old bog road that circles Girley Bog. Girley is one of Ireland's raised bogs, so named because

they are dome-shaped and receive their nutrients only from rainwater, not groundwater. Raised bogs are a rare and threatened habitat.

Girley Bog is home to an abundance of flora and fauna, as well as a variety of birdlife, including the willow warbler, whose sounds walkers often hear along the trail. Interpretive panels along the self-guided walk tell the history of Irish bogs, provide information on wildlife in the area, and display photos of the carnivorous great sundew and other plants.

The trail takes most walkers approximately two hours to complete. For a trail map and a detailed description of the walk, visit *discoverireland.ie*.

ROCK OF DUNAMASE

Broken walls, arches, and runs of masonry, outlined against the sky, rise from flowery grass banks on the Rock of Dunamase in County Laois. Two and a half thousand years of history can be read in these high and poignant remnants of fortifications.

The middle ward, the ruin of the main gate, and the hilly landscape of County Laois

Rock of Dunamase

235 D2

Visitor Information

Lyster Sq.,
Portlaoise,
Co. Laois

057/862-1178

laoistourism.ie

The landscape in the eastern half of County Laois, which borders County Kildare to the east and Counties Kilkenny and Carlow to the south, is generally either flat plain or rolling valleys. As a result, the abrupt limestone crag of the Rock of Dunamase, 3 miles (5 km) east of Portlaoise, draws the eye. The jagged ruins of the fortifications that cover the crag look doubly intriguing because of their elevation and the way they stand out of jungly banks of bracken and scrub. Towers and walls appear as natural extensions of the broken rock on which they stand.

The Egyptian astrologer Ptolemy was probably referring to Dunamase when he reported on an Irish stronghold he called Dunum. If the rock was fortified as long ago as 500 B.C., it was a natural choice, given its eagle-eye command of 50 miles (80 km) of country. Iron Age men walled the summit with stone. By 845, the fortification was significant enough for the Vikings to plunder it. In the 12th century, Dermot MacMurrough (see sidebar opposite), King of Leinster, built a castle on the rock, which was strengthened by the formidable Anglo-Norman warlord Richard de Clare. In 1650, Cromwell's forces destroyed it.

What you see, looking up from the little parking lot, seems like a jumble beyond interpretation, but a quick glance at the explanatory board by the entrance gate will soon give you your bearings. Essentially the rock is divided by walls into **three wards** or defended enclosures through which you climb to reach the summit.

Outer Ward: You climb across ditches and up banks shaggy with feathery grasses and bracken and spattered with wildflowers to reach the **outer gate** that pierces the first wall. Walk through the gate's tall arch and continue your climb

---

INSIDER TIP:

Visit the dramatic ruins of the 12th-century castle on the Rock of Dunamase for a sweeping panorama across the rolling farmland of the central plain.

—TOM JACKSON
National Geographic Society

---

up the steep, uneven slope of the outer ward, defended from above and below by stronghold gates. Soon you reach the curtain wall that encloses the top of the rock; its tremendously strong main gate has slit spyholes in each of its flanking towers so that the garrison could keep a watch on all incomers.

Middle Ward: Once through the main gate, you are in the wide middle ward. To your right are the square foundations of an excavated gate; to the left, a path curves up to a corner of the middle ward's upper wall, with the arched and offset remains of a sally port, from where defenders could rush out and surprise attackers.

Fatal Attraction

It was Dermot MacMurrough, King of Leinster and builder of the castle on the Rock of Dunamase, who was responsible for bringing the English—or at any rate the Anglo-Normans—over to Ireland in 1169.

MacMurrough's affair with Dervorgilla, wife of Tiernan O'Rourke, had resulted in exile at the decree of O'Rourke's patron Rory O'Connor, High King of Ireland. England's King Henry II had obtained a Papal Bull in 1155 that authorized him to conquer and subjugate Ireland, and when the exiled MacMurrough approached him for help in his quarrel, Henry had exactly the excuse he needed.

Inner Ward: If you prefer the direct approach, climb up through nettles and scrub into the inner ward on the top of the rock. The separating wall has all but vanished; but three angles of Strongbow's Norman **keep** stand firm, with round-arched windows in plain, massive walls. The view is wonderful, from the Slieve Bloom Mountains in the west, 15 miles (24 km) away, to the peaks of the Wicklow Mountains 35 miles (56 km) off in the east. ■

WALKS: SLIEVE BLOOM MOUNTAINS

The Slieve Bloom Mountains rise from the level grassy plains of County Laois, a range of heathery hills with tremendous views from their windswept tops. Tucked into their flanks are secret valleys with waterfalls, woodlands, and plenty of sheltered paths. Here are two walks to introduce you to these splendid hills—one in a hidden valley, the other up on the crest.

The Slieve Bloom Mountains provide wonderful walks for strong and determined hikers.

Walk 1—Clamphole Falls

From the **Glenbarrow parking lot,** walk down a track marked "Tinnahinch 3 km." In about 200 yards (200 m), bear left at a yellow arrow through the trees for 1 mile (1.6 km). This forest plantation of mainly spruce and pine is a beautiful shady walk. Watch for red squirrels, which sadly have become extremely rare in Britain but are still quite widespread in Ireland.

After about 0.5 mile (1 km), you will reach an area of bare rock along the riverbed, an old **quarry ❶** where the sandstone floor has been shaped into square flags. Shortly, you will reach **Clamphole Falls ❷,** a lovely stretch of water tumbling over sandstone boulders where locals come to picnic. In the sandstone of the riverbed, you'll be able to distinguish some rippling lines—marks hewn by the constant action of waves when the Slieve Bloom Mountains were a flat floodplain in ancient times. From the falls, simply retrace your steps to the parking lot.

NOT TO BE MISSED:

A paddle in the pools at Clamphole
• Red squirrels in the plantations
• "Wave" lines in the rock of the riverbed

Walk 2—Ridge of Capard

From the **Ridge of Capard parking lot,** pass the waymark for the **Slieve Bloom Way** ①. This fine long-distance footpath makes a 31-mile (50 km) circuit of the peaks and ridges of Slieve Bloom. It's a tough but enjoyable hike.

Follow the Slieve Bloom Way, a moorland track labeled "Monicknew 8 km," through the heather for about 500 yards (450 m). Turn right along a graveled road for 100 yards (100 m) before bearing left across the heather, following pole markers southwest for 1.5 miles (2 km) to the **Stoney Man cairn** ②, seen ahead as you approach.

The Slieve Blooms swell out of a wild area of low-lying midlands country, and views from the Ridge of Capard are superb, extending over scores of miles out across the flat landscape of hayfields and woodland some 1,000 feet (300 m) below. Don't spurn the wildlife of the heather: There are beautiful mosses and lichens of different types. The tall cairn called the Stoney Man is a great place to picnic.

From the cairn, either retrace your steps to the parking lot or bear right and descend over thick heather and through trees to the forest road in the valley bottom. Turn right, and where the road divides, take the left fork to return to the parking lot.

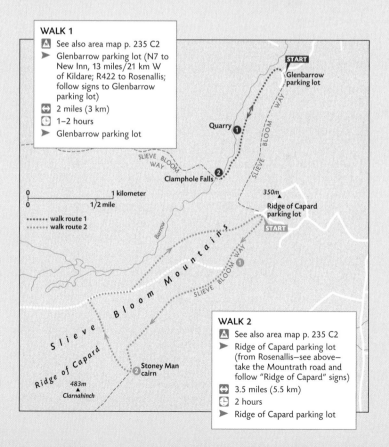

WALK 1

⛰ See also area map p. 235 C2

➤ Glenbarrow parking lot (N7 to New Inn, 13 miles/21 km W of Kildare; R422 to Rosenallis; follow signs to Glenbarrow parking lot)

↔ 2 miles (3 km)

🕓 1–2 hours

➤ Glenbarrow parking lot

START
Glenbarrow parking lot

Quarry ①

SLIEVE BLOOM WAY

SLIEVE BLOOM WAY

Clamphole Falls ②

350m ▲

Ridge of Capard parking lot

START

SLIEVE BLOOM WAY

SLIEVE BLOOM WAY ①

Barrow

S l i e v e   B l o o m   M o u n t a i n s

Ridge of Capard

483m ▲
Clarnahinch

Stoney Man ② cairn

0 —————— 1 kilometer
0 —————— 1/2 mile

•••••• walk route 1
•••••• walk route 2

WALK 2

⛰ See also area map p. 235 C2

➤ Ridge of Capard parking lot (from Rosenallis—see above—take the Mountrath road and follow "Ridge of Capard" signs)

↔ 3.5 miles (5.5 km)

🕓 2 hours

➤ Ridge of Capard parking lot

| KELLS & TRIM

The modest country town of Kells in the northwest of County Meath is famous for just one thing: the Book of Kells, created in the monastery here about A.D. 807. Kells people are proud of the connection, so don't raise the possibility that the "world's most beautiful book" might actually have been made in St. Columba's monastery on the Scottish island of Iona! Although the glorious book is kept in Trinity College, Dublin (see pp. 54–55), Kells is worth exploring for its magnificent high crosses and tiny oratory known as St. Columba's House.

Kells

⚄ 235 D4

Visitor Information

✉ Kells Tourist Information Point, Kells Civic Offices, Headfort Pl., Kells, Co. Meath

☎ 046/924-8856

🕐 Closed Sat.–Sun.

meath.ie/tourism

Trim

⚄ 235 E3

Visitor Information

✉ Town Hall, Castle St., Trim, Co. Meath

☎ 046/943-7227

🕐 Seasonal

Kells

St. Columba founded Kells Monastery in 559. A tenth-century **round tower** stands in a churchyard on the site now, a fine but capless cylinder 100 feet (30 m) high.

Just up from the churchyard is **St. Columba's House,** a little oratory with a steep corbeled roof and a ladder to a tiny room under the roof space. It probably dates to the tenth century, but it might be contemporary with the arrival of the Iona monks at the turn of the ninth century.

The four ninth-century **high crosses** in the churchyard are worth close inspection. The **South Cross,** or **"Cross of St. Patrick and St. Columba,"** is the finest, carved with scenes typical of high-cross art, including the Burning Fiery Furnace, Doomsday, and the Crucifixion. The **North Cross** is only a stump. The **West Cross** is a shaft with Noah's ark and the Judgment of Solomon, while the **East Cross** displays a Crucifixion.

The tenth-century **Market Cross** stands outside the **Kells Heritage Centre,** home to replicas of the Market Cross and Book of Kells. Stories say that United Irish rebels were hanged from the cross in 1798.

Trim

Set on the River Boyne some 15 miles (24 km) south of Kells, the historic town of Trim has two castles, two cathedrals, and enough monastic remains to keep you interested for a day. The main sights are grouped north and south of the Boyne, with another group a mile (1.6 km) to the east around the cemetery and St. Peter's Bridge.

Trim Castle, the largest fortress in Ireland, looms over the south side of the river. It was built mostly in the early 13th century on the site of an earlier castle burned by Rory O'Connor, King of Connacht, in 1174.

INSIDER TIP:

Several scenes from the 1995 Mel Gibson movie *Braveheart* were filmed at Trim Castle. A tour of the keep with a castle guide is a must.

—STEPHANIE ROBICHAUX
National Geographic contributor

By the mid-13th century, the new castle had a curtain wall almost 500 yards (450 m) long that enclosed 3 acres (1.2 ha) of ground, a huge square keep

70 feet (20 m) tall with walls 11 feet (3 m) thick, several sally ports, and ten D-shaped towers.

Opposite the castle on the north bank of the Boyne stands **Talbot's Castle,** a fine fortified manor built in 1415 by Sir John Talbot, battlefield opponent of St. Joan of Arc. Behind it the 14th-century **Yellow Steeple** is all that remains of St. Mary's Abbey. Along the Boyne east of town is **St. Peter's Bridge,** a handsome Norman span. South of the river here is the **Crutched Friary—**a 13th-century chapel and keep that belonged to the Crossed Friars.

North of the river and a little west is the ruined early 13th-century **Cathedral of St. Peter and St. Paul.** In the cemetery alongside lie the effigies of Sir Lucas Dillon (died 1593) and his wife, Jane. The sword separating them symbolizes the rift caused when Jane had a fling with her brother-in-law.

Slane Castle

Surrounded by a 2.5-square-mile park, the impressive Slane Castle, home to the Conyngham family since 1703, overlooks the River Boyne.

With guided tours, guests can visit the elegant 19th-century rooms and the whiskey distillery in the old castle stables and discover the curious history of the manor that became one of Ireland's most famous venues for the great rock bands that perform on its front lawn. ∎

Slane Castle

🅐 235 D4

✉ Slane, Co. Meath

☎ 041/988-4477

🕐 Tours all year round. Closed for events.

💲 $$

slanecastle.ie

▪ **Giant Trim Castle stands above the River Boyne, an enduring expression of Norman power.**

HILL OF TARA

The Hill of Tara rises from the Meath plains and commands 100 miles (160 km) of view. For a thousand years, all through the first millennium, the High Kings of Ireland based themselves at Tara, and it became the symbol and seat of Irish government. It is a powerfully moving place, soaked in history and heroic myth.

■ In the Royal Enclosure, Cormac's House stands to the right of the Royal Seat, with the Stone of Destiny at the hub. Beyond lies the smaller Mound of the Hostages.

History & Legend

It was here that beautiful Gráinne persuaded Diarmuid of the Fianna to elope with her on the eve of her wedding to Fionn MacCumhaill. Tara was also the venue for the great war council of Nuada the Silver-handed, king of the magical De Danaan, when defeat by the fierce Fomorians looked inevitable. The god Lugh the Long-handed turned up providentially and proved his right to act as the De Danaan's champion by slinging heavy flagstones over the palace wall and beating all comers at *fidchell,* a kind of mythic chess. When the time came for single combat, Lugh felled the Fomorian champion, Balor of the Evil Eye—his own grandfather—with a well-aimed *tathlun,* or magic stone.

Another tale tells of Conn the Hundred Battles standing on the Lialh Fáil, the Stone of Destiny on the Royal Seat, and causing it to let out a great scream—the sign by which the rightful High Kings of Ireland could be identified.

In 435, St. Patrick lit an Easter fire on the nearby Hill of Slane to challenge the pagan fires on Tara. Then he came across to negotiate with Laoghaire, the High King, for the right to preach Christianity—not in a spirit of confrontation but with a suggestion of partnership.

Tara Fictions

- In the 1890s a group of British Israelites became convinced that the Ark of the Covenant lay hidden in a graveyard abutting the Rath of the Synods. The mounds caused by their excavations in search of the Ark can still be seen.
- Some believe that the Lialh Fáil, or Stone of Destiny, was Jacob's pillow when he had his dream of angels on a ladder.
- Others feel the stone was brought to Tara by the immortal De Dannan from Falias, one of the four cities of Tir na nÓg, the Land of the Young, where they had previously lived and learned their craft of poetry and magic.

Exploring the Site

Archaeologically speaking, the Hill of Tara was occupied for at least 3,000 years before its abandonment in 1022. Entering the site from the **visitor center** (a former church), you are aware of multiple lumps and bumps, and with the center's booklet in hand, your imagination will quickly clothe them with both fact and fancy.

The northern part of the hill contains the huge trenches of a sunken entrance to Tara, 750 feet (230 m) long, known as the **Banquet Hall**—a thousand men could feast in it together, say the legends. Nearby is **Gráinne's Fort,** a ditched mound, and the circular **Sloping Trenches** where Dúnlaing,

King of Ulster, massacred 30 princesses of Tara in 222.

Going south along the hill, opposite the visitor center you pass the three-ringed Iron Age hill fort called the **Rath of the Synods,** where two superb gold collars or torques were found in 1810 (now in Dublin's National Museum of Ireland–Archaeology; see pp. 56–59). The largest embanked area, the **Royal Enclosure,** comes next and encloses three sites. **Dumha na nGiall,** the Mound of the Hostages, a grassy hummock with a low doorway, is a Stone Age passage grave where High King Cormac MacArt (A.D. 227–266) imprisoned captives from Connacht until they died.

INSIDER TIP:

Get in touch with your inner Gael at the Hill of Tara, ancient seat of the High Kings of Ireland and the center of power for the island's pre-Celtic dwellers.

—JUSTIN KAVANAGH
*National Geographic
Travel Books editor*

Side by side to the south are **Cormac's House,** a Bronze Age burial mound, and the ring fort called the **Royal Seat,** where the **Lialh Fáil** or Stone of Destiny—a fine pillar stone—stands alone. Farther south from the Royal Enclosure you reach another ring fort, **Rath Laoghaire,** where King Laoghaire is said to be buried upright in full battle gear. ■

Hill of Tara

⬛ 235 E3

Visitor Information

✉ Off the M3, 7.5 miles (12 km) S of Navan, Co. Meath

☎ 046/902-5903

🕐 Closed mid-Sept.–mid-May; hill accessible at all times

💲 $

hilloftara.org

BRÚ NA BÓINNE

In a long bend of the River Boyne lies Brú na Bóinne, the Palace by the Boyne—more than 50 ancient monuments that record the beliefs and religious practices of pre-Christian ancestors, in Europe's most concentrated site. Though most of that record is indecipherable, the sheer power of these tombs, henges, forts, and standing stones—especially the giant passage grave of Newgrange—is overwhelming.

On the winter solstice, the rising sun pierces into the heart of the burial mound of Newgrange.

Brú na Bóinne

235 E4

Boyne Valley
Archaeological
Park, 7 miles
(11 km) SW
of Drogheda,
Co. Meath

041/988-0300

$

heritageireland.ie

Visiting the Site

Most of the monuments of Brú na Bóinne stand on private land and are inaccessible to the public, and it is the three great passage graves of New-grange, Knowth, and Dowth that attract all the attention. Of these, **Dowth** is open only to archaeological excavators for the foreseeable future, while **Knowth**—its stones richly carved with circles, arcs, snake patterns, and one extraordinary "sundial" motif—can be visited only on an external tour.

So the kernel of a visit to Brú na Bóinne consists of the exhibition in the **visitor center,** followed by a tour to the heart of the Newgrange tomb. This tour is

immensely popular, so arrive early in the day to secure a place.

Newgrange

Across Europe, the period between 4000 and 3000 B.C. saw the building of passage graves— tombs of stone, with a passage leading from the entrance to a burial chamber or complex of chambers at the heart of the structure. They varied from small tombs only a few feet long to vast mounds that took decades to complete.

Newgrange is one of the big-gest, a man-made hill 280 feet (85 m) in diameter and 35 feet (11 m) high. The core of the mound consists of stones, at least 200,000 tons (182,000 tonnes), layered with clay and shells from the Boyne, while a row of 97 massive stone blocks secures the circular external wall of the tomb. The small Stone Age farming community living around this curve of the Boyne Valley 5,000 years ago—average life expectancy 30 years—would probably have taken between 40 and 80 years to erect the tomb.

But this was no haphazard mounding of material. The huge hill of stone is a covering for the internal structure of the tomb—a stone-lined and stone-roofed passage 62 feet (19 m) long that leads from the doorway, with its threshold stone elaborately carved in spirals, to a corbeled **chamber** deep inside. Off this chamber lie three recesses, holding two big shallow sandstone bowls or dishes. Passage and recesses are heavily carved with whorls, spirals, and wavy lines.

More remarkable still is the slit-shaped aperture above the door, known as the **roof-box.** The mound's doorway is precisely aligned with the position of the sun at dawn on December 21, the winter solstice, in such a way that

INSIDER TIP:

Entrance into Brú na Bóinne and many other key sites in Ireland is covered by the Irish Heritage Card. Good for a year, you can buy the card at any of the participating sites—visit *heritageireland.ie* for a complete list.

—LISA MCCLOUGHRY
National Geographic Society

on that day, and a couple of days on either side of it, a ray of the rising sun penetrates the roof-box and pierces into the very heart of the tomb. For about a quarter of an hour, the central chamber is flushed with golden light; then the finger of light withdraws along the passage. It is an intensely moving experience for the lucky few who are admitted each winter solstice. So keen is the competition to witness the phenomenon that a lottery system has been set up to handle the many requests (see sidebar below).

The white stones that face the walls of the monument are of Wicklow quartz and must have

EXPERIENCE: Witness the Winter Solstice Sunrise

Tens of thousands of people want to witness the winter solstice illumination from inside the Newgrange tomb, but the central chamber holds only 20. So places are allocated by lottery. Each September local children draw 50 names, ten for each of the five days around December 21 that the phenomenon occurs. Each winner can bring a guest. A reserve list of 50 is also drawn, in case winners can't attend or can't be contacted. To apply for tickets, either fill in a form at the visitor center or, if you can't show up there in person, e-mail your address and a contact telephone number to *brunaboinne@opw.ie,* and the staff will complete an application form on your behalf. Remember, there's no guarantee— if it's cloudy, you'll see nothing!

been brought by sea raft or coracle. **Standing stones** guard the tomb in a loose ring.

What the tomb-builders intended is open to speculation, but clearly something irresistible drove them to take on the huge task of planning and building. A

■ The entrance to the Newgrange burial chamber with its iconic triple spiral and diamonds stone engravings

Mound of stones and earthwork

Newgrange in its restored condition today

Front retaining wall of white quartzite stones

Remains of stone circle surrounding mound

clue may lie in the ashes found in the central recesses' shallow dishes. They formed the remains of only half a dozen people, and it is surmised that the tomb may have been periodically cleared of remains to make way for the next few months' cremations.

Perhaps the people believed that, on the shortest day of the year, the spirits of their dead rode the shaft of light out of the tomb to help ensure the return of spring. ■

Cruciform central chamber with recesses

Corbeled roof

Orthostats lining entrance passage

Roof-box

Decorated entrance curbstone

DRIVE: DROGHEDA TO DUNDALK ALONG THE COAST

You could zip from Drogheda to Dundalk in half an hour by way of the M1 highway, but the aim of following this meandering route northward up the coast of County Louth is to take your time, dipping in and out of the coastline and the little villages en route with neither time nor other visitors on your heels.

Fishing boats in port along the shore of the Irish Sea in County Louth

Built of gray stone beside the River Boyne, historic **Drogheda** ❶ *(visitor information, Tholsel, West St., Drogheda, tel 041/987-2843, drogheda.ie)* offers plenty to see and do. From **Millmount,** the ancient mound south of the river, you get a good panorama over Drogheda. Millmount is topped by a **Martello tower** built in 1808 as a defense against a possible invasion by the French under Napoleon Bonaparte. Below the tower, the fine **Millmount Museum** *(millmount.net, $)* displays the splendid 19th-century painted canvas banners of the Drogheda trade guilds.

In the town itself, **St. Peter's Church** on West Street is notable for displaying the prison letters, cell door, and leathery brown severed

NOT TO BE MISSED:

Millmount Museum • Relics of St. Oliver Plunkett, St. Peter's Church • Termonfeckin high cross

head of St. Oliver Plunkett (1629–1681), Archbishop of Armagh, who was hanged, drawn, and quartered for treason. He was canonized three centuries later.

From Drogheda, take the N1 Belfast road and turn off to **Termonfeckin** ❷ *(signed on the right just uphill from the bridge in Drogheda).* In the churchyard of St. Fechin's Church in

Coastal Strolls & Picnics

Far from the rush and roar of the M1, you can stroll along the strands and cliffs of Ireland's unfrequented northeast coast. A beautiful sandy beach runs south from Clogherhead toward Termonfeckin; anywhere along here is great for a leg stretch or a picnic. North of Clogherhead, the R166 cuts across the hinterland behind Dunany Point; several side roads and lanes lead to the lonely coast beyond the villages of Dunany and Salterstown, great for strolling and eating, with superb views north across Dundalk Bay to the hills of the Cooley Peninsula.

Termonfeckin *(entrance on the right some 150 yards/135 m past the bridge)* stands a tenth-century **high cross,** blotched with lichens, with Christ in Glory on the west face and fine interlacing on the east. In front of the cross is set another ancient piece of sculpture–a much-weathered **Crucifixion** featuring a soldier piercing Christ with his spear.

Beyond the church *(signed)* stands the rugged three-storied **Termonfeckin Castle** *(key from the bungalow opposite),* whose corbeled roofs still hold up. Previous owners, including the Archbishop of Armagh, had the right to first choice of the local fishermen's catch.

From Termonfeckin, continue along the R166 to the small town of **Clogherhead ③**; bear right in the village to reach the sandy **beach,** great for exploring rock pools and walking. Back on the road, a right turn *(blue "Port Oriel" sign)* leads in a mile (1.6 km) to the little **harbor** with its rusty trawlers. Here stands a roadside shrine to Mary, Queen of the Sea, built

in memory of locals who lost their lives at sea.

Back on the R166, in 1.5 miles (2.5 km) a right turn *(blue "scenic route" sign)* leads to a beautiful lonely **scenic drive** by sandy beaches and through forgotten farmland where long straight tracks lead to houses hidden among trees.

Turn left on the R166 *("Annagassan 4" sign),* with superb views of the Mourne Mountains ahead, to **Annagassan ④**, with its friendly **Glyde Inn** next to **O'Neill's Bakery.** The little **harbor**—with creel boats, an old ivy-covered kiln, and huge iron anchor—is signed off the village street. Continue to the N1 at Castlebellingham, then head north to Dundalk.

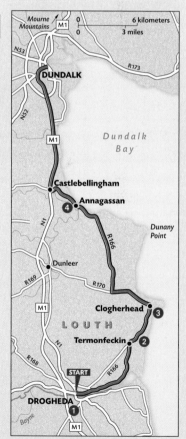

MONASTERBOICE

In this compact site in County Louth northwest of Drogheda, many superb early Christian monuments rub shoulders. Muiredach's Cross, in particular, is the finest high cross in Ireland, a tenth-century masterpiece of the stone-carver's art.

The tower at Monasterboice was built in the tenth century as a stronghold against the Vikings.

Monasterboice

235 E4

Collon,
Co. Louth,
6 miles
(10 km) NW
of Drogheda.
Turn left off
the M1 from
Drogheda near
Monasterboice
Inn

Monasterboice stands in a beautiful rural location among rolling green fields, although trees mask the full glory of the site until you are right up close. Then you see the round tower, the high crosses, and the shells of the churches and realize that this is one of Ireland's most striking collective monuments.

A disciple of St. Patrick, a hermit named Buite (or Buithe, Boethius, or Boyce—even Boyne: It's claimed that the river was named after him) founded the monastery late in the fifth century. Buite died in 521; the angels lowered a ladder from the sky to enable him to climb straight into heaven. His monastery became a famous center of learning.

Round Tower

Monasterboice survived a Viking occupation in 968, during which the marauders were driven out by a force from Tara led by the High King himself, Donal. After that, the 110-foot (33 m) round tower was constructed, a tremendously tall structure tapering toward the top, built with curved stones. The windows are no more than impenetrable defensive slits, and the door is 6 feet (2 m) off the ground. The monks entered via a ladder, which could be pulled up in times of attack. The interior of the tower burned in 1097, along with many of Monasterboice's valuables, and shortly afterward, the monastery declined as the newly built Mellifont Abbey (see p. 274) prospered.

Churches & Crosses

Ancient graveslabs, some perhaps from monastic times, surround the round tower and the two ruined churches—**An Teampall Theas,** the South Church, and **An Teampall Thuaidh,** the North Church.

In pride of place, though, are the three tenth-century high crosses. The **North Cross,** standing beside the graveyard wall, has a weatherbeaten, whorly pattern to its head. The **West Cross,** beside An Teampall Thuaidh, is 21 feet (6 m) tall and composed of separate shaft, wheel cross, and cap. Many of the carved panels have eroded, but the Crucifixion in the center of the west-facing wheel is clear, and on the east face are scenes of Christ walking on the Sea of Galilee, the giant Goliath, and the children of Israel worshipping the golden calf.

Muiredach's Cross

The **South Cross** near the site entrance—otherwise known as Muiredach's Cross—stands 18 feet (5 m) tall. Wheel and shaft were carved from the same piece of sandstone, with a cap shaped like a gabled house and a base inscribed "*Or do Muiredach Lasndernad Chros—*A prayer for Muiredach, for whom this cross was made." Muiredach (died 923) was abbot of Monasterboice, and the high cross was erected shortly after his death as a memorial and symbol of the wealth of Monasterboice.

The cross is heavily carved with biblical scenes. On the east face, Christ sits in judgment in the central boss of the wheel. Beneath his feet, St. Michael weighs souls, while the devil yanks down the scales. On

St. Buite & Monasterboice

St. Buite owed much of his fame and certainly his monastery to his supposed powers of healing. After he was said to have cured the mortally sick daughter of the King of Dalriada, the grateful father paid for Buite to found the monastery at Monasterboice late in the fifth century. When the saint died on December 7, 521, he foretold on his deathbed the imminent birth of "a child illustrious before God and men"—and St. Columba was born that very day.

the shaft below, the four Wise Men worship the Infant Jesus; Moses knocks water out of a desert rock while ranks of Israelites look on; David readies a slingshot for Goliath; and Eve offers Adam the fateful apple, while Cain smacks Abel with a cudgel. On the west side is a central Crucifixion; Christ presenting St. Peter with the keys of heaven; Doubting Thomas having his misgivings disproved by a rank of tablet-wielding apostles; and Judas delivering a betrayer's kiss in the Garden of Gethsemane. ∎

WALK: THE COOLEY PENINSULA & TÁIN TRAIL

This is a straightforward there-and-back walk with the most spectacular coastal and mountain views as reward for a little effort. The Cooley Peninsula in County Louth is a largely unfrequented corner of Ireland so you are more than likely to have all this beauty to yourself.

Carlingford village ❶ *(visitor information, Old Dispensary, Main Rd., tel 042/941-9692, closed Oct.–May, carlingford.ie)* looks out on Carlingford Lough, a superb wide inlet that separates County Louth in the Republic of Ireland from the Mourne Mountains in County Down, Northern Ireland.

Carlingford stands on the northern shore of the Cooley Peninsula, a glorious humpbacked piece of country with a mountainous spine and fertile green skirts. The village's neat, white-washed streets stand under 1,930-foot (588 m) Slieve Foye, highest point of the knobbly ridge of Carlingford Mountain.

By the water's edge is the 12th-century

King John's Castle, clinging romantically to its rock overlooking the fishing harbor. On the waterfront street stands **Taaffe's Castle,** a 16th-century tower house of grim aspect.

Begin your walk at the **Village Hotel** on the square in Carlingford. Walk up the road that rises

> ## NOT TO BE MISSED:
>
> **Carlingford village and its castles • View of Carlingford Lough and the Mourne Mountains from the Táin Trail • View to the southwest from the pass**

The wild moorland hills of the Cooley Peninsula offer superb, uncrowded walks.

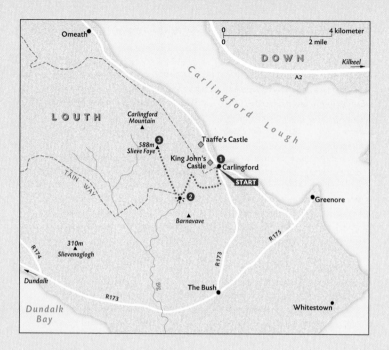

Omeath

DOWN   Kilkeel

0   4 kilometer
0   2 mile

Carlingford Lough

A2

LOUTH   Carlingford Mountain ▲

588m ▲ Slieve Foye   ❸   Taaffe's Castle

TÁIN WAY   King John's Castle ◇   ❶   Carlingford

START

Greenore

❷   R175

▲ Barnavave   R173

310m ▲ Slievenaglogh

R174

Big   The Bush

Dundalk   R173   Whitestown

Dundalk Bay

from the top of the square, and in about 300 yards (250 m), turn left for 0.5 mile (0.75 km). At a T-junction, you'll see a "Táin Trail" marker post with its "walking man" logo. Turn right and follow the Táin Trail posts up onto a grassy path that bends back to the right above the village as it climbs the mountainside.

Be sure to stop and look around frequently because the views get better all the time. Across Carlingford Lough, you will see the **Mourne Mountains** rise in ruggedly beautiful shapes, 1,600-foot (485 m) Slievemartin toward the left above the northern lough shore, the bulks of Eagle Mountain (2,090 feet/635 m) and Slieve Muck (2,210 feet/672 m) miles back in center frame, and over to the right the 2,450-foot (745 m) peak of Slieve Binnian. Up the lough, the twin villages of Rostrevor and Warrenpoint lie by the water.

The view is at its best from the **saddle of the pass ❷** at the top of the path, and another spectacular southwesterly view opens from this

> 🗺 See also area map p. 235 F5
> ► Village Hotel, Carlingford, Cooley Peninsula
> ⟷ 5 miles/8 km (7 miles/11 km with ascent of Slieve Foye)
> ⏱ 2 hours (3 hours)
> ► Carlingford

vantage point as well. The slopes of Carlingford Mountain rise away to your right, the lower shoulder of Barnavave to your left. In front, the broad green valley of the Big River falls away toward Dundalk Bay, with a great sweep of coastline running away south for 15 miles (24 km) to Dunany Point.

You can retrace the Táin Trail down to Carlingford from here, but if you have the energy it is worth bearing northeast for the steep but easy climb to the **summit of Slieve Foye ❸** (around another 950 feet/300 m), where the views are even better.

From here, return the way you came.

More Places to Visit in Central Ireland

Abbeyleix

Viscount de Vesci, 18th-century lord of Abbeyleix House, had a model village laid out at his gates—wide streets lined with trees, handsome buildings, and a Georgian sense of order and calm. The **Abbeyleix Heritage House** *(tel 057/873-1653, abbeyleix heritage.com, $)* in the former school gives a good run-through of the place's history. Walk around the village, then enjoy a pint in **Morrissey's** pub on Main Street, an old-fashioned bar dating from 1735. 235 D1 On the N8 Portlaoise–Kilkenny road, 9 miles (14 km) S of Portlaoise, Co. Laois

Emo Court

James Gandon, designer of Dublin's fabulous Custom House, designed Emo House in 1792 for Lord Portarlington, creating a superb neoclassical house under a big dome. The main rooms, beautifully restored, form the focus of a tour around the house. In the immaculate gardens, classical statues stand among azaleas and rhododendrons; paths lead down to a gorgeous lakeside walk. *heritageireland.ie* 235 D2 Off the N7 Kildare–Portlaoise road, at New Inn, 6 miles (10 km) NE of Portlaoise, Co. Laois 057/862-6573 House closed early Nov.–Easter; gardens open year-round $

Lough Boora Parklands & Sculpture Park

The low-lying Lough Boora Parklands form a truly remarkable landscape. Forty years ago these 5,000 acres (2,000 ha) were a hideous, black, and sludgy wasteland after decades of peat harvesting; now, after painstaking restoration, they present a wide and varied countryside of woodland, bog, heather, waterways, reedbeds, and lakes, crisscrossed by footpaths and bikeways. Wildlife thrives, including swans, geese, songbirds, hares, otters, dragonflies, and Ireland's only colony of gray partridge. Walk the trail around the park's huge modern sculptures—children are welcome to clamber! *loughboora.com* 235 C2 Off N52 bet. Tullamore & Birr, Co. Offaly 057/934-0010

Loughcrew Passage Graves

Up on the peaks of Sliabh na Caillighe, the Hill of the Witch, 32 passage cairns (3000–2500 B.C.) await. Many have their stones incised with markings—mazy circles and zigzags, snaky lines, and what seem to be flowers. Take a flashlight, and be prepared for a 15-minute uphill climb. *knowth.com /loughcrew.htm* 235 D4 On Sliabh na Caillighe hill (parking lot), signed from the R154 5 miles (8 km) SE of Oldcastle (13 miles/21 km NW of Kells by the R163/R154), Co. Meath Closed Oct.–May Deposit required for key: Collect from Loughcrew Coffee Shop, Loughcrew Gardens (tel 049/854-1356)

Mellifont Abbey

At its peak, Mellifont Abbey supported a community of 400. It was the center of the Cistercian order in Ireland, having been the order's pioneer house when established in 1142 by St. Malachy, Archbishop of Armagh. By the 1550s, the abbey was a fortified house. In 1727, it was abandoned, and by the 19th century, it was used as a pigsty. These days you can admire the big gatehouse, a gorgeous 14th-century vaulted chapter house, and something unique among Irish monastic remains: an octagonal 12th-century lavabo, or monks' washing place. Four of the eight sides remain, with beautifully carved Romanesque archways. 235 E4 5 miles (8 km) NW of Drogheda, signed off the R168 and N2, Co. Louth 041/982-6459 Closed Oct.–May $

The mordant wit of Belfast and Londonderry, the easy pace of conversations in the country towns, and humor wherever you go

NORTHERN IRELAND

Liquid gold at the Old Bushmills Distillery

NORTHERN IRELAND

Northern Ireland has had a troubled past and for a long time, it remained on the fringes of traditional tourist itineraries. Nonetheless, it holds an allure well worth discovering. Its people are extraordinarily cordial and rightfully proud of the enchanting landscapes, enormous lakes, rolling hills, and breathtaking coastline that have attracted the growing interest of both tourists and filmmakers.

NOT TO BE MISSED:

Having a drink in Belfast's beautiful Crown Liquor Saloon   282

Wandering through the galleries of the Ulster Museum in Belfast   284-285

A Black Taxi tour of Belfast's history and gable-end art   285-290

Visiting the Giant's Causeway, a storm of dramatic spray   302-303

The ancient stone circles near An Creagan   317

Cruising Lower Lough Erne   323

Enjoying spectacular views from the top of Slieve Gullion   327

The six counties of Northern Ireland fan out like segments of a wheel from the central hub of Lough Neagh, the biggest lake in the British Isles. County Antrim is the best known because of its glorious coastline stretching north from Belfast–a succession of east-running glens ending in superb cliffs, with the 37,000 hexagonal basaltic columns of the Giant's Causeway as the icing on the cake.

County Londonderry (or Derry), west of Antrim, possesses Northern Ireland's second city, Londonderry (Derry), a lively and forward-looking town whose heart is enclosed within the best-preserved set of city walls anywhere in Ireland. On the cliffs of the north-facing Londonderry coast you'll find

the 18th-century country estate of Downhill, while inland are forests and the northern range of the Sperrin Mountains.

County Tyrone is the setting for the bulk of the Sperrins, glorious hills for striding over or for exploring by car. At the waist of Tyrone, a wide belt of bogland holds a rich collection of archaeological sites.

Out to the west, County Fermanagh boasts Upper and

Lower Lough Erne, which offer superb cruising, fishing, and island-hopping.

County Armagh has the Lough Neagh Discovery Centre, the historic city of Armagh, drumlin hills, and volcanic Slieve Gullion.

Northward toward Belfast is County Down, last of the six, with the beautiful Mourne Mountains in the south, St. Patrick's Country in the center, and the wildfowl paradise of Strangford Lough in the north.

| BELFAST

Belfast's past was one of manufacturing and industry but in recent years, the city has decided to make the most of its potential for tourism by improving its image and offering modern attractions and facilities. Today, after a long, uncertain pacification process, Belfast's citizens (like the citizens from every corner of Northern Ireland) want to show tourists just how welcome they are and how they represent better times to come for the entire area.

■ Belfast's "RISE" sculpture symbolizes a brighter future.

Belfast

🅰 277 F3 & 279

Visitor Information

✉ Belfast Welcome Centre, 8-9 Donegall Sq. North, Belfast

☎ 028/9024-6609

visitbelfast.com

Belfast sits handsomely at the inner end of Belfast Lough, with a fine ridge of hills on the west—Black Hill, Black Mountain, Divis, Squire's Hill, and Cave Hill. The city is divided by the River Lagan, which winds its way north into Belfast Lough.

From the late 19th century Belfast was made prosperous by the textile and shipbuilding trades, and it maintains the appearance of a Victorian manufacturing city still today. There are grandiose 19th-century public buildings and churches, canyonlike shopping streets, acres of redbrick terraced housing, and tree-lined avenues.

Since 1998, to mark the end of 30 years of infighting, "peace allocations" have made the reconstruction and modernization possible. The city has worked toward improving its image with new facilities and attractions and has been repaid with a growing influx of tourists.

The once stinking River Lagan in particular has been cleaned up, and Titanic Belfast's mixture of exhibitions and events celebrates the iconic, Belfast-built transatlantic liner. The grandest buildings—the Town Hall, the Opera House, and St. Anne's Cathedral—stand in the heart of the city, with the Botanic Gardens, that splendid symbol of Victorian philanthropic provision, and an interesting Ulster Museum to the south.

The best way to see all this is slowly. Talk to as many people as possible. Chat to the driver as you ride in a Black Taxi to see the sectarian murals, have a drink and a plate of champ (mashed potato and spring onions) in the ornate Crown Liquor Saloon, or stroll up on Cave Hill or along the Lagan towpath. Belfast generosity and black humor make a potent tonic.

Donegall Square

Belfast city center has two distinct characters: the solemn

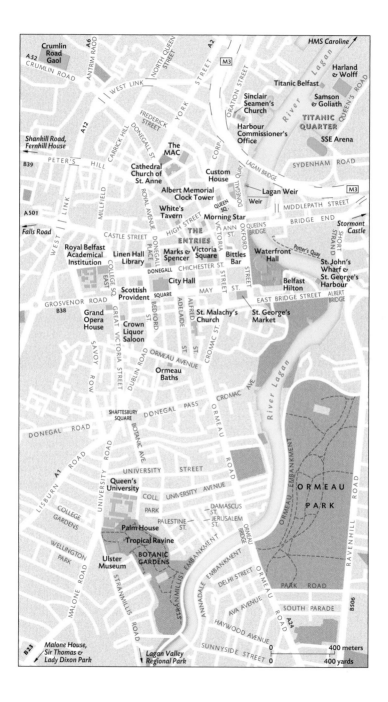

Crumlin Road Gaol
A52
A6 ANTRIM ROAD
CRUMLIN ROAD
WEST LINK
NORTH QUEEN STREET
STREET
M3
A2
HMS Caroline
Lagan
Harland & Wolff
QUEEN'S ROAD
Titanic Belfast
ORATION STREET
CORP
FREDERICK STREET
YORK
Sinclair Seamen's Church
Samson & Goliath
River
TITANIC QUARTER
CARRICK HILL
DONEGALL ST
A12
Harbour Commissioner's Office
Shankill Road, Fernhill House
PETER'S HILL
B39
MILLFIELD
SSE Arena
The MAC
Cathedral Church of St. Anne
ROYAL AVENUE
Custom House
DONEGALL QUAY
LAGAN BRIDGE
SYDENHAM ROAD
A501
WEST LINK
Albert Memorial Clock Tower
QUEEN SQ.
Lagan Weir
M3
Weir
MIDDLEPATH STREET
White's Tavern
Morning Star
BRIDGE END
Falls Road
HIGH STREET
THE ENTRIES
ANN ST.
OXFORD
QUEEN'S BRIDGE
SHORT STRAND
Stormont Castle
CASTLE STREET
DONEGALL PLACE
VICTORIA ST.
Potter's Quay
Royal Belfast Academical Institution
COLLEGE EAST
Linen Hall Library
Marks & Spencer
Victoria Square
Bittles Bar
Waterfront Hall
St. John's Wharf & St. George's Harbour
WEST
CHICHESTER ST.
DONEGALL
VICTORIA STREET
Scottish Provident
City Hall
MAY ST.
Belfast Hilton
ALBERT BRIDGE
GROSVENOR ROAD
B38
COLLEGE SQ
SQUARE
BEDFORD ST
ADELAIDE
ALFRED
St. Malachy's Church
EAST BRIDGE STREET
Grand Opera House
GREAT VICTORIA STREET
ST.
ST.
St. George's Market
Crown Liquor Saloon
CROMAC ST.
SAVOY ROW
DUBLIN ROAD
ORMEAU AVENUE
Ormeau Baths
CROMAC
River Lagan
SHAFTESBURY SQUARE
DONEGAL PASS
ORMEAU
BOTANIC AVE.
DONEGAL ROAD
ROAD
ORMEAU EMBANKMENT
ORMEAU PARK
UNIVERSITY STREET
ROAD
Queen's University
COLL
UNIVERSITY AVENUE
DAMASCUS ST.
RAVENHILL ROAD
LISBURN
A1
ROAD
PARK
PALESTINE ST.
JERUSALEM ST.
COLLEGE GARDENS
UNIVERSITY
Palm House
ORMEAU BRIDGE
WELLINGTON PARK
Tropical Ravine
MALONE ROAD
Ulster Museum
BOTANIC GARDENS
STRANMILLIS ROAD
ANNADALE EMBANKMENT
DELHI STREET
ORMEAU
PARK ROAD
B506
A24
AVA AVENUE
SOUTH PARADE
B23
Malone House, Sir Thomas & Lady Dixon Park
Lagan Valley Regional Park
HAYWOOD AVENUE
SUNNYSIDE STREET

0   400 meters
0   400 yards

■ Impressive City Hall, downtown Belfast's Victorian masterpiece

City Hall

🅐 Map p. 279

✉ Donegall Sq.

☎ 028/9027-0456

🕐 Public tours: all
year round

belfastcity.gov.uk

grandeur of great Victorian public buildings and the quick-fire humor and friendliness of the locals. Any stroll should start in Donegall Square, in the very heart of the city. This fine wide plaza, with its central lawns and gardens, contains many of Belfast's best civic buildings.

City Hall: Pride of place goes to City Hall, a great white wedding cake of a building in pale Portland stone. Begun in 1898 and opened in 1906, its sheer size—a mighty portico in a facade 300 feet (90 m) long, a verdigris-green central dome of copper that rises 173 feet (53 m)—and

the elaborate confection of its four corner turrets exude Edwardian confidence. Queen Victoria stares stolidly from her plinth out front.

Other fine monuments encircle City Hall, notably the **memorial to the crew of the Belfast-built *Titanic*** and the splendid **statue of Frederick Temple,** Lord Dufferin, and Ava (1826–1902). Anyone who needs a reminder of the inter-twined histories of Britain and Ireland should look at Lord Dufferin's effigy. Imperious but humorous-looking in his breeches and waxed moustache, he personifies the Empire-ruling Briton of the Victorian era. He was viceroy of India from 1884 to 1888 (a turbaned Sikh flanks him), governor-general of Canada, and ambassador to Moscow.

Walk below the huge **pediment** (where Hibernia presides over figures emblematic of Belfast's success in industry and the arts) and enter the **great hall,** highly decorated with three different kinds of Italian marble. Ornate plasterwork of swags and medallions decorates the walls and the interior of the **great dome**—this is viewed from below, crowning a cylinder of circular galleries and murals depicting the city's history.

The **Council Chamber** is the highlight of the guided tours of City Hall. It is a sumptuous room, paneled in hand-carved Austrian oak, with red **benches** for the city councilors and a heavily carved **throne** for the Lord Mayor under **stained-glass windows** and a splendid crimson-and-white **dome.** Here, too, is the plain wooden **table** at which Sir Edward Carson signed the Solemn League and Covenant against Home Rule on September 28, 1912, a document later signed by thousands of Orangemen (see pp. 306–307), some in their own blood.

In a nearby corridor hangs a vigorous and moving **painting** of Ulstermen in a conflict that united Irishmen across the political and religious divides. Thousands of Northern Irish Catholics and Protestants, unionists and nationalists, joined up to fight with British Crown forces during World War I. The picture shows 17-year-old 2nd Lieutenant Thornley and his men of the Ulster Division on July 1,

1916, the opening day of the Battle of the Somme, rushing forward from a captured trench, fresh blood on their bayonets. If you'd like to know more about the history of the city, visit the exhibit in the east wing of the ground floor. Admission is free.

Around Donegall Square: Notable commercial and civic buildings flank Donegall Square. The ornate, sculpture-encrusted **Scottish Provident building,** on the west side, shows dolphins, queens, and lions, while the red sandstone **Marks & Spencer** building, on the north, looks fabulously Italianate.

At the northwest corner of the square stands the **Linen Hall Library,** housed in what was a Victorian linen warehouse—stone swaths of the stuff are bunched over the doorway. This is a real old-fashioned library, where hushed voices are in order and books stand on wooden shelves by the tens of thousands. You can explore it on your own or take one of the themed guided tours.

Linen Hall Library

- ⓐ Map p. 279
- ✉ 17 Donegall Sq. North, Belfast
- ☎ 028/9032-1707
- ◷ Closed Sun.

linenhall.com

EXPERIENCE:
Quiet Reading

If you're looking for a quiet place to settle in with the newspaper or a good book, a place where conversations and cell phones are not tolerated, head to Belfast's wonderful **Linen Hall Library** (see below). The strict no-noise policy here means you can read in peace. Of course, if you want a bit of chatter, make for the library's fabulous coffeehouse or the children's area.

Royal Belfast Academical Institution

🅰 Map p. 279

✉ College Sq. East, Belfast

☎ 028/9024-0461

rbai.org.uk

Grand Opera House

🅰 Map p. 279

✉ Great Victoria St., Belfast

☎ 028/9024-1919

goh.co.uk

Crown Liquor Saloon

🅰 Map p. 279

✉ 46 Great Victoria St., Belfast

☎ 028/9024-3187

nicholsonspubs.co.uk

A beautiful wooden staircase takes you upstairs where you can lose yourself in other bookshelves. You will find crusty old books, both rare and curious, in the **Governor's Room,** and there are bound copies of the *Belfast Newsletter*—the oldest newspaper in the country—dating back to 1738. The **Political Collection,** on the second floor, documents the course of the contemporary Troubles through newspaper clippings, posters, and other material. At the end of the visit, you can sip a cup of tea in the **Tea Room.**

INSIDER TIP:

The Crown Liquor Saloon is a must. Go before 3 p.m. and eat in the pub downstairs—it's the same great food as the upstairs restaurant but with better ambience.

—KAREN MARTINEZ
National Geographic Society

Beyond Donegall Square

A counterclockwise stroll from Donegall Square around the city center sights could start with a westward walk along Wellington Place to College Square, where the handsome brick-built **Royal Belfast Academical Institution** stands in a green setting. It was built in 1814 to a design by Sir John Soane, who also designed the Bank of England and many other London buildings.

Going south from the "Inst" (as its pupils, and most of the rest of Belfast, call it), College Square East

leads to Great Victoria Street and the wonderfully overblown **Grand Opera House** of 1894–1895. Smiley (comedy) and frowny (tragedy) symbolic theatrical masks adorn the outside, while inside it is all crimson plush and huge gilt plasterwork elephants, cherubs, and thespians. The Opera House was restored in 1980, partially wrecked by bombs in 1991 and 1993, and restored to glory once more.

Opposite the Opera House is a Belfast drinking institution, the **Crown Liquor Saloon,** such a remarkable example of extravagant late Victorian pub design that the National Trust now looks after it. Note the crown mosaic at the entrance. The story goes that during an 1895 refurbishment of what was then the Railway Tavern by the owners, Mr. and Mrs. Patrick Flanagan, the lady—a keen loyalist—demanded that the pub be renamed the "Crown" and that a crown image be created and installed. Patrick Flanagan, a dedicated nationalist as well as a wise husband, agreed to carry out his wife's wishes but had the crown put on the floor so that everyone would wipe their feet on it. You can order a drink at the curved, tiled bar under the plaster foliage and scrollwork of the brown ceiling and sip it in one of the carved wooden snugs with their frosted glass and handy metal matchstrikers. Try the Crown's famous champ, a delicious mess of mashed potato and scallions (spring onions), often with pork and leek sausages.

On Ormeau Avenue (due south of Donegall Square by way

For imbibing amid high Victorian decor, head to the Crown Liquor Saloon.

of Linenhall Street), you'll find the former **Ormeau Baths,** located on Ormeau Avenue (south of Donegall Square, after Linenhall Street), are an imaginative reconversion of the old, defunct bathhouses. They were closed for a long time and reopened in 2017 as a co-working space and event venue. Just northeast of the gallery, on Alfred Street, is a Victorian gem, Catholic **St. Malachy's Church.** A plain exterior of dark brick and pink paint hides an exuberant interior with fan-vaulting, plasterwork, and art nouveau stained-glass windows.

Northeast again stands the redbrick **St. George's Market** *(12–20 East Bridge St.),* a late Victorian-style covered market of red bricks open from Friday to Sunday. Among the items for sale in its colorful stalls are flowers, fish, fruit and vegetables, and local handicrafts. It's home to art events and concerts, mostly on Sundays.

Northeast of Donegall Square is another group of architectural jewels. **Victoria Square** is a modern, four-floor shopping center topped

with an iconic, futuristic dome *(accessible by guided tour)* that offers a spectacular 360-degree view of the city.

North and east of Donegall Square is another clutch of delights. **The Entries** is a tangled area of alleyways just south of High Street, the heart of old Belfast and full of characterful pubs.

At the top of High Street stands an unmistakable Belfast landmark, the 113-foot (35 m) **Albert Memorial Clock Tower,** built in 1865. The tower inclines 4 feet (1.25 m) out of perpendicular; it had to be founded on wooden piles because of the marshy ground, and these foundations have shifted over the years.

The same stretch of boggy ground is responsible for the bumpy nave floor in the **Cathedral Church of St. Anne** on Donegall Street, west of the Albert Tower. St. Anne's, consecrated in 1904, is founded on 80 feet (25 m) of log piling, which has moved around. The floor is beautiful, though, with Canadian maple and Irish marble, its shapeliness enhanced by the

Ormeau Baths
🗺 Map p. 279
✉ 18 Ormeau Ave., Belfast
☎ 028/9076-7266
ormeaubaths.com

Victoria Square
🗺 Map p. 279
✉ 1 Victoria Sq., Belfast
☎ 028/9032-2277
victoriasquare.com

Cathedral Church of St. Anne
🗺 Map p. 279
✉ Donegall St., Belfast
☎ 028/9032-8332
🕐 Open all year round (Sun. tours only 1-3 p.m.)
💲 $
belfastcathedral.org

The MAC

Map p. 279

✉ 10, Exchange St. W., Belfast

☎ 028/9023-5053 (box office); 028/9089-2960 (other enquiries)

💲 Theater shows: $$–$$$$

themaclive.com

upward sweep of pillars that rise to capitals carved with scenes of the "Occupations of Mankind"—spinning flax, weaving, shipbuilding, seed-sowing. Stone from each of Ireland's 32 counties was used in the construction of St Anne's. There are three fine modern east windows full of Christian symbols. Against the north wall, you'll find a bronze memorial above the grave

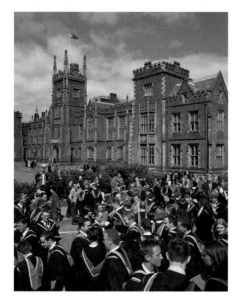

■ Graduation Day at Queen's University

of Lord Carson (1854–1935), the Unionist leader of Ulster from 1911 to 1921.

Behind St Anne's stands **The MAC** (Metropolitan Arts Centre), heart of the city's vibrant art scene. The six-floor building has three art galleries and two theaters where guests can see exhibits and dance and music performances.

South of the City Center

Queen's University: The prestigious Queen's University, located in University Road, was inaugurated in 1849 in a Gothic building designed by Charles Lanyon.

Beyond Queen's, on Stranmillis Road, you reach the splendid **Botanic Gardens** with their high Victorian iron-and-glass monsters of greenhouses. The hot and steamy **Palm House** of 1839–1840 with its rounded prow and long wings is also superb, as is the Victorian glass-roofed **Tropical Ravine.** A raised balcony lets you wander at forest canopy level among banana and cinnamon trees, ferns and orchids, Dutchman's Pipe, and guava.

Ulster Museum: Next door to Queen's is the excellent Ulster Museum. Take the elevator to the top floor and work your way down.

Third floor: In the **Art Zone** you'll find the Gallery of Applied Art (superb Irish glass, delicate Belleek pottery, modern pieces from around the world, costume from 1730 to the present) and eight art galleries with changing exhibitions.

Second floor: In the **Nature Zone** are fossil skeletons of dinosaurs, with plenty of hands-on exhibits for children to explore, including a blue whale vertebra as big as a dockside capstan. *The Sea Around Us* shows a coelacanth in a tank, with beautiful sponges and corals. *The Elements* shares strange stories of inadvertent poisonings, and a *Discover Nature* display has child-friendly exhibits, including a stuffed Bengal tiger, elephant tusks and teeth to handle, and lots of creepy-crawlies.

First floor: In the **History Zone** you are taken on a discovery tour from the earliest migrations into Ireland to modern-day Ulster by way of polished stone tools and gold hoards, peat-bog bodies and Iron Age tools, early Christian gravestones, and Viking swords. Then comes the story of the ill-fated Spanish Armada, and the treasure of cannon, cutlery, buttons and gold chains, salt cellars, and meat forks retrieved from the wrecked galleass *Girona*. On the exhibit goes, through Protestant plantations, rebellions, and famine, to independence and the two World Wars.

Ground floor: The recent Troubles are tackled in black-and-white photos, the preamble acknowledging that some of the themes "may be upsetting—most of them remain contentious." Here are Catholic marches and Protestant parades, bombings and shootings, soldiers on Belfast streets, Derry's Bloody Sunday victims, and the Omagh bomb of 1998 that killed people of all ages and political and religious persuasions. It's a stark way to end your visit, and sends you out into present-day Belfast in a thoughtful mood.

Black Taxi Tours

The Black Taxi tour of Belfast is the best way to see the city from an insider's perspective. You can discuss the route with your driver, who can customize your tour. The standard route takes in some of the waterfront—generally the Lagan Weir and Lagan Lookout, with glimpses of the striking Titanic Belfast building and the big Samson & Goliath cranes in Harland & Wolff's shipyards (see p. 291)—as well as **city center sights** such as the Crown Liquor Saloon, City Hall, and the Grand Opera House (see pp. 280–282). But the main interest comes when you swing off toward the Shankill and Falls Roads and the frontline Troubles enclaves of West Belfast.

Crumlin Road: Protestant West Belfast starts here where the **Crumlin Road Courthouse** stands forbiddingly, designed by Belfast's paramount Victorian architect, Sir Charles Lanyon, to personify the Dignity of the Law, with its statue of Justice on top.

Facing it is the even more oppressive dark brick **Crumlin Road Gaol;** a tunnel beneath the road connects the two. In the 1970s and '80s the Diplock

(continued on p. 290)

Botanic Gardens

- Map p. 279
- Stranmillis Rd., Belfast
- 028/9031-4762

belfastcity.gov.uk

Ulster Museum

- Map p. 279
- Botanic Gardens, Belfast
- 028/9044-0000
- Closed Mon.

nmni.com/um

Black Taxi Tours

- Depart from Belfast city center
- 028/9064-2264
- Tours every 30 minutes (book ahead)
- 1–2 passengers: $$$$;
  3–6 passengers: $$$ per person

belfasttours.com

Titanic Facts

The "Belfast Symphony" was the name for the pulsating, incessant rhythm of riveters' hammers that rang out from the Belfast shipyard during the building of the *Titanic*. The great ship consumed 3 million rivets, weighing 1,200 tons (1,090 tonnes). Her rudder alone used 101 tons (92 tonnes) of steel. The makers needed 23 tons (21 tonnes) of tallow, soft soap, and railway grease to lubricate the slipway at her launch on May 31, 1911. When fully equipped she carried 29 boilers, 159 furnaces, 8,000 tons (7,250 tonnes) of coal, 40 tons (36 tonnes) of potatoes, and five grand pianos.

GABLE-END ART & THE TROUBLES

As "political" murals—the euphemism employed by the tourist trade—many of the famed sectarian murals of Belfast are way over the top. But as folk art expressing raw emotion, they have great power. Murals come and go as buildings are demolished and new developments inspire fresh commentary, but the sites remain roughly the same.

Militaristic loyalist artists credit their paramilitary heroes with the organization of a formal army.

Your first sight of the murals can be a shock. They seem to pump anger and the threat of violence across the city, with their balaclava-clad gunmen and intolerant assertions— "Irish Out," "England's Genocide," "No Surrender"—blazoned house-high across gable ends and street walls. At the same time, there is a kind of playground machismo about these paintings that robs them of some of their menace.

Republican & Loyalist Murals

Republican murals are thickest on the ground around Falls Road and Springfield Road, the streets around the Ballymurphy estate and the Ardoyne farther north, and in the Short

Strand district of East Belfast. Loyalist murals tend to be around the Shankill and Crumlin Roads and in East Belfast around Lower Newtownards Road.

The character of the murals reflects the nature of the 30-year confrontation known as the Troubles. Loyalists with their siege mentality and desire to keep the status quo tend to produce aggressive, die-hard images of bully-boy paramilitaries hefting guns, advertising a bewildering number of outlawed organizations: UDA (Ulster Defence Association), UVF (Ulster Volunteer Force), UFF (Ulster Freedom Fighters), LVF (Loyalist Volunteer Force), and many more. Republican murals are more aspirational, romantic, and imaginative. Smiling hunger strikers exhort everyone to play a part, figures from Ireland's mythological past imperiously dispatch British soldiers back across the Irish Sea. The standard of execution varies from schoolboy crude to extremely skillful.

History of the Troubles

Discriminated against in housing, work, policing, and social services, and with local political representation fixed in favor of Protestants, Catholic activists began a series of civil rights marches in 1968 that soon turned into confrontations with the police and with loyalists—especially around Londonderry's Bogside, an impoverished Catholic ghetto quickly renamed "Free Derry" in pioneer republican murals. British troops appeared on the streets of Londonderry on August 14, 1969, and in Belfast two days later. At first, Catholics saw the soldiers as protectors, but they soon had them lumped in with the Royal Ulster Constabulary as oppressors—and foreign ones at that.

The 1980s hunger-striker Bobby Sands remains a hero to many in the Catholic community.

INSIDER TIP:

Don't miss a personalized Black Taxi tour through Belfast's divided neighborhoods, but make sure your driver is comfortable going through both Catholic and Protestant areas.

—CHRISTOPHER KLEIN
National Geographic Traveler
magazine writer

EXPERIENCE:
Viewing the Murals

The Troubles are still too recent for many museum exhibitions to have been organized around them. Exhibits at the **Ulster Museum** in Belfast (see pp. 284–285) and the **Tower Museum** in Londonderry (see pp. 305, 308) are the most complete as yet. As a result, the best way for you to catch the authentic flavor of the Troubles is to view the gable-end murals for yourself. **Belfast City Taxi Tours** (*tel 078/7979-5445, belfastcitytours.com*) offers a complete 800-year history of Belfast with particular concentration paid to the city's gable-end and wall murals. The tour also includes a stop at the city's peace wall.

Escalating Violence

In 1971, the IRA campaign of shooting and bombing to force a British withdrawal began. A government crackdown saw the imposition of internment without trial and direct rule from Westminster. On January 30, 1972—"Bloody Sunday"—British paratroopers shot 13 people dead in Londonderry. Three years later, the IRA began a bombing campaign on the British mainland, killing 21 youngsters with pub bombs in Birmingham. Loyalists retaliated by activating their own paramilitary groups, and two bitter decades of tit-for-tat killings ensued. Loyalists

ASKATASUNA

★ 1959 fifty years of revolution 2009

700 Political Prisoners!
Political Parties banned!
Incidents of torture!
Civil Rights abused!

UN GENERAL ASSEMBLY
RESOLUTION OCT 2008
COUNTRIES OPPOSED TO
US BLOCKADE 185
COUNTRIES IN FAVOUR:3
(U.S. ISRAEL, PALAU)

THE WORLD OPPOSES US BLOCKADE
OF CUBA
TIME FOR CHANGE MR OBAMA

NOT SPAIN   NOT FRANCE
Self determination for the Basque country

Murals along the Falls Road side of the divide

wanted Northern Ireland to stay within the United Kingdom; nationalists wanted civil justice and to be part of a united Ireland. Neither would budge nor listen to the other side. It was as simple, and as complicated, as that.

In 1975, internment without trial was suspended, but republican prisoners had their status as "political" detainees withdrawn. "Blanket protests" (refusal to wear prison clothes) and "dirty protests" (refusal to "slop out" the cell toilets and the consequent smearing of cells with excrement) followed. Prison protests escalated to their awful conclusion in 1981, when ten hunger strikers, led by Bobby Sands MP, starved themselves to death in the Maze prison south of Lisburn in an abortive attempt to regain political status. Their faces appear on the Falls Road murals.

Movement Toward Peace

In the 1980s, more extremist splinter groups split off from the main paramilitary organizations. But political moves were being made. A 1973 attempt to set up a

INSIDER TIP:

Though Belfast residents are among the friendliest— and most talkative—you'll ever meet, resist the temptation to bring up religion, politics, or the recent Troubles.

—ROBIN CURRIE
National Geographic author

power-sharing executive to govern Northern Ireland had been brought down the following year by a province-wide Protestant worker's strike. In 1982, a power-sharing Northern Ireland Assembly was established on a very limited basis. The year 1985 saw the signing of the Anglo-Irish Agreement, which brought Dublin on board to some extent. The involvement of the Republic's government, for so long negatively anti-British and reiterative of its supposed claim to sovereignty over the North's six counties,

in the Downing Street declaration; ended the Republic's claim over the six counties; promised the release of paramilitary prisoners, the decommissioning of paramilitary weapons, and the establishment of an independent commission on policing in Northern Ireland; and proposed a Northern Ireland Assembly elected by proportional representation. All signatories committed to "exclusively democratic and peaceful means" of resolving differences.

Future of Northern Ireland

Problems remain for Northern Ireland. The centuries-old, Troubles-exacerbated differences between the two sections of the community, Protestant/Unionist and Catholic/Republican, are not going to dissolve overnight. There are still political posturings and times of tension. But constructive moves toward a permanent peace have been made, with the IRA

was vital to long-term resolution.

Signs of moderation grew in the 1990s. The 1993 Downing Street declaration saw the British government renounce any "selfish strategic or economic interest" in Northern Ireland, while Dublin accepted that any change in constitutional status would have to be subject to the agreement of a majority of the people. On August 31, 1994, the IRA declared a "complete cessation" of violence. Loyalist paramilitary groups followed suit. The British responded with some troop withdrawals and the demolition of roadblocks and border crossings.

An End to Violence

The seeds of hope were briefly frozen in 1996, when the IRA resumed mainland bombing. Then, in May 1997, a Labour government was elected in the United Kingdom, and the mood changed. The new government's majority was big enough to shrug off Unionist opposition. On April 10, 1998, the Good Friday Agreement was announced, a historic accommodation by all sides. It reasserted the points made

■ **A republican artist makes her point along Falls Road in Belfast.**

declaring an end to its armed campaign in July 2005. The Northern Ireland Assembly, after a shaky start, has evolved into a credible government. And most importantly, the vast majority of the people are—as they always have been—interested only in getting along with their neighbors and living in peace.

■ Black Taxi tours are the best way to see the famous murals.

Crumlin Road Gaol

🗺 Map p. 279

✉ 53–55 Crumlin Rd., Belfast

☎ 028/9074-1500

💲 $$

crumlinroadgaol. com

Courts held their enclosed trials here; in some circumstances a prisoner on remand could be incarcerated for years before coming to trial. In 1996, the jail fell into disuse. It has recently been transformed into a museum and can be visited with one of the daily guided tours.

Shankill Road: A block farther south, Shankill Road runs parallel with Crumlin Road. The Shankill is the main artery of Protestant West Belfast, essentially an old-fashioned suburban thoroughfare of small family-run shops, pubs, betting shops, and sole-proprietor businesses. You won't fail to notice the barbed wire and reinforced steel around the bookies'

premises, though, a telltale sign of a community that feels itself under siege.

The fierce Loyalist sense of identity is expressed in the enormous murals that cover gable ends and whole house walls (see pp. 286–289). Your Black Taxi driver is quite happy to stop while you photograph. He'll also tell you about what went on here—in garish detail if you want, but with thoughtful insight if he sees that you are prepared to listen. The area of sectarian violence in Belfast was astonishingly small. Just 100 yards (100 m) separates Shankill Road from the Catholic-dominated Falls Road and Springfield Road to the south. Here the **"Peace Line"** was built to keep both sides' extremists, and their firebombs, out of the opposing enclave. You can add your own message of peace on this ugly, depressing, but necessary, 20-foot (6 m) wall of concrete, wire, and corrugated tin.

Falls Road: In much of its appearance and atmosphere Falls Road mirrors the Shankill, though here the curbstones and flags are orange and green, the nationalist colors. You'll find the same small shops and businesses, the same kind of pubs, and a tremendous array of murals. It will be strange indeed if you don't finish your tour with more of an understanding of this historic city and its problems, and an admiration for the stoicism and decency of ordinary Belfast people.

River Lagan Cruise

The Lagan was a stinking, moribund open sewer until the building of the Lagan Weir in 1994. It's hard to believe nowadays, with salmon and sea trout coming upriver and anglers to be seen along the banks. The River Lagan cruise on M.V. *Joyce* shows you a peaceful side of Belfast. From Donegall Quay there are two options, up or down river.

Downriver Cruise: The downriver cruise takes you past the big new **SSE Arena** entertainment complex, Abercorn basin, and the giant cranes and slipways of the once-great **Harland & Wolff shipyards,** where the *Titanic* was built in 1909–1911 and where the new **Titanic Belfast** experience now stands.

Upriver Cruise: On the upriver cruise, the boat goes under the **Queen's Bridge,** Sir Charles Lanyon's first major Belfast project, with its ornate triton lamp standards. Andy Scott's "**Beacon of Hope,**" a great 50-foot (15 m) sculpture of a woman made of silver wire, now stands at the end of the bridge. Then the boat passes the old **Custom House** (see p. 297) and recent west bank developments that include the circular **Waterfront Hall** (1997). On the opposite bank you catch a glimpse of the giant shipyard cranes, **Samson & Goliath.** Things get greener past the big trees of **Ormeau Park.** Oystercatcher, sandpiper, and curlew can be seen on the gravelly river beaches, and the river supports eels, grey mullet, and even sea bass and baby plaice. The overall impression is of a river coming back to life.

Titanic Belfast

This area on Belfast Lough was once occupied by the now defunct Harland & Wolff shipyards. It has been home to the Titanic Belfast museum since 2012 and has brought back prestige to an area that had fallen into disuse. Its four sharp, upswept angles represent the four points

---

INSIDER TIP:

A budget-friendly alternative to a Black Taxi tour is to buy an all-day public bus pass and take a double-decker bus to Shankill.

—ALEXANDRA BURGUIERES
National Geographic contributor

---

of the star that symbolized the White Star Line, the company that built the doomed R.M.S. *Titanic*—but they also call to mind ships' prows, and in their reflective silver cladding one can imagine the glitter of an iceberg. Inside, exposed rivets, rusted metal plates, and tiny lights like mid-Atlantic stars continue the allusions. An enormous compass rose set into the floor becomes apparent as you ascend the floors of the building.

Gallery 1: Boomtown Belfast: The shipyards of Harland & Wolff were noisy, clangorous, dangerous places where the White Star Line's great passenger

---

River Lagan Cruise

✉ Lagan Boat Company, Donegall Quay, Belfast

☎ 028/9024-0124

🕐 Cruises daily March–Dec.; call for times

💲 $$

laganboatcompany.com

Titanic Belfast

🗺 Map p. 279

✉ 1 Olympic Way, Queen's Rd., Titanic Quarter, Belfast

☎ 028/9076-6386

🚌 Bus: Metro lines 26, 26A, 26B; Glider G2; Airport Express: 600

💲 $$

nmrn.org.uk

vessels—*Oceanic, Olympic, Britannic, Titanic*—were forged.

Gallery 2: The Shipyard Ride's cars take you among the legs of the giant 228-foot-high (70 m) **Arrol Gantry,** which straddled the slipways where the ships were built. You see *Titanic's* keel being laid, the steel girders of her frame twisted into shape, her iron-plated hull, her double bottom and 15 supposedly watertight bulkheads. There's a goosebump-inducing photo of *Titanic* and her sister ship *Olympic* side by side on their slipways, *Oceanic* gleaming in white paint, *Titanic* spectral black and shrouded in a skeletal gantry.

Gallery 3, The Launch: Some 100,000 people lined the banks of the River Lagan on May 31, 1911, to see *Titanic* slide into Belfast Lough.

Galleries 4 & 5, The Fit-Out and The Maiden Voyage: Boilers, engines, funnels, propellers; tables, chairs, bunks, sofas; saloons, staterooms, grand staircase, stokers' quarters; inlaid wood, crystal, porcelain, sanitary china. Fitting out *Titanic* was like fitting out a city, a stately home, a hospital, and an engineering works all rolled into one. The rigid distinctions between First, Second, and Third Class passengers are examined, and *Titanic's* prolonged departure on her maiden voyage is followed.

Belfast Tours

In addition to the famous Black Taxi tours (see pp. 285–290), Belfast boasts a wealth of tours. If you'd like a short guided walk around the city, try Official Belfast iTours, free downloadable podcasts from *podcast.com.* Check with **Belfast City Guided Walking Tours** *(belfast-city-walking-tours.co.uk)* for other tours. Perhaps the most agreeable form of guided city walk is the **Historical Pub Tour of Belfast** *(tel 028/9268-3665, belfastpub tours.com, $),* which leaves from the Crown Dining Rooms upstairs at the Crown Liquor Saloon (see pp. 282–283) and ends at **White's Tavern** in Winecellar Entry off Lombard Street, Belfast's oldest pub (it dates back to 1630), a black-beamed, stone-floored drinking den with great character; during the tour, you will stop at the splendid peninsula wooden bar and railed-off snugs in the stylish old **Morning Star** in Pottinger's Entry; and **Bittles Bar** on Victoria Square, a sharp triangular building filled with paintings of literary figures by local artist Joe O'Kane.

The best shows W. B. Yeats, James Joyce, Brendan Behan, George Bernard Shaw, and Samuel Beckett drinking at a bar, with Oscar Wilde manning the beer pumps and Flann O'Brien looking on from a picture frame. With the help of **Discover Hidden Belfast** *(tel 079/7189-5746, belfasthiddentours.com),* you can explore the best-hidden corners of the city but if you'd rather not walk, you can take one of the myriad bus tours available.

If the weather is good, take a tour in one of **City Sightseeing**'s open buses *(tel 028/9032-1321, belfastcitysightseeing.com)* or take one of the tours offered by **City Tours Belfast** *(tel 028/9032-1921, citytoursbelfast.com),* which organizes tours out of the city as well.

If you're looking to try something out of the ordinary, **Taste and Tour** *(tel 028/9045-7723, tasteandtour.co.uk)* offers themed tours for lovers of gin, whiskey, beer, or traditional Irish cuisine—there's something for everyone.

The Titanic Museum echoes the great Belfast-built ship's impressive presence.

Gallery 6, The Sinking: In a darkened gallery you hear the recorded testimony of survivors of *Titanic*'s fatal collision with an iceberg shortly before midnight on April 14, 1912. "Slowly she reared up on end," remembers the liner's second officer Charles Lightoller, "till at last she was absolutely perpendicular. Then quite quietly, but quicker and quicker, she seemed just to slide away under the surface and disappear." There are terse Morse messages, tales of deeds heroic and cowardly, and black despair when the full extent of the losses becomes clear—1,513 dead, and only 711 survivors.

Gallery 7, The Aftermath: This deals with the subsequent U.K. and U.S. inquiries into the disaster, accusations of cowardice and callousness, and privilege versus the lower classes.

Gallery 8, Myths and Legends: This looks at filmic and other treatment of the *Titanic*

story. The *Titanic* **Beneath The-atre** shows fascinating film footage of the great ship lying broken in two, 12,415 feet (3,784 m) down on the bed of the Atlantic, her rails and hatches, foremast, and anchor chain clearly visible. You hear the tale of her rediscovery in 1985 by oceanographer Robert Ballard.

Outside the building among skateboarders and rollerbladers you can walk the **old dock and slipway** where *Titanic* was built, now configured with outlines to represent her shape, and benches arranged in the dot and dashes of the Morse messages sent out by the stricken ship as she sank.

H.M.S. *Caroline*: The H.M.S. *Caroline,* a British Royal Navy warship used in World War I, is docked along the Alexandra Dock, just over half a mile from the Titanic Belfast. Inside the ship, visitors can use interactive displays to discover its history. ∎

HMS Caroline

🅰 Map p. 279

✉ Alexandra Dock, Queen's Rd., Titanic Quarter, Belfast

☎ 023/9289-1370

🚌 Bus: Metro lines 26, 26A, 26B; Glider G2; Airport Express: 600

💲 $$$

titanicbelfast.com

WALK: CAVE HILL

This fine walk, a favorite with Belfast folk, takes you up the mountain behind the city to visit prehistoric caves, to the promontory where United Irishmen pledged their lives in 1795, and to the heritage center in Belfast Castle.

The tremendous view over Belfast Lough is worth every step up Cave Hill.

Start from the parking lot on the south side of Belfast Castle. Follow the **Blue Route footpath** *(blue arrows)* and walk up to a T-junction and turn right. After about 550 yards (500 m), bear left and then turn uphill under the great basalt cliff of **Napoleon's Nose ❶**. In about 300 yards (275 m), at a stone with two blue arrows and "McArt's Fort" sign, bear uphill through trees.

Emerge from the wood, and in another 300 yards (275 m) or so, turn left, aiming for a large **cave ❷** in the cliff face. With care you can scramble up the rock face into the cave. Up here the view is tremendous—Belfast spread out along Belfast Lough, with the dark bulk of the Ards Peninsula hills rising beyond, crowned by the rocket shape of Scrabo Tower.

NOT TO BE MISSED:

Napoleon's Nose • Cave
• View from McArt's Fort
• Cave Hill Heritage Centre

The cave itself is one of five Neolithic excavations—Stone Age men found flint in the chalk under the basalt hill cap. Iron was mined here, too, opening up the delvings. "The Wages of Sin Is Death," warns a painted message on the cave wall. It may have been here, or at **McArt's Fort ❸** on the summit, that Wolfe Tone, Henry Joy McCracken, Dr. William Drennan, and a small band of friends—mostly Presbyterians—met in

1795 to swear an oath that Irishmen of every creed should unite for independence. It was the birth of the United Irishmen, a rebel organization whose leaders came to a bloody end in the 1798 rising.

To reach McArt's Fort, bear right as you face the cave on a narrow path along the grass slopes under the cliff. It soon trends uphill. At the top of the slope, cross a cattle grid near a post with blue and yellow waymarks. Bear left uphill. In about 300 yards (275 m), cross a cattle grid and continue uphill with a fence on your right, bearing left to reach the fort at 1,182 feet (360 m). This old earthwork was named after Brian McArt O'Neill, one of the last Irish chieftains to die in the Tudor repressions—he was killed by Lord Mountjoy in 1601.

From the fort, retrace your steps and descend through the woods to the stone with two blue arrows. Bear left downhill here; in about 150 yards (135 m), go straight ahead at a meeting of woodland tracks.

Follow the blue arrow on a stone at the **Volunteers' Well ④** to meet a road. Bear right along it; at a parking area, bear right to reach **Belfast Castle ⑤**, built in 1867–1870 in baronial style for the Marquis of Donegall.

The **Cave Hill Visitor Centre** *(Belfast Castle, tel 028/9031-9629)*, on the second floor, gives fascinating insights into the wildlife, geology, and history of the area.

🅰 See also area map p. 277 F3

➤ Belfast Castle parking lot, Cave Hill Country Park— signed off the A6 Antrim road, 4 miles (6 km) N of city center. City bus 8, 9, 10, 45–51 from Donegall Square

🕐 2 hours. Free trail map and literature available from Cave Hill Heritage Centre

↔ 2 miles (3.5 km)

➤ Belfast Castle

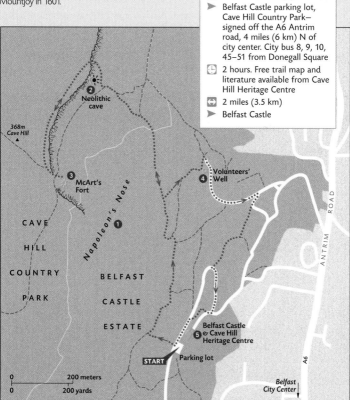

More Places to Visit Around Belfast

Lagan Towpath

If you want to explore the River Lagan on foot upriver from Belfast, there is an 11-mile (18 km) **Lagan Towpath Walk** through the beautiful, wooded Lagan Valley Regional Park. Pick up one of the brochure guides available from the Belfast Welcome Centre.

The walk starts at the parking lot on Lockview Road. Leaving the gates of the Botanic Gardens, turn left beside the Ulster Museum and continue up Stranmillis Road. Then turn right onto Lockview Road. The old towpath takes you through a 4,000-acre (1,600 ha) mixture of woodland and pasture, wetlands and forest, to its end at Union Locks in Lisburn.

In 3 miles (5 km) from the start of the Lagan towpath, you reach two of Belfast's most pleasant green oases. **Malone House** *(Barnett Park, Upper Malone Rd., Belfast, tel 028/9068-1246, city bus 8A, 8B, malonehouse.co.uk),* south of the city center, is a fine restored late Georgian house with an excellent café and restaurant. It stands on 100 acres (40 ha) of grounds ablaze with azaleas and rhododendrons in spring.

A mile (1.6 km) along the Upper Malone Road from Malone House lies **Sir Thomas and Lady Dixon Park** *(Ulsterbus 21 from Europa Bus Station),* a varied mosaic of meadows, woodland, and water with the City of Belfast International Rose Gardens at its heart—11 acres (4 ha) of more than 30,000 shrub roses. These are spectacular beginning in mid-July, and in spring daffodils fill the park. ▲ Map p. 279

The Waterfront

Belfast's waterfront areas have been revitalized since the 1994 building of the Lagan Weir's five steel sluice gates. The weir has stabilized river levels, eliminated offensive smells, and made Laganside a pleasant area to explore.

Sir Edward Carson (1854–1935), vehement Unionist, shakes a defiant fist outside Stormont.

The Lagan Weir itself straddles the river just upstream of Belfast's Titanic Quarter. Beside the weir lies the "Big Fish," created by sculptor John Kindness in 1999 to celebrate the regeneration of the River Lagan. Its blue and white ceramic "scales" carry images and texts of Belfast history. You can look across to the giant twin cranes of Samson & Goliath in Harland & Wolff's ship-yards, their gaunt yellow frames towering more than 300 feet (91 m) high and 450 feet (137 m) long. They symbolize a shipbuilding power that is all but gone from the yards where *Titanic* was built and launched in 1912. At their height, the shipyards employed more than 25,000 men; today, barely a couple of hundred work there.

Just behind the Lagan Lookout, you'll see the Sir Charles Lanyon–designed **Custom House** of 1854–1857, its pediment crowded with nauti-cal statuary—Neptune, Britannia, dolphins, and anchors.

East of the Lagan: Across the river, playing Impudence to the Custom House's Dignity, stands **SSE Arena** *(Queen's Quay, tel 028/9076-6000, ssearenabelfast.com)*, a $150 million sports and culture venue of the most modern kind—evidence of the confidence Laganside Development Corporation has engendered.

Walking seaward from the Lagan Lookout along Donegall Quay and under the motor-way bridge, with Titanic Belfast's silver prows gleaming across the river, you'll find the 1854 **Harbour Commissioner's Office** *(Corporation Sq., tel 028/9055-4422, group visits by prior arrangement, belfast-harbour.co.uk)*. The interior is rich in stained glass and elabo-rate plasterwork. Upstairs highlights include fine paintings of sailing ships in heavy seas, paintings of old Belfast harbor scenes by well-known turn-of-the-20th-century painter Eyre Macklin, and the Barnet Room, with its painted stucco barrel roof and stained-glass windows portraying the arms of Belfast's trad-ing partners in days of the Empire—Australia, Canada, Russia, the United States, India, Italy,

and the Cape Colony of South Africa.

Just along the street, look for the **Sin-clair Seamen's Church** *(Corporation Sq., tel 028/9080-1240, sinclairchurch.co.uk, open Wed. 2–4:30 p.m. except Jan.–Feb. & Sun. for services*

Stormont

A great place for walks is around Stormont, 5 miles (8 km) east of Bel-fast city center (see map p. 279). The 1928 Portland stone **Stormont Castle** *(tel 028/9052-1802, city bus 20A, 23, parliamentbuildings.org)*, seat of the Northern Ireland Assembly, is spectac-ularly sited at the crown of a mile-long (1.6 km) drive. The castle itself is only open to the public by appointment, but you are free to wander the 300 acres (120 ha) of parkland and woods. The castle can be visited only with twice-daily guided tours *(Mon.–Fri. at 11 a.m. & 2 p.m.)* but you can walk around the park on your own.

at 11 a.m. & 6:30 p.m.)*, designed by Sir Charles Lanyon and opened in 1857. Throughout the furnishings of this remarkable L-shaped Presbyterian church, with its separate Italianate tower, a nautical theme predominates, from the semaphore flags that spell out "Welcome" at each door to the ship's binnacle used as a font. Fishing boats and tugs feature in the stained-glass windows, the collection boxes are miniature lifeboats, and the pulpit is shaped like a ship's prow. On the walls hang the mast of a Guinness barge, port and starboard ship lights, and a silver flashlight with which some shipwreck victims summoned help. Fifty seats are kept empty for visiting sailors every Sunday, and the start of the service to which they are welcomed is signaled by six strokes on the brass ship's bell of H.M.S. *Hood,* sunk at the mouth of Portsmouth Harbour, England, in World War I. ▲ Map p. 279

COUNTY ANTRIM

The pride and glory of County Antrim resides in its spectacular coast and green hinterland. Stretching 75 miles (120 km) from Carrickfergus to Portrush and forming the northeastern rim of Northern Ireland, this playground of basalt and sandstone is like a giant natural sculpture park. Driving the Antrim coast road is one of the great highlights of any trip to Ireland.

Carnlough displays all the neatness, order, and architectural harmony of a planned village.

Carrickfergus

🗺 277 F3

Visitor Information

✉ Carrickfergus Castle, Marine Hwy., Carrickfergus, Co. Antrim

☎ 028/9335-8222

midandeastantrim. gov.uk

Carrickfergus Castle

✉ Marine Hwy., Carrickfergus, Co. Antrim

☎ 028/9335-1273

💲 $

Carrickfergus

The A2 coast road, heading north out of Belfast, passes through the suburb of Newtownabbey to reach Carrickfergus. Big and well preserved, **Carrickfergus Castle** stands on a rocky promontory by the harbor, a 90-foot (28 m) keep rising from gray battlemented walls. Sir John de Courcy built the castle in 1180 as a deterrent to any attacker advancing up Belfast Lough. It suffered various sieges and captures in its time, by Scots and French forces, as well as the English—all owing to its vital strategic position at the lough entrance.

In the town center, you can explore the 12th-century **Church of St. Nicholas** off the marketplace. The church contains notable late medieval glass and the beautifully carved 17th-century tomb of Sir Arthur and Lady Chichester, 1st Earl and Countess of Belfast, and their poignantly tiny son.

Just north of Carrickfergus, you'll see the **Andrew Jackson Cottage and U.S. Rangers Centre.** Though this thatched cottage offers a collection of Jackson-related material, fans and family of the former U.S. president (1767–1845) should be aware that his connection to the house is tenuous. Jackson's parents emigrated from the town two years before Andrew was born, and this house was not their home.

Islandmagee Peninsula

Beyond Carrickfergus, you can take a worthwhile detour around the 7-mile-long (11 km) **Island-magee Peninsula** (reached by the B150, off the A2 just north of Whitehead). The tidal inlet of **Larne Lough,** all but enclosed by the eastward arm of Islandmagee, is good for bird-watching and boating, while the peninsula itself has the very fine **cliffs of the Gobbins** looking out east into the Irish Sea. In late Victorian times, railway engineer and architect Berkeley Deane Wise (1853–1909) designed the Gobbins Path *(thegobbinscliffpath.com, $$),* a splendid walkway of cast-iron tubes and ladders, rock-cut steps, and tunnels that allowed intrepid ladies and gentlemen to venture along these sheer cliff faces. Wise's walkway eventually fell into disrepair, but recently a modern version replaced it.

The Coast Road

A ferry connects Ballylumford at the northern end of the peninsula with **Larne,** a bustling coastal ferry port. But Larne is the gateway to the real delights of the Antrim coast, which you skirt all the way north on the A2. Sir Charles Lanyon, chief architect of 19th-century Belfast, designed the road in 1834 as a project to enable destitute locals to earn some money.

Built by Scottish engineer William Bald, the coast road hugs the cliffs and passes the mouth of each of the nine Antrim Glens. Before the road was built, the inhabitants of the coast villages of Carnlough, Glenariff, Cushendall, and Cushendun had been all but cut off by intervening cliffs from each other and from Ballycastle to the north and Larne to the south. Trade and tourism quickly improved once the coast road opened.

INSIDER TIP:

The drive from Belfast along the Antrim coast is an essential road trip for any visitor to Northern Ireland. It's one of the most stunning scenic drives in the world.

—ALLY THOMPSON
National Geographic contributor

Antrim Glens

From Ballygalley, the coast rises to some fine limestone cliffs at **Carnlough,** a pretty fishing village around Carnlough Bay. But they are only the prelude to the dramatic Antrim coast. There are many glens or valleys in Antrim; nine in particular are recognized as the Antrim Glens—from south to north they are Glenarm, Glencloy, Glenariff, Glenballyeamon, Glenaan, Glencorp, Glendun, Glenshesk, and Glentaisie.

Carved by rivers and shaped by Ice Age glaciers and meltwaters, frosts, and other weathering processes, the Antrim Glens veer northeast as they bend and wriggle

Church of St. Nicholas

✉ 3 Lancasterian St., Carrickfergus, Co. Antrim

☎ 028/9336-0061

saintnicholas.org.uk

Andrew Jackson Cottage and U.S. Rangers Centre

✉ Boneybefore, Larne Rd., 2 miles (3 km) E of Carrickfergus on the A2

☎ 028/9335-8222

🕐 Closed on Mon.–Tue.

Larne

🗺 277 F4

Visitor Information

✉ Narrow Gauge Rd., Larne, Co. Antrim

☎ 028/2826-2495

midandeastantrim. gov.uk

Causeway Coast and Antrim Glens

🗺 277 F4

Visitor Information

☎ 028/7034-4723

visitcausewaycoast andglens.com

EXPERIENCE: Taste Treats at the Fair

Two delicacies you can't avoid at the **Ould Lammas Fair** *(Ballycastle, Co. Antrim, last Mon. & Tues. in Aug., visitcauseway coastandglens)* are yellowman and dulse. Yellowman is basically that brittle fairground toffee known as honeycomb, with a dash of vinegar to give it some bite. In his classic ballad "The Ould Lammas Fair," John Henry MacAuley is overcome with nostalgia as he recalls: "The scene that haunts my memory is kissing Mary Ann / Her pouting lips all sticky from eating Yellow Man," a rather charming image.

Another long tradition in Ireland is savoring the beautiful crimson seaweed *Palmaria palmata* ("dulse" or "dilisk" to

locals, *creathnach* or *duileasc* to Irish speakers)—not in its leathery shoreline state but after it has been thoroughly dried. Apart from its crunchy texture and salty, slightly citrus taste, it has a reputation for expelling parasite worms, guarding against "women's longing," and curing hangovers while giving a relish to the taste of beer—all useful properties at the Ould Lammas Fair.

Other Irish delicacies worth trying are colcannon (potato, onion, and cabbage), boxty (griddled potato cakes), champ (potatoes, chives, spring onion), soda bread, farls (Northern Ireland's fabulous flatbread), porter cake (fruitcake with stout), and barm brack (fruit bread).

Glenariff Forest Park

⛰ 277 E4

✉ On A43
Ballymena–
Waterfoot Rd.

☎ 028/7034-0870

**nidirect.gov.uk/
glenariff-forest-park**

through limestone, sandstone, and basalt to the coast. There is something magical in their quiet depths, all well grown with woodlands, and in the moorland and bare rock that rims them.

The glens are a very popular visitor destination, but few visitors leave their cars. If you set out to explore these delectable valleys on foot, you should have the landscape more or less to yourself.

Glenarm & Glencloy: Glenarm and Glencloy reach the sea at **Carnlough Bay,** from where the coast road curls on at the feet of the cliffs around **Garron Point.** Here the limestone hands over to dusky red sandstone as the cave-burrowed cliffs shoot up some 800 feet (250 m).

Glenariff: Around the corner from Garron Point begins the most striking section of the

Antrim coast as the coastal plain flattens into a green apron of land 3 miles (5 km) long. Glenariff, Glenballyeamon, and Glenaan converge here, their mouths separated by the dominant flat-topped 1,153-foot (350 m) prow of Lurigethan.

Turn left inland from the coast village of **Waterfoot** on the aptly named **Red Bay,** its shore stained with the iron ore mined in Glenariff until the turn of the 20th century. Continue up Glenariff, widest and grandest of the glens, under dark granite slabs, over which waterfalls pour after heavy rain.

Glenariff Forest Park is signposted high up the glen. You can enjoy a number of short nature trails, a medium-size scenic trail, and the 3-mile (5 km) **Waterfall Trail** around some of Glenariff's best falls.

Glenballyeamon to Glendun: Back on Red Bay, the road continues to **Cushendall,** where the B14 leads up Glenballyeamon. From Cushendall, a country road leads past the golf course over the hill of Cross Slieve, a short route to Cushendall's sister village of Cushendun at the foot of Glendun.

But if you bear inland with the A2, you can turn off in 1 mile (1.6 km) on a marked road to **Ossian's Grave.** Leave your car at the foot of the steep farm track that climbs to the monument; the reward for 10 or 15 minutes of upward walking is a wonderful view over glens, mountains, and coasts from Ossian's Grave. This is a 4,000-year-old horned cairn, a court grave, with pointed "horns" guarding its sacred enclosure; legend names it as the burial place of Fionn MacCumhaill's son, Ossian.

A side road climbs **Glenaan** to a junction of roads in wild moorland; bear right to return seaward down the beautiful wooded **Glendun.** You pass the triple-arched red sandstone viaduct by which Sir Charles Lanyon brought the main coast road over the Glendun River, and then **Craigogh Wood,** where an 18th-century Mass rock carries an incised Crucifixion scene.

Cushendun, just below, is a charming model village (now cared for by the National Trust) created for Lord Cushendun in the early 20th century by the visionary architect Clough Williams-Ellis. Its rugged cottages feature plenty of whitewash and slate as they peep out of the trees.

Ballycastle & Rathlin Island

The A2 now takes off inland for a 10-mile (16 km) moorland run to Ballycastle. A much more enjoyable alternative, however, is the rough, bumpy coast road *(signed "Scenic Route"),* which snakes and switchbacks through a high, rolling coastland of farms and sloping fields by way of **Torr Head** (there's a parking area here and wonderful sea views to add spice to a picnic lunch) to rejoin the A2 at Ballyvoy.

From here, it's a short run into **Ballycastle,** a handsome little seaside resort that comes alive at Lammastide, the last Monday and Tuesday of August. This is the date of the **Ould Lammas Fair**

Ballycastle

🗺 277 E5

Visitor Information

✉ 14 Bayview Rd., Ballycastle, Co. Antrim

☎ 028/2076-2024

■ **Carrick-a-Rede rope bridge**

Kebble Cliffs National Nature Reserve

🗺 277 E5

✉ W end of Rathlin Island

☎ 028/7035-9963

daera-ni.gov.uk

Boathouse Centre

🗺 277 E5

✉ Rathlin Island Harbor

☎ 028/2076-2024

🕐 Closed Sept.– March

(see sidebar p. 300), held here for the last 400 years, when lovers of seaweed, shellfish, and yellowman toffee arrive for an orgy of tasting. The seaweed is dulse, picked off the rocks locally and dried—eaten au naturel or lightly toasted according to taste. Yellowman toffee, available in the town, is a bright yellow, hard toffee that has to be broken up with a hammer.

From Ballycastle, a ferry leaves daily for **Rathlin Island** *(rathlin community.org),* a friendly and beautiful place that you certainly shouldn't miss. The L-shaped island, roughly 5 miles (8 km)

from east to west and 3 miles (5 km) from north to south, is home to about 70 islanders who rely on tourism, farming, and fishing—in that order—for their survival. Chief attraction is the **Kebble Cliffs National Nature Reserve** out at the west end of the island, where 250,000 seabirds—fulmars, kittiwakes, puffins, razorbills, guillemots—whirl and shriek during the April to July nesting season. In the village, there's a pub, and a fine museum in the **Boathouse Centre.**

Carrick-a-Rede Rope Bridge

Located near Ballintoy, the Carrick-a-Rede rope bridge is a scary cat's cradle of ropes and planking slung each salmon-fishing season (traditionally by local fishermen) between the mainland cliffs and a huge offshore rock—almost an island. The rock stands right in the path of salmon on their spawning run, forcing them to divert course into the nets that were cunningly set by the fishermen. The 60-foot (20 m) bridge, administered by the National Trust, is a great visitor attraction. Although it sways, bucks, and lurches as you walk 80 feet (25 m) above the sea, it's quite safe.

Giant's Causeway

Seven miles (11 km) beyond Carrick-a-Rede, and very well signposted, lies Northern Ireland's most celebrated tourist site, the Giant's Causeway, 37,000 hexagonal columns of

The hexagonal columns of the Giant's Causeway

The Old Bushmills Distillery

Just inland of the Giant's Causeway is the village of Bushmills, where Northern Ireland's finest whiskey is made at the Old Bushmills Distillery *(2 Distillery Rd., Bushmills, Co. Antrim, tel 028/2073-3218, bushmills.com)*. Bushmills is the world's oldest licensed distillery, first operating in 1608. Take a tour and view the gleaming copper stills and quaking brew in the giant mash tuns. The delightful warehouse is full of the sweet fragrance of the "angels' share"—whiskey vapor evaporating from the seams of the piled wooden barrels. You get a sample or two and the chance to buy a bottle of blended or single-malt Bushmills.

cooled basalt, formed from lava after a volcanic eruption some 60 million years ago. The cooled lava flow can be seen in the form of dark columns remarkably like closely stacked pencils, up to 40 feet (12 m) high, in the face of the 300-foot (92 m) cliffs. Victorian guides named the most striking of these formations the Giant's Organ Pipes, a very apt title. The giant was—who else?—the mighty Fionn MacCumhaill, and the best known part of the lava flow, the long shelf of tessellated columns that noses into the sea, is the causeway he laid down to reach his girlfriend on the Hebridean island of Staffa.

The mythology and geology of the Giant's Causeway is explained in the strikingly designed **visitor center** *(tel 028/2073-1855, giantscauseway tickets.com)* on the cliffs above. From here you can take a road train down to the causeway, or stroll down in 10 minutes. Walkers can continue from the causeway to the Organ Pipes, then turn back to the visitor center along a cliff path with fine views down onto the causeway and back along the basalt cliffs.

Dunluce Castle

Before reaching the resort of Portrush and the border with County Londonderry, turn for one of Ireland's most evocative sights: the extensive ruins of Dunluce Castle perched on the edge of the cliffs in a wonderfully romantic setting. In 1584, its gallant and bloody-handed

---

INSIDER TIP:

The Giant's Causeway is one of only a handful of geological formations of its kind in the world—another is directly across the sea in Staffa, Scotland.

—JIM FEENEY
National Geographic contributor

---

owner, Sorley Boy MacDonnell, recaptured the castle from the English in a fantastically daring attack. MacDonnell later fortified it with cannon from the wreck of the Spanish Armada galleon *Girona* (see p. 285). In 1639, the castle kitchens fell into the sea during a storm. Dunluce was abandoned and left in ruin. ∎

Carrick-a-Rede Rope Bridge
- 277 E5
- 5 miles (8 km) W of Ballycastle off B15
- 028/2073-3335
- $

nationaltrust.org.uk/ carrick-a-rede

Giant's Causeway
- 277 E5
- On B147 Causeway Rd., near Bushmills
- 028/2073-1855
- Park & Ride: March–Oct. from Bushmills, every 20 mins.
- $$
- Bus: Ulsterbus 172, Goldline 221, Open Top 177, Causeway Rambler 402, Antrim Coaster 252

nationaltrust.org. uk/giants-causeway

Dunluce Castle
- 277 D5
- 87 Dunluce Rd., Bushmills, Co. Antrim, 3 miles (4.8 km) E of Portrush
- 028/2073-1938
- $

COUNTY LONDONDERRY

County Londonderry (or Derry) forms the northwestern segment of Northern Ireland. A stretch of coast less dramatic than that of neighboring Antrim, but with its own charm, leads along the east and south shore of Lough Foyle to Londonderry city. Inland, the Sperrin Mountains spill over the border from County Tyrone, and a great stretch of hilly, forested country rises above the farmlands along Londonderry's eastern boundary of the River Bann.

■ Maurice Harron's "Hands Across the Divide" statue overlooks the Waterside area of Londonderry.

Londonderry City

🏛 276 C4

Visitor Information

✉ 44 Foyle St., Londonderry, Co. Londonderry

☎ 028/7126-7284

visitderry.com

Londonderry City

Generally, you will hear the city called Londonderry if the speaker is a Protestant or a mainland Briton, Derry if the speaker is a Catholic and/or a nationalist. Londonderry, or Derry (designated "City of UK Culture" in 2013), is Northern Ireland's "second city" after Belfast—a vibrant, lively, small city, very conscious of its past as a springboard to its future.

Maybe it's the more rural surroundings that make Londonderry conversation and humor seem lighter and less caustic than their Belfast counterparts. Or maybe it's

just the effect of being a very small city that has moved on a long way from the dark days of the 1960s and early '70s. Whatever the cause, Londonderry breathes a most attractive energy and optimism. This is a great place to spend a day or two, and the locals are only too happy to bend your ear or lend an ear—whichever you choose.

History of the City: Londonderry, meaning the "Place of the Oaks Where Londoners Live," stands on the River Foyle at the point where the river begins to widen into the sea outlet of Lough Foyle, a prime location for trade and defense. In 1613–1618, at the start of the plantation of Ulster with Protestant outsiders (see p. 26), the London trade guilds that had taken over Londonderry built a tight lozenge of defensive walls around the heart of the city. The walls had a testing trial toward the end of that century when, in April 1689, the deposed Catholic king of Britain, King James II, laid siege to the town. Londonderry had in fact been in a state of siege since the previous December, when 13 apprentice boys had locked the city gates against the Jacobite army. By the time the siege was broken in July 1689, 7,000 of the 30,000 defenders lay dead of disease, wounds, and starvation.

The Great Siege fueled centuries of provocation and bitterness. These flared in the 1960s as the city's Catholic majority, resentful of their lack of civil rights, found no redress from a city council dominated by supremacist Protestants. Bloody Sunday 1972 (see sidebar p. 34 & p. 287), when British paratroopers shot dead 13 civil rights marchers, was a Londonderry tragedy. Levels of violence soared, especially in the hard-line extramural Catholic ghetto of the Bogside. At one point, three-quarters of all buildings outside the walls had been damaged or destroyed by fire, bombs, or neglect.

City Sights: You'll be hard put to recognize any sign of past miseries in today's Londonderry. The bars along **Waterloo Street,** just outside the walls to the west,

are thronged at night. The **Craft Village** (tel 028/7126-0329, derrycraftvillage.com), inside the northern angle of the walls, is flourishing, with craft workshops, eateries, wine bars, and cafés around little paved squares.

The town's splendid 1890

Touring Londonderry

If you are interested in learning more about the city's nationalist Bogside neighborhood or its fierce and funny contemporary murals, try **Martin McCrossan's City Tours** (derrycitytours. com), or **Michael Cooper** (tel 028/7136-1311, derrybluebadgeguide.com), the only Blue Badge tourist guide in Derry. Based in the Bogside, **Free Derry Tours** (tel 077/9328-5972, freederry.tours) offers political walking tours that include the city's famous walls and St. Columb's Cathedral, while **Tours and Trails** (tel 028/7136-7000, toursntrails.co.uk) leads a walk along the walls that includes stories, songs, and even sweets!

Guildhall, built in local red sandstone under a monstrous clock tower, has the 1689 Siege of Derry depicted vividly in its stained-glass windows, and more stained glass in its Council Chamber and Main Hall. An exhibit on the ground floor tells the story of the colonization of Ulster that started at the beginning of the 17th century.

The **Tower Museum,** in Union Hall Place inside the walls, built in the 1970s, gives a balanced history of Londonderry. You learn of 17th-century prosperity, 18th-century industrialization, and the Home Rule movement of Victorian

(continued on p. 308)

Guildhall

✉ Guildhall Sq., Londonderry

☎ 028/7137-6510

visitderry.com

Tower Museum

✉ Union Hall Pl., Londonderry, Co. Londonderry

☎ 028/7137-2411

$ $

derrystrabane.com/ towermuseum

THE ORANGE & THE GREEN

Every July 12, the city streets and country lanes of Northern Ireland resound with the thump of Lambeg drums (marching drums with a painted skin) and the squeal of flutes as the Orange Order men go marching. For outsiders, it can be hard to understand the passionate commitment that these sober-faced, bowler-hatted Protestants in their orange sashes feel for this ritual and the bitter resentment it provokes in Catholic onlookers.

Orangemen on the march, the very picture of Unionist pride and defiance

A Source of Conflict

At Drumcree on the outskirts of Portadown, County Armagh, the July 12 marches have caused enormous anger and some bloodshed in recent years—so much so that successive Drumcree marches have been banned by the Parades Commission set up to control such explosive situations. Other venues across the province have been flash points for trouble, too.

If you ask an Orangeman, he will tell you that he is marching for two reasons. The first is to commemorate the victory of Protestant King William III over the deposed Roman Catholic King James II at the Battle of the Boyne on July 12, 1690. The second reason is to uphold Protestant tradition. If a nationalist Catholic gives an opinion, it will be that the

Orange marches are a show of triumphalism, a reinforcement of the traditional Protestant upper hand. There is truth in both assertions.

History of the Orange Order

The Orange Order was formed in September 1795 after a Protestant vigilante group, the Peep O'Day Boys, repulsed a raid made by the Defenders, a Catholic group, on Dan Winter's farm at Loughgall in County Armagh. An Orange Order museum has now been established at the house (see sidebar opposite). The July 12 march first took place the following year, 1796, and has continued as a Protestant tradition ever since.

Plenty of salt has been rubbed in Catholic wounds along the way, especially with the making of offensive gestures during the march and the playing of inflammatory sectarian tunes as the marchers pass through predominantly Catholic areas. Yet most Protestants in Northern Ireland deplore such provocation and are greatly distressed at the image the outside world has of them as insensitive supremacists.

Marches in Londonderry

Other Orange marches have been used to taunt Catholics, too, particularly the parades held around the walls of Londonderry on the Saturday nearest August 12 (the anniversary of the 1689 relief of the Great Siege; see p. 305) and the Saturday nearest December 18 (the date of the locking of the city gates by the 13 apprentice boys in 1688; see p. 305). Overlooking the Catholic enclave of Bogside, these marches symbolized the

■ **The other side of the coin, on St. Patrick's Day**

Orangemen's possession of the political and economic, as well as the physical, high ground. But with the recent hope of better interdenominational relations, the Derry Walls parades have dwindled in size and contentiousness.

Catholic Reaction

The Ancient Order of Hibernians, a Catholic organization, was founded in 1838, although it has its origins way back in Tudor times. The green-sashed members of the order continue to mount two of their own marches each year—on St. Patrick's Day, March 17, and on the Feast of the Assumption, or Lady's Day, August 15. But these marches are lower-key affairs than their Orange Order counterparts, more rural and more church-based, and provoke little or no aggression and bad feeling.

Partisan Museums

Although the violence of the Troubles has abated, the historical division between the two factions is still evident. Four museums offer an interesting, though clearly biased, view of the history of the region.

The **Museum of Orange Heritage** (Main St., Loughgall, Co. Armagh, tel 028/3889-2048, danwinterscottage.com, closed Sun.–Mon., $) is located in a house that once belonged to James Sloan, who founded the Orange Order together with James Wilson and Daniel Winter. The museum is dedicated to the history of the organization. Visitors can then stop at **Dan Winter's House** (9 Derryloughan Rd., Loughgall, Co. Armagh, tel 028/3885-1344, danwinterscottage.com), said to be the birthplace not only of Mr. Winter, but of the Orange Order itself.

Imprisoned in Armagh Gaol from 1973 to 1977, Eileen Hickey died before realizing her dream of a museum dedicated to Irish republican history. The **Eileen Hickey Museum** (Conway Mill Complex, Conway St., Belfast, tel 028/9024-0504, eileenhickey museum.com), opened in 2007, houses a collection of artifacts and handicrafts from the time of the Troubles, including republican posters and paintings.

The **Museum of Free Derry** (55 Glenfada Park, Bogside, Derry, tel 028/7136-0880, museumoffreederry.org, $, closed Sun. Nov.–June), located in the Catholic neighborhood of Bogside, focuses on the tragic events of Bloody Sunday and the history of the Northern Ireland Civil Rights Association that campaigned for civil rights in the 1970s (see p. 305).

■ Frederick Hervey, Bishop of Londonderry, built Mussenden Temple on the cliffs at Downhill.

St. Columb's Cathedral

✉ London St., Londonderry, Co. Londonderry

☎ 028/7126-7313

🕐 Closed on Sundays (open only for services)

stcolumbscathedral. org

The Siege Museum

✉ 13 Society St., Londonderry, Co. Londonderry

☎ 028/7126-1219

🕐 Closed Sundays

💲 $

thesiegemuseum.org

times. Last comes an exploration of the Troubles.

Walking the Walls: By far the best way to appreciate Londonderry is to walk the **Walls of Derry,** starting the 1-mile (1.6 km) circuit from the Tower Museum. Looking outward, you'll see the slogan-painted Bogside, poor Protestant estates, new shopping areas, the graceful new Peace Bridge for cyclists and walkers across the River Foyle, and a gorgeous view of the surrounding hills. Inward are shiny new shops and restaurants and regenerated housing. Make time to look into **St. Columb's Cathedral** inside Bishop's Gate, a shrine to the Great Siege and to Protestant nostalgia. The Walls are spectacularly lit by night. Lastly, you can explore the **Siege Museum,** an interactive exhibit dedicated to the siege of the city in 1689 and a section dedicated

to the formation of the Protestant fraternal society, the Apprentice Boys of Derry.

Downhill Demesne & Mussenden Temple

Five miles (8 km) west of Coleraine via the A2, on the northern Antrim border, a strange collection of buildings stands on the cliffs above the golfing resort of Castlerock. This is **Downhill Demesne,** an estate that once belonged to Frederick Hervey, 4th Earl of Bristol and Protestant Bishop of Londonderry. Erected on the cliffs in the 1780s, Downhill was built with a vast gallery to accommodate Hervey's art collection.

You can wander the sprawling ruins of the castle and its walled garden complete with icehouse and dovecote. Then stroll to the cliff edge to view the domed **Mussenden Temple** (1783–85), built by Hervey—some say for one of his mistresses. Also visit Hezlett House, a restored 17th-century thatched cottage.

West from Downhill the shark's-nose peninsula of **Magilligan Point** almost closes Lough Foyle—only a mile (1.6 km) of water separates it from the Inishowen shore in County Donegal. Side roads will give you access to this flat, fertile curve of coast, much of it reclaimed from the sea for agriculture.

Limavady

Inland and due south of Magilligan Point sits Limavady, a neat little Georgian town on the River Roe—"roe" means red, and the river does run a dusky crimson-brown. You can see it at its most spectacular just south of Limavady in **Roe Valley Country Park** *(tel 028/7772-1925, visitor center open all year round Apr.–Sept., Sun. only Oct.–March)*, a 3-mile (5 km) stretch of gorge and valley. Preserved remnants of Londonderry's linenmaking industry are scattered along the park—scutch mills where the flax fibers were separated for weaving, bleaching meadows in which the coarse woven cloth was spread to dry, and beetling mills where water-powered wooden hammers beat the linen to flatten and smooth it.

South to Maghera

The B68 leads south from Roe Valley Country Park to **Dungiven.** Just south of the town, off the A6 Maghera road, the impressive ruins of the early 12th-century

Augustinian **Dungiven Priory** perch on a bluff above the River Roe. In the church, you'll find one of the best tombs in Ireland, that of "Cooey of the Foreigners," Cooey-na-Gal O'Cahan (died 1385), who lies ready for battle in his armor, guarded by carvings of six soldiers in kilts—"gallowglasses," or mercenaries, from Scotland, whose hire gave Cooey his nickname.

The A6 leads southeast to **Maghera,** where you can head north for 2 miles (3 km) on the A29 before turning left on the Grillagh road. In 1.5 miles (2.5 km), bear left after Rockfield Farm on a track to a parking lot, the entrance to **Drumlamph Wood.** This is one of Northern Ireland's few remaining pieces of ancient woodland—45 acres (18 ha) of hazel and oak, rustling with red squirrels, where walkways lead through a mosaic of bog, river, and rushy pasture. ∎

Downhill Demesne, Hezlett House, & Mussenden Temple

- 277 D5
- Mussenden Rd., Castlerock, Co. Londonderry
- 028/7084-8728
- Hezlett House open daily mid-April–mid. Sept., weekends mid-March & mid-Apr. Downhill Demesne open all year round

nationaltrust.org. uk/downhill-demesne-and-hezlett-house

Limavady

- 277 D4

Visitor Information

- Roe Valley Arts & Cultural Centre, 24 Main St, Limavady
- 028/7776-0650

roevalleyarts.com

Bellaghy Bawn

Lovers of poetry should continue from Maghera, via the A42 and the B182, to Bellaghy. There, the fortified farmhouse of Bellaghy Bawn *(Castle St., Bellaghy, Co. Londonderry, tel 028/9082-3207, open Sun.),* built in 1613, contains a display on the life and work of Seamus Heaney, the recipient of the 1995 Nobel Prize in Literature (see p. 310). Born in 1939, Heaney grew up at nearby Mossbawn Farm. At Bellaghy Bawn, you can see first editions and manuscripts of his work.

EXPERIENCE: Visiting Seamus Heaney Country

It is quite remarkable how many poets such a small island has produced—and continues to produce. For lovers of Irish literature, exploring Seamus Heaney country is a must. Heaney (1939–2013), who won the Nobel Prize in Literature in 1995, is Ireland's most celebrated and widely read poet of recent decades. You can visit the places that inspired his works and attend events with readings of Heaney's poetry on his own home ground.

Seamus Heaney HomePlace

The museum dedicated to Seamus Heaney (*45 Main St., Bellaghy, tel 028/7938-7444, seamusheaneyhome.com, $*) is the ideal place to begin exploring the townland of this great poet. The museum, inaugurated in 2016 in an old building, is beautifully modern and rich in interactive, multimedia displays. It's divided into two sections—"People and Place," which includes the poet's personal objects and videos of him reading his work, and "Imagination and Inspiration," dedicated to the things and places that inspired him.

Laurel Villa

Laurel Villa Townhouse (*60 Church St., Magherafelt, Co. Derry, tel 028/7930-1459, laurel-villa.com;* see also Travelwise p. 377), a bed-and-breakfast on the outskirts of Magherafelt, is a mecca for poetry lovers in the heart of Seamus Heaney country. You'll notice the photographs and paintings lining the walls: James Joyce, Samuel Beckett, Seamus Heaney. There are poems printed on linen, first editions in glass cases.

Proprietor Gerardine Kielt keeps things immaculate and cooks quite wonderful breakfasts, too. Her husband, Eugene, organizes poetry readings at Laurel Villa and maintains contact with poets far and wide—including, during his lifetime, Seamus Heaney himself.

Heaney, a local boy born on a farm a few miles from Magherafelt, had a great admiration for the Kielts' love and respect for poetry and came to the unassuming Magherafelt house to give a reading of his poetry in front of an audience of 50. In addition to Laurel Villa's wide and varied collection of Heaney works and memorabilia, you can be sure of a varied program of readings by poets from across Ireland, and beyond.

Guided Tours

Readings are not the only poetical happenings associated with Laurel Villa. Eugene Kielt also offers guided tours around Seamus Heaney country, taking visitors to places that inspired the poet in some of his best known poems. Along with Bellaghy Bawn (see sidebar p. 309), these locations include **Barney Devlin's forge** at the Hillhead near Magherafelt ("The Forge"); the **old railway** cutting in the townland of Broagh ("The Railway Children"); **Church Island** on the shores of Lough Beg ("The Strand at Lough Beg," Heaney's eulogy for his second cousin, Colm McCartney, murdered by sectarian killers in 1975); **Anahorish,** where Heaney went to school ("Testimony"); and the graveyard where the poet, his brother Christopher, and cousin Colm lie near each other.

Exhibition at Seamus Heaney HomePlace

ULSTER-AMERICAN FOLK PARK

South across the Londonderry border in County Tyrone, this admirable collection of buildings gives an authentic flavor of life in bygone rural Ulster, while exploring the poverty and insecurity of tenure that forced families to emigrate. Another area of the park shows the kinds of houses that emigrants built for themselves in America and the life they took up there.

History brought to life: Authentic costumes and props help re-create scenes from Irish history.

Thomas Mellon was five years old when he emigrated in 1818 with his family from the simple house at Camphill, just north of Omagh, around which the Ulster-American Folk Park has grown since its inauguration in 1976. The young emigrant grew up to be Judge Thomas Mellon, whose son, Andrew, founded the steel industry in Pittsburgh. His descendants wanted to create a memorial to him, and to millions like him, forced from their native land by poverty and lack of opportunity.

The main benefactor, Dr. Matthew T. Mellon, flew over for the opening of the park's visitor center in 1980. He delighted everyone by recounting the tales he had heard his great-grandfather, Judge Thomas Mellon, tell of the Atlantic crossing he made in 1818, a dreadful three-month voyage.

Old World Collection

The **Mellon house** is typical of 19th-century peasant dwellings—dark and low with smoke-pickled yellow walls and creaky wooden beds, smelling of turf smoke and damp. Women in period costume bake and offer bread; ducks and hens quack and cluck around the door. It's a good introduction to this bucolic way of life, though the brisk waft of sanitization remains. An earlier house, of the kind lived in by most peasants in

Ulster-American Folk Park

🗺 276 C3

✉ 2 Mellon Rd., Castletown, Omagh, Co. Tyrone

☎ 028/8224-3292

🕐 Closed Mon., except bank holidays

💲 $$

nmni.com

the 18th century, is a single-room cabin into which parents and their children would have crammed.

Most of the buildings of the Old World collection were rescued from demolition and brought here. There's a dark, cobwebby **blacksmith's forge,** piled with bricks of turf, and a **weaver's cottage,** where a costumed spinner sits outside the door, busy at her wheel. Inside is one of the big looms that made possible the cottage weaving that sustained Ulster's linen industry until industrialization.

Nearby is the **Hughes house,** birthplace of John Joseph Hughes, who emigrated in 1817 as a child. Hughes rose to become the first Catholic Archbishop of New York, and he founded St. Patrick's Cathedral there in 1858.

The **National School from Castletown** is a great favorite with visiting school parties. Lessons are put on twice a day under the "firm but fair" schoolmarm, who instructs the children as they sit at cramped wooden desks.

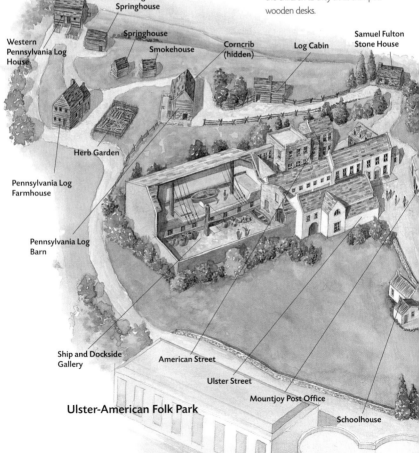

Cunningham Springhouse

Springhouse

Western Pennsylvania Log House

Smokehouse

Corncrib (hidden)

Log Cabin

Samuel Fulton Stone House

Herb Garden

Pennsylvania Log Farmhouse

Pennsylvania Log Barn

Ship and Dockside Gallery

American Street

Ulster Street

Mountjoy Post Office

Schoolhouse

Ulster-American Folk Park

A complete 19th-century **street** has been created from small-town premises all over Ulster—the little Mountjoy post office, a saddler's shop, a printer and stationer, Devlin the pawnbroker, Murray the draper, Hill the chemist (drugstore), and a pub brought from Newtownbutler.

The street leads to a dark and gloomy dockside with a ticket office, where a cobbled quay hosts a full-size reproduction of the central section of an **emigrant sailing ship.** You pass down a gangway into the ship's hold, with its low beams, tables, and wooden box berths 4 feet (1.2 m) wide and 5 feet (1.5 m) long into which a whole family would have squeezed.

A mock-up of a **New World dockside,** with tumbledown houses advertising "Cheap Logins" and plenty of cheats and sharpers ready to exploit the exhausted emigrants, reinforces a sense of the struggle most of them had when they did get to the other side.

New World Collection

The New World collection shows the kinds of log cabin built by those emigrant settlers who tried their luck in the huge open spaces of the Midwest. ■

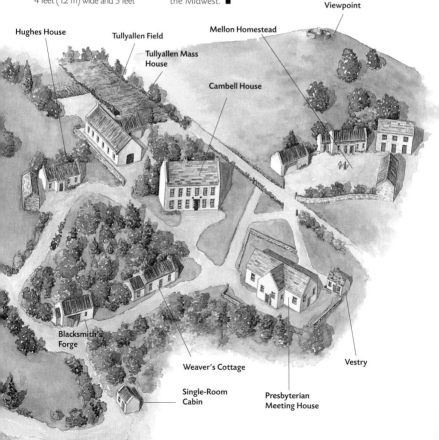

Viewpoint

Hughes House

Tullyallen Field

Mellon Homestead

Tullyallen Mass House

Cambell House

Blacksmith's Forge

Weaver's Cottage

Single-Room Cabin

Presbyterian Meeting House

Vestry

DRIVE: SPERRIN MOUNTAINS

The Sperrin Mountains are wild, lonely, and beautiful. They rise in a series of waves on the Tyrone/Londonderry border, seamed with the parallel east–west valleys of the Owenkillew and Glenelly Rivers. Settlements are tiny, views far and wide. This is the haunt of birds of prey, mountain hares, and the occasional hiker.

From Omagh, take the B48 north toward Gortin. In 6 miles (10 km), the road enters Gortin Glen between heavily wooded slopes. A 5-mile (8 km) track along the marked scenic drive of **Gortin Glen Forest Park ❶** (tel 028/8167-0666) takes you to beautiful corners of this coniferous forest. There are fine views ahead as the B48 dips into **Gortin ❷**, a small village at the foot of the **Owenkillew Valley.** The **Hidden Pearl Restaurant** (tel 028/8164-8157), at 16 Main Street, is a great place for hungry walkers (and drivers) to refuel.

From Gortin, take the B46 eastward for 4 miles (6 km); a mile (1.6 km) beyond Drumlea Bridge, bear left on a twisty mountain road along the south side of the valley. In 4.5 miles (7 km), at Monanameal, the road bends right for Greencastle; keep straight instead. After one mile (1.6 km), you'll pass a field on your left with two ancient stones, one a standing stone, the other a pillar known as the **Aghascrebagh Ogham Stone ❸**, with an inscription at least 1,500 years old in the ancient Irish

> ## NOT TO BE MISSED:
>
> **Gortin Glen Forest Park • Aghascrebagh Ogham Stone • Views from Barnes Gap • Sawel Mountain**

writing called Ogham—the only specimen in County Tyrone.

At Crouck Bridge, 10 miles (16 km) from Gortin, bear left and left again to return up the Owenkillew Valley on the north side of the river. In 6 miles (11 km), bear right at Scotch Town on a road through the spectacular viewpoint of **Barnes Gap ❹**, with fabulous views ahead across the Glenelly Valley to the highest Sperrin peaks—**Sawel Mountain** (2,225 feet/678 m) to the right, with its satellite **Dart Mountain** (2,030 feet/619 m), and straight ahead, the bulge of **Mullaghclogha** (2,080 feet/635 m). Down in Glenelly, turn right onto the road that keeps to the south side of the valley. In 3.5 very snaky miles (5.5

The rolling landscape of County Tyrone's beautifully untamed Sperrin Mountains

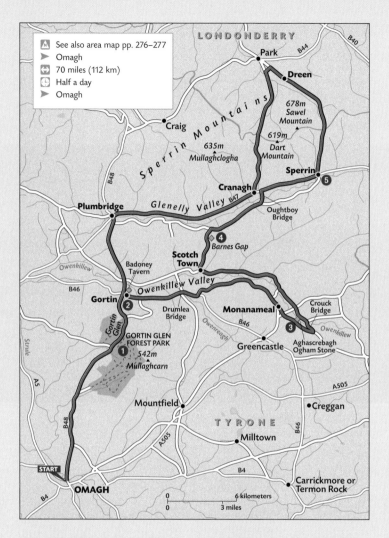

See also area map pp. 276–277
► Omagh
🔄 70 miles (112 km)
🕐 Half a day
► Omagh

LONDONDERRY

Park

Dreen

678m
Sawel
Mountain

619m
Dart
Mountain

Sperrin

Craig

S p e r r i n   M o u n t a i n s

635m
Mullaghclogha

Cranagh

Oughtboy
Bridge

Plumbridge

G l e n e l l y   V a l l e y   B47

Barnes Gap

Scotch
Town

Badoney
Tavern

O w e n k i l l e w   V a l l e y

Gortin

Drumlea
Bridge

Monanameal

Crouck
Bridge

Aghascrebagh
Ogham Stone

Greencastle

GORTIN GLEN
FOREST PARK

542m
Mullaghcarn

Mountfield

Creggan

T Y R O N E

Milltown

START

OMAGH

Carrickmore or
Termon Rock

0   6 kilometers
0   3 miles

km) turn left to descend and cross the river at Oughtboy Bridge. Bear right on the B47 along the north side of Glenelly. In 2.5 miles (4 km) turn left at **Sperrin** ⑤ and cross the moorland heart of the hills. This narrow mountain road takes you under the eastern flank of Dart Mountain (2,031 feet/619 m), and then **Sawel Mountain,** at 2,224 feet (678 m) the highest summit in the Sperrins.

Watch for birds of prey—big buzzards, little dark peregrines, and pale hen harriers. On the far side of the hills, the mountain road descends to meet the B44 at Park. Just before the B44, bear sharply left to return over the Sperrins into the **Glenelly Valley.** At Cranagh, turn right along the B47 for the 7-mile (11 km) run to Plumbridge, from where the B48 returns you to Gortin and Omagh.

AN CREAGAN & THE TYRONE BOGLAND

To the south of the Sperrin Mountains, the waist of County Tyrone wears a thick belt of blanket bog—a peat bog mostly composed of dead grasses and dependent on high rainfall. Hauntingly beautiful, it hides a marvelous archaeological treasure—a vast Stone Age and Bronze Age landscape only now beginning to emerge.

The mysterious stone circles and avenue at Beaghmore

An Creagan
🗺 277 D3
an-creagan.com

Start your trip around the blanket bogs of Tyrone at **An Creagan Visitor Centre** *(tel 028/8076-1112),* on the A505 road, midway between Omagh and Cookstown. The center gives an excellent overview of the area—its culture and traditions, the bogs themselves, the way they were formed, their great variety of wildlife, and the rare archaeological landscape that surrounds An Creagan. You'll also get a meal here and pamphlets that will direct you to the best sites within a 5-mile (8 km) radius of the center, some

reachable on foot and others by recommended cycling routes. To rent bikes, inquire at the Omagh visitor information office *(Strule Arts Centre, Townhall Sq., tel 028/8224-7831, closed Sun.).*

History of the Bogs

The blanket bogs began to develop during a cold and wet climatic phase around 1000 B.C. They crept in on a partly wooded landscape of birch, oak, hazel, and alder, much of it already cleared for farming thousands of years before. Stone Age farmers had erected standing stones, field walls, wedge tombs, and court tombs, and the Bronze Age people who followed them circa 2000 B.C. added stone circles, cist cairns, and artificial *crannog* islets in the bog lakes. The bog smothered all these and a moody landscape came into being: heathery and grassy bog and oily pools undulating to the horizon.

Farming ceased until dispossessed Catholics were forced to make the best of the boglands during the 18th and 19th centuries. Their attempts to cultivate the peat can be seen in the ruins of lime kilns and telltale ridges of earth beneath which potatoes were stored. The bog turf proved more useful for fuel, and turf cutters unearthed treasures like the Beaghmore Stone Circles.

Beaghmore

Beaghmore is the best known of the Tyrone archaeological sites, lying northeast of the center. The site contains an extraordinary number of stone alignments set up between 2000 and 1200 B.C.—three pairs of circles formed of stones varying from craggy chest-high boulders to prone chunks of rock, one solo circle filled with more than 800 little stone lumps, a dozen or so round cairns, and several stone rows running off to various unfathomable destinations.

Around An Creagan

Due north of An Creagan lies **Peadar Joe Haughey's Cottage,** the restored home of one of Tyrone's last native Gaelic speakers and the large patch of raised bog known as the **Black Bog.** Much deeper than the surrounding blanket bog, it formed over the remains of a deep lake. North again is **Dun Ruadh,** the Red Fort, a horseshoe-shaped cairn in which Bronze Age people buried 13 of their number.

South of the A505 lie several sites, pride of which are three remarkable tombs. Most westerly is **Loughmacrory wedge tomb,** built around 2000 B.C. with great capstones perched on curbstones. Southeast of An Creagan Visitor Centre, overlooking lonely Lough Mallon, **Creggandevesky court**

INSIDER TIP:

The bar at the An Creagan Visitor Centre has live traditional Irish music every weekend.

—MEREDITH WILCOX
*National Geographic Books
Director, Administration
and Rights Clearance*

---

tomb predates Loughmacross by at least 1,500 years and is one of Ireland's finest examples of its type. About 60 feet (18 m) long and composed of tons of tiny stones, it has three chambers. The burned bones of 21 people were excavated here.

Two miles (3 km) east, up a gravelly lane beyond a farmhouse, lies **Cregganconroe court tomb.** A giant capstone stands tilted to the sky among its curbstones and the remains of two sizable galleries and two small side chambers. ∎

Beaghmore
▲ 277 D3

Peader Joe Haughey's Cottage
▲ 277 D3

Dun Ruadh
▲ 277 D3

Loughmacrory Wedge Tomb
▲ 276 C3

Creggandevesky Court Tomb
▲ 277 D3

Cregganconroe Court Tomb
▲ 277 D3

COUNTY FERMANAGH

According to legend, the whole of County Fermanagh used to be dry plain. At its center was a well that the locals kept covered for fear that fairies had cursed it. One day, a girl and her lover happened by. Feeling thirsty, they took a drink from the well but forgot to replace the lid. Next dawn, as the rising sun hit the well, the water overflowed and would not stop. Soon much of Fermanagh was filled with water, and that's how things still stand today.

Belleek

276 A2

Belleek Pottery

Belleek, Co. Fermanagh

028/6865-8501

Closed weekends Jan.–Feb.

$

belleek.com

Almost all the water in the county belongs to the great twin lake system known as **Lower** and **Upper Lough Erne.** Together, the two lakes stretch for some 50 miles (80 km), hinged together by the isthmus on which stands Fermanagh's county town of Enniskillen. Lower Lough Erne is one mighty sheet of water, while Upper Lough Erne is more like a complicated system of small rivers winding around tiny islands, peninsulas, and headlands.

From here, via the Ballynamore and Ballyconnell Canal (renamed the Shannon-Erne Waterway; see p. 231), it is possible to cruise all the way south to the Shannon Estuary. As for the two lakes themselves, providing cruising and fishing for visitors is their economic lifeblood.

Belleek

At the westernmost end of the Lower Lough sits Belleek (Beleek), a lively village right on the border between County Fermanagh in Northern Ireland and County Donegal in the Republic. Belleek is a pretty place, with cast-iron street furniture and renovated wooden shop fronts. Its claim to fame is the glittering white parian ware that has been turned out since the 1850s by **Belleek Pottery.**

A tour around the factory shows you the process, in which a mixture of Cornish china clay and glass is beaten with wooden paddles to squeeze out air bubbles. Then, craftsmen shape the mixture into various forms before decorating them, perhaps with minute birds or flowers. The craftsmen tend to use homemade tools; they say a humble 5-inch (13 cm) nail

Nothing but the finest craftsmanship at Belleek Pottery

EXPERIENCE: Fishing in Ireland

Ireland is justly famed for its fishing. Atlantic waters, warmed by the Gulf Stream, yield a variety of marine fish species, from Mediterranean to North Atlantic, while the abundant lakes and brisk, highly oxygenated rivers give great trout and coarse fishing.

Information on regulations and fishing sites in Northern Ireland can be found at *www.dcal-fishingni.gov.uk*. South of the border, the **Central Fisheries Board** *(tel 01/884-2600, fishinginireland.info)* is a one-stop shop for anyone interested in fishing in Ireland, from coarse and sea fishing to pike, trout, and salmon. The board maintains a list of fishing tackle shops, guides and gillies, and charter boats. Check the website for regulations and licenses, information on regional boards, maps, and announcements of festivals and events.

---

with one end flattened is the key to success.

Naturally, you can buy examples of Belleek ware in the pottery showroom, though your pockets will need to be deep to afford the best basketware. Some pieces are decorated with lucky shamrocks, although it's doubtful whether these will bring you the kind of good fortune that attended one of the men who helped build the pottery. During construction, he slipped and fell from the roof to the ground but somehow landed on his feet, unharmed. He was given a stiff tot of whiskey and a pat on the back and sent straight back up to carry on with the job.

At Belleek, you can rent a cruiser for the Lower Lough, a lovely entryway to the world of the lakes.

South of Lower Lough Erne

A long ridge of hills crowned and collared by two big forests— Lough Navar Forest and Big Dog Forest—dominates the wide, hilly area south of Lower Lough Erne. **Lough Navar Forest** is well set out for forest driving and for waymarked walking. Most paths and tracks seem to lead eventually to the big panoramic map at **Lough Navar Forest viewpoint**, right on the dramatic bluffs of the **Cliffs of Magho**, where you can see not only the islands and straggly peninsulas of Lower Lough Erne but also Benbulben in County Sligo, 25 miles (40 km) to the west, and the pale 2,467-foot (750 m) triangle of Mount Errigal rising northward, 40 miles (60 km) away in northwest Donegal.

Two fine castles from the early 17th-century plantation days stand to the south: Tully Castle, beside the lough shore, and Monea Castle, on a rocky bluff farther inland. **Tully Castle** was built around 1610 by the Scottish Hume family. In 1641, Roderick Maguire, whose Catholic clan had had all their Fermanagh land confiscated after Hugh O'Neill's disastrous 1601 rising (see p. 26), enthusiastically joined in a general rebellion and burned Tully. Its garrison perished, in spite of Maguire's assurances of safe conduct to Enniskillen.

Tully Castle

🗺 277 B2

✉ Derrygonnelly, on Enniskillen–Belleek road, Co. Fermanagh

☎ 028/9082-3207

🕐 Open daily June–Sept., Sun. Oct.–May

The tall, gaunt ruins still have the turreted walls of their *bawn,* or defensive enclosure, and a delightful herb garden with a clipped hedge has been laid out in early 17th-century style.

Monea Castle, with its tall, baronial drum towers, looks as if it has been transported from the Scottish Highlands. It, too, was burned in 1641 and again by Jacobite troops in 1689 during their abortive attempts to take Enniskillen. After another fire in 1750, it was finally left to decay.

North of Lower Lough Erne

The north side of Lower Lough Erne possesses two fine forest parks, both with extensive shorelines. **Castle Caldwell Forest** *(tel 028/6634-8855),* 4 miles (6 km) east of Belleek, has beautiful walks along two long wooded lake peninsulas. There's excellent bird-watching here. By the lodge at the park entrance on the A47 is a **memorial stone,** shaped like an outsize violin, to Denis McCabe, a fiddle player who drowned on August 13, 1779, after falling off Sir James Caldwell's barge into the lough while drunk.

Castle Archdale Forest Park, halfway down the lough, has a herd of red deer, a marina where boats can be rented, and more walks.

Five miles (8 km) south, toward Enniskillen, it's worth turning aside into the village churchyard at Killadeas to look at the

Journey into the depths of the Earth—the wonders of Marble Arch Caves are viewed by boat.

Marble Arch Caves

The southern border of Fermanagh bulges into the panhandle of northwest County Cavan. Down here, south of lovely Lough Macnean Lower, the hills are riddled with caves. In the northern flank of Cuilcagh Mountain, you can visit Marble Arch Caves *(5 miles/8 km W of Florence Court, off the N16 Enniskillen–Sligo road, tel 028/6634-8855, marblearchcaves geopark.com, closed Jan.–mid-March, $$).* The exciting tour—which starts with a boat ride along an underground river—ends with a walk among stalagmites, stalactites, and other weird calcite formations, an unforgettable experience not to be missed.

Bishop's Stone. This memorial stone, probably carved around the eighth century, commemorates an abbot with a profile portrait on one side. On the other side of the stone, a very pagan-looking face stares out fixedly. It is as if the carver was reflecting the contemporary changeover (or maybe the early Celtic church's live-and-let-live policy) between paganism and Christianity.

Enniskillen

Both the north and south routes along the shores of Lower Lough Erne converge at Enniskillen, on the narrow isthmus separating the lower from the upper lake. Fermanagh's chief town sits right at the heart of the county, socially and economically as well as geographically. There's an excellent tourist office here, several decent hotels, and all the main facilities of a sizable town. The straggling main street—which changes name six times in its mile-long (1.6 km) course—contains a gem of a watering hole in the unreconstructed Victorian pub known as **Blake's of the Hollow** *(tel 028/6632-2143,*

blakesofthehollow.com). From the whiskey tuns and wood-paneled snugs to the excellent Guinness and frequent traditional music sessions, this is a treasure of a place.

Along the River Erne, you'll find **Enniskillen Castle,** with its handsome twin-towered water gate; a regimental museum here deals with the history of the Inniskilling Fusiliers, and a good heritage center covers Fermanagh history. You can buy local crafts in the converted Buttermarket and watch Fermanagh dealers and farmers in the lively cattle market.

The town's **war memorial** commemorating World Wars I and II, at the top of East Bridge Street, gained worldwide notoriety as the scene of the murder of 11 people by the IRA in a bomb explosion on Remembrance Day, November 11, 1987.

North of the memorial is Forthill Park, where **Cole's Monument** rises from the center of a star-shaped 17th-century fort. The fluted column, erected in 1857, honors Gen. Sir Galbraith Lowry Cole (1772–1842), brother of the 2nd Earl of Enniskillen and one of the Duke of Wellington's generals

Enniskillen

🗺 276 B2

Visitor Information

✉ Wellington Rd., Enniskillen, Co. Fermanagh

☎ 028/6632-5000

fermanaghlakelands. com

Enniskillen Castle

✉ Castle Barracks, Enniskillen, Co. Fermanagh

☎ 028/6632-5000

🕐 Call for opening times

💲 $

enniskillencastle. co.uk

The Tudor water gate of Enniskillen Castle, looking out over the River Erne

Crom Estate

🗺 276 C1

✉ 3 miles (5 km) W of Newtownbutler off A34, Co. Fermanagh

☎ 028/6773-8118

🕐 Closed Nov.– Feb.

💲 $

nationaltrust.org. uk/crom

in the Napoleonic Wars. Climb the 108 spiral steps inside the column for a wonderful view over Enniskillen and Lough Erne.

Around Upper Lough Erne

South of Enniskillen the landscape explodes into a crazed maze of water and land as the River Erne wriggles through the countless windings and backwaters of Upper Lough Erne. **Derrylin** ("the friendliest place in Fermanagh"), on the south side of the Upper Lough, and **Lisnaskea,** on the north side, are two pleasant small towns where you can catch your breath.

In the south part of the lough, near the Cavan border and 3 miles (5 km) west of Newtownbutler, the National Trust administers the **Crom Estate** on the east shore of

INSIDER TIP:

Foodies should pick up a "Taste of Ulster" brochure at any local tourist office. It lists all the province's restaurants and cafés that use local produce and traditional cooking.

—ALLY THOMPSON
National Geographic contributor

the lake (note: New Crom Castle is a private residence). The 1611 plantation castle is a picturesque ruin by the lakeshore, with two giant and gnarled 17th-century yews growing in the garden. Here you will find woodland and lough shore walks, deer, and pine martens. ■

EXPERIENCE: Cruising Lough Erne

Though you can catch many charming glimpses of the Upper and Lower Loughs from the shore, you can only enjoy the full picture by cruising their island-dotted waters. The two main boating centers are Belleek (see pp. 318–319) and Enniskillen (see pp. 321–322).

There are reputed to be 93 islands in Lower Lough Erne (or is it 97?) and 152 (or is that 177?) in Upper Lough Erne. No one's counting—but there are plenty of options.

Lower Lough Erne

The Lower Lough's best known island is **Devenish,** just downstream of Enniskillen *(Erne Water Taxi, ferry from Lakeland Forum Building, tel 077/1977-0588, ernewatertaxi.com, closed mid-Nov.–Feb.),* with its superb round tower, ruins of monastic churches, and finely carved high cross.

In Caldragh Cemetery, on **Boa Island** *(causeway bridges on the A47),* you'll find the enigmatic fifth- or sixth-century Janus figure, its two pagan faces staring wildly in opposite directions.

On **White Island** *(ferry from Castle Archdale Country Park, tel 028/6862-1892, castlearchdaleboathire.com, closed Oct.–Easter, weekdays Easter–June & Sept.)* stand some stone carvings that experts have puzzled over. Look for a *sheela-na-gig* (the figure of a grinning woman holding open her vulva), two probable representations of Christ, a scowling head, along with a bishop, and someone who may be King David. The carvings may date back to the sixth century.

Upper Lough Erne

In Upper Lough Erne, three islands with ancient pagan or monastic carvings are easily reached by either car or boat. **Inishkeen** *(causeway off the A4 just S of Enniskillen)* has strange carved stones in the cemetery of St. Fergus's Church—an antlered head and someone in a vessel. On **Cleenish,** reached by a bridge 2 miles (3 km) east of Bellanaleck, several finely carved gravestones can be found, while in the south, on **Galloon** *(causeway from Landbrock crossroads, 2 miles/3 km S of Newtownbutler),* are more macabre 18th-century gravestones with designs that include skull-and-crossbones and hourglass motifs.

Boat Rentals & Cruises

Enniskillen:
Guided cruises and day-boat rentals on Lower Lough Erne are offered by **Erne Tours Ltd.** *(028/6632-2882, ernetours.com);* contact **Lochside Cruisers** *(tel 028/6632-4366, lochsidecruisers.com)* for rentals.

Belleek (Beleek):
Contact the **Belleek Angling Centre** *(tel 028/6865-8181)* for day-boat rentals.

Linsaskea:
Lisnaskea Share Discovery Centre *(tel 028/6772-2122, sharevillage.org)* offers guided tours of the Upper Lough Erne in addition to an array of water activities.

The round tower and monastic buildings on Devenish Island are one of the chief attractions for boaters on Lough Erne.

TWO GREAT FERMANAGH HOUSES

The 18th century was the golden age of grand landscaping and domestic architecture in Ireland. The rich commissioned the very biggest and best country houses that money could buy. County Fermanagh boasts two of the most enchanting.

■ Florence Court stretches its arcaded wings wide, as if embracing its beautiful parkland.

Florence Court

🏛 276 B1

✉ Signed off the A32 Enniskillen–Swanlinbar road, 8 miles (13 km) SW of Enniskillen

☎ 028/6634-8249

🕐 House: Seasonal; visit website for hours. Grounds: Open year-round

💲 $

nationaltrust.org. uk/florence-court

Florence Court

Florence Court is a secluded 18th-century house, tucked away in beautiful wooded grounds looking southwest to the jagged ridge of Cuilcagh Mountain. The Cole family (later Earls of Enniskillen) built it in stages from the 1750s—first the three-story central block and then the arcaded wings.

In the summer, these grounds provide the setting for various outdoor events, from Victorian garden parties and country fairs to a children's teddy bear picnic. One interesting feature is the **sawmill**

that was established by the 3rd Earl of Enniskillen during the Great Famine to give paid work to some of his destitute tenants.

Among various lovely woodland walks, one leads toward Cuilcagh Mountain. It passes the **Florence Court Yew,** a tattered old thing shaped like a rocket that was found growing on Cuilcagh in the mid-18th century. Its offspring cuttings have established a distinct species, the Irish yew.

In 1955, the National Trust had to restore the entire house interior—only five years after it acquired the property—following a fire. Wonderful rococo plasterwork can be seen on the staircase walls and the dining ceiling, where puff-cheeked cherubs represent the Four Winds of Heaven and birds fly among flowers.

Upstairs, family prints, drawings, and photographs are displayed. In the bedside table beside the elegant four-poster in the Countess's bedroom is a rare piece of Belleek Pottery (see pp. 318–319)—a chamber pot with a picture of 19th-century British prime minister William Gladstone strategically placed on the bottom. Gladstone forfeited the allegiance—indeed, inspired the hatred—of many Irish Ascendancy families (those with British backgrounds who lived and owned land in Ireland) with his support

INSIDER TIP:

Florence Court's Glen Wood Trail is a spectacular hike that passes the Florence Court Yew. Trail maps are available at the gift shop or at *walkni.com*.

—LARRY PORGES
*National Geographic
Travel Books editor*

for the Home Rule bill that threatened to destroy their comfortable supremacy.

Castle Coole

The Lowry-Corry family, Earls of Belmore, built Castle Coole at the end of the 18th century. A flock of greylag geese has been resident in the park for at least 300 years, and legend says that the Belmores will remain at Castle Coole as long as the geese do. The present earl lives in another house on the estate.

Regency architectural supremo James Wyatt designed the great Palladian mansion. Completed in 1798, it is reckoned to be the finest neoclassical house in Ireland. It was commissioned by Armar Lowry-Corry, a country squire who got lucky in 1741 when he inherited the estate along with streams of money, property, and lands throughout Fermanagh, Tyrone, and Donegal. The house was built as a grand statement of his capacity to exercise power and influence over the Irish political scene. He was created 1st Earl of Belmore in 1797, but vicissitudes of life brought him no joy—his dark-haired beauty of a wife ran off and left him miserable. He died in 1802, so much in debt that his son, the 2nd Earl, had to wait 20 years before finishing the decorations and furnishings.

The house with its **portico** of four immense columns stands on a ridge on 1,500 acres (600 ha) of beautiful parkland. Almost all the original furnishings are here, still in the rooms for which they were designed and built. The oval **saloon,** with its elaborate cast-iron stoves, the **dining room,** and the **drawing room** are floored with Irish oak and opulently furnished. The canopied bed in the **State Bedroom** was created for a visit by King George IV in 1821 (he never showed up, reportedly because he was dallying elsewhere with one of his mistresses). ∎

Castle Coole

🗺 276 B2

✉ On the A4 Enniskillen–Belfast road, 1.5 miles (2.5 km) SE of Enniskillen

☎ 028/6632-2690

🕐 House: Seasonal; visit website for hours. Grounds: Open year-round

💲 $

nationaltrust.org.uk/ castle-coole

Florence Court Mill

It is the Victorian domestic details that bring the heyday of the grand country houses vividly to life. In the gardens of Florence Court, a dripping wooden aqueduct or headrace feeds a big cast-iron waterwheel. In the shed alongside, a wicked-looking circular saw whirs around. Roughly sawn planks lie nearby. Lingering here and savoring the resinous smell of sawdust, the quiet clanking of the wheel, and the rattle of the slack old driving belt, one can easily imagine it is the 19th rather than the 21st century.

COUNTY ARMAGH

County Armagh, with its oppressive republican reputation, is few people's idea of a visitor destination. Yet historic houses and towns, landscape beauty, and local friendliness are to be found in plenty in this most maligned of the six counties.

■   At the Armagh Planetarium on College Hill in Armagh city

Oxford Island

🏛 277 E2

✉ Oxford Island, Lough Neagh, Craigavon, Co. Armagh

☎ 028/3832-2205

oxfordisland.com

The Argory

🏛 277 D2

✉ Derrycaw Rd., Moy, Dungannon, Co. Armagh

☎ 028/8778-4753

🕒 Visit website for opening times

💲 $$

nationaltrust.org.uk/the-argory

Oxford Island

The southern shore of Lough Neagh closes the northern boundary of County Armagh, and here, at the **Lough Neagh Discovery Centre** on Oxford Island, you can learn about the natural history and traditions of the biggest lake in the British Isles. From the bird-watching blinds, you can enjoy the sight of dozens of bird species.

The Argory & Ardress House

South of the M1 Dungannon–Belfast motorway stands **The Argory,** signed from junctions 13 and 14. Built in 1820, the

house has an atmosphere and furnishings that have remained frozen in the year 1900. **Ardress House,** 3 miles (5 km) southeast of the Argory, is a 17th-century farmhouse swollen into an 18th-century mansion. Children love the working farmyard attached to the house.

Armagh City

The ancient capital of Ulster and seat of both Catholic and Anglican Bishops of Ireland, Armagh city has two cathedrals, one for each denomination, on opposite hills—symbolic of their intransigent positions during the recent Troubles.

Fionn MacCumhaill on Slieve Gullion

When you climb to the top of Slieve Gullion in South Armagh, you'll find a dark little lake, the Calliagh Beara Lough, just by the north cairn. Legend has it that Fionn MacCumhaill met Miluchra, an enchantress in the shape of a beautiful young woman, here. She begged him to dive into the lake to retrieve her gold ring. Gallant Fionn did as the maiden asked, but on climbing out of the water, the hero found himself transformed into a feeble old man. The damsel, meanwhile, had turned into a withered hag, the Calliagh Beara.

Some say it was Fionn's men who found the Calliagh Beara hiding in the summit cairn and forced her to undo the mischief. Others tell of how Fionn's dog, Bran, fetched the hero's grandson Oscar, who caught a fairy man who gave Fionn a drink of youth to revitalize him.

The building of the Gothic **Catholic Cathedral of St. Patrick** began in 1838, stopped during the famine, and was completed in 1873. Standing proud at the top of a long flight of steps, it's a marvel of ornate marble and mosaic, with gold-winged angels soaring high in the vaulted nave roof.

Across the valley, the **Anglican cathedral**—also dedicated to St. Patrick—is lower, smaller, and far older than its Catholic counterpart. Built in medieval times and restored in 1765, it holds fine monuments, including the splendid Tandragee Idol, an Iron Age effigy grinning under his fat cheeks and clutching one arm. He might be a representation of Nuada the Silver-handed (see p. 262). Outside, on the west wall of the north transept, is a memorial to Brian Boroimhe or Boru, mightiest of all Ireland's High Kings, who died in 1014 at the Battle of Clontarf, the final victory over the Vikings. Brian lies buried "in the north side of the great church," according to contemporary accounts.

Armagh's **public library** (tel 028/3552-4072), on Abbey Street near the Anglican cathedral, is an antiquarian's dream of old leather books in a solemn and splendid room. **Armagh Planetarium** has different shows to suit stargazing fans of all ages, plus lots of space exhibits, hands-on children's crafts, and real live rocket-launching sessions. The **County Museum,** in the Mall East, has a fabulous collection of artifacts, wooden drinking cups, Bronze Age jewelry, and tools. Two miles (3 km) west of Armagh is **Navan hill fort,** the ancient Eamhain Mhacha, or Queen Mhacha's Palace. The Kings of Ulster ruled from this great mound for 1,000 years.

South Armagh

In South Armagh, you will find regular music and storytelling at the **Tí Chulainn Cultural Activity Centre** (see p. 45), in Mullaghbane. The **Slieve Gullion Forest Park** (5 miles/8 km SW of Newry, tel 028/3031-3170, open all year round) is signed off the B113 between Meigh and Fork-hill; from here you can drive or walk. The final scramble to the Bronze Age cairns on the summit of Slieve Gullion is short but steep, the view spectacular. ∎

Ardress House
- 🅰 277 E2
- ✉ Annaghmore, Co. Armagh, on B28, 7 miles (11 km) W of Portadown
- ☎ 028/8778-4753
- 🕐 Visit website for opening times
- 💲 $

nationaltrust.org.uk/ardress-house

Armagh
- 🅰 277 D2

Armagh Planetarium
- ✉ College Hill, Armagh, Co. Armagh
- ☎ 028/3752-3689
- 🕐 Closed Sun.
- 💲 Exhibition: $; show: $$

armagh.ac.uk

County Museum
- ✉ The Mall East, Armagh, Co. Armagh
- ☎ 028/3752-3070
- 🕐 Closed Sun.

visitarmagh.com

WALK: TRASSEY TRACK TO HARE'S GAP, MOURNE MOUNTAINS

The Mountains of Mourne sweep down to the sea at the southern extremity of County Down—beautifully shaped pink-gray granite peaks, 12 of them over 2,000 feet (610 m), all packed into an area measuring 15 by 8 miles (24 by 13 km). Lakes hide in the heart of the Mournes, and there are famous beauty spots such as the narrow and dramatic Spelga Pass. These are accessible by car, but the Mournes are above all walkers' country.

The spectacular views from the high places of the Mourne Mountains make the climb worthwhile.

You need to dress in suitable hill-walking gear and take with you a map, a compass, and food and drink. Weather conditions can change quickly, and though the highest peak, Slieve Donard, is only 2,788 feet (850 m), these are proper mountains. Once on the peaks, though, it's hard to get lost, thanks to the Mourne Wall, a 22-mile (35 km) circuit of drystone wall that links the main inner summits. It was built between 1904 and 1922 to help poverty-stricken, hungry men earn enough to feed their families.

NOT TO BE MISSED:

Views back from the Trassey Track
• Views forward from Hare's Gap

The walk to Hare's Gap starts from the little parking lot under the forest-covered Clonachullion Hill. From the entrance, walk left along the road, and after about 70 yards (64 m), bear left through a gate and follow the Mourne Way up the **Trassey Track,** a well-trodden route that

Walking in the Mourne Mountains

The Ordnance Survey of Northern Ireland publish an excellent 1:25,000 Activity Map, "The Mournes," which gives the detail that allows you to enjoy every part of these beautiful mountains on foot. Buy the map and books of Mourne walks at **Newcastle Visitor Information Centre** *(10–14, Central Promenade, tel 028/4372-2222)*. You can get local information about conditions on the Trassey Track (and a cup of tea and snack) at **Meelmore Lodge** *(tel 028/4372-5949)*, just down the road from the starting parking lot.

climbs gradually, keeping the large **forestry plantation ❶** on your left. At the top edge of the trees, the Mourne Way long-distance footpath bends away to the right. But keep walking straight ahead, swinging a little to the left and then straightening to climb on steepening ground, with the Trassey River on your right.

The section of the track you are on now is known as the **Brandy Pad ❷**, with good reason: It is part of an old smuggler's path by which contraband goods (including brandy) were brought by pack pony through the heart of the Mournes from the coast south of Newcastle. Once down in the lowlands on the inland side of the mountains, they could be hidden around any number of farms before onward transportation.

⚐ See also area map p. 277 F1
► Parking lot just NE of Trassey Bridge, below Clonachullion Hill (1 mile/1.6 km off the B180, 4 miles/6 km W of Newcastle), Co. Down
↔ 4 miles (6 km), with 850 feet (260 m) of ascent
🕑 3 hours
► Parking lot just NE of Trassey Bridge

In 1 mile (1.6 km) the Trassey Track crosses the river and bears away right toward some old granite **quarries ❸**, but you should keep straight ahead here on a path that climbs, at first gently and then steeply among boulders, to reach the **Mourne Wall ❹** in **Hare's Gap.** Take plenty of time to walk forward and admire the stunning views over the end of Ben Crom Reservoir to the bulk of Slieve Commedagh (2,515 feet/767 m) and Slieve Donard.

From here, retrace your steps back down to the parking lot, with still more wonderful views in prospect.

ST. PATRICK'S COUNTRY

The spirit of Ireland's patron saint infuses the region known as St. Patrick's Country. For it was in this lovely but rather overlooked corner of County Down, between Strangford Lough and the Mourne Mountains, that St. Patrick landed in 432 to begin his great mission of converting Ireland to Christianity.

The Life of St. Patrick

Did St. Patrick even exist? The answer to this question varies depending on who you talk to, but it is most probable that he did. The best guess is that he was born in Scotland or Wales, perhaps the son of a Roman centurion at the end of the Roman Empire's tenure in the British Isles. At the age of about 16, he was captured by Irish marauders and taken to County Antrim, where he was put to work herding sheep on Slemish Mountain for six years or so. It seems that some pioneer missionary converted him to Christianity during this period of enslavement.

Patrick finally escaped on a ship that was carrying a cargo of wolfhounds and made his way to Gaul (France). Perhaps a quarter of a century of wandering and preaching across the Continent followed. Then, in 431, Patrick was appointed bishop and, the following year, made his landing in County Down. He probably sailed up the estuary of the Slaney River and landed at Ringbane near Saul, which is located just east of present-day **Downpatrick.**

Patrick, always a practical missionary, hastened to convert the local chief, Dichu, the man with the greatest on-the-spot influence, and Dichu gave Patrick use of a barn (*sabhal* in Irish, hence "Saul") as a temporary base. Though the saint was to move on and travel all through the north

Each spring, fresh daffodils are placed on the great incised graveslab of St. Patrick outside Downpatrick Cathedral.

West of Downpatrick

Two more ecclesiastical sites a little to the west of Downpatrick are well worth visiting. **Inch Abbey** (tel 028/9082-3207), off the A7 just beyond the river bridge, is a Cistercian monastery with a fine triple-lancet east window that is beautifully sited beside the River Quoile.

At Loughinisland (take the B2, then the Loughinisland road), three old churches stand on a drumlin island in a lake cradled by hills. You can cross via a causeway to explore these churches. The most notable of the three is **MacCartan's Chapel** with its tiny door, inscribed PMC (for its builder, Phelim MacCartan), and dated 1636—a time when to build a Catholic church was to invite persecution, and maybe even death.

of Ireland, it was to Saul that he returned to die in 461, in the monastery he had founded there.

In 1932, the 1,500th anniversary of Patrick's arrival, a church and round tower in traditional Gaelic style were built on the spot. The **Saint Patrick Centre** contains a very good exhibition about the saint's life and work, with emphasis on local Patrick-related sites. You can climb the purgatorial Stations of the Cross path up the nearby hill of Slieve Patrick to the altar and 30-foot (9 m) cross on top. From the summit there are great views over Strangford Lough and the Lecale Peninsula.

Sites Associated With St. Patrick

In common with all early Christian missionaries, Patrick was a great mortifier of the flesh. At **Struell Wells** (information from Downpatrick visitor information), 2 miles (3 km) south of Saul (signed off the Downpatrick–Ardglass road), the saint tested his own fortitude by immersing himself in freezing water and spending "a great part of the night, stark naked, singing psalms and spiritual songs." The wells in their green valley gained a great reputation for healing powers and were developed in the 18th century into a pilgrimage complex.

Today you can explore the roofless women's bathhouse and the men's bathhouse, with its benches and dark, cold bathing tank under a heavy stone roof. Look, too, for the well whose water cures eye disease, and the domed drinking well—long known as the Tub—in which St. Patrick spent his prayerful night of immersion.

Downpatrick Cathedral, on its rise of ground, is mostly 19th- and 20th-century work. In the shadow of its walls lies the vast slab of rock, inscribed "Patric," that was laid over St. Patrick's grave in 1901 to stop pilgrims removing the sacred earth. Late 12th-century Norman lord Sir John de Courcy vowed he had reburied Patrick's bones here, along with those of St. Columba, who died on Iona in 597, and St. Brigid, who died in Kildare in 523. Whether all or any of them really lie under the great rock is open to question. ∎

Downpatrick

🗺 277 F2

Visitor Information Centre & Saint Patrick Centre

✉ St. Patrick's Sq., Market St., Downpatrick, Co. Down

☎ 028/4461-9000

🕐 Closed Sun., except July–Aug.

💲 $

saintpatrickcentre.com

STRANGFORD LOUGH & THE ARDS PENINSULA

East of Belfast lies one of Ireland's most beautiful and haunting landscapes—the long southward-curving arm of the Ards Peninsula and the great bird-thronged sea inlet of Strangford Lough. Two fine National Trust houses, a spatter of islands, and some dramatic coastline complete the picture of County Down.

House and garden form a fine composition at Mount Stewart on the shores of Strangford Lough

Bangor

🗺 277 F3

Visitor Information

✉ 34 Quay St., Bangor, Co. Down

☎ 028/9127-0069

visitardsand northdown.com

Strangford Lough

🗺 277 F3–G2

visitstrangford lough.co.uk

The Ards Peninsula begins at the seaside town of **Bangor**, in northern County Down, and runs south for some 25 miles (40 km). Its coast looks east to the Irish Sea, over splendid sandy beaches often heaped with seaweed and interspersed with rocky coves and fishing villages. At the southern tip, a glorious 5-mile (8 km) coastal walk leads around the hamlet of **Kearney.** The National Trust maintains both village and coast.

Strangford Lough

The inner coastline of Ards is entirely different; Strangford

Lough, onto which it looks, has a muddy, mysterious, estuarine feel. The lough is 19 miles (30 km) from innermost corner to the peninsula tip, a great tidal inlet full of drumlin islands, whose waters recede at low tide to expose mighty mudflats and sandbanks.

The bird-watching here is unequaled in Northern Ireland (see sidebar opposite); some 12,000 light-bellied brent geese fly from Greenland to overwinter here, and regular gatherings occur of huge numbers of golden plover, lapwing, curlew, godwit, and redshank, as well as vast clouds of ducks.

Mount Stewart: The Stewarts have their seat at Mount Stewart, a beautiful country house on the east shore of the lough now in the care of the National Trust. There's a family feel to the house, with original bird paintings by English artist and humorist Edward Lear casually stuck to a fire screen and copies of playwright Sean O'Casey's works dedicated in his own hand to Edith, wife of the 7th Marquis of Londonderry. Edith laid out the superb gardens and the Dodo Terrace, with animal statues dedicated to members of her informal "Ark Club" of politicians and soldiers.

Grey Abbey, 4 miles (6 km) farther south, is a fine 12th-century ruin by the shore.

Around Strangford Lough

At Portaferry, an attractive waterside village, catch a ferry to reach Strangford village and the southern and western shores of Strangford Lough. In 2 miles (3 km), a signed right turn leads to the National Trust property of **Castle Ward** *(on A25, 1.25 miles/2 km W of Strangford, Co. Down, tel 028/4488-1204, call ahead for opening times, nationaltrust.org.uk/castle-ward, $$),* beautifully set on wooded parkland at the southern end of the lough.

The house is an architectural oddity, with the front half in sober Palladian style and the back half all exuberant Gothic. The 18th-century owners, Bernard and Lady Anne Ward, disagreed bitterly over the design of the house, so each took half. Bernard's front half is a model of classical restraint on the outside with wonderful plasterwork within; Lady Anne's rear half features pointed windows and door frames, fan vaulting, and Moorish decorations.

There are fine river and wetland walks at **Quoile Countryside Centre** *(tel 028/4461-5520, closed winter),* just north of Downpatrick, and far up the western lough shore is some excellent birdwatching at **Castle Espie Wildfowl and Wetlands Trust** *(tel 028/9187-4146, wwt.org.uk).*

Between the two lies **Mahee Island** *(signed),* a lonely islet at the end of several causeways. St. Patrick preached here at the monastery of St. Mochaoi. Ancient stone walls, ruins of a round tower and church, and rugged monastic graveslabs are all that remain. ∎

Mount Stewart
- 277 G3
- 5 miles (8 km) SW of Newtownards on A20, Co. Down
- 028/4278-8387
- House: Nov.–March open only weekends; gardens: open year round
- $$

nationaltrust.org.uk/mount-stewart

Grey Abbey
- 277 G3
- Grey Abbey, Co. Down
- 028/9082-3207

EXPERIENCE:
Bird-watching

Ireland has about 400 bird species, roughly three-quarters of the number in mainland Britain. Raptors include peregrine, merlin, and the reintroduced golden eagle. Some species—such as blackcap, stonechat, and goldfinch—are on the increase, while others, like the skylark, robin, and wheatear, are declining. Be sure to always take your binoculars wherever you go! Consult the **Birds of Ireland News Service** *(birdsireland.com)* for information on tours, recent sightings, and the rare birds of Ireland. Other valuable sources of information are the **Royal Society for the Protection of Birds** *(rspb.org.uk)* and **Birdwatch Ireland** *(birdwatchireland.ie).*

CÚCHULAINN, ULSTER'S WARRIOR HERO

The ancient kingdom of Ulster, of which Northern Ireland comprises a major part, is steeped in colorful legend. Much of it revolves around the indomitable warrior Cúchulainn, the only hero who might have given that other Irish mythical daredevil, Fionn MacCumhaill (Finn McCool), a run for his money.

Son of the god Lugh the Long-handed, Cúchulainn was given the birth name Setanta. At the age of seven, he slew a ferocious hound that had attacked him on the slopes of Slieve Gullion by jamming his *sliotar* (hurling ball) into its jaws and then beating it with his *camán* (hurley stick). The hound's owner, Culainn the Smith, was not pleased, so Setanta offered to guard his house until he had trained another dog. Thus he acquired his proper name: Cúchulainn, the Hound of Culainn.

■ **Cúchulainn, in his warrior glory, strides toward the Shadow Land.**

Haughty but beautiful Emer set him impossible tasks in order to win her hand: to leap the salmon leap, to slay eight men with a single blow—not once, but three times over—and to carry off two women along with their weight in gold and silver. He accomplished all with ease. Before battle, fearsome changes came upon him. He would swell to giant stature and turn different colors, while one eye bulged to enormous size and his body burned so hot that snow melted, sparks showered from his mouth, and a mist of blood spurted from the crown of his head.

The Cattle Raid of Cooley

Cúchulainn's finest hour came when treacherous Queen Medb of Connacht launched the Cattle Raid of Cooley upon Ulster. Envious of a fabulous bull, the White-horned One, that belonged to her husband King Ailill, she was determined to steal a beast that would match it—Ulster's famed Brown Bull of Cooley. The men of Ulster were under an enchantment that made them weak, so the 17-year-old Cúchulainn defended Ulster single-handedly. With sword, slingshot, and the dreaded spear Gae, he defeated Medb's armies. The wicked queen did manage to get back to Connacht with the Brown Bull of Cooley, only to have her prize kill the White-horned One and rampage through Ireland before dropping dead of sheer rage.

Queen Medb's Revenge

Queen Medb had the last laugh, though. Ten years after the Cattle Raid of Cooley, she enlisted three witches—their enchanter father had been killed by Cúchulainn—to put the warrior hero under a spell. Believing that Ulster was being attacked, Cúchulainn set out to defend his homeland.

Soon he met the sons of the Kings of Munster and Leinster. Unfortunately, Cúchulainn had killed those kings, too. In the ensuing

Cúchulainn rides his war chariot into battle.

battle, the hero was mortally pierced with a spear thrust. Binding himself for support to a standing stone, he wielded his sword until he died. But even then the Hound of Culainn was not quite finished. As young King Lughaidh of Munster stepped up and sliced off Cúchulainn's head, the sword fell from the hero's grasp and cut off his enemy's right hand. So passed Ulster's doughtiest champion, a mighty warrior to the last.

EXPERIENCE: Walk in the Footsteps of Legends

The name and fame of Cúchulainn are known to every person who grows up in Ireland, but the Ulster hero is only one of dozens of mythical figures around which the early history and fireside stories of Ireland were built. Centuries of Ireland's storytellers have preserved the mighty adventures and sayings of not only Cúchulainn but also Fionn MacCumhaill, Deirdre of the Sorrows, Diarmuid and Gráinne, Queen Medb of Connacht, Lugh the Long-handed, and many more.

You can hear these and other myths and legends told aloud at **Tí Chulainn**

Cultural Activity Centre (see sidebar p. 45) in Mullaghbane, County Armagh. Or consult **Storytellers of Ireland** (*storytellersofireland.org*), which maintains a directory of expert traditional storytellers throughout Ireland, as well as a list of upcoming events. To hear the ancient stories recounted in Dublin, check online at *legendarytours.com*.

If you want to see the sites that figure in Irish myth, book a tour of the Boyne Valley or the area around Newgrange with **Mythical Ireland** (*mythicalireland.com*). You can also create your own tour.

More Places to Visit in Northern Ireland

Barrontop Fun Farm

With all the sounds, sights, and smells of the farm, this is the perfect place for children. They get the opportunity to hold fluffy chicks, feed the goats, lambs, and ducks, cuddle a friendly puppy or a baby rabbit, and go up close to llamas, deer, and pot-bellied pigs.

For those with a lot of energy to burn, there is an adventure playground and a bouncy castle. Cart rides are another attraction. There are picnic areas and a tearoom—and also plenty of indoor facilities if it's raining.

discovernorthernireland.com 🔺 276 C3 ✉ 35 Barron Rd., Donemana, Strabane, Co. Tyrone ☎ 028/7139-7767 🕐 Open weekends only 💲 $$

Castlederg

It's worth taking a drive on the B72 out to Castlederg in the west of County Tyrone because, while it has no spectacular visitor attractions, it's a good example of a friendly working village that's still dependent on agriculture. The Tuesday morning sheep sales in Forbes Livestock Mart out on the Killen road are a great gathering place for hill farmers, whose weather-beaten faces ring the auctioneer with his machine-gun patter. West of Castlederg, County Tyrone makes a bulging salient into County Donegal. There's great walking and leisurely motoring here along the quiet and lonely back roads and lanes around **Killeter Forest** on the border. 🔺 276 B3

Dark Hedges

Around 1775, near Gracehill House, the Stuart family planted two rows of beech trees along the drive that led to the house. Over time, the trees curved inward over the drive and their branches intertwined to form a natural tunnel – a sort of enchanted path– that today is one of Ireland's most photographed attractions. The site became

■ Wrinkled rocks of Ardglass overlook the uncrowded sands of the Lecale Peninsula.

Ancient Architecture

Ireland is an island particularly rich in the architecture of the ancients. Stone and Bronze Age peoples left us few artifacts to judge and understand them by, but their massive monuments in stone are markers that the passage of many millennia has failed to erase. Most notable are the court tombs from around 4000 B.C., with their partly enclosed courts or ritual spaces fronting the burial chambers. Wedge tombs (wedge-shaped court tombs) were built perhaps a thousand years later. Hard on their heels

came the passage graves, man-made mounds with a passage leading to central chambers; these could be any size, with the largest—such as Newgrange (see pp. 264–267)—being as big as a small hill.

Stone circles were erected by both Stone Age and Bronze Age people, some as boundary markers around burial sites, others apparently to form enclosed spaces for rituals. Some possess much larger stones that seem to have had a guardian role.

famous as one of the locations for the filming of the television series *Game of Thrones*. Fans can visit the location on the **Game of Thrones Tours** (gameofthronestours.com) that depart from Belfast, Dublin, and Tollymore. 🅰 277 E5 ✉ Ballinea Rd., 8 miles (12.8 km) N of Ballymoney, Co. Antrim

Knockmany Chambered Cairn

Southeast of Omagh, not far from the border with County Monaghan, the Clogher Valley is a forested, secret glen. Signposted at the summit of a steep wooded hill here is Knockmany chambered cairn, a Bronze Age passage tomb whose pink stones are carved with wonderful whorls and spiral patterns, parallel lines like Ogham script, and mazelike shapes. The view from here over miles of forest and hilly country is superb. 🅰 276 C2 **Omagh Visitor Information** (see p. 338)

Lecale Peninsula

The blunt-nosed Lecale Peninsula, east of Downpatrick, has plenty of delights and surprises. The 22-mile (35 km) coast drive, starting at Strangford village, turns south through **Kilclief**, where there is a fine 15th-century tower house. It was built by a naughty Bishop of Down, John Cely—he

was defrocked in 1443 for living with Lettice Savage, a married woman, in the tower.

In 5 miles (8 km) you reach **Ardglass,** a lively fishing town that in its day was the most important fishing port in Ulster—hence the large number of towers, minicastles, and other fortified buildings. **Killough,** 3 miles (5 km) on, was laid out neatly in the 18th century by Lord Bangor of Castle Ward as a port to ship out lead and farm produce from his estate. The rule-straight 8-mile (13 km) road he made to connect port and estate is still there. From Killough you can drive or walk the couple of miles (3 km) to the ruined tenth-century chapel on **St. John's Point.** From the tip of the point awaits a fabulous view of the Mourne Mountains. 🅰 277 F2–G2 ✉ E of Downpatrick, Co. Down **Downpatrick Visitor Information** ✉ St Patrick Sq., Market St., Downpatrick, Co. Down ☎ 028/4461-9000

Lough Neagh

On the eastern border of Tyrone, Lough Neagh stretches its vast, flat shore. Coarse fishing for lough eels, bream, roach, perch, and pike is superb: The Sperrin Tourism Partnership issues a pamphlet guide.

On the shores of Lough Neagh east of Cookstown stands the **Ardboe high cross,** a magnificently carved tenth-century cross 18.5

▪ Sailboats prepare for a good night's sleep on Lough Neagh.

feet (5.5 m) tall featuring the Judgment of Solomon, Cain bashing Abel with a flail, and Daniel with two lions. Nearby stands a wishing tree, poisoned to death by thousands of votive coins pushed into its trunk. *discoverloughneagh.com*
🖼 276 E3 **Magherafelt Visitor Information**
✉ The Bridewell, 6 Church St., Magherafelt, Co. Londonderry ☎ 028/7963-1510

Murlough Bay

This is a glorious bay, and though it lies between the popular Antrim Coast Road and the Giant's Causeway area, it remains unspoiled because of the absence of a major road along this shoulder of the Antrim coast.

Rocks and silvery sand lie under cliffs and slopes clothed in silver birch and mountain ash. From the upper parking lot, various walks are indicated; one of them goes along the cliffs to Fair Head and a wonderful view north to Rathlin Island. From the lower parking lot, there is a choice of beautiful beach and hill slope rambles. 🖼 277 E5–F5 ✉ 5 miles (8 km) E of Ballycastle, off the coast road between Fair

---

Ulster's Presidential Ancestral Homes

Several U.S. presidents could trace their lineage to Northern Ireland and there are several associated sites worth visiting.

In the northwest of County Tyrone, 2 miles (3 km) east of Strabane, you can visit President Wilson Ancestral Home *(Spout Rd. Dergalt, 2 miles (3.2 km) SE of Strabane, Co. Tyrone, tel 028/7138-4444)*. The whitewashed cottage that Woodrow Wilson's grandfather James Wilson left in 1807 is kept by the curators, who are members of the Wilson family, still farming the ancestral land.

The ancestral home of 21st U.S. president (1881–1885) Chester Alan Arthur can be found at **Arthur Cottage.** Arthur's father emigrated in 1815.

The parents of Andrew Jackson, seventh U.S. president (1829–1837), left Carrickfergus for America in 1765. The **Andrew Jackson Cottage** *(Boneybefore, Carrickfergus, Co. Antrim, tel 028/9335-8049)*, a traditional cottage of the period, is beautifully restored and furnished with various Jackson exhibits and displays.

John Simpson, the maternal great-grandfather of Ulysses S. Grant, 18th U.S. president (1869–1877), was born in the mud-floored **Grant Ancestral Home** *(Dergina, Ballygawley, Co. Tyrone, tel 028/8555-7133)* in 1738 and emigrated to the U.S. at the age of 22.

Head and Torr Head, Co. Antrim **Ballycastle Visitor Information,** *visitcausewaycoastandglens. com* ✉ 14 Bayview Rd., Ballycastle, Co. Antrim ☎ 028/2076-2024

Omagh

Tyrone's county town of Omagh was known only as a shopping and local business center until the infamous day of August 15, 1998. Then a republican splinter group opposed to the Good Friday Agreement (see pp. 288–289) and calling itself the Real IRA exploded a car bomb in a street crowded with Saturday shoppers; 29 people were killed. This appalling act brought condemnation across the board, and paradoxically sealed determination to make the peace process work. *fermanaghomagh.com* ▲ 276 C3 **Visitor Information** ✉ Strule Arts Centre, Townhall Sq., Omagh ☎ 028/8224-7831

INSIDER TIP:

The very best time to visit County Down's Rowallane Garden is in the spring, when you'll see thousands of rhododendrons and azaleas in full bloom. The colors are amazing—it's a glorious sight.

—ALLY THOMPSON
National Geographic contributor

Rowallane Garden

This is a gorgeous, natural-looking garden on a 50-acre (20 ha) site with no artificial landscaping whatsoever. The Rowallane estate was bequeathed to Hugh Armytage Moore by his uncle, the Reverend John Moore, in 1903, and he tended it for the next half century, planting specimens from all over the world.

You can wander through the walled garden

full of azaleas—gorgeous in May—and down to the natural outcrop rock garden by way of the shallow glen of New Ground between banks of orange, scarlet, pink, yellow, purple, and white rhododendrons. *nationaltrust.org.uk/ rowallane-garden* ▲ 277 F2 ✉ Signed off the A7 Belfast–Downpatrick road near Saintfield, 11 miles (18 km) from both Belfast & Downpatrick, Co. Down ☎ 028/9751-0131 $ $

Scrabo Tower

An eye-catching landmark for many miles around, Scrabo Tower rises 135 feet (41 m) from the summit of Scrabo Hill, at the northern end of **Strangford Lough** (see pp. 332–333). It was erected in 1857 as a gesture of thanks to the 3rd Marquis of Londonderry for his efforts to relieve the suffering of his tenants during the Great Famine.

Nowadays, the tower houses an exhibition about the natural and social history of the area, including Strangford Lough, and if you have the energy to climb up the 122 steps to the top of the tower, it is definitely worth it. The view is wonderful, one of the most impressive in Northern Ireland, taking in the Mountains of Mourne, the hills of the Antrim Coast, Belfast, the great swath of Strangford Lough itself, and the Ards Peninsula. On particularly clear days, you might even be able to get a glimpse of the Isle of Man and the hills of Scotland across the Irish Sea.

The tower is at the heart of the Scrabo Hill Country Park, where woodland gives way to open areas where the dark volcanic rock that overlies the sandstone makes dramatic shapes of outcrops and quarry scars in the green surroundings. ▲ 277 F3 ✉ 6 miles (10 km) SW of Newtownards, Co. Down ☎ 028/9181-1491 🕐 Open Fri.–Sun., May–mid-Sept. $ $

Springhill

Springhill is an excellent example of a plantation house. Built by the Conyngham family from Scotland around 1690, the house was enlarged with two wings in the 18th

■ Colors, shapes, and sizes of plants blend and contrast at Rowallane Garden.

century. Inside is a well-stocked 18th-century library; some splendid 18th- and 19th-century furniture, including ladder-back chairs and delicately crafted cabinets; a gun room with some historic weapons displayed (flintlock muskets used by defenders at the Siege of Derry and some pikes captured at the Battle of Vinegar Hill, County Wexford, in 1798); and a costume exhibition. Outside is a walled garden and well-marked walks through park and woodland. *nationaltrust.org.uk/springhill* 🗺 277 D3 ✉ Signed on the B18 Money-more–Coagh road, 5 miles (8 km) NE of Cookstown, Co. Londonderry 🕐 House: open weekends only, Sept.–mid-Apr.; Garden: open all year round 🛢 $

Toomebridge Eel Fishery

Call in on this fishery in the west of County Antrim, near County Londonderry, and enjoy the astonishing sight of eels in the mil-lions. It's a commercial concern, but you are welcome to drop in and visit. The fishery, at the point where the River Bann flows out of the northernmost point of Lough Neagh, is a prime site for eel catching—mostly for

export, since Ulster people seem not too fond of these wriggly delicacies. Lough Neagh eel fishermen make their living from the trade, however, and lower along the Bann in summer eel-fishing for sport is a very popular pastime. *loughneagheels.com* 🗺 277 E3 ✉ Lough Neagh Fishermen's Coop-erative Society, Toomebridge, Co. Antrim 🕿 028/7965-0618 🕐 Closed Sat. & Sun.

Wellbrook Beetling Mill

The mill was one of six built in this narrow valley from 1767 onward. Their function was to beat linen cloth to a fine sheen with water-powered wooden hammers. You can admire the noisy "beetles," or hammers; the waterwheel; and the rest of the original machinery, and also learn about Ulster's once thriving linen industry in the drying loft display. *nationaltrust.org.uk/wellbrook-beetling-mill* 🗺 277 D3 ✉ Signed off the A505 Cookstown–Omagh road at Kildress, 4 miles (6.5 km) W of Cookstown, Co. Tyrone 🕿 028/8674-8210 or 028/8674-1735 🕐 Open weekends only, March.–Oct. 🛢 $

TRAVELWISE

A modern Dublin tram

TRAVELWISE

PLANNING YOUR TRIP

When to Go

The best time of year to visit Ireland is spring and early summer. April to June tend to be the sunniest and mildest months, the population is not yet suffering from tourist overload, and the countryside is green and fresh from the winter rain. Visitor numbers have not yet peaked, so the roads are quiet, but most attractions have opened after the winter layoff.

However, the biggest concentration of the festivals for which Ireland is famous is in summer. The Cork and Dingle Regattas, Galway Arts Festival and Races, Dublin Horse Show and Connemara Pony Show, International Rose of Tralee Festival, and Fleadh Cheoil na h'Éireann (All-Ireland Music Festival) all take place in July or August.

The months of September and October tend to see better weather and beautiful colors in woods and moors; prices are on the way down by October, too. Winter weather is generally mild but can be dark and gloomy. This is the season of low prices and indoor fun—many attractions have closed, but fire-warmed pubs come into their own.

What to Take

Pack clothes that take account of the informal, mostly outdoor nature of a holiday in Ireland. It's certainly wise to take good waterproof clothing, a hat, and an umbrella, as it's bound to rain at least some of the time during your visit. As for other clothing, the keynote is informality unless you intend to stay or dine at the very classiest five-star places.

An English-Irish dictionary or phrase book will help you appreciate the place-names. You may also find bird and flower identification books to be helpful. You can buy these in leading towns and cities countrywide.

If you want to join in with the music, a couple of harmonicas or a tin whistle (keys G and D) will fit easily into your suitcase. These are the best instruments for unobtrusively "faking it." And bring a couple of songs, too, in case someone invites you to oblige the company in the pub. There's no better icebreaker than singing your party piece, even if your voice is itself a rusty instrument.

A wide range of over-the-counter and prescription medicines is available in Irish pharmacies (sometimes called chemists), but you should seriously consider bringing any specialized medication with you.

HOW TO GET TO IRELAND

By Air

Flying time between the U.S. and Ireland is between six and nine hours. Scheduled flights link many North American airports to Dublin, Shannon, Cork, Knock (Co. Mayo), and Belfast. The Republic's national carrier (operating to Belfast, too) is Aer Lingus (*tel 800/223-6537*).

Arrival by air in the Irish Republic is most likely to be at either Dublin or Shannon Airport; in Northern Ireland, either Belfast International or Belfast City airport. All have foreign exchange bureaus (generally open by 7 a.m.), the major car rental firms, and taxi ranks—fares are about five times the bus fares.

Getting to the City Centers

Journeys to city centers all take about 0.5–1 hour, depending on traffic. From Belfast City airport, allow 10–15 minutes to reach the city.

Dublin Airport to Dublin

By car—take the M1 south
By bus—Airlink and AirCoach bus every 20 minutes (moderate fare) via central bus station and Connolly railway station to Heuston railway station
By taxi—expensive

Shannon Airport to Limerick

By car—take the N18 east
By bus—Irish Bus (Bus Éireann) runs a frequent, inexpensive airport–Limerick service
By taxi—moderate/expensive

Cork Airport to Cork

By car—take the N27 north
By bus—Bus Éireann line 226 runs to the city center (moderate fare)
By taxi—moderate/expensive

Belfast International Airport to Belfast

By car—take the A52 east
By bus—Airbus service (moderate fare, children free) runs to the city center every half hour
By taxi—expensive

Belfast City Airport to Central Belfast

By car—follow city-center signs
By taxi—moderate

GETTING AROUND

Getting Around in Dublin

By Bus

Dublin Bus (*tel 01/873-4222, dublinbus.ie*) runs bus services in Greater Dublin (extends to the outskirts of Counties Meath, Kildare, and Wicklow).

Tickets—Buy cheaper prepaid tickets en bloc from the CIE information desk in Dublin Airport, from the Dublin Bus head office at 59 Upper O'Connell Street, or from several hundred ticket outlets across the city.

By Rail

DART *(irishrail.ie)* is an efficient rail service connecting outer Dublin with the city center. There are 31 stations—the three most central are Connolly (north of the river, a ten-minute walk to O'Connell Street), and Tara Street and Pearse Street (both south of the river, five minutes to Trinity College). Buy tickets at any DART station.

The **Luas** *(luas.ie)* tram system's Green Line goes southeast from Broombidge to Bride's Glen through St. Stephen's Green; the Red Line goes east from Connolly station to The Point, and west from Connolly to Heuston station, then southwest to Saggart or Tallaght. (Note: There are no subways in Ireland.)

By Taxi

The main city-center taxi ranks are at St. Stephen's Green, College Green, O'Connell Street, and Westland Row to the east of the Trinity College grounds. Dublin taxis are mostly metered; agree on fares in advance with drivers of those that are not.

Leaving Dublin by Car

Dublin is ringed by the M50 motorway. Main roads out of the city are:

M1 to Dublin Airport, Drogheda, Dundalk, and Belfast
N2 to Slane, Monaghan, and Derry
N3 to Navan, Cavan, Enniskillen, and Donegal
N4 to Kinnegad (where the N6 leaves for Galway), Longford (where the N5 leaves for Westport), and on to Sligo
N7/M7 to Naas (where the N9 leaves for Waterford), Portlaoise (where the N8 branches off for Cork), and Kildare
N11 to Bray, Wicklow, Wexford, and Rosslare car ferry

Traveling Around the Republic

By Air

Aer Lingus, Ireland's national airline *(U.S. tel 800/474-7424, Ireland tel 01/886-8202, aerlingus. com),* flies from Dublin to Shannon and to Donegal.

By Car Ferry

Two short car ferry trips that will save you hours on the road are:
Across the Shannon (20-minute crossing, every hour) between Killimer, County Clare, and Tarbert, County Kerry *(shannonferries.com)*
Across Waterford Harbour (10-minute crossing, continuous operation) between Ballyhack, County Wexford, and Passage East, County Waterford *(passageferry.ie)*

By Public Transportation

CIE *(cie.ie)* is the company that runs bus and train services in the Republic of Ireland through its subsidiaries Irish Rail (Iarnród Éireann), Irish Bus (Bus Éireann), and Dublin Bus (Bus Átha Cliath).

By Bus

Irish Bus *(tel 01/850-836-611, buseireann.ie),* with its distinctive Red Setter logo, services all towns and cities and many rural villages. The daily express buses between Dublin and Belfast are good value and can beat the train for time if traffic conditions permit.

By Train

Irish Rail *(tel 01/836-6222, irishrail.ie)* runs the Republic's train services—efficient north and south of Dublin, slow and in need of investment farther west. Major cities are all connected by rail. The excellent Dublin–Belfast express (eight per day) takes two hours. Reserve in the peak holiday season and for traveling on the very crowded last trains on Friday and Sunday nights.

Tickets

Buy them from any train or bus station. Under-16s and other concessions are up to half off. There are various good ticket deals available, many of them including bus and train. A number of discount bus/rail tickets and passes are available, including the **Explorer** tickets (5-day) and **Trekker** (4-day)—enquire at Irish Bus, Irish Rail, or at stations. Student discounts are available for long distance train and bus travel with a valid Student Card.

Driving

Car Rental

You'll need a full valid driver's license from your home country, held for two years without endorsement. Age limits are generally 23–70. A credit card is required to rent a car and online price comparisons and reservations prior to departure are recommended.

Fly-drive deals offer the best prices. Reservations are essential for mid-July to mid-August. High season prices are much higher than in low season; they usually include third-party, fire, theft, and passenger indemnity insurance, unlimited mileage, and VAT.

Driving in the Irish Republic

Driving in the Republic, generally speaking, is still a pleasure. Out of the big towns, the roads are uncrowded and most drivers observe the courtesies. The farther west you go, the more roads get narrow, steep, and twisty. Distances on signposts take some getting used to—essentially, Irish Eurocrats have switched to kilometers (shown on green-and-white signs) and the other 99 percent of the population still operates on miles (black-and-white signs).

Drive on the left; overtake on the right.

Don't park illegally in Dublin; you'll be wheel clamped.

Drivers and passengers must wear seat belts.

Speed limits: 31 mph (50 kph) in towns, 50 mph (80 kph) on regional/local roads (ones that don't have an "N" designation), 62 mph (100 kph) on national roads and dual roadways, 75 mph (120 kph) on motorways.

Alcohol limit: 50 mg of alcohol per 100 ml of blood (one pint of medium-strength beer, one small glass of wine), and 20 mg/100 ml for learner and novice drivers (less than two years with a full license).

What to Do in the Event of a Car Accident

1. Dial 999 for fire, police, or ambulance services.
2. Remain at the scene.
3. Exchange names, addresses, and insurance details with anyone else involved.
4. Do not admit liability, whatever the circumstances.
5. Most car rental firms detail in their documentation the steps they require. These may include a requirement to use a specified towing and repair service; use of another service may invalidate your insurance coverage, so check up.

Maps

Ordnance Survey of Ireland (osi.ie) 1:50,000 Discovery Series covers all of Ireland in 75 sheets, good for driving. Information offices and car rental firms supply general road maps.

Getting Around in Belfast

By Bus

Metro (tel 028/9066-6630, translink.co.uk/Services/Metro-Service-Page) operates buses within Belfast. Buy tickets on the bus or from Europa Bus Centre (Glengall Street) or Laganside Bus Centre (Oxford Street near Central Station). Cheap multiple tickets/concessions are available.

By Taxi

Black "London" cabs with yellow identifying discs are metered; others may not be. City-center taxi ranks are at Yorkgate and Central train stations, at bus stations, and at City Hall. Taxi firms are listed in the Yellow Pages.

Leaving Belfast by Car

Main routes are:

A2 north up the coast to Antrim and the Giant's Causeway, east through Bangor and around the Ards Peninsula

M1 to Dungannon/A4 to Enniskillen

M1 to Jct7/A1 to Dundalk and Dublin

M2/A6 to Derry

Getting Around Northern Ireland

By Bus

Ulsterbus (tel 028/9066-6630, translink.co.uk/Services/Ulsterbus-Service-Page) operates to all towns and most villages across Northern Ireland. Buy tickets at bus stations or on-board buses. Cheap day returns, unlimited travel tickets, bus/rail options, or child/student/senior discounts are available.

By Rail

Northern Ireland Railways (tel 028/9066-6630, translink.co.uk/Services/NI-Railways) runs trains from Belfast to Larne and to Derry, Bangor, and Dublin (O'Connolly Station). Buy tickets at train stations.

Driving

Car Rental

Requirements are the same as for the Republic except that the driver's license need only have been held for one year. If you plan to drive in both the Republic and Northern Ireland, ensure the insurance covers you.

The roads in Northern Ireland are uncrowded, and drivers are generally relaxed and courteous. Road surfaces are good, and signpost distances are given in miles. Rules and laws apply as in the Republic.

Maps

Ordnance Survey of Northern Ireland 1:50,000 series of 18 sheets covers all of Northern Ireland (along with Donegal and parts of Counties Cavan, Leitrim, Louth, Monaghan, and Roscommon). Ireland North at 1:250,000 is a useful driving map, available from visitor information centers.

PRACTICAL ADVICE

Children

Well-behaved children are made welcome everywhere. In practice, pubs operate individual admittance policies—just ask.

Discounts on transportation and entrance fees are usually available.

Communications

Postal Service

The Republic's mailboxes and postal vans are green. You can buy stamps from a post office or machine. Letters take roughly two days to reach the United Kingdom, three to four days to get to the United States. In the North, the mailboxes and vans are red; British stamps are used.

Mobile Phones & Wi-Fi

Using your own phone in Ireland could prove very expensive. Before travelling, check on your provider's roaming charges for making and receiving calls. A way to avoid roaming charges is to buy an Irish SIM card (if your phone is not locked) or alternatively, a cheap local prepay phone with its own SIM card.

Wi-Fi is available in nearly all hotels, guesthouses, public establishments, museums, some visitor's centers, pubs, and cafés. In most cases it's free.

Telephones

Republic: Phone booths in the Republic tend to be either gray or green and white. You'll find them at train and bus stations, near post offices, and on street corners. Mos of the phone booths use phone-cards, sold by newsagents, post offices, and bigger shops such as supermarkets. You can phone anywhere in the world.

The international code for the Republic of Ireland is 353.

To call Northern Ireland from the Republic, dial 048, then the local number.

Northern Ireland: Northern Ireland has red telephone boxes, along with a plethora of flimsy plastic ones.

The international code for Northern Ireland is 44. Dial 100 for the domestic operator, 155 for the international operator.

Conversions

Distance	multiply by
kilometers to miles	0.62
miles to kilometers	1.6

Length	multiply by
centimeters to inches	0.39
inches to centimeters	2.54
meters to feet	3.28
feet to meters	0.30
meters to yards	1.09
yards to meters	0.91

Area	multiply by
hectares to acres	2.47
acres to hectares	0.40

Weight	multiply by
kilograms to pounds	2.21
pounds to kilograms	0.45
kilograms to U.S. tons	0.001
U.S. tons to kilograms	907

Volume	multiply by
liters to U.S. gallons	0.26
U.S. gallons to liters	3.79

Temperature	
°C to °F multiply by 1.8, add 32	
°F to °C subtract 32, multiply by 0.55	

Currency Restrictions

You can bring as much money as you like into Ireland, but amounts of Irish or other currency taken out of the country are restricted. It is a good idea to complete a currency declaration upon arrival.

Customs

The usual prohibited goods, including illegal drugs, are forbidden in Ireland. Travelers in the EU can carry, duty-paid, up to 110 liters of beer, 90 liters of wine, and 800 cigarettes in and out of Ireland. Duty-free goods allowances (Republic only) include 200 cigarettes, 1 liter of spirits, and 2 liters of fortified wine.

Electricity

Electricity is at a standard 230-volt AC (50 cycles). Wall sockets are for plugs with either three flat or two round pins. U.S. visitors will need a transformer/adaptor.

Embassies & Consulates

Canada: 7–8 Wilton Terrace, Dublin 2, tel 01/234-4000
United States: U.S. Consulate General, Danesfort House, 223 Stranmillis Rd., Belfast BT9 5GR, tel 028/9038-6100
U.S. Embassy, 42 Elgin Rd., Dublin 4, tel 01/668-6770

Entry Formalities

All non-EU nationals need a passport to enter Ireland. U.S. citizens do not need a visa. No ID is needed to cross between southern and Northern Ireland.

Etiquette & Local Customs

There are no formal rules of etiquette in Ireland. Irish people love to talk, banter, sound off, give forth, and take part in the great game of conversation, and the more you join in, the better it all goes round. The Irish love to include strangers and find out all about them. This isn't nosiness, just genuine warmth and curiosity. Such personal interest may be less evident in crowded tourist spots in the high season or in cities in big towns, where, like everywhere else these days, busy inhabitants tend to skip over such an enjoyable way of passing the time.

Don't be afraid to join in with a session of music in a pub. Sing along with the chorus if everyone else is doing so, and if you want to join in with your own instrument, don't forget that it's good manners to ask first! Be sure that you can keep up with (and not spoil) the tune. Don't forget, too, that smoking has been banned in pubs and every other sort of public room.

The old adage about not initiating conversations about sex, politics, and religion is a good one to have in mind, particularly in some areas of the North. In Northern Ireland, you need to be especially sensitive about offering your own ideas on religion and politics unless you have been invited to do so. But nowadays many northerners are keen to talk about the past, present, and future of their troubled country with anyone who is interested. Once the topics are on the table, it's usually best just to listen.

Health

No inoculations are necessary. Tap water is safe to drink. Insurance: see below.

Holidays

January 1 (New Year's Day)

March 17 (St. Patrick's Day)
March/April (Good Friday–
     Easter Monday)
First Monday in May
     (May Holiday)
Last Monday in May (Spring
     Holiday–Northern Ireland)
First Monday in June (June
     Holiday–Republic)
July 12 (Orangemen's Day–
     Northern Ireland; nearest
     Monday is a holiday; parades
     take place on nearest Saturday)
First Monday in August (August
     Holiday–Republic)
Last Monday in August (Late
     Summer Holiday–Northern
     Ireland)
Last Monday in October
     (October Holiday–Republic)
December 25 (Christmas Day)
December 26 (Boxing Day/
     St. Stephen's Day)

Most businesses are closed on
national holidays.

Insurance

Medical and dental treatment are
available on the Irish health service for nationals of EU countries
and certain others on production
of a European Health Insurance
Card (EHIC), but U.S. and most
other nationals should arrange
comprehensive health and travel
insurance before traveling to
Ireland.

Liquor Laws

Licensing hours are rapidly
changing to reflect demand,
and 24-hour drinking may be
just around the corner. Already
in Dublin and Belfast there are
plenty of places with late licenses,
up to 1 a.m. or later. Technically,
you can buy alcohol in the Republic between 10:30 a.m. and 10:00
p.m., Monday–Saturday; and
12:30–11 p.m. on Sunday.

In Northern Ireland, pubs can
open whenever they choose, but
alcohol can only be served between

11:30 a.m. and 11 p.m. (12:30 p.m.–
10:00 p.m. on Sun.) unless the pub
has a special extension license and
offers food and/or entertainment.

Lost Property

If you lose something, report it to
the nearest police station. Don't
forget to ask for a signed and
dated acknowledgment that you
have reported the loss, to show
your insurance company.

Media

Among the Republic's serious
national papers, two dailies
stand out: the *Irish Times*
(irishtimes.com) and the *Irish Inde-*
pendent (independent.ie). There's
one authoritative regional paper,
the southwest's *Irish Examiner*
(examiner.ie), as well as dozens of
local papers.

RTÉ *(rte.ie)*, the state broadcast-
ing corporation, has two television
channels in English and one in Irish,
and four radio stations (one in Irish).

Northern Ireland receives
some of the Republic's transmis-
sions and is served with mainland
British newspapers, television, and
radio, as well as its own regional
varieties. It's instructive to read the
opposing views of the two strongly
aligned Belfast daily papers, the
pro-Unionist *News Letter (newsletter*
.co.uk) and the nationalist *Irish News*
(irishnews.com). One of the most
widely distributed newspapers is the
Belfast Telegraph (belfasttelegraph.
co.uk). Conceived as a unionist
paper in the second half of the
19th century, it filed down its sharp
edges over time and won over a
reading audience from both sides
of the aisle.

Money Matters

The currency in the Republic is
the euro. There are 100 cents to 1
euro. Bills come in denominations
of 5, 10, 20, 50, 100, 200, and 500
euros, although the latter two are
seldom seen. The coins come in

1 and 2 euros and 1, 2, 5, 10, 20,
and 50 cents.

In Northern Ireland, the British
pound is used, with 100 pence to
the pound. Coin and note denominations are the same as for euros.

The two currencies are not
interchangeable, although a number
of Northern Ireland attractions will
accept euros for admission fees,
especially close to the border, and
vice versa, but don't depend on it.

Most major international credit
cards and many debit cards are generally accepted and usable in ATMs.
The smaller and more rural the
establishment, the more prudent it
is to have cash at hand.

Opening Times

Republic: Banks are generally open
Monday–Friday 10 a.m.– 4:30 p.m.
In smaller towns, they may close
for lunch. Bigger banks in Dublin
are open until 5 p.m. on Thursdays
and on Saturday mornings.

Shops are generally open
Monday to Saturday 9 a.m.–6 p.m.;
in central Dublin, many stay open
later. On Sundays, supermarkets and
some big stores open from noon to
5 or 6 p.m. Shopping centers often
stay open until 8 or 9 p.m. Shops in
smaller towns may close at 1 p.m. on
Wednesdays or Thursdays.

Northern Ireland: Banks are
generally open Monday–Friday
9:30 a.m.–4:30 p.m. **Shops** are
generally open during the same
hours as in the Republic.

Pharmacies

All large towns and many small
ones have pharmacies (sometimes
called chemists); they should all
display a notice on the door giving
directions to nearby pharmacies
scheduled to be open after hours.

Places of Worship &
Religion

Church of Ireland (Protestant)
and Roman Catholic churches
abound in Ireland. Methodist,

Baptist, and other nonconformist congregations are scarce, as are Jewish, Sikh, Muslim, and Hindu places of worship.

Restrooms

You'll find public restrooms in all the places you'd expect—airports, train and bus stations, and city centers. Some are free; in others, you gain entry with a small coin. Restrooms are available also in hotels, public establishments, museums, and some visitor's centers.

Senior Citizens

Discounts on transportation and entrance fees are usually available to senior citizens.

Time Differences

Ireland is on Greenwich Mean Time (e.g., at noon in Ireland, it is 7 a.m. in New York and 4 a.m. in Los Angeles). Clocks are set forward one hour between late March and late October.

Tipping

Tipping is very much a matter for you to decide. Generally speaking, the only people who will be upset at the lack of a tip are restaurant waiters and waitresses and cab drivers.

The owners/management of some establishments have developed the regrettable habit of keeping a proportion—or all—of a tip for themselves if the customer includes it when paying the bill with a credit or debit card. Don't be afraid to ask your waiter or waitress if that is the case. If it is, then consider paying the tip directly to the server in cash.

Visitor Information

Republic of Ireland

Faîlte ("Fawl-che") Ireland (Welcome to Ireland) is the Irish Republic's tourist board (Baggot St. Bridge,

Baggot St., Dublin 2, tel 01/602-4000, discoverireland.ie). The only number to call for information is 01/890-324-583. while principal Faîlte Ireland offices are:

Dublin: Dublin Discover Ireland Centre, Suffolk St.
Tourist Information Centre, 14 Upper O'Connell St.
Kilkenny: Rose Inn St.
Waterford: 120 Parade Quay
Cork: 125 St. Patrick st.
Killarney: Beech Rd.,
Limerick: 20 O'Connell St.
Shannon Airport: Arrivals Hall
Athlone: Athlone Castle
Galway: Aras Faîlte, Forster St.
Westport: James St.
Sligo: Old Bank Building, O'Connell St.

Northern Ireland

The **Northern Ireland Tourist Board** (discovernorthernireland.com & visit-belfast.com) has welcome centers in Belfast (9 Donegall Sq. N.) and in Dublin (Discover Ireland Centre, Suffolk St., Dublin 2, visitdublin.com).

Principal Northern Ireland Tourist Board offices in Northern Ireland are:
Antrim: The Old Courthouse, Market Sq., tel 028/9442-8331
Armagh: 40 English St., Armagh, tel 028/3752-9644
Londonderry: 44 Foyle St., tel 028/3752-1800
Down: 34 Quay St., Bangor, tel 028/9127-0069
Fermanagh: Wellington Rd., Enniskillen, tel 028/6632-3110
Tyrone: Strule Arts Centre, Townhall Sq., Omagh, tel 028/8224-7831

Visitors With Disabilities

Increasing numbers of hotels and public buildings are being adapted or built to cater to travelers with disabilities. Helpful sources of information are the **National Disability Authority** (Republic of Ireland; tel 01/608-0400, nda.ie)

and **Disability Action** (Northern Ireland; tel 028/9029-7880, disabilityaction.org).

Women

Women travelers are as safe in Ireland as anywhere in the world, provided standard common sense is followed. Serious harassment is extremely rare.

EMERGENCIES

For all emergencies in Ireland, telephone 999.

Crime & Police

The Republic of Ireland has a well-deserved reputation for being one of the safest countries in Europe. Northern Ireland earned a name for violent disruption during the Troubles, but even then the vast majority of incidents occurred far from any place a visitor was likely to be. These days no one need be especially concerned about safety issues in the North.

The kind of crime likely to affect visitors—petty theft, pocket-picking—is largely confined to the more disadvantaged areas of Dublin and Belfast. Outside of these enclaves, the usual general precautions are all you need to observe. If you do get into trouble, help and support are available from the **Irish Tourist Assistance Service** (Mon.–Fri.: 6–7 Hanover St. E., Dublin 2, tel 01/661-0562; weekends & holidays: Pearse St. Garda Station, Pearse St., Dublin 2, tel 01/666-8109, itas.ie).

In the Republic, the police are known as the **Gardai** (pronounced "gard-ee"; garda.ie) or the "gards"; they normally work unarmed. In Northern Ireland, the police force is called the **Police Service of Northern Ireland** (PSNI; psni.police.uk).

HOTELS & RESTAURANTS

Time was—and not so long ago—when the traveler outside Dublin would need to look long and hard for a good place to stay. The norm, especially in small towns, was a run-down hotel with bad beds. But things have changed, and today there is an enormous range of accommodations, from magnificent castles on beautiful grounds to simple hostels, and standards rarely fall below what's acceptable.

HOTELS

In the Republic, tourist offices have lists of accommodations approved by Bord Fáilte (Irish Tourist Board; discoverireland .ie); north of the border, tourist offices have the same, with establishments approved by the NITB (Northern Ireland Tourist Board; discovernorthernireland .com). The consumer website tripadvisor.com is extremely helpful—it contains personal reviews, and also links through to online booking sites, often offering reduced rates.

Converted castles and stately homes can be very atmospheric and great fun, though the quality is variable and you may have to put up with some of the inconveniences (lack of elevators, odd-shaped rooms, steep staircases) that come with a rambling old building. Large, very well-organized country houses and golf hotels are another option at the luxury end. There is also a growing number of small, owner-run hotels with very high standards of care and attention.

Bed-and-Breakfast

It is the famous Irish bed-and-breakfast (B&B), though, that for most visitors offers the most enjoyable accommodations, where you are welcomed with true Irish warmth. Generally the owners are only too pleased to share their insiders' knowledge about the best attractions, music pubs, and places to eat. Those approved by Bord Fáilte display a shamrock sign; you can expect very high standards at these places.

Another trustworthy organization is B&B Ireland (tel 071/982-2222, bandbireland.com), which has more than 1,600 properties. And there are thousands of nonaffiliated B&Bs, where standards are very high. The village pub, shop, or post office is a good place to make inquiries.

One word of caution—many small businesses are closed in the winter, so it is always best to make a reservation. And one more word—the Irish breakfast (in the North known as the Ulster Fry) is an enormous, artery-unfriendly cholesterol blast, absolutely irresistibly bad for you. But you are on holiday, and, in any case, with one of those on board, you won't want lunch.

Christmas & Off-Season

Increasingly, these dates are decided year by year. Patrons are best advised to check in advance by email about seasonal and off-season closings.

Hotel Parking

Parking near hotels in cities is changing rapidly. Parking lots are sold for development, and valet parking is now the norm in grander hotels. If it's important, guests should check in advance. Hotels are starting to charge and have deals with private local parking lots whereby a reduced rate is given to guests. This can still be very expensive.

RESTAURANTS

It used to be a thankless task trying to find a decent place to eat in Ireland, but as with hotels, things have changed. Demand has created supply, and now you'll find a huge range of really good restaurants in every corner.

Although menus and cooking styles across Ireland vary, the claims of the top Irish restaurants to be among the best in Europe have solid foundations—fresh produce from the land and sea.

Meat has been the mainstay of Irish cooking for the past hundred years; Irish-reared beef, lamb, and pork are excellent, the art of the sausage flourishes, and Ireland has extended a cautious but now snowballing welcome to the organic meat movement.

Many places grow their own, or buy in, organic vegetables and herbs nowadays, too, and Irish cheese

---

PRICES

HOTELS

An indication of the cost of a double room in the high season is given by **$** signs.

$$$$$	Over $330
$$$$	$200–$330
$$$	$150–$200
$$	$100–$150
$	Under $100

RESTAURANTS

An indication of the cost of a three-course meal without drinks is given by **$** signs.

$$$$$	Over $80
$$$$	$50–$80
$$$	$35–$50
$$	$20–$35
$	Under $20

boards, long confined to soapy cheddar, have taken on a rapidly growing selection of delicious Irish cheeses.

As for seafood, Ireland is, of course, an island, and there are any number of excellent fish and seafood specialists making diners happy from Kinsale to Portrush.

The Irish cellar has kept up with the improvements in the kitchen, and small Irish breweries are introducing flavorsome "craft beers" into what used to be a sea of bland, fizzy lager.

Don't neglect the café at afternoon teatime for Irish baking. Don't spurn the pub for an inexpensive meal—many pubs now put on a range of dishes that can outclass the local restaurants. And don't forget that your B&B may offer a home-cooked evening meal that might well be more enjoyable than the fanciest restaurant in town.

CREDIT CARDS, ORGANIZATION, & ABBREVIATIONS

Apart from in a very few rural backwaters, MasterCard and Visa debit and credit cards are pretty much universally accepted (there may be a minimum spend/administration charge for credit cards). But American Express and Diner's Club are frequently refused these days. For this reason, the term "Major cards," as used in the following listings, includes only MasterCard and Visa. For all other cards, travelers are advised to call ahead to establishments to check which cards are accepted.

All sites are listed first by price, then in alphabetical order.

The abbreviations used are:
L = lunch   D = dinner
AE = American Express;
DC = Diner's Club;
MC = MasterCard; V = Visa

▶ **DUBLIN**

HOTELS

⊞ INTERCONTINENTAL DUBLIN
$$$$$
SIMMONSCOURT RD.
DUBLIN 4
TEL 01/665-4000
intercontinentaldublin.ie

This elegant five-star hotel is situated in the quiet, upscale district of Ballsbridge on the way to Dublin Bay and offers all the amenities including pool, gym, and spa.
🛈 197 🅿 Valet ⊜ ❄ 🎽 ⊠
🗞 Major cards

⊞ RADISSON BLU ST. HELEN'S HOTEL
$$$$$
4A STILLORGAN RD.
BLACKROCK, DUBLIN 4
TEL 01/218-6000
radissonblu.com

This hotel is located in an elegant and luxurious Georgian out-of-town house, overlooking terraced gardens, which retains many of its original 18th-century features.
🛈 151 🅿 230 ⊜ ❄
🗞 Major cards

⊞ THE MERRION
🍴 **$$$$–$$$$$**
UPPER MERRION ST.
DUBLIN 2
TEL 01/603-0600
merrionhotel.com

This Georgian building surrounding a garden offers first-class cuisine, immaculate service, and the likelihood of rubbing shoulders with stellar personalities. **Restaurant Patrick Guilbaud** (see p. 352) provides a grand setting for fine food rooted in French tradition.
🛈 145 🅿 60 ⊜ ❄ ⊠
🗞 Major cards

⊞ NUMBER 31
$$$$–$$$$$
31 LEESON CLOSE
DUBLIN 2
TEL 01/676-5011
number31.ie

Located beside St. Stephen's Green, this Georgian residence and coach house is ideally placed for exploring Dublin. It offers a lovely green garden, beautiful fresh food at breakfast, and a typically warm Irish welcome.
🛈 21 🅿 20 🗞 Major cards

SOMETHING SPECIAL

⊞ RENAISSANCE SHELBOURNE
$$$$–$$$$$
27 ST. STEPHEN'S GREEN
DUBLIN 2
TEL 01/663-4500
marriott.com

The Shelbourne, an elegant Georgian on St. Stephen's Green, oozes atmosphere, as befits a hotel that played a part in the 1916 Easter Rising (see pp. 30–32). Staying here, in the centuries-old heart of Dublin, you'll eat, drink, and sleep with the shades of everyone who was anyone in Ireland's historic and literary life.
🛈 190 🅿 45 ⊜ ⊠
🗞 Major cards

⊞ THE CLARENCE
🍴 **$$$$**
6–8 WELLINGTON QUAY
DUBLIN 2
TEL 01/407-0800
theclarence.ie

Owned by members of the rock band U2, this beautifully refurbished hotel looks out on the River Liffey, with Temple Bar at its back door. The hotel also hosts the renowned **Tea Room**.
🛈 49 🅿 15 🕐 Closed Christmas ⊜ ❄ 🗞 Major cards

🗞 Nonsmoking ❄ Air-conditioning ⊜ Indoor Pool 🌊 Outdoor Pool 🎽 Health Club ⊠ Wi-Fi 🗞 Credit Cards

🏨 FITZWILLIAM HOTEL

🍴 $$$$

ST. STEPHENS GREEN
DUBLIN 2
TEL 01/478-7000
fitzwilliamhoteldublin.com

This luxury hotel in the most beautiful part of Dublin boasts a modern decor and a truly attentive staff. Starred chef, Andy McFadden's **Glovers Alley Restaurant** (see p. 252) is located in the hotel.

🛏 130 🅿 85 🔼 📶
📳 Major cards

🏨 THE MORRISON

$$$$

ORMOND QUAY
DUBLIN 1
TEL 01/887-2400
morrisonhotel.ie

Cool, chic, and stylish, this is one of the nicest places to stay in the city center.

🛏 90 🔼 📶 📳 Major cards

🏨 PREMIER SUITES DUBLIN

$$$$

STEPHENS HALL
14–17 LOWER LEESON ST.
DUBLIN 2
TEL 01/638-1111
premiersuitesdublin.com

Located near St. Stephen's Green, this is an interesting idea that works well—a hotel containing several types of accommodations ranging from penthouses and suites to studios, all of them very well appointed.

🛏 34 🅿 40 🔼
📳 Major cards

🏨 SCHOOLHOUSE HOTEL

$$$$

2–8 NORTHUMBERLAND RD.
BALLSBRIDGE, DUBLIN 4
TEL 01/667-5014
schoolhousehotel.com

School phobics have no cause to be alarmed! The enjoyably atmospheric decor does indeed reflect the building's original incarnation as a Victorian school, but there's nothing at all spartan about the well-appointed bedrooms.

🛏 31 🅿 21 🔼 Closed Christmas 🔼 📶 📳 Major cards

🏨 CLONTARF CASTLE

$$$–$$$$

CASTLE AVE.
CLONTARF, DUBLIN 3
TEL 01/833-2321
clontarfcastle.ie

There is something a little preposterous, but endearing, about the unashamed extravagance of Clontarf Castle, where stone lions and suits of armor greet you.

🛏 180 🅿 134 🔼 📶
📳 Major cards

🏨 WESTBURY HOTEL

$$$–$$$$

BALFE ST.
DUBLIN 2
TEL 01/679-1122
doylecollection.com

This luxury city-center hotel offers chandeliers, valet parking, and tea on the terrace around the grand piano.

🛏 205 🅿 100 🔼 📶
📳 Major cards

🏨 ABERDEEN LODGE

$$$

53–55 PARK AVE.
BALLSBRIDGE, DUBLIN 4
TEL 01/283-8155
aberdeenlodgedublin.com

A classy Edwardian building houses one of Dublin's best private hotels, where high standards of comfort and efficiency are not allowed to get in the way of friendly service.

🛏 20 🅿 16
📳 Major cards

🏨 BROOKS HOTEL

$$$

DRURY ST., DUBLIN 2
TEL 01/670-4000
brookshotel.ie

Located between the buzz of Temple Bar and the tranquillity of St. Stephen's Green, Brooks is a comfortable modern hotel.

🛏 98 🅿 Pay 🔼 📶
📳 Major cards

🏨 BUSWELLS HOTEL

$$$

23–27 MOLESWORTH ST.
DUBLIN 2
TEL 01/614-6500
buswells.ie

Located very close to the National Museum (see pp. 56–59), just north of St. Stephen's Green, this 18th-century town house has been stylishly converted into a comfortable hotel in a surprisingly peaceful location.

🛏 69 🔼 Closed Christmas 🔼 📶 📳 Major cards

🏨 THE GIBSON HOTEL

$$$

POINT SQ., DUBLIN 1
TEL 01/681-5000
thegibsonhotel.ie

Comfortable hotel, all glass walls and chic furnishings, just east of the city center in trendy Point Village on the River Liffey.

🛏 252 🅿 Pay 🔼 📶
📳 Major cards

🏨 THE MARKER HOTEL

$$$

GRAND CANAL SQ.
DOCKLANDS, DUBLIN 2
TEL 01/687-5100
themarkerhoteldublin.com

Docklands is Dublin's coolest new quarter, and this stylish modern hotel is at the heart of it.

🛏 187 🅿 Valet 🔼 📶 📺 📶
📳 Major cards

🏨 ARIEL HOUSE

$$–$$$

50–54 LANSDOWNE RD.
BALLSBRIDGE, DUBLIN 4
TEL 01/668-5512
ariel-house.net

🏨 Hotel 🍴 Restaurant 🛏 No. of Guest Rooms 🔼 No. of Seats 🅿 Parking 🔼 Closed 🔼 Elevator

This beautifully kept period Victorian house, which is located near the Lansdowne DART station, is run to very high standards.

🚪 37 🅿 30 💳 Major cards

🏨 PORTMARNOCK HOTEL
$$–$$$

STRAND RD., PORTMARNOCK
TEL 01/846-0611
portmarnock.com

This is a really comfortable out-of-town hotel, set overlooking the sea in a beautiful beachside location only 20 minutes by train from central Dublin, with its own championship links golf course (designed by two-time Masters winner Bernhard Langer) among the dunes.

🚪 138 🅿 150 ⬅➡ ❄
🕘 Closed Christmas
💳 Major cards

🏨 TEMPLE BAR HOTEL
$$–$$$

13 FLEET ST.
TEMPLE BAR, DUBLIN 2
TEL 01/677-3333
templebarhotel.com

This cozy, centrally located hideaway shares its name and location with Dublin's trendiest quarter—right on the doorstep—for ambling around by day and living it up by night.

🚪 129 🕘 Closed Christmas
⬅➡ 💳 Major cards

🏨 WATERLOO HOUSE
$$–$$$

8–10 WATERLOO RD.
BALLSBRIDGE, DUBLIN 4
TEL 01/660-1888
waterloohouse.ie

Behind the handsome brick facade of this luxury town house, on a quiet street, you'll find an elegant and peaceful haven. Wonderful breakfasts set you up for the fray.

🚪 17 🅿 8 🕘 Closed Christmas 💳 Major cards

🏨 THE ASHLING HOTEL
$$

PARKGATE ST., DUBLIN 8
TEL 01/677-2324
ashlinghotel.ie

Dublin city center lies a 20-minute stroll along the Liffey quays from this very comfortable hotel near the gates of Phoenix Park.

🚪 225 🅿 Pay
⬅➡ ❄ 🏊
❄ Some rooms
🕘 Closed Christmas
💳 Major cards

🏨 CROKE PARK HOTEL
$$

JONES'S RD., DUBLIN 3
TEL 01/871-4444
doylecollection.com
A lively, family-run hotel handily placed for sports lovers opposite Croke Park GAA stadium.

🚪 232 🅿 176 ⬅➡ ❄ 🎽
💳 Major cards

🏨 FITZPATRICK CASTLE HOTEL DUBLIN
$$

KILLINEY, DUBLIN
TEL 01/230-5400
fitzpatrickcastle.com

From its flamboyant mock castle exterior to its helpful and friendly staff, the Fitzpatrick Castle is a real treat, and conveniently placed for the DART railway ride into town.

🚪 113 🅿 220
⬅➡ ❄ 🎽 🏊
💳 Major cards

🏨 THE GRESHAM
$$

23 UPPER O'CONNELL ST.
DUBLIN 1
TEL 01/874-6881
gresham-hotels.com

Just north of the River Liffey, the Gresham offers comfort and a high standard of service.

🚪 288 🅿 150 ⬅➡ ❄
💳 Major cards

🏨 MARINE HOTEL
$$

SUTTON CROSS, DUBLIN 13
TEL 01/839-0000
marinehotel.ie

This comfortable gabled hotel, built in a traditional seaside style, is on the north side of Dublin Bay and situated only a few minutes from central Dublin by DART railway.

🚪 48 🅿 150 🕘 Closed Christmas ⬅➡ 🏊 💳 Major cards

🏨 CHARLEVILLE LODGE
$–$$$

268–272 NORTH CIRCULAR RD.
PHIBSBOROUGH, DUBLIN 7
TEL 01/838-6633
charlevillelodge.ie

A short terrace of fine Victorian houses has been skillfully combined to create this congenial refuge near the northern perimeter of Phoenix Park.

🚪 30 🅿 18 🕘 Closed Christmas 💳 Major cards

🏨 CLAYTON HOTEL
$–$$

MERRION RD.
BALLSBRIDGE, DUBLIN 4
TEL 01/668-1111
claytonhotelballsbridge.com

Clayton prides itself on its relaxed ambience, with staff striking a welcoming note from the outset.

🚪 304 🅿 240 ⬅➡
💳 Major cards

🏨 THE MARTELLO
$–$$

47 STRAND RD., BRAY
TEL 01/286-8000
themartello.ie

A classic seaside hotel right on the front of Dublin's "home resort" of Bray, very convenient for the DART railway into the city. Nightclub, vibrant atmosphere, and youngsters partying good-naturedly are part of the fun!

🚪 44 ❄ 🕘 Closed Christmas
💳 Major cards

❄ Nonsmoking ❄ Air-conditioning 🏊 Indoor Pool 🏊 Outdoor Pool 🎽 Health Club 📶 Wi-Fi 💳 Credit Cards

RESTAURANTS

🍴 GLOVERS ALLEY
$$$$$
FITZWILLIAM HOTEL
128 ST. STEPHEN'S GREEN
DUBLIN 2
TEL 01/478-7008
fitzwilliamhoteldublin.com/
glovers-alley

Starred chef, Andy McFadden's refined cuisine is served in a refined dining space in the Fitzwilliam Hotel. The à la carte menu offers thoughtful, original dishes from both land and sea for an extraordinary combination of flavors.
🕐 Closed Sun.–Wed. L, Mon.–Tues. D
💳 Major cards

🍴 RESTAURANT PATRICK GUILBAUD
$$$$$
21 UPPER MERRION ST.
DUBLIN 2
TEL 01/676-4192
restaurantpatrickguilbaud.ie

Faultless French cuisine and immaculate service have won Patrick Guilbaud more awards than any other restaurant in Ireland. Impeccable culinary creations here include succulent Connemara lobster ravioli and sole and duck confit. Housed in the **Merrion Hotel** (see p. 349), with a fine collection of original Irish art, the restaurant is an upscale dining experience with considerable Irish charm.
🕐 Closed Mon. & Sat. D
💳 Major cards

🍴 LOCKS BRASSERIE
$$$$
1 WINDSOR TERRACE
PORTOBELLO, DUBLIN 8
TEL 01/416-3655
locksrestaurant.ie

Portobello has a few good restaurants and this is one of the best, a canalside place with great views, offering

French-influenced cooking. Sample fresh fish from Kilmore Quay, locally sourced beef, and oysters out of Carlingford Lough, complimented with a carefully chosen French wine list.
🕐 Closed Tues.–Thurs. L, Mon. & Sun. D
💳 Major cards

🍴 MV CILL AIRNE
$$$$
QUAY 16, NORTH WALL QUAY
DUBLIN 1
TEL 01/817-8760
mvcillairne.com

A short stroll from the O2 concert arena, this beautifully restored training vessel, with its gleaming wooden floors and bar, makes a characterful place to eat and drink, before or after a show. Dine in style in the **Quay 16 Restaurant,** or snack in the laid-back bistro.
🕐 Closed Sun.

🍴 CHAPTER ONE
$$$
18–19 PARNELL SQ.
DUBLIN 1
TEL 01/873-2266
chapteronerestaurant.com

The Dublin Writers Museum sits on top of this excellent Michelin star restaurant, which uses both French and Irish influences in its cooking to great effect.
♿ 🕐 Closed Sun.–Mon., Sat. L
💳 AE, DC, V

🍴 HUGO'S
$$$
6 MERRION ROW
DUBLIN 2
TEL 01/676-5955
hugos.ie

With its awning and bright colors, Hugo's puts you in mind of a small restaurant in a French provincial town. And the French/Irish/touch-of-the-Mediterranean cooking doesn't disappoint. A good selection

of wines complements a menu that's not overlong. Two favorites are pork neck fillet with sweet potato mash, and the lunchtime classic *croque madame* with gruyere and béchamel.
🕐 Closed Sat.–Sun. L
💳 Major cards

🍴 KITES
$$$
15–17 BALLSBRIDGE TERRACE
BALLSBRIDGE, DUBLIN 4
TEL 01/660-7415
kitesrestaurant.ie

A very good Chinese restaurant with a pleasant, low-key atmosphere, serving a wide variety of dishes.
🕐 Closed Sat., Sun. L, Good Friday, Dec. 25–26
💳 Major cards

🍴 L'ECRIVAIN
$$$
109A LOWER BAGGOT ST.
DUBLIN 2
TEL 01/661-1919
lecrivain.com

A deservedly famous Dublin restaurant, full of good culinary ideas based on the best fresh ingredients, executed brilliantly but simply. Monkfish, oysters, prawns, and scallops are all wonderful, and meat-lovers will love the Irish lamb and beef. As a bonus: a particularly interesting wine list.
♿ 🕐 Closed Sun. & Sat.–Thurs. L
💳 Major cards

🍴 ROLY'S RESTAURANT & CAFÉ
$$$
7 BALLSBRIDGE TERRACE
BALLSBRIDGE, DUBLIN 4
TEL 01/668-2611
rolysbistro.ie

A tremendous atmosphere of Dubliners enjoying themselves, and an unfussy approach to food (notably the Dublin Bay prawns and the hearty "keep-out-the-cold" puddings) that lets basic flavors and textures speak for themselves.

🖼 Major cards

🍴 SHANAHAN'S ON THE GREEN

$$$

119 ST. STEPHEN'S GREEN, DUBLIN 2

TEL 01/407-0939

shanahans.ie

Behind the very Irish name is very American cooking: huge steaks done to perfection—a rare art. There's something for everyone on the menu, but carnivores with heroic appetites will think they have died and gone to Dallas.

🕐 Closed L Sat.–Thurs. & Sun.

🖼 Major cards

🍴 BON APPÉTIT

$$–$$$$

9 JAMES TERRACE

MALAHIDE, CO. DUBLIN

TEL 01/845-0314

bonappetit.ie

A proper fine-dining experience in trendy Malahide. The set menus are pricey yet still good value for beautifully cooked lobster and prawns, Irish beef and rabbit, and superbly flavorsome vegetables, all meticulously presented. Perfect for afternoon tea on weekends (after your seaside stroll).

🕐 Closed Sun. D, Mon.–Fri. L

🖼 AE, MC, V

🍴 PORT HOUSE PINTXOS

$$–$$$

12 EUSTACE ST.

TEMPLE BAR, DUBLIN 2

TEL 01/672-8590

porthouse.ie

This lively tapas bar in the heart of bouncing Temple Bar has an open kitchen and more racked wine bottles than you can count. Offerings include paella, patatas bravas, sausage, and octopus, along with Spanish and Portuguese wines, beers, and sherries.

🖼 MC, V

🍴 THE TEMPLE BAR PUB

$$–$$$

47/48 TEMPLE BAR, DUBLIN 2

TEL 01/672-5286 OR 01/672-5287

thetemplebarpub.com

Just the place to grab a quick and tasty bite (Guinness and oysters a specialty) before jumping into the night's fun. Try their O'Hara's, Dungarvan, and Carrig craft beers.

🖼 Major cards

🍴 101 TALBOT

$$

100–102 TALBOT ST., DUBLIN 1

TEL 01/874-5011

101talbot.ie

Far East (vegetable coconut curry), Middle East (spanakopita), and Near East (Clonakilty black pudding) collide to all-encompassing effect on the menu of this Northside restaurant. It's very convenient for pre-theater fueling—both the Abbey and the Gate theaters are within strolling distance.

🕐 Closed Sun.–Mon., L

🖼 Major cards

🍴 CAVISTONS

$$

58–59 GLASTHULE RD.

SANDYCOVE, CO. DUBLIN

TEL 01/280-9245

cavistons.com

Quite simply, an unpretentious, family-run restaurant whose Irish-style seafood and other cooking is so superb that connoisseurs will visit Ireland specifically to eat here. Yet everyone feels welcome, and no one feels excluded.

🕐 Closed Sun.–Mon. L; Sun.–Wed. D 🖼 Major cards

🍴 ELEPHANT & CASTLE

$$

18 TEMPLE BAR, DUBLIN 2

TEL 01/679-3121

elephantandcastle.ie

The Elephant & Castle opens early and closes late, so you could eat three (or four) square meals a day here. And why not, when the food's good from breakfast to dinner (enormous baskets of chicken wings, homemade hamburgers with an array of sauces, and a mighty Caesar salad) and the atmosphere is so enjoyable?

♿ 🖼 Major cards

SOMETHING SPECIAL

🍴 O'CONNELL'S

$$

135 MOREHAMPTON RD.

DONNYBROOK, DUBLIN 4

TEL 01/269-6116

oconnellsrestaurant.com

O'Connells has moved to this new location from the Ballsbridge Court Hotel, but still obtains all its ingredients and its wine from top-class sources (organic, free range, fresh almost goes without saying), and the menu lets you know exactly who and where it all came from. It adds a certain something to your enjoyment of salmon, for example, if you can visualize the cold blue waters off magical green Clare Island where the fish was raised.

🕐 Closed Mon.–Thurs. L

🖼 Major cards

🍴 THE VINTAGE KITCHEN

$$

7 POOLBEG ST., DUBLIN 2

TEL 01/679-8705

thevintagekitchen.ie

Next to Mulligan's famous pub, this is a cheerful, informal place. Bring your own wine—and your own vinyl to play, too!

🕐 Closed 2 weeks Jan., Sun.–Mon. 🖼 Major cards

🍴 THE WINDING STAIR

$$

40 ORMOND QUAY

DUBLIN 1

TEL 01/872-7320

winding-stair.com

This combination eatery and bookshop overlooks Ha'penny Bridge. Read or watch the crowds over Connemara lamb, smoked Cork sausage, or traditional bacon and cabbage.

🕒 Closed Christmas
🖸 MC, V

🍴 BEWLEY'S GRAFTON STREET

$–$$

78 GRAFTON ST., DUBLIN 2
TEL 01/564-0090
bewleys.com

A Dublin institution in the heart of the city, it was recently restored to its original splendor. Have a cup of coffee or a snack in this elegant café as you enjoy its oriental charm, its centenary history, and its works of art, including Harry Clarke's beautiful stained-glass windows.

🖸 Major cards

🍴 KINARA

$–$$

318 CLONTARF RD., DUBLIN 3
TEL 01/833-6759
kinara.ie

A tremendous Pakistani restaurant looking out across Dublin Bay, its food rich in all the flavors you'd expect, but adjustable in spiciness to your individual palate.

♿ 🕒 Closed Mon.–Wed. L
🖸 Major cards

🍴 SILK ROAD CAFÉ

$–$$

CHESTER BEATTY LIBRARY
DUBLIN CASTLE, DUBLIN 2
TEL 01/407-0770
silkroadkitchen.ie

Located inside the Chester Beatty Library (see pages 65–67), this is the ideal place to stop after visiting the museum or the nearby castle. It offers a variety of specialties including exquisite dishes from the Mediterranean and the Middle East

such as moussaka, baklava, spiced chicken, and Lebanese pancakes.

♿ 🕒 Closed D, Mon. L (Oct.–May) 🖸 Major cards

🍴 ABBEY TAVERN

$

28 ABBEY ST., HOWTH
CO. DUBLIN
TEL 01/839-0307
abbeytavern.ie

Sticky bangers and mash, boxty cake with smoked salmon, beef from cattle reared on nearby Lambay Island—these are some of the Abbey's specialties, often with a background of live Irish music and dancing. Don't leave without sampling their delicious McGrath's craft beers, brewed in Craigavon, County Armagh.

🖸 Major cards

🍴 BESHOFF RESTAURANT

$

6 UPPER O'CONNOLL ST.
DUBLIN 1
TEL 01/872-4400
beshoffrestaurant.com

You can't leave Ireland without tasting the local fish and chips. This simple but welcoming restaurant occupies two floors with windows overlooking the very busy O'Connell Street. It's been a local institution since 1913 and has an excellent quality/price ratio.

♿ 🖸 Major cards

🍴 BUTLER'S CHOCOLATE CAFÉ

$

24 WICKLOW ST., DUBLIN 2
TEL 01/671-0591
butlerschocolates.com

Butler's has done for hot chocolate what Seattle did for coffee, and you can either drink it neat or add one of a variety of flavored syrups. There's great coffee, too, along with freshly baked cakes and croissants and

PRICES

HOTELS

An indication of the cost of a double room in the high season is given by $ signs.

$$$$$	Over $330
$$$$	$200–$330
$$$	$150–$200
$$	$100–$150
$	Under $100

RESTAURANTS

An indication of the cost of a three-course meal without drinks is given by $ signs.

$$$$$	Over $80
$$$$	$50–$80
$$$	$35–$50
$$	$20–$35
$	Under $20

a selection of handmade chocolates.

🖸 Major cards

▶ EAST IRELAND

COUNTY KILDARE

ATHY

🏨 COURSETOWN COUNTRY HOUSE

$$

STRADBALLY RD.
TEL 059/863-1101

This is a luxurious country-house hotel set on a 250-acre (100 ha) farm, which is also a wildlife sanctuary. The owners are only too happy to share their knowledge with their guests. Lovely walks.

🛈 5 🅿 22 🕒 Closed mid-Nov.–mid-Feb.
🖸 MC, V

BALLYMORE EUSTACE

🍴 BALLYMORE INN
$$

BALLYMORE EUSTACE
TEL 045/864-585
ballymoreinn.com

From tempting starters to the excellent cheese board, this pub-style restaurant and bar offers top-quality fare, based on carefully selected ingredients—all served, of course, with a welcoming smile.

🗟 AE, MC, V

KILDARE

🏠 MARTINSTOWN HOUSE
$$$

THE CURRAGH
TEL 045/441-269
martinstownhouse.com

This upmarket, but comfortable and relaxed, family-run haven is located close to the Curragh and the heart of Ireland's horse-racing world.

🛈 6 🕒 Closed Christmas

LEIXLIP

🏠 LEIXLIP HOUSE HOTEL
🍴 $$

CAPTAINS HILL
TEL 01/624-2268
leixliphouse.com

In this fine Georgian house, the enjoyable ambience is more than matched by the Irish-style cooking. With great attention to locally sourced seasonal produce, it sets the standard for other hotel restaurants in the area.

🅿 64 🗟 Major cards

STRAFFAN

🏠 THE K CLUB
$$$$$

STRAFFAN
TEL 01/601-7200
kclub.ie

A top-notch, five-star hotel with its own Arnold Palmer–designed golf course—the 2005 Ryder Cup was contested here. Efficient staff offers polished, attentive service. A luxury stopover for those who need not count the cents—nor the dollars.

🛈 69 plus 10 annex 🅿 205
🔁 🗟 🗟 Major cards

COUNTY WICKLOW

ASHFORD

🏠 BALLYKNOCKEN HOUSE
$$–$$$

GLENEALY
TEL 0404/44-627
ballyknocken.ie

This first-class guesthouse makes a convenient base for visiting the Wicklow Mountains. Ask for one of the rooms with the vast Victorian baths. There is also an excellent cooking school.

🛈 7 🕒 Closed mid-Dec.–Jan.
🗟 MC, V

BRAY

🍴 OCEAN BAR & GRILL
$$

7 STRAND RD.
TEL 01/286-5071
oceanbarandgrill.ie

After a morning run along Bray's promenade, pop into the seafront Ocean Bar & Grill for a breakfast of porridge, French toast, pancakes with berries, or eggs Benedict. For lunch on a cold day there's Atlantic seafood chowder or a spicy cajun prawn sizzler, while dinner menus include such specialties as squid in a squid-ink risotto, or a tian of lemony salmon and cream cheese.

🗟 Major cards

GLENDALOUGH

SOMETHING SPECIAL

🏠 BROOKLODGE &
🍴 WELLS SPA
$$$$

MACREDDIN VILLAGE
TEL 0402/36-444
brooklodge.com

A luxury hotel within easy reach of the Wicklow Mountains. De-stress in the sauna, then savor organic, locally sourced food in the **Strawberry Tree** restaurant.

🛈 90 🗟 AE, MC, V

🏠 GLENDALE
$

LARAGH E.
TEL 0404/45-410
glendale-glendalough.com

The exceptionally friendly and helpful Christy and Valerie Merrigan run this selection of purpose-built self-catering cottages just down the road from the beautiful valley, historic monastic site, and twin lakes of Glendalough. The accommodation is spotless and very well appointed, and the locally born and bred Merrigans know most of the best walks and pubs hereabouts.

🛈 15 🅿 🗟 Major cards

KILMACANOGUE

🍴 AVOCA HANDWEAVERS
$

KILMACANOGUE
TEL 01/274-6900
avoca.com

What real food is all about—fresh ingredients, combined into uncomplicated dishes, and served with charm. The restaurant is attached to the famous knitwear store.

♿ 🕒 Closed D, Sun.–Wed.
🗟 Major cards

RATHNEW

🏨 TINAKILLY COUNTRY HOUSE HOTEL
$$$$–$$$$$
RATHNEW
TEL 0404/69-274
tinakilly.ie

A Victorian house in terraced gardens, with beautiful sea views on this unfrequented coast north of Wicklow town.

ⓘ 51 🅿 60 ⏲ Closed Christmas ⬛ Major cards

🏨 HUNTER'S HOTEL
$$$
NEWRATH BRIDGE
TEL 0404/40-106
hunters.ie

A long-established, family-run coaching inn set in beautiful gardens. Wood beams, open fires, beautiful old staircases, and a wealth of antique furniture set a lovely scene.

⏲ Closed Christmas ⬛ Major cards

WOODENBRIDGE

🏨 WOODENBRIDGE
$$–$$$
VALE OF AVOCA
TEL 0402/35-146
woodenbridgehotel.com

A friendly hotel at the foot of the delectable Vale of Avoca in the south Wicklow Mountains. Some of the rooms date to the 17th century, others are new; all are very comfortable.

ⓘ 23 🅿 100 ⬛ Major cards

COUNTY CARLOW

BAGENALSTOWN

🏨 LORUM OLD RECTORY
$$$
KILGRANEY
TEL 059/977-5282
lorum.com

A stylish and welcoming place famous for its wonderful home cooking. Fresh flowers throughout the house, croquet and peacocks on the lawn.

ⓘ 4 ⏲ Closed Dec.–Feb. ⬛ Major cards

🏨🍴 MOUNT WOLSELEY HOTEL, SPA & GOLF RESORT
$$$
TULLOW
TEL 059/918-0100
mountwolseley.ie

A handsome old house on the southern outskirts of Tullow has been transformed into an extremely comfortable hotel—stylish, without being stuffy (that applies to the staff, too). The 18-hole golf course was designed by Masters, Classic, and Ryder Cup winner Christy O'Connor.

ⓘ 143 🅿 160 ⬛ 🌀 📺 🏊 ⬛ Major cards

CARLOW

🏨🍴 AVLON HOUSE
$–$$
GREEN LANE, DUBLIN RD.
TEL 059/917-4222
carlowbedandbreakfast.com

Gerard McCormack and Tom Donagher have created exactly what Carlow needed, a top-notch B&B. Everything is kept in immaculate order, and the mighty breakfasts include fresh fruit and all the desirable trimmings.

ⓘ 5 🅿 7

COUNTY KILKENNY

KILKENNY

🏨 BUTLER HOUSE
$$–$$$$
16 PATRICK ST.
TEL 056/772-2828
butler.ie

The former Dower House of Kilkenny Castle provides elegant accommodations right in the heart of the town. It has magnificent marble fireplaces and sweeping staircases, and the larger rooms have views over the peaceful garden and the castle. Breakfast is included in the price, either a Continental, served in the rooms, or full hot breakfast provided just across the garden.

ⓘ 13 🅿 24 ⬛ Major cards

🏨 LANGTON HOUSE HOTEL
$$–$$$
67 JOHN ST.
TEL 056/776-5133
langtons.ie

Four times national pub of the year, Langton's now has a stylish hotel extension with the same high standards and attention to detail that won accolades for the bar and restaurant.

ⓘ 30 🅿 80 ⬛ Major cards

🏨🍴 KILKENNY ORMONDE HOTEL
$–$$$
ORMONDE ST.
TEL 056/775-0200
kilkennyormonde.com

Consistently good food is on offer in both restaurants of this new hotel with large lounge and reception areas.

ⓘ 118 ⬛ Major cards

🍴 CAMPAGNE
$$$$
THE ARCHES, 5 GASHOUSE LN.
TEL 056/777-2858
campagne.ie

The fish, meat, and vegetables of this bright, modern restaurant come from local suppliers. Try the creamy Knockdrinna goat cheese.

⏲ Closed Mon.–Tues. & D Sun. ⬛ MC, V

THOMASTOWN

🏨 MOUNT JULIET
$$$$–$$$$$
THOMASTOWN
TEL 056/777-3010
mountjuliet.ie

Fine stucco, Adam fireplaces, 18th-century furniture, and

objets d'art feature within this handsome Palladian mansion. Jack Nicklaus designed the hotel's golf course, and there are 1,500 acres (600 ha) of parkland to explore.

🛏 32 plus 27 annex 🅿 200
🖥 🖨 Major cards

COUNTY WEXFORD

ARTHURSTOWN

🏨 **DUNBRODY COUNTRY**
🍴 **HOUSE HOTEL**
$$$$–$$$$$
ARTHURSTOWN
TEL 051/389-600
dunbrodyhouse.com

Individually styled bedrooms with marble bathrooms in a Georgian country house set in parkland near the sea. You can enjoy award-winning cuisine in the **Harvest Room,** in the most beautiful surroundings on Waterford Harbour.

🛏 22 🅿 40 🕐 Closed Christmas 🖨 Major cards

ENNISCORTHY

🏨 **BALLINKEELE HOUSE**
$$$$
BALLYMURN
TEL 053/917-7436
ballinkeele.ie

Bedrooms are extremely comfortable, the ambience relaxed at this upscale Victorian farmhouse at the heart of a working farm.

🛏 5 🅿 20 🖨 AE, MC, V

GOREY

🏨 **MARLFIELD HOUSE**
$$$$–$$$$$
COURTOWN RD.
TEL 053/942-1124
marlfieldhouse.com

This luxurious hotel, once a fine Regency house, was home to the Earl of Courtown. The conservatory looks out on lovely gardens.

🛏 20 🅿 50 🖨 Major cards

ROSSLARE

🏨 **KELLY'S RESORT HOTEL**
🍴 **& SPA**
$$$
TEL 053/913-2114
kellys.ie

A seafront hotel with a stylish modern approach, down to its imported French zinc bar. The same goes for the food in **La Marine Bistro,** as superbly tasty as really direct contemporary cooking should be. The seafood chowder and the Wexford beef hot off the grill are outstanding.

🛏 118 🅿 99 🖥 🖨
🖨 AE, MC, V

COUNTY TIPPERARY

BALLINDERRY

SOMETHING SPECIAL

🍴 **BROCKA-ON-THE-**
WATER
$$$
KILGARVAN QUAY
TEL 067/22-038

Forget the whistles and bells of more pretentious restaurants. This one concentrates on the three things that matter—atmosphere, location, and, oh yes, food. Brocka-on-the-Water is a relaxed and delightful place beside Lough Derg in northernmost County Tipperary. The freshest fish and meat are complemented by herbs and vegetables from the restaurant's own garden.

🕐 Closed Sun. 🖨 Major cards

CASHEL

🏨 **CASHEL PALACE HOTEL**
$$$$–$$$$$
CASHEL
TEL 095/31-001
cashelhouse.ie

This hotel is the former palace of the Bishops of Cashel, with the spectacular backdrop of

the Rock of Cashel (floodlit at night). Luxury bedrooms in the palace itself; family or group needs are catered for in mews accommodations alongside.

🛏 13 plus 10 annex 🅿 35
🕐 Closed Christmas 🖨
🖨 Major cards

CLONMEL

🏨 **HOTEL MINELLA**
$$$
COLEVILLE RD.
TEL 052/612-2388
hotelminella.com

This is a cozy, family-run hotel with tastefully decorated bedrooms in its own extensive grounds by the River Suir.

🛏 90 🅿 100
🕐 Closed Christmas
🖥 🖨 Major cards

COUNTY WATERFORD

BALLYMACARBRY

🏨 **GLASHA FARMHOUSE**
$$–$$$
BALLYMACARBRY, VIA CLONMEL
TEL 052/613-6108
glashafarmhouse.com

Paddy and Olive O'Gorman have made a country haven in their dairy farmhouse. With pretty cottage-style furnishings, Glasha is well placed for exploring the Comeragh and Knockmealdown Mountains.

🛏 8 🅿 10 🕐 Closed Christmas 🖨 MC, V

🏨 **HANORA'S COTTAGE**
🍴 **$$–$$$**
NIRE VALLEY
TEL 052/613-6134
hanorascottage.com

Guests feel like friends here, where the cooking is superb and Mary Wall, her son Eoin, and his wife Judith offer a warm welcome and all the advice you need on walking in the Comeragh Mountains.

🛏 10 🅿 15 🕐 Closed Christmas 🖨 MC, V

DUNGARVAN

🍴 TANNERY RESTAURANT

$$$

10 QUAY ST.

TEL 058/45-420

tannery.ie

People travel a long way to eat at the Tannery—small wonder, because this is a restaurant for hungry folk, not precious aesthetes. Plates are nice and full, the atmosphere is lively, and the staff are friendly. Try the fish, especially the crab crème brûlée, or snack on delicious tapas.

🕐 Closed Mon.; Sun. D except July–Aug.; Mon.–Thurs. L
🖎 Major cards

TRAMORE

🍴 VICTORIA HOUSE

$$

12 QUEEN'S ST.

TEL 051/390-338

thevic.ie

A wood-paneled bar, wooden beams, wood-burning stove—a cozy place to tuck into steaks, seafood marinara, or chicken sourdough.

🕭 🖎 MC, V

WATERFORD

🏨 WATERFORD CASTLE

$$$$–$$$$$

THE ISLAND, BALLINAKILL

TEL 051/878-203

waterfordcastle.com

A chance to stay in a Norman castle, reached by ferry and set up to ensure the most romantic sojourns. Realists will enjoy the 18-hole golf course, clay shooting, and other outdoor activities.

🛈 19 🅿 50 🔁
🖎 Major cards

🍴 HARLEQUIN CAFÉ & WINE BAR

$–$$

37 STEPHEN ST.

TEL 051/877-552

Run by an Italian couple, this is a great place to pop in for pungent coffee to wake you up or some pasta later in the day.

🕐 Closed Mon. & Christmas
🖎 MC, V

▶ SOUTHWEST IRELAND

CORK CITY

🏨 HAYFIELD MANOR

$$$$$

PERROTT AVE., COLLEGE RD.

TEL 021/484-5900

hayfieldmanor.ie

A snug retreat where you can shut the world away (and work on your fitness in the exclusive health club), Hayfield Manor is a comfortable, upscale hotel toward the western outskirts of Cork city.

🛈 88 🅿 100 🔁 🖎 🖴
🖎 Major cards

🏨 PARADISO
🍴

$$$

16 LANCASTER QUAY

TEL 021/427-7939

paradiso.restaurant

This vegetarian café with rooms is great for pre-theater dining, with such delicacies as caramelized beetroot tart or a cake of couscous, feta cheese, and pistachio.

🛈 3 🕐 Closed Sun.
🖎 Major cards

🏨 THE RIVER LEE HOTEL

$$$

WESTERN RD.

TEL 021/425-2700

doylecollection.com/hotels/the-river-lee-hotel

Situated on the southern arm of the River Lee, a few minutes

walk from the town center, this striking modern hotel has a nice, relaxed atmosphere, helped by the friendliness of the staff.

🛈 182 🅿 🔁 🖎 🖴
🖎 Major cards

🏨 IMPERIAL HOTEL

$$–$$$$

76 SOUTH MALL

TEL 021/427-4040

flynnhotels.com

The individually styled en suite rooms of this recently refurbished hotel offer comfort and a quiet atmosphere in central Cork.

🛈 125 🅿 40 🕐 Closed Christmas 🔁 🖎 Major cards

🍴 JACOB'S ON THE MALL

$$$

30A SOUTH MALL

TEL 021/425-1530

jacobsonthemall.com

Sophisticated cuisine such as roast cod with champ—mashed potato with a touch of magic—or oysters with shallots are served in a relaxed atmosphere in the heart of Cork city.

🕭 🕐 Closed Sun.; L 🖎 AE, MC, V

🍴 JACQUES

$$$

23 OLIVER PLUNKETT ST.

TEL 021/427-7387

jacquesrestaurant.ie

Dishes from around the world, each treated with care and attention to detail—beetroot and quinoa cakes, Thai swordfish with yellow chili sauce, or tapas of *patatas bravas* and chipotle.

🕐 Closed Sun.–Mon.
🖎 AE, MC, V

🍴 CRAWFORD ART GALLERY CAFÉ

$$

CRAWFORD ART GALLERY, EMMET PL.

TEL 021/427-4415

crawfordartgallery.ie

You wouldn't necessarily expect to find a fabulous eating experience in an art gallery's café, but that's what this is—largely because the celebrated Ballymaloe House kitchens, gardens, and bakery supply most of what's on offer. That could mean local lamb and fish with intriguing herbs, a big vegetarian stew, or just a pile of freshly baked bread, the house chutney, and some Cork farmhouse cheese.

🕐 Closed Sun.; D 🅺 MC, V

🍴 SOUTH COUNTY BAR AND CAFE
$$
WEST VILLAGE, DOUGLAS
TEL 021/489-1574
thesouthcounty.com

Enjoy a breakfast, lunch, or early dinner in this nice cheerful pub, before turning your attention to the wonderful traditional music sessions four nights a week.

🅺 Major cards

🍴 CAFÉ GUSTO
$
3 WASHINGTON ST.
TEL 021/425-4446
cafegusto.com

Far more than a simple café, the Gusto whips up sandwiches made in heaven. If you want something a little fancier, try the mezze, antipasti plates, or a good chunky Moroccan lamb stew.

🕐 Closed Sun.; D

COUNTY CORK

BALTIMORE

🍴 CASEY'S OF BALTIMORE
$$$
BALTIMORE
TEL 028/20-197
caseysofbaltimore.com

Famed seafood restaurant (the steaks and local lamb are

excellent, too!) with a great appetizer of a sea view. Enjoy mussels out of Roaringwater Bay, seafood and fish caught locally, tangy smoked haddock, and Casey's justly popular crab claws.

🅺 Major cards

BANTRY

🏨 BANTRY HOUSE & GARDENS
$$$$–$$$$$
BANTRY
TEL 027/50-047
bantryhouse.com

Guests of the B&B, ten minutes from Bantry town, have full access to the famous gardens and historic house and its impressive collections of furniture and art. Guest rooms overlook the gardens and Hundred Steps, worth the climb for the breathtaking view over the house and to the bay. A self-catering house is also available year-round.

ℹ️ 7 plus guesthouse 🅿️
🕐 B&B closed Nov.–March
🅺 MC, V

🍴 BLAIRSCOVE HOUSE
$$$$
DURRUS
TEL 027/61-127
blairscove.ie

A free-and-easy ambience allied to beautifully tasty but unfussy cooking.

🕐 Contact for off-season closures. 🅺 Major cards

🍴 O'CONNOR'S SEAFOOD RESTAURANT
$$$
WOLFE TONE SQ.
TEL 027/55-664
oconnorseafood.com

This was the first restaurant in Ireland to specialize in mussels, and all the seafood is excellent. Starters could include seafood chowder, mixed seafood with

lemongrass or hand-dived scallops, with pan-fried hake and cod, paupiette of plaice, or black Angus beef to follow. Children get a complimentary cola float or jelly and ice-cream—but only if they finish their mains (sausages and mash, fish and chips, flash fried calamari) first!

♿ 🅺 MC, V

FERMOY

🏨 BALLYVOLANE HOUSE
$$$
CASTLELYONS
TEL 025/36-349
ballyvolanehouse.ie

You will enjoy an exceptionally warm welcome at this fine 18th-century Italianate country house, set in famous gardens within parkland. Stroll around the lakes; one has been stocked for fishing and might yield you a brown trout.

ℹ️ 6 🅿️ 25 🕐 Contact for off-season closures
🅺 Major cards

🍴 THE FORGE
$$
DUNTAHEEN RD.
TEL 025/40-351

A pub and restaurant with a cheerful atmosphere. The menu offers typical Irish cuisine with a variety of specialties, primarily soups and meat dishes.

🕐 Closed Mon., Tues.–Wed. D
🅺 Major cards

FOTA ISLAND

🏨 FOTA ISLAND HOTEL & SPA
$$$$$
FOTA ISLAND
TEL 021/488-3700
fotaisland.ie

This full-scale luxury operation comprises a wooded estate on a private island, extremely comfortable and carefully furnished rooms with subtle modern lighting, suites with private terrace balconies, and a spa with a hydrotherapy suite that boasts more than 60 treatments. Outside is a championship-standard golf course and golf academy.

ⓘ 131 ⊡ Closed Christmas
⊠ Major cards

KILBRITTAIN

🏠 BRIDGEVIEW FARMHOUSE B&B
$

COOLMAIN HARBOUR
TEL 023/884-9723
bridgeviewfarmhouse.com

Bridgeview Farmhouse commands a fabulous view over Courtmacsherry Bay from its terrace. You arrive to welcoming tea and home baking, and the rooms are cozy and furnished farmhouse style.

⊡ Contact for off-season closures

KINSALE

🏠 OLD BANK TOWN HOUSE
$$–$$$

11 PEARSE ST.
TEL 021/477-4075
oldbankhousekinsale.com

A hospitable Georgian house meticulously restored by the owners, who can arrange sea fishing, riding, and sailing for guests. Bedrooms are country house in character, furnished with fine antiques.

ⓘ 17 ⊡ Contact for off-season closures ⊟
⊠ AE, MC, V

🍴 FISHY FISHY CAFÉ
$$

GUARDWELL
TEL 021/470-0415
fishyfishy.ie

Like the name says, fish is king here. You can choose the one you prefer and it will be cooked exactly to your desire, or you can put yourself into the hands of the chef and opt for fish soup, fresh prawns, hake, or any one of the special treats the menu has to offer. The restaurant is proud to say that it relies on local fishermen, smokers, and suppliers. Among the delicacies on the menu, diners will always find crab, lobster, shrimp, cod, monkfish, and rake as well as clams and periwinkle.
⊡ Closed D

🍴 HAMLETS OF KINSALE
$$

THE GLEN
TEL 021/477-2209
hamletsofkinsale.com

The restaurant is elegant and modern with an open-air space where you can have a beer or a cocktail. The menu has a bit of everything including pasta and pizza but its specialties are undoubtedly the oysters and its Irish steaks.
⊠ Major cards

MACROOM

🏠 GOUGANE BARRA HOTEL
$$$

GOUGANE BARRA,
BALLINGEARY
TEL 026/47-069
gouganebarrahotel.com

Neil Lucey and his team have got a really good thing going here: a family-run hotel in a superb lakeside location. The watchword is comfort and a relaxed, friendly atmosphere. Hidden in the nearby forests is a clutch of wonderful walks.

ⓘ 26 ⊡ Closed Nov.–March
⊠ Major cards

PRICES

HOTELS
An indication of the cost of a double room in the high season is given by $ signs.

$$$$$	Over $330
$$$$	$200–$330
$$$	$150–$200
$$	$100–$150
$	Under $100

RESTAURANTS
An indication of the cost of a three-course meal without drinks is given by $ signs.

$$$$$	Over $80
$$$$	$50–$80
$$$	$35–$50
$$	$20–$35
$	Under $20

MALLOW

🏠 LONGUEVILLE HOUSE HOTEL
$$$–$$$$$

MALLOW
TEL 022/47-156
longuevillehouse.ie

A very handsome and elegant Georgian house with Italian stucco and many other original features. Upscale accommodation in lovely secluded parkland.

ⓘ 20 🅿 30 ⊠ Major cards

MIDLETON

🏠🍴 BALLYMALOE HOUSE
$$$$–$$$$$

SHANAGARRY
TEL 021/465-2531
ballymaloe.ie

Probably the best known restaurant in the south of Ireland. Homemade pâté, Cobh smoked fish, local beef with original sauces, fabulous

Cork cheeses as a complement to the famous Ballymaloe bread—everything is exactly right.

☎ 22 plus 10 annex **P** 30
⊕ Closed Christmas &
2 weeks in Jan. **☎**
☒ Major cards

ROSSCARBERY

🍴 O'CALLAGHAN WALSHE
$$$

NORTH SQ.
TEL 023/884-8125

Oysters, mussels, and lobster to turbot, cod, and Dover sole—all salty-fresh and served in a cozy environment. (No children under 12 after 7:30 p.m. during the summer.)

⊕ Closed L, Mon. Weekends only Oct.–May but call to check
☒ MC, V

SCHULL

🏨 MOSSIE'S RESTAURANT
🍴 & ULUSKER HOUSE
$$

ADRIGOLE, BEARA
TEL 027/60-606
mossiesrestaurant.com

This delightful place, a beautifully restored 17th-century house in a charming garden, is just the setting for tapas in the conservatory, an evening meal based around fresh fish or local meat, or just a strawberry cream tea on the lawn.

☎ 4 **⊕** Closed L & Jan.
☒ Major cards

SKIBBEREEN

🏨 LISS ARD ESTATE
$$$

CASTLETOWNSEND RD.
TEL 028/40-000
lissardestate.com

The Victorian estate just outside Skibbereen offers a wide variety of accommodation—in the big house, the garden mews, or the lodge down by the lake.

⊕ Closed Christmas
☒ Major cards

SOMETHING SPECIAL

🍴 ISLAND COTTAGE
$$

HARE (HEIR) ISLAND
TEL 028/38-102
islandcottage.com

A romantic boat ride to an island restaurant—sounds good? Island Cottage is entirely idiosyncratic, but in a good way. There's no choice of menu, because you don't need one with such out of this world source material (all local, most organic) and beautiful, uncomplicated cooking. Lunch is offered on weekends. Telephone well in advance, though, and note there's a separate charge for the boat trip.

⊕ Open April–June only weekends L; open mid-June–mid-Sept. Wed.–Sat. D (on Sun. pre-booked groups only)

YOUGHAL

🏨 AHERNE'S
🍴 $$$–$$$$

163 N. MAIN ST.
TEL 024/92-424
ahernes.net

Family-run for several generations, this is a place that simply exudes traditional Irish hospitality, from the warm welcome to the fond farewell. The restaurant is very strong on fresh seafood and meats.

☎ 13 **&** **P** 20 **⊕** Closed Christmas **☒** Major cards

COUNTY KERRY

BALLYDAVID

🍴 OLD PIER RESTAURANT
$$

FEOTHANACH
TEL 066/915-5242
oldpier.com

In a wonderful location on the north shore of the Dingle Peninsula, with a big bay window overlooking the sea, this is a stylish modern restaurant (and guesthouse). The extensive menu includes plenty of wonderfully fresh and tasty local seafood.

& **⊕** Closed L; Tues. Nov.–Feb.
☒ MC, V

DINGLE

🏨 GREENMOUNT HOUSE
$$$

UPPER JOHN ST., GORTONORA
TEL 066/915-1414
greenmounthouse.ie

Set on beautiful Dingle Harbour, Greenmount House offers warm hospitality and a relaxed atmosphere.

☎ 14 **P** 12
☒ MC, V

🍴 OUT OF THE BLUE
$$$

WATERSIDE
TEL 066/915-0811
outoftheblue.ie

Out of the Blue only serves fresh fish and only when local fishermen have fish to sell—Atlantic salmon, cod, turbot, monkfish; oysters, mussels, scallops; crab, crayfish, lobster.

⊕ Closed Mon.–Sat. L except bank holiday weekends; Nov.–Feb. **☒** MC, V

GLENBEIGH

🏨 KERRY OCEAN LODGE
$–$$

GLENBEIGH
TEL 066/976-9666
kerryoceanlodge.com

You don't have to be a walker to stay here, but it helps. With the famed Macgillycuddy's Reeks nearby, the lodge offers friendly, warm service and delicious breakfasts.

☎ 20

⊗ Nonsmoking **❄** Air-conditioning **▦** Indoor Pool **▨** Outdoor Pool **♥** Health Club **☎** Wi-Fi **☒** Credit Cards

KENMARE

SOMETHING SPECIAL

🏨 PARK HOTEL KENMARE
$$$$$
KENMARE
TEL 064/664-1200
parkkenmare.com

A smart and luxurious Victorian country-house hotel that is set in landscaped gardens, where strollers enjoy superb views over the Kenmare River's broad estuary.

🛏 46 🅿 60 🕒 Closed Dec.–Feb.; open two weeks around Christmas & New Year's 🔼
🔘 Major cards

🍴 PACKIE'S
$$$
HENRY ST.
TEL 064/664-1508
packiesrestaurant.ie

Desserts are rich and delicious here, particularly the homemade ice cream—but make sure you leave room for the main courses, which marry first-class ingredients to unpretentious cooking. The menu includes such dishes as potato cakes with garlic butter.
🔘 MC, V

KILLARNEY

🏨 AGHADOE HEIGHTS HOTEL & SPA
$$$$$
LAKES OF KILLARNEY
TEL 064/663-1766
aghadoeheights.com

This luxury hotel commands stunning views of the lakes and mountains of Killarney National Park. Service is personal, friendly, and helpful, and the hotel is superbly appointed. The stylish bedrooms are air-conditioned, and many have their own sundecks.
🛏 73 🅿 120 🔼 🔘
🎦 🔘 Major cards

🏨 KILLARNEY PARK
$$$$–$$$$$
TOWN CENTRE
TEL 064/663-5555
killarneyparkhotel.ie

Purpose-built for the luxury end of the Killarney visitor market, the Killarney Park gives you a soft landing and a stylish ride all the way.
🛏 71 🅿 70 🕒 Closed Christmas 🔼 🔘 🎦
🔘 Major cards

🍴 BEAUFORT BAR & RESTAURANT
$$
TEL 064/664-4149
beaufortbar.com

This historic bar has been run by the O'Sullivan family since it opened in 1841, and from 1911 to 1914 it was the base of the American Kalem Film Company, which shot about 70 movies in the area (still photographs hang on the walls here). The restaurant is a more recent addition, but soon acquired a reputation for excellent cuisine.
🕒 Contact for off-season closures 🔘 Major cards

KILLORGLIN

🍴 NICK'S SEAFOOD RESTAURANT & PIANO BAR
$$$
LOWER BRIDGE ST.
TEL 066/976-1219
nicks.ie

A restaurant that would run a hundred miles rather than take itself too seriously, Nick's fills your ears with music, your mouth with rollicking choruses, and your belly with good grub. The menu leans cheerily on local meat and fish—Kerry-reared beef, say, or local shellfish such as mussels done in a superb Franco-Irish style.
🕒 Contact for off-season closures 🔘 Major cards

SHEEP'S HEAD PENINSULA

🏨 GALLÁN MÓR
$$
KEALTIES, DURRUS
TEL 027/62-732
gallanmor.com

A boutique B&B with individually furnished rooms, a superb outlook to the Mizen Peninsula hills across Dunmanus Bay, and great food—including honey from the owners' bees.
🛏 4 🔘 Major cards

WATERVILLE

🏨 BUTLER ARMS HOTEL
$$$–$$$$
WATERVILLE
TEL 066/947-4144
butlerarms.com

A spacious hotel that occupies a splendid location overlooking the sea. Most of the bedrooms have sea views, and all have en suite marble bathrooms.
🛏 40 🅿 50 🕒 Closed Oct.–March 🔼 🔘 Major cards

COUNTY LIMERICK

ADARE

🏨 DUNRAVEN ARMS
$$$–$$$$
ADARE
TEL 061/605-900
dunravenhotel.com

Relax in the easygoing atmosphere of this traditional country inn in Adare, one of Ireland's most attractive preserved estate villages.
🛏 86 🅿 90 🔼 🎦
🔘 Major cards

🍴 WILD GEESE RESTAURANT
$$$
ROSE COTTAGE
TEL 061/396-451
thewild-geese.com

A gorgeous cottage is the setting for this extremely

well-regarded restaurant, where first-class ingredients are used to please a discerning and enthusiastic clientele. Light lunches only in summer.

🕓 Closed Sun. D, Mon. 🈐 AE, MC, V

BALLINGARRY

🍴 THE MUSTARD SEED AT ECHO LODGE
$$$
BALLINGARRY
TEL 069/68-508
mustardseed.ie

Fine cooking based on local, organic, and seasonal produce, for example, pheasant and venison or a rack of Irish mountain lamb—all done with a warmly hospitable touch. You can stay here, too.

🈐 🕓 Closed Dec. 24–26, mid-Jan.–Feb. 1 🈐 Major cards

KILMALLOCK

🏨 FLEMINGSTOWN HOUSE
$$
KILMALLOCK
TEL 063/98-093
flemingstownhouse.com

Just outside the country town of Kilmallock, the Georgian farmhouse of Flemingstown House offers a winning combination of elegance and style—antiques in the drawing room, stained-glass windows in the dining room—together with the warmth of the staff and the owner.

🈐 5 🅿 12 🈐 MC, V

LIMERICK

🏨 NO. 1 PERY SQUARE HOTEL & SPA
$$$–$$$$
PERY SQ.
TEL 061/402-402
oneperysquare.com

This boutique hotel in a beautiful Georgian townhouse has huge beds and luxurious furnishings. Eat and drink in the first-floor brasserie, and bask in the spa's herb and seaweed treatments.

🈐 20 🕓 Closed Christmas 🈐 🈐 Major cards

🏨 CASTLETROY PARK HOTEL
$$–$$$
DUBLIN RD.
TEL 061/335-566
castletroypark.ie

A fine modern hotel with extensive leisure and banqueting facilities.

🈐 188 🅿 160 🈐 🈐 Major cards

🍴 HOOK & LADDER
$–$$
7 SARSFIELD ST.
TEL 061/413-778
hookandladder.ie

In a cozy and informal atmosphere, from breakfast time until late afternoon, guests can savor dishes prepared with ingredients from the Irish countryside: sandwiches, porridge, quiches, salads, and much more.

🕓 Closed D 🈐 Major cards

▶ THE WEST OF IRELAND

COUNTY CLARE

BALLYVAUGHAN

🏨 GREGAN'S CASTLE
$$$$
BALLYVAUGHAN
TEL 065/707-7005
gregans.ie

In a superb location in the heart of Clare's Burren region, the medieval tower house of Gregan's Castle stands at the foot of the famous Corkscrew Hill. Accommodations

are up to date in amenities, however. Each bedroom is individually furnished in country-house style—all have wonderful countryside views, and some have their own private gardens. The emphasis is very much on peace and quiet; bedroom televisions are conspicuous by their absence.

🈐 22 🅿 25 🕓 Closed mid-Dec.–mid-Feb. 🈐 AE, MC, V

BUNRATTY

🏨 BUNRATTY CASTLE HOTEL
$–$$$
BUNRATTY
TEL 061/478-700
bunrattycastlehotel.com

A comfortable, traditional-style hotel, very conveniently located near Shannon Airport and on the doorstep of Bunratty Castle & Folk Park.

🈐 144 🅿 🈐 🈐 🈐 Major cards

COROFIN

🏨 FERGUS VIEW GUESTHOUSE
$
KILNABOY
TEL 065/683-7606
fergusview.com

An excellent family-run guesthouse, where Mary Kelleher's cooking of local meat and fish and homegrown vegetables is scrumptiously set off by her amazing puddings. Very well positioned for exploring the Burren or the coast.

🈐 6 🅿 8 🕓 Closed Nov.–Easter

DOOLIN

🏨 ARAN VIEW HOUSE HOTEL
$$$
COAST RD.
TEL 065/707-4061
aranview.com

A friendly hotel. Each bedroom is beautifully furnished, equipped with TV, en suite bathrooms, and superb views out across Galway Bay to the Aran Islands. Traditional music is performed at the Aran View several times a week. The vaulted bar is a great spot for mulling over the day's events.

🛏 13 plus 6 annex 🅿 40
🕐 Closed Nov.–March
💳 Major cards

🍴 BALLINALACKEN COUNTRY HOUSE & RESTAURANT

$$$

BALLINALACKEN CASTLE
TEL 086/361-3719
ballinalackencastle.com

Ballinalacken Castle is a famous local landmark with a restaurant that is popular with locals who appreciate good food from the sea and land nearby. Doolin-caught crab, Clare-bred lamb, and locally produced St Tola's goat cheese are all delights of the menu.

🕐 Closed Nov.–mid-April

ENNIS

🏨 THE OLD GROUND

$$–$$$

O'CONNELL ST.
TEL 081/836-5036
oldgroundhotelennis.com

A fine traditional hotel in the heart of the county town of Ennis, with a calm and discreet ambience. Bedrooms have been refurbished and feature crisp white sheets, subtle colors, and lots of cushions.

🛏 10 💳 Major cards

KILFENORA

🍴 VAUGHAN'S

$

KILFENORA
TEL 065/708-8004
vaughanspub.ie

Vaughan's is a most delightful pub where the Guinness is great, the music is brilliant, and the "plain Irish cooking" uses the best local ingredients for local dishes (bacon and cabbage, beef and stout pie) that locals eat with relish.

🕐 Closed Good Fri., Christmas
💳 MC, V

KILLALOE

🍴 GOOSERS

$$

BALLINA
TEL 061/376-791
goosers.ie

The menu in this warm, cozy establishment is traditionally Irish with soups and meat dishes, especially stews. The tables outside offer a panoramic view of the River Shannon.

💳 Major cards

KILRUSH

🏨 HILLCREST VIEW

$

DOONBEG RD. (OFF N67)
TEL 065/905-1986
hillcrestview.com

This family-run B&B has an inviting atmosphere and its comfortable rooms have all the amenities. The bright patio is a great place to have breakfast and guests can enjoy the tables outdoors on sunny days.

🛏 6 🅿 7
💳 AE, MC, V

LAHINCH

🍴 BARRTRÁ SEAFOOD RESTAURANT

$$

BARRTRÁ
TEL 065/708-1280
barrtra.com

If the local boats have taken it out of the sea that day, the chances are it'll be on the table at Barrtrá, looking and tasting even better thanks to the fabulous sea views.

🕐 Closed Sun.–Thurs. March–May; Thurs. in June; Mon.–Fri. Oct.–Dec. (call for off-season hours); & Jan.–Feb. 💳 AE, MC, V

LISDOONVARNA

🏨 DROMOLAND CASTLE

$$$$–$$$$$

NEWMARKET-ON-FERGUS
TEL 061/368-144
dromoland.ie

This is every multimillionaire's dream of a Gothic revival castle with turrets, irregular rooflines, and battlements. It may have been built many centuries after such defenses were actually necessary, but this fairy-tale pile is not about grim reality.

🛏 100 🅿 120 🛗
💳 Major cards

🏨🍴 SHEEDY'S COUNTRY HOUSE HOTEL

$$$

LISDOONVARNA
TEL 065/707-4026
sheedys.com

Comfortable and friendly, this small, family-run hotel is attached to an excellent restaurant (try the succulent casserole of local lamb with rosemary and organic vegetables) in one of Clare's most characterful towns.

🛏 11 🅿 40 🕐 Closed mid-Oct.–mid-March 💳 AE, MC, V

🍴 WILD HONEY INN

$$

KINCORA RD.
TEL 065/707-4300
wildhoneyinn.com

Modern cooking is dished up in the very pleasant bar. Choices include Liscannor crab claws, rare breed pork belly, fish of the day, or chicken breast with ceps.

🕐 Closed Jan.–mid-Feb.; call for details 💳 Major cards

COUNTY GALWAY

ARAN ISLANDS

🏨 SOUTH ARAN HOUSE
$$
INISHEER
TEL 099/75-073
southaran.com

A whitewashed stone cottage set in a flowery garden near the sea, with simple blue-painted furniture and unfussy, comfortable rooms. Wake up to scrambled eggs with fresh coriander, or a newly caught mackerel if the fishermen have been lucky.
🛏 3 ⏱ Contact for off-season dates 💳 Major cards

BALLYNAHINCH

🏨 BALLYNAHINCH
🍴 **CASTLE**
$$$–$$$$$
BALLYNAHINCH
TEL 095/31-006
ballynahinch-castle.com

A cheery, outdoorsy place on the banks of a famous sporting river (most of the comfortable bedrooms enjoy river views). You don't have to catch your own dinner here—though the chef will be only too delighted to cook anything you do bring in from lake, river, or sea. Otherwise, just settle back to enjoy one of Ireland's most agreeable castle settings.
🛏 40 🅿 ⏱ Closed Feb., Christmas 💳 Major cards

BUSHYPARK

🏨 GLENLO ABBEY
$$$$$
BUSHYPARK
TEL 091/519-600
glenloabbeyhotel.ie

A hotel full of character, incorporating a restored church and early Georgian abbey buildings, on the shores of Lough Corrib. A modern wing houses the very comfortable bedrooms, many of which have fabulous lough views.
🛏 46 🅿 150 ⏱ Closed Christmas 😊 💳 Major cards

CASHEL

🏨 CASHEL HOUSE HOTEL
$$$$–$$$$$
CASHEL
TEL 095/31-001
cashelhouse.ie

Stunningly set in 50 acres (20 ha) of superb gardens on one of Connemara's most beautiful bays, Cashel House offers elegant, luxurious accommodation.
🛏 32 🅿 40 ⏱ Contact for off-season dates
💳 Major cards

🍴 ZETLAND COUNTRY HOUSE
$$$
CASHEL BAY
TEL 095/31-111
zetland.com

Unpretentiously delicious cooking in a beautifully appointed room with one of Connemara's classic sea and coastal views to aid digestion.
⏱ Closed L, Dec.–Jan.
💳 Major cards

CLARENBRIDGE

🍴 PADDY BURKE'S
$$
CLARENBRIDGE
TEL 091/796-226
paddyburkesgalway.com

Simply the most famous oyster house in Ireland, *fons et origo* of the Clarenbridge Oyster Festival, where the glitterati and the literati rub shoulders with denizens of the real world over excellent seafood and stout.
⏱ Closed Good Friday, Christmas
💳 Major cards

CLIFDEN

🏨 ABBEYGLEN CASTLE HOTEL
$$$$
SKY RD.
TEL 095/21-201
abbeyglen.ie

Abbeyglen Castle is just west of Clifden on the fabulously scenic Sky Road. A highly dedicated family team puts both comfort and cuisine in the top bracket, but also with antennae tuned to what might please the guests—hence many music sessions in the bar.
🛏 45 🅿 50 ⏱ Closed early Jan.–early Feb. 💳 Major cards

🏨 ARDAGH HOTEL
$$$–$$$$
BALLYCONNEELY RD.
TEL 095/21-384
ardaghhotel.com

Beautifully located on Ardbear Bay near Clifden, this is a well-run family setup where guests' comfort and well-being come first. Well-furnished bedrooms with either sea or country views.
🛏 19 🅿 35
💳 Major cards

🏨 MALLMORE COUNTRY HOUSE
$$
BALLYCONNEELY RD.
TEL 095/21-460
mallmore.com

A very stylish house, beautiful furnishings, and wonderful views. Amid all this, owners have not forgotten the essential ingredient of any Irish B&B—a warm, welcoming atmosphere.
🛏 6 ⏱ Closed Nov.–Feb.
💳 No credit cards

🍴 MITCHELL'S RESTAURANT
$$$
MARKET ST.
TEL 095/21-867
mitchellsrestaurantclifden.com

This family-run restaurant on Clifden's main street has many loyal devotees—and no wonder, with mouthwatering favorites such as fish and chips, shepherd's pie, and fish cakes.

🕒 Closed Nov.–Feb.
🃏 Major cards

GALWAY CITY

🏨 HARBOUR HOTEL
$$$–$$$$$
NEW DOCK RD.
TEL 091/894-800
harbour.ie

Forming part of the development of Galway's harbor frontage, this hotel may be modern in design, but it offers all the traditional comfort of open fires and plush furnishings.

ⓘ 96 🅿 64 ⬆ 🃏 Major cards

🏨 ALMARA HOUSE
$–$$
2 MERLIN GATE, DUBLIN RD.
TEL 091/755-345
almarahouse.com

The proprietors of Almara House also own a butcher's shop, so fresh bacon and sausages for breakfast are guaranteed. Cozy bedrooms and a warm welcome are assured, and there's a bus stop for city-center services right outside.

ⓘ 4 🅿 8 🃏 Major cards

🍴 GEMELLE'S
$$
23 QUAY ST.
TEL 091/568-821

This small restaurant in the center of Galway with a welcoming atmosphere offers Irish specialties as well as tapas and vegetarian dishes.

🕒 Closed Christmas
🃏 AE, MC, V

🍴 OSTERIA ITALIANA DA SIMONE
$$
3 ST. FRANCIS ST.
TEL 091/564-850

osteriaitalianagalway.com

Just paces from Eyre Square, you can experience a real slice of authentic Italian cuisine. Huge portions, excellent food, warm atmosphere. Desserts, such as panna cotta and tiramisu, are the cherry on top.

🕒 Closed Mon.–Thurs. L
🃏 Major cards

🍴 TIGH NEACHTAIN & ARTISAN RESTAURANT
$$
CROSS ST.
TEL 091/568-820
tighneachtain.com

This smallish restaurant does things with a Gallic twist and is all the better for it. Meat comes from local sources and fish out of Galway Bay.

🕒 Closed Christmas
🃏 Major cards

🍴 GOYA'S
$
2–3 KIRWAN'S LN.
TEL 091/567-010
goyas.ie

Stickies, slices, and sweet nothings to ruin your waistline and keep out the cold—even if it's a Galway heat wave.

🕒 Closed Sun., D
🃏 MC, V

LETTERFRACK

SOMETHING SPECIAL

🏨 ROSLEAGUE MANOR
$$$$$
LETTERFRACK
TEL 095/41-101
rosleague.com

Rosleague Manor preserves remarkably the atmosphere of a highly relaxed, slightly eccentric country house. The house looks out over beautifully kept gardens, mature trees, and a lake-like sea inlet to a memorable prospect of the Connemara Mountains. There

---

PRICES

HOTELS
An indication of the cost of a double room in the high season is given by **$** signs.

$$$$$	Over $330
$$$$	$200–$330
$$$	$150–$200
$$	$100–$150
$	Under $100

RESTAURANTS
An indication of the cost of a three-course meal without drinks is given by **$** signs.

$$$$$	Over $80
$$$$	$50–$80
$$$	$35–$50
$$	$20–$35
$	Under $20

are four-poster beds, huge baths, antique furniture, and sumptuous breakfasts.

ⓘ 20 🕒 Contact for off-season dates
🃏 MC, V

OUGHTERARD

🏨 ROSS LAKE HOUSE HOTEL
$$$–$$$$$
ROSSCAHILL
TEL 091/550-109
rosslakehotel.com

A handsome Georgian house in a quiet setting among the miles of beautiful woodland. Rooms are furnished in keeping with the elegant 18th-century ambience, including comfortable beds and big fireplaces. Rowing, sailing, and fishing on Ross Lake are easily arranged.

ⓘ 13 🅿 150
🕒 Closed Nov.–mid-March
🃏 Major cards

RECESS

⊞ LOUGH INAGH LODGE
$$$–$$$$
INAGH VALLEY
TEL 095/34-706
loughinaghlodgehotel.ie

A delightful lakeside retreat, formerly a 19th-century hunting lodge, set in a beautiful valley with the Twelve Bens rising mystically on one side and the Maumturk Mountains on the other. All bedrooms have lovely views, and five are deluxe standard.

ℹ 12 🅿 16 🕒 Closed mid-Dec.–mid-March 🅢
🅢 Major cards

COUNTY MAYO

ACHILL ISLAND

⊞ ACHILL CLIFF HOUSE
$$–$$$
KEEL
TEL 098/43-400
achillcliff.com

Enjoy breathtaking views of the mountains and seacoasts of Achill Island from this comfortable modern guesthouse, run by a warm and hospitable hostess who is full of good ideas and insider knowledge.

ℹ 10 🅿 20 🕒 Contact for off-season dates
🅢 AE, MC, V

CASTLEBAR

⊞ BREAFFY HOUSE RESORT
$$$$
CASTLEBAR
TEL 094/902-2033
breaffyhouseresort.com

Breaffy House Resort is excellent for children with its Breaffy Buddies Kids Club, outdoor playground and activities, leisure swimming area, and woodlands to play in. There are two hotels—one in

Breaffy House, the other in Breaffy Woods Hotel.

ℹ 62 🅿 300 🅢 🅢 AE, MC, V

🍽 BAR ONE
$$
RUSH ST.
TEL 094/903-4800
barone.ie

Up-to-the-minute decor and atmosphere with a menu far removed from the usual gastropub fare. Try the flavorful and tangy fisherman's pie or the beer-battered fish, chips, and mushy peas.

🕒 Closed Sun. 🅢 MC, V

CONG

⊞ RYAN'S HOTEL
$$$
MAIN ST.
TEL 094/954-6243
ryanshotelcong.ie

Located in the center of this quiet little town, its rooms are simple but comfortable. The pub next door, the Crowe's Nest, is a good place to try some Irish beers and chat with the very hospitable locals.

ℹ 13 🅢 Major cards

SOMETHING SPECIAL

🍽 ASHFORD CASTLE
$$$–$$$$$
CONG
TEL 094/954-6003
ashfordcastle.com

To really feel like a queen or a king while in Cong, sit back and enjoy the Connaught Room's spot-on service and cuisine—one of a handful of absolutely top-drawer Irish restaurants, set in the surroundings of the country's grandest castle. The George V Dining Room—the Connaught's brother restaurant at the castle—offers equally exalted standards in a slightly less rarified atmosphere.

🅢 Major cards

MULRANNY

⊞ MULRANNY PARK HOTEL
$$
MULRANNY
TEL 098/36-000
mulrannyparkhotel.ie

Comfortable and welcoming—perfect for exploring Clew Bay and Achill Island, walking and cycling on the Great Western Greenway, and following the Gourmet Greenway to discover local cheeses, honey, seafood, chutneys, cakes, and charcuterie.

ℹ 61 🅢 🅢
🅢 Major cards

WESTPORT

⊞ ARDMORE COUNTRY HOUSE
$$$–$$$$$
THE QUAY
TEL 098/25-994
ardmorecountryhouse.com

With superb views over Westport Quay, Clew Bay, and Croagh Patrick, Ardmore Country House is a relaxed and enjoyable place to stay close to the town center.

ℹ 13 🅿 40 🅢 AE, MC, V

⊞ CLEW BAY HOTEL
$$–$$$
JAMES ST.
TEL 098/28-088
clewbayhotel.com

The Clew Bay Hotel is family-run, extremely friendly, and located in the center of Westport close to the Mall and the music pubs.

ℹ 48 🕒 Contact for off-season dates 🅢 Major cards

🅢 Nonsmoking 🅢 Air-conditioning 🈴 Indoor Pool 🈺 Outdoor Pool 🆈 Health Club 🛜 Wi-Fi 🅢 Credit Cards

▶ **NORTHWEST IRELAND**

COUNTY SLIGO

BALLYMOTE

🏨 **MILLHOUSE B&B**
$–$$
BALLYMOTE
TEL 071/918-3449
Email: millhousebb@eircom
.net

The Millhouse is a modern house set in beautiful gardens. The hosts are delighted to direct you to the places worth exploring that "only the locals know!"

ⓘ 5 🅿 Major cards

COLLOONEY

🏨 **MARKREE CASTLE**
$$$$
COLLOONEY
TEL 071/916-7800
markreecastle.ie

You could probably eat a boiled boot and enjoy it in surroundings like these—a gorgeous old castle now turned into a fine hotel, with en suite luxury rooms and its own riding stables. It's run by a family who has owned it since Methuselah was a lad.

ⓘ 30 🅿 60 🕐 Closed Christmas ⬆
Major cards

ENNISCRONE

🏨 **DIAMOND COAST**
$$–$$$
BARTHRAGH
TEL 096/26-000
diamondcoast.ie

This nice 4-star hotel is ideal for a relaxing stay along the Wild Atlantic Way. It also has family rooms and suites, a restaurant, sports facilities, and a play area for children.

ⓘ 94 Major cards

GRANGE

🏨 **ROWANVILLE LODGE**
$
MONEYGOLD
TEL 071/916-3958
rowanville.com

Beautifully situated within full view of W. B. Yeats's magnificent mountain of Benbulben, this cheerful and very friendly house makes an excellent base for exploring Yeats Country (see pp. 210–215).

ⓘ 3 🅿 8 🕐 Closed Oct.–Feb.
MC, V

SLIGO TOWN

🏨 **SLIGO CITY HOTEL**
$$$
QUAY ST.
TEL 071/914-4000
sligocityhotel.com

This pleasantly relaxed hotel is conveniently located on the old quays in the center of Sligo town. All of the bedrooms are comfortable and smartly furnished in a modern style; some are of luxury standard with plenty of space and huge beds, and some have been adapted to suit wheelchair users.

ⓘ 58 🅿 20 🕐 Closed Christmas ⬆ ♿
Major cards

🏨 **SLIGO PARK HOTEL**
$$$
PEARSE RD.
TEL 071/919-0400
sligoparkhotel.com

Standing in 7 acres (3 ha) of beautiful parkland on the southern outskirts of Sligo town, the Sligo Park is well placed for exploring the countryside associated with the Yeats brothers. This is a well-appointed, smartly run hotel, with big en suite bedrooms furnished in a straightforward, modern style.

ⓘ 135 🅿 200
🕐 Closed Christmas ♿
Major cards

🏨 **CHESTNUT LAWN**
$
CUMMEEN, STRANDHILL RD.
TEL 071/916-2781
chestnutlawn.com

A comfortable, carefully maintained house with modern, attractively furnished bedrooms on the way out from Sligo town to Strandhill—within a short distance of the Sligo Bay beaches, Knocknarea Mountain, and the megalithic cemetery at Carrowmore.

ⓘ 3 🅿 4
🕐 Closed Nov.–Feb.
MC, V

🍴 **EALA BHAN**
$$$
ROCKWOOD PARADE
TEL 071/914-5823
ealabhan.ie

Eala Bhan specializes in old favorites done very well (fish cakes, chicken wings, seafood chowder, duo of lamb, roast squash risotto). Sunday lunch here is a favorite with locals, and there's a well-thought-out and tempting kids menu, too.

🕐 Closed Sun.–Mon. L
Major cards

🍴 **HARGADON'S**
$
4–5 O'CONNELL ST.
TEL 071/915-3714
hargadons.com

The food in Hargadon's is fine, from good steaks to traditional bacon and cabbage—but this remarkable town-center pub, famous throughout the northwest, is really about relaxation and great conversation in one of the private snugs or up at the characterful old bar.

🕐 Closed Sun.

🏨 Hotel   🍴 Restaurant   ⓘ No. of Guest Rooms   ➕ No. of Seats   🅿 Parking   🕐 Closed   ⬆ Elevator

COUNTY DONEGAL

ANNAGRY

SOMETHING SPECIAL

🍴 **DANNY MINNIE'S**
$$
ANNAGRY, THE ROSSES
TEL 074/954-8201
dannyminnies.ie
A superb refuge from wind, weather, and wild country out in Donegal's western margins, Danny Minnie's offers warm hospitality and a menu that makes the most of local produce. Examples are delicious local lobster and tender mountain lamb specialty.
🕐 Closed Christmas; Sun., call for opening times Sept.–May
💳 DC, MC, V

ARDARA

🏨 **NESBITT ARMS**
$$–$$$$
THE DIAMOND
TEL 074/954-1103
nesbittarms.com
A very characterful, central hotel offering comfortable en suite accommodations, with friendly staff and some great musical sessions.
🛏 19 💳 MC, V

BALLYBOFEY

🏨🍴 **KEE'S**
$$$
STRANORLAR
TEL 074/913-1018
keeshotel.ie
A family-run hotel with a good reputation for solid, competent cooking. In spite of the fact that there's a mountain or two between Stranorlar and the sea, the fish is great—try Kee's pan-fried cod or smoked haddock chowder for a delicious smack of the briny.
🛏 53 🅿 90 🏊 💳 Major cards

🏨 **VILLA ROSE HOTEL**
$$
MAIN ST.
TEL 074/913-2266
villarose.ie
The Villa Rose is a comfortable family-owned hotel with all sorts of activities from spa breaks to ballroom dancing, live entertainment in the bars, and a traditional music session on Sunday nights.
🛏 57 💳 Major cards

BALLYLIFFIN

🏨 **BALLYLIFFIN LODGE & SPA HOTEL**
$$$
INISHOWEN
TEL 074/937-8200
ballyliffinlodge.com
Ballyliffin Lodge with its warm atmosphere makes a good base for exploring Ireland's most northerly corner. If the sharp Donegal air makes you hungry, try a Ballyliffin cream tea!
🛏 40 🏊 💪 💳 Major cards

DONEGAL TOWN

SOMETHING SPECIAL

🏨🍴 **HARVEY'S POINT COUNTRY HOTEL**
$$$
LOUGH ESKE
TEL 074/972-2208
harveyspoint.com
This very friendly hotel, beautifully set on the sheltered shores of Lough Eske, runs like clockwork. Nothing is too much trouble for the dedicated staff. The classic cooking is superb. Harvey's Point inspires tremendous loyalty among its visitors —they voted it Trip Advisor's No. 1 Hotel in Ireland for 2013 and 2014, and no wonder.
🛏 60 🅿 300 💳 DC, MC, V

DUNFANAGHY

🏨 **ARNOLDS HOTEL**
$$
MAIN ST., DUNFANAGHY
TEL 074/913-6208
arnoldshotel.com
Arnolds Hotel occupies a lovely position on the harbor at Dunfanaghy Bay. This is a really fine example of an Irish family-run hotel—very friendly, extremely helpful to guests, and cozily comfortable.
🛏 32 💳 Major cards

GREENCASTLE

🍴 **KEALY'S SEAFOOD BAR**
$$$
THE HARBOUR
TEL 074/938-1010
kealysseafoodbar.ie
This is a great restaurant for those who like a laid-back atmosphere in which to enjoy unfussy but perfectly cooked and presented food—not just seafood, but that's what Kealy's particularly shines at.
♿ 🕐 Closed Mon.–Wed.
💳 Major cards

LETTERKENNY

🏨🍴 **SILVER TASSIE HOTEL**
$$–$$$
RAMELTON RD.
TEL 074/912-5619
silvertassiehotel.com
The Silver Tassie is a very popular place to eat, and the hotel caters to a good variety of customers. There's a daily lunch carvery which gives way to a bar menu later in the day, or finer dining in the restaurant (specialty: delicious steaks).
🕐 Closed Christmas
💳 Major cards

RAMELTON

🏨 **FREWIN HOUSE**
$$
RAMELTON

TEL 074/915-1246
frewinhouse.com

A dignified Victorian rectory, solid and stone-built, beautifully furnished, whose owners Regina and Thomas Coyle go out of their way to make you feel welcome.

🕐 Closed Christmas week
💳 Major cards

RATHMULLAN

🏨 **RATHMULLAN HOUSE**
$$$$$
RATHMULLAN
TEL 074/915-8188
rathmullanhouse.com

Whether a game of tennis, a dip in the pool, a massage with herbal essences, or a stroll on the beach, Rathmullan House, overlooking beautiful Lough Swilly, guarantees relaxation.

🛏 32 🕐 Closed Christmas
💳 Major cards

ROSSNOWLAGH

🏨 **SANDHOUSE HOTEL**
$$$-$$$$
ROSSNOWLAGH, DONEGAL BAY
TEL 071/985-1777
sandhouse.ie

The welcoming, easy-paced Sandhouse commands one of southwest Donegal's best sea views, around the bay at Rossnowlagh. Bedrooms are in classical country-house style, and some have four-poster beds and sea views.

🛏 55 🅿 40 🕐 Contact for off-season dates
💳 Major cards

COUNTY LEITRIM

CARRICK-ON-SHANNON

🏨 **THE LANDMARK**
$$$$
CARRICK-ON-SHANNON
TEL 071/962-2222

landmarkhotel.com

A very luxurious and elegant hotel overlooking the River Shannon at the heart of this prime boating and angling area; cruising, fishing, riding, and golf can be arranged.

🛏 50 🅿 60 ⬆
💳 Major cards

▶ CENTRAL IRELAND

COUNTY ROSCOMMON

BOYLE

SOMETHING SPECIAL

🏨 **KILRONAN CASTLE**
🍴 **ESTATE**
$$
BALLYFARNON
TEL 071/961-8000
kilronancastle.ie

In a beautiful location with a magical, romantic atmosphere, this elegant pristine castle has a hotel, restaurant, cocktail bar, and spa. Various types of rooms are available, including family rooms and suites.

🛏 3 🕐 Nov.–March
💳 Major cards

COUNTY LONGFORD

LONGFORD

🏨 **VIEWMOUNT HOUSE**
$$$
DUBLIN RD.
TEL 043/334-1919
viewmounthouse.com

Viewmount House is early Georgian, foursquare, and elegant. The bedrooms have beautiful antique beds and command superb countryside views. The old stables have been converted into an atmospheric restaurant.

🛏 13 🕐 Contact for off-season dates 💳 Major cards

SOMETHING SPECIAL

🍴 **GREEN APPLE RESTAURANT**
$$
18 MAIN ST.
TEL 043/334-7027

This is one of the few places to eat really well in Longford County. In addition to typical Irish dishes, there is a wide choice of vegetarian specialties.

🕐 Closed Mon., D
💳 Major cards

COUNTY CAVAN

BAILIEBOROUGH

🏨 **BAILIE HOTEL**
$$$
MAIN ST.
TEL 042/966-5334
bailiehotel.com

Bailieborough is a neat, proud little town, and the Bailie Hotel is right in that tradition—well run, friendly, efficient, and welcoming with a pleasant and helpful staff.

🛏 18 💳 Major cards

BALLYCONNELL

🏨 **SLIEVE RUSSELL HOTEL**
$$$$
BALLYCONNELL
TEL 049/952-6444
slieverussell.ie

A grand hotel with a championship golf course, attentive service, and all the modern amenities.

🛏 219 🅿 600 ⬆ 🏊
💳 Major cards

BLACKLION

SOMETHING SPECIAL

🍴 **MACNEAN HOUSE & RESTAURANT**
$$$$$
MAIN ST.

TEL 071/985-3022
macneanrestaurant.com

In the MacNeans' small family-run restaurant in a village on the North/South border is a five-star culinary experience from the young maestro, Irish master chef Neven Maguire. Perish the day he moves on to bigger—though not necessarily better—surroundings.

🕐 Closed Mon.–Tues.
💳 MC, V

KINGSCOURT

🏨 CABRA CASTLE
$$–$$$$
CARRICKMACROSS RD., KINGSCOURT
TEL 042/966-7030
cabracastle.com

Fish, golf, or practice your archery at this refurbished castle amid 100 acres (40 ha) of parkland and let the friendly but well-drilled staff help you to enjoy a stylish few nights. Bedrooms are all decorated in keeping with the Georgian surroundings—chandeliers, luxurious furnishings, and all.

🛏 80 🅿 200 🕐 Closed Christmas 💳 Major cards

COUNTY MONAGHAN

CARRICKMACROSS

🏨 NUREMORE HOTEL
🍴 $$$$–$$$$$
CARRICKMACROSS
TEL 042/966-1438
nuremore.com

A large Victorian mansion skillfully brought up to date: deluxe demisuites with separate sitting areas, extremely comfortable single bedrooms, or large family rooms. The ambience in the restaurant is rather formal, though perfectly friendly. Cooking is excellent throughout the menu (quails' eggs, duck, locally gathered mushrooms) with plenty

of style. There also are sports facilities, including an 18-hole golf course, in a peaceful country setting.

🛏 72 🅿 200 � 🏊 💳 Major cards

GLASLOUGH

🏨 CASTLE LESLIE
$$–$$$
GLASLOUGH
TEL 047/88-100
castleleslie.com

An old-style luxury hotel in a country house with superb rococo plasterwork, carved marble fireplaces, a huge billiards room, and bedrooms in sensuous reds and greens.

🛏 62 🕐 Contact for off-season dates 💳 Major cards

MONAGHAN

🍴 ANDY'S BAR & RESTAURANT
$$$
12 MARKET ST.
TEL 047/82-277
andysmonaghan.com

This is where the locals go to eat fine pub grub in the bar downstairs. The menu here might feature dishes such as sausages and mashed potato, or bacon and cabbage. There's also a decent middlebrow restaurant upstairs, where a more upscale selection could run to fish and steaks.

🕐 Closed Mon.; contact for other closures 💳 MC, V

COUNTY WESTMEATH

ATHLONE

🏨 ATHLONE SPRINGS
🍴 HOTEL
$$$$–$$$$$
MONKSLAND
TEL 090/644-4444
athlonespringshotel.com

The hotel is located in a modern structure and offers every

comfort. Its restaurant, cocktail bar, covered pool, sauna, and wellness center guarantee a relaxing vacation.

🛏 68 🏊 🕐 Closed 25–26 Dec. 💳 Major cards

🏨 HODSON BAY HOTEL
$$$–$$$$
HODSON BAY
TEL 090/644-2004
hodsonbayhotel.com

Commanding a wonderful panorama of Lough Ree, the Hodson Bay Hotel has been refurbished and extended to provide high levels of comfort and service. Some of the bedrooms overlook the lake, and the views from their big picture windows are absolutely stunning. The hotel has its own golf course and lake marina.

🛏 133 🅿 300 � 🏊 💳 Major cards

🏨 PRINCE OF WALES HOTEL
$$–$$$$
CHURCH ST.
TEL 090/647-6666
theprinceofwales.ie

Located in the center of Athlone, the hotel is simple but perfectly kept. Its rooms are comfortable and clean, its restaurant and bar are acclaimed, and the city's shopping and nightlife are both nearby.

🛏 73 🅿 35 💳 Major cards

🍴 WINEPORT LODGE
$$$
GLASSON
TEL 090/643-9010
wineport.ie

One of the great restaurants of Ireland, in an area not exactly oversupplied with them. Wonderful lake views sharpen the appetite for a menu that's dictated by what's available locally, fresh and with regard to the season, e.g., all sorts of

---

💳 Nonsmoking 🆎 Air-conditioning 🏊 Indoor Pool 🏊 Outdoor Pool 🏋 Health Club 📶 Wi-Fi 💳 Credit Cards

game, newly picked mushrooms, smoked eels; also Irish beef and delicious farmhouse cheeses. Ask about lakeside accommodations.

🕒 Closed L & Christmas
🔾 Major cards

🍴 LEFT BANK BISTRO
$$
FRY PLACE
TEL 090/649-4446
leftbankbistro.com

Veggies in Ireland have traditionally fared about as well as sun-worshippers, but here's one place where the art of the vegetable is understood. Not that carnivores are left unsatisfied; sharp modern ideas shine a light on every corner of the menu at the Left Bank.

♿ 🕒 Closed Sun.–Mon.
🔾 AE, MC, V

MULLINGAR

🏨 LOUGH OWEL LODGE
$$
CULLEENMORE
TEL 044/934-8714
loughowellodge.com

A very welcoming B&B on an organic farm beside Lough Owel. Homemade jams and preserves, home baking, everything sourced within 10 miles (16 km) of the farm. Fishing, tennis, walking are all available.

🛏 5 🕒 Closed Nov.–March
🔾 Major cards

COUNTY OFFALY

BANAGHER

🏨 HARBOUR MASTER'S HOUSE
$–$$
SHANNON HARBOUR
TEL 087/922-0853
harbourmastershouse.com

Open fires, splendid breakfasts, and a warm welcome, not to mention a great pub a short

stroll away—this is a haven in the bleakly beautiful boglands, right on the Grand Canal.

🛏 6 🕒 Nov.–March 🔾 MC, V

BIRR

🍴 THE THATCH
$$
MILITARY RD., CRINKILL
TEL 057/912-0682
thethatchcrinkill.com

A great pub, bursting with atmosphere. The menu here caters to those looking for a zest of the exotic (kangaroo steaks, anyone?), devotees of local game (rabbit, pigeon), and those who just want good traditional pub grub.

🕒 Closed Good Friday, Christmas 🔾 DC, MC, V

KINNITTY

🏨 ARDMORE COUNTRY HOUSE
$$
THE WALK
TEL 086/278-914
kinnitty.com

You haven't tasted potato cakes until you've sampled Chris Byrne's. But that's not the only talent of the hospitable hostess of Ardmore House—she is a stalwart of the local walking club, knows all the best walks in the Slieve Blooms, and plays the fiddle like a demon, too!

🛏 5 🕒 Closed Christmas
🔾 MC, V

COUNTY LAOIS

BALLICKMOYLER

🏨 COOLANOWLE COUNTRY HOUSE
$$
COOLANOWLE
TEL 059/862-5176
coolanowle.com

Coolanowle Country House specializes in delicious, home-produced organic food.

PRICES

HOTELS
An indication of the cost of a double room in the high season is given by **$** signs.

$$$$$	Over $330
$$$$	$200–$330
$$$	$150–$200
$$	$100–$150
$	Under $100

RESTAURANTS
An indication of the cost of a three-course meal without drinks is given by **$** signs.

$$$$$	Over $80
$$$$	$50–$80
$$$	$35–$50
$$	$20–$35
$	Under $20

Organic beef, pork, lamb, chicken, and duck are all on the dinner menu, and breakfast makes full use of the establishment's own bacon, sausages, eggs, and black and white puddings.

🛏 8 🕒 Closed Christmas
🔾 Major cards

DURROW

🏨🍴 CASTLE DURROW HOTEL
$$$–$$$$
DURROW
TEL 057/873-6555
castledurrow.com

This fabulous 300-year-old country-house hotel is set in beautiful gardens and grounds offering woodlands and riverbank strolls. A relaxed and friendly atmosphere, with luxury rooms in the house or something a bit simpler in the converted stable block.

🛏 60 🕒 Closed first 2 weeks in Jan. 🆇 Major cards

PORTLAOISE

🏨 IVYLEIGH HOUSE
$$
BANK PLACE, CHURCH ST.
TEL 057/862-2081
ivyleigh.com

A friendly welcome awaits at this Georgian house, which is meticulously maintained and efficiently run, making it a very comfortable stopover in Portlaoise. The bedrooms are light and airy, with a striking decor of bright color schemes.

🛏 6 🅿 6 🕒 mid-Dec.–early Jan. 🆇 MC, V

COUNTY MEATH

KELLS

🍽 VANILLA POD RESTAURANT
$$$
HEADFORT ARMS HOTEL
TEL 046/924-0084
headfortarms.ie

Although it's housed in the same building as the Headfort Arms Hotel, the Vanilla Pod is a separate setup and attracts a large following for its wine nights as well as great food, including the best charcoal-grilled steaks in the region.

🕒 Closed L except Sun.; Christmas 🆇 Major cards

NAVAN

🏨 BELLINTER HOUSE
$$$$$
NAVAN
TEL 046/903-0900
bellinterhouse.com

Very elegant and charming 18th-century house with varied accommodations, from grand bedrooms to cozy couple-friendly hideaways and

bedroom-plus-living-room apartments in the stable block, perfect for families.

🛏 34 🆇 Major cards

🏨 ARDBOYNE HOTEL
$$$
DUBLIN RD.
TEL 046/902-3119
ardboynehotel.com

An efficiently run, well-equipped hotel on the edge of town that offers comfort and good service in a relaxed atmosphere. The pleasantly upbeat bedrooms are well lit and have garden views.

🛏 29 🅿 186 🕒 Closed Christmas
🆇 Major cards

SLANE

🏨 TANKARDSTOWN HOUSE
$$$$$
RATHKENNY
TEL 041/982-4621
tankardstown.ie

Tankardstown House aims to be a home away from home—and indeed it is, if your home happens to be a magnificent country house set on 80 acres (32 ha) of tree-lined parkland. Luxury bedrooms, courtyard cottages, spa treatments, an outdoor hot tub, and iPod-friendly trees (ask when you get there).

🛏 18 🆇 Major cards

COUNTY LOUTH

BETTYSTOWN

🍽 RELISH
$–$$
COAST RD.
TEL 041/981-3344
relishcafe.ie

Fabulous café food with a great sea view. Try breakfast smoothies, fruit bowl, and organic porridge; a Big Brunch Bap

to fill that gap; or sandwiches such as the Humdinger (roast vegetables) and the Favourite (chicken 'n' crispy bacon).

🕒 Closed Mon.–Thurs. & Sun. D 🆇 Major cards

CARLINGFORD

🏨 GHAN HOUSE
🍽 **$$$–$$$$$**
CARLINGFORD
TEL 042/937-3682
ghanhouse.com

Famous for its warm hospitality, Ghan House sits on Carlingford Lough between mountains and the sea. This quiet but very social retreat features open fires and super-comfortable bedrooms. The food is superbly prepared, from local beef and lamb to Carlingford Lough fish and free-range eggs.

🛏 12 🕒 Reserve in advance 🆇 Major cards

🏨 MCKEVITTS VILLAGE HOTEL
$$$
MARKET SQ.
TEL 042/937-3116
mckevitts.ie

This hospitable hotel is in a great location on the Cooley Peninsula, surrounded by beautiful, relaxing landscapes. Its charming restaurant is open every day.

🛏 14 🆇 Major cards

🍽 P. J. O'HARE'S BAR & RESTAURANT
$$
THOLSEL ST.
TEL 042/937-3106
pjoharescarlingford.com

A genuine "black and white" pub, with low ceilings, beams, black woodwork, white walls, open fires, live music, and a wonderful atmosphere. Great Guinness and delicious seafood pie.
🆇 Major cards

DROGHEDA

🏨 BOYNE VALLEY HOTEL AND COUNTRY CLUB
$$$

STAMEEN, DUBLIN RD.
TEL 041/983-7737
boyne-valley-hotel.ie

A leisure center, tennis court, gym, and putting green are just some of the attractions of this well-run hotel, with pleasant modern guest rooms.

🛏 73 🅿 200 ⊟ ☎
Ⓢ Major cards

🏨🍽 SCHOLARS TOWNHOUSE HOTEL
$$–$$$

KING ST.
TEL 041/983-5410
scholarshotel.com

Relax in the Gastrolounge, browsing on local seafood chowder, Moroccan tagine, or Fivemiletown goat cheese with orzo. There's a fine selection of craft beers, whiskeys, and sophisticated coffees.

🛏 418 Ⓢ Major cards

🏨 WESTCOURT HOTEL
$$–$$$

WEST ST.
TEL 041/983-0965
westcourt.ie

One of those traditional hotels at the heart of the community where you can drink, eat, dance, meet, or get married.

🛏 29 🅿 Ⓢ Major cards

▶ NORTHERN IRELAND

BELFAST

🏨 EUROPA HOTEL
$$$–$$$$

GREAT VICTORIA ST.,
BELFAST BT2 7AP
TEL 028/9027-1066
hastingshotels.com/
europa-belfast

Quite simply, this is Belfast's most famous hotel, scene of many a drama and romance—a very efficient and well-run luxury hotel with friendly and helpful staff. The Opera House and famed Crown Liquor saloon are adjacent.

🛏 240 🅿 ⊟ ☎ 📺
Ⓢ Major cards

🏨🍽 MALMAISON BELFAST
$$$

34–38 VICTORIA ST.,
BELFAST BT1 3GH
TEL 028/9022-0200
malmaison.com

All Malmaison hotels have started life in a different role; this handsome building was once a grand seed warehouse. Rooms are done out in black, cream, and red. There's a bar and a brasserie offering such delights as salmon, wood pigeon, and smoked haddock.

🛏 62 Ⓢ Major cards

🏨 MALONE LODGE
$$$

60 EGLANTINE AVE.,
BELFAST BT9 6DY
TEL 028/9600-1405
malonelodgehotelbelfast.com

In a quiet, leafy street south of the city center, Malone Lodge offers a warm welcome, a friendly atmosphere, and very pleasant surroundings. This is one of the nicest hotels in the city, with extremely comfortable guest rooms.

🛏 51 🅿 35 ⊟
Ⓢ Major cards

🏨🍽 MERCHANT
$$$

16 SKIPPER ST.,
BELFAST BT1 2DZ
TEL 028/9023-4888
themerchanthotel.com

The Merchant Hotel is located in the heart of the city's cool Cathedral Quarter. It's a grand place, full of art deco touches, with friendly staff. The afternoon teas are a Belfast

institution—finger sandwiches, scones and cream, silver pastry stands.

🛏 62 🅿 Valet ⊟ 🔆
Ⓢ Major cards

🏨 CRESCENT TOWNHOUSE HOTEL
$$–$$$

13 LOWER CRESCENT,
BELFAST BT7 1NR
TEL 028/9032-3349
crescenttownhouse.com

A decent, comfortable hotel where the welcome is warm and staff are friendly and efficient. It's a stylish Regency townhouse next to the Botanic Gardens station; lively bars below, smart bedrooms above.

🛏 17 Ⓢ Major cards

🏨 CAMERA
$–$$

44 WELLINGTON PARK,
BELFAST BT9 6PD
TEL 028/9066-0026
camera-guesthouse.co.uk

A stylish guesthouse with bright, airy, modern rooms in the peaceful, well-maintained area close to the university.

🛏 9 Ⓢ Major cards

🍽 RESTAURANT MICHAEL DEANE
$$$$

36–40 HOWARD ST.,
BELFAST BT1 6PF
TEL 028/9033-1134
michaeldeane.co.uk

If you are out to catch the real formal dining tiger by the tail, there's only one place north of the border to go hunting, and that's at Michael Deane's. Far and away the most accomplished cook in the North, Deane has set out every detail—room, service, wine list—to complement his marvelous skills at the stove with impeccable fish (monkfish, scallops) or meat (Irish mountain lamb, local beef).

Just around the corner, his Meat Locker restaurant is more informal, but just as good.

⏰ Closed Mon.–Tues., Christmas, 2 days in July
💳 AE, MC, V

🍴 JAMES STREET SOUTH
$$$
21 JAMES ST. S.,
BELFAST BT2 7GA
TEL 028/9560-0700
jamesstandco.com

There's a timeless and very welcoming atmosphere to this former linen mill. The menu includes local fruit and vegetables, Antrim-reared beef and lamb, game from nearby estates, and fish out of the Irish Sea—all complemented by a well-balanced wine list.

💳 AE, MC, V

🍴 SHU
$$$
253 LISBURN RD.,
BELFAST BT9 7EN
TEL 028/9038-1655
shu-restaurant.com

Excellent brasserie-style cooking, where traditional values of first-class ingredients and true flavors are what matter. Try their duck confit or a tasty dish of smoked hake with special chips.

♿ ⏰ Closed Sun., Christmas
💳 AE, MC, V

🍴 HADSKI'S
$$–$$$
33 DONEGALL ST., COMMERCIAL CT., BELFAST BT1 2NB
TEL 028/9032-5444
hadskis.co.uk

Hadski's lies in wait in the Cathedral Quarter. Dine in laid-back style in the dining room, or sit at the kitchen counter watching the cooks at work on your black pudding and polenta, salt-baked bream, or giant T-bone.

💳 Major cards

🍴 THE PANTRY CAFÉ AND KITCHEN
$$
2–4 UNIVERSITY RD.,
BELFAST BT7 1NH
TEL 075/8117-5164

Located inside The Crescent cultural center near Queen's University, this bright, cheery café offers an array of sweets, sandwiches, salads, and other imaginative specialties created with local quality ingredients. Vegan and gluten-free dishes are available.

⏰ Closed Sat.–Sun. D
💳 Major cards

🍴 FIBBER MAGEE'S, AT ROBINSON'S SALOON
$$
38–42 GREAT VICTORIA ST.,
BELFAST BT2 7BA
TEL 028/9024-7447
robinsonsbar.co.uk

Spit-and-sawdust old-style pub, with brilliant traditional music sessions every night.

💳 Major cards

🍴 THE KNIFE & FORK RESTAURANT
$$
60 EGLANTINE AVE.,
BELFAST BT9 6DY
TEL 028/9038-8000
malonelodgehotelbelfast.com/dining/knife-and-fork-restaurant

A downbeat name for a great new restaurant in the leafy suburb of Malone. Meat from County Fermanagh, vegetables from North Down, fish from Ardglass—even the tea is blended in Northern Ireland. The menu ranges from tear-and-share breads through spiced pork fillet with bubble and squeak to lime leaf crème brûlée.

⏰ Closed Mon.–Wed.; Thurs.–Sat. L
💳 Major cards

🍴 THE MAC CAFÉ
$–$$
10 EXCHANGE ST. W.,
BELFAST BT1 2NJ
TEL 028/9023-5053
themaclive.com

The MAC café in the modern art center serves excellent dishes and is open every day from 8.30 a.m. until late evening. Savor a bowl of (sustainable) fish soup with a slice of Guinness and molasses bread while the children devour a plate of spiced chicken with noodles and a lime yogurt.

💳 Major cards

SOMETHING SPECIAL

🍴 CROWN LIQUOR SALOON
$
46 GREAT VICTORIA ST.,
BELFAST BT2 7BA
TEL 028/9024-3187
nicholsonspubs.co.uk

The Crown is a Belfast institution, and so firmly on the tourist trail that it must be superglued there. And it's no wonder—this fabulously ornate pub, impeccably cared for by the National Trust, is the best example anywhere in the city of an authentic Victorian imbibing emporium. The food is great, and most of it is traditional Irish cuisine—eat sausages and champ here before you leave Ireland, and you'll pine until you're back in the Crown once more.

💳 DC, MC, V

🍴 ESTABLISHED COFFEE
$
57 HILL ST., BELFAST BT1 2LD
TEL 028/9031-9416
established.coffee
When you're in need of a good cup of coffee, this is the place to go. The cakes and lunch dishes are good, too. Its modern, vaguely industrial chic decor is alluring and very comfortable.

⏰ Closed D   💳 Major cards

🚭 Nonsmoking ❄️ Air-conditioning 🏊 Indoor Pool 🏊 Outdoor Pool 💪 Health Club 📶 Wi-Fi 💳 Credit Cards

COUNTY ANTRIM

BALLYCASTLE

🍴 CENTRAL WINE BAR
$$–$$$
12 ANN ST.
TEL 028/2076-3877
centralwinebar.com

An absolutely fabulous place, and a bit of a surprise to find such a snappy atmosphere and general excellence in a sleepy seaside town. Family-run with wonderful food and a cheerful, personal air about the service.

🐾 Major cards

BALLYMENA

🏨 GALGORM RESORT & SPA
$$$
BALLYMENA
TEL 028/2588-1001
galgorm.com

Horseback riding, water-skiing, and fishing are some of the activities you can enjoy at this handsome Victorian manor-house hotel, set on 85 acres (35 ha) beside the River Maine—with river views from comfortable guest rooms.

🛏 24 🅿 170 🐾 Major cards

🏨 MARLAGH LODGE
$–$$
71 MOORFIELDS RD.
TEL 028/2563-1505
marlaghlodge.com

The musicians Rachel and Robert Thompson saved Marlagh Lodge from disrepair. Their love and care for the lodge is evident in everything from the top-notch ingredients they use to the bookcases in the rooms. Meals are served in a warm, friendly dining room where a fireplace warms the atmosphere on cool days.

🛏 3 🕐 Call during off-season
🐾 MC, V

BUSHMILLS

🏨🍴 BUSHMILLS INN
$$$$
9 DUNLUCE RD.
TEL 028/2073-3000
bushmillsinn.com

The Bushmills Inn has a great reputation for character, whether it's the wonky old floors, the real coal and turf fires, or the individually decorated bedrooms. The perfect stopover for your tour of the Old Bushmills Distillery.

🛏 41 🐾 Major cards

CARNLOUGH

🏨🍴 LONDONDERRY ARMS
$$$
20 HARBOUR RD.
TEL 028/2888-5255
londonderryarmshotel.com

A comfortable old Georgian inn in a fishing village on the spectacular Antrim coast. Paintings of local scenes and antique furnishings combine to make this hotel a memorable place to stay. A relaxed approach and plenty of skill in the kitchen makes this a good restaurant to stop on your way up the Antrim Coast Road.

🛏 35 🅿 50 🕐 Closed Christmas 🛗
🐾 Major cards

PORTRUSH

🍴 RAMORE WINE BAR
$$
THE HARBOUR
TEL 028/7082-4313
ramorerestaurant.com

The Ramore made its name as an upscale place for sophisticated dining, but it has turned into a cheap(ish) and very cheerful space serving superior grills, steaks, and pasta to a relatively young crowd.

🐾 MC, V

COUNTY LONDONDERRY

COLERAINE

🏨 THE GRANGE
$$
2E GRANGE RD.,
AGHADOWEY
TEL 028/7034-4961
thegrangecoleraine.com

The facility has a rustic, homey atmosphere with a number of comforts and elegant touches that are part of the warm hospitality. It's near Portstewart and Castlerock, a good position for visiting the Antrim Coast.

🛏 5 🐾 Major cards

COOKSTOWN

🏨 TULLYLAGAN COUNTRY HOUSE HOTEL
$$–$$$
40B TULLYLAGAN RD.
TEL 028/8676-5100
tullylaganhotel.com

This is a very handsome country-house hotel set in 30 acres (12 ha) of gardens and grounds, with all the comfort and service you'd expect. A great base for exploring the nearby Sperrin Mountains.

🛏 15 🕐 Closed Christmas
🐾 Major cards

GARVAGH

🏨 GORTIN GLEN HOUSE
$
52 BALLYAGAN RD.
TEL 028/7086-8260
gortinglen.co.uk

Bedrooms are located in carefully converted outbuildings at Gortin Glen House, situated in the beautiful rolling countryside of east Derry.

🛏 3 🅿 6

🏨 Hotel 🍴 Restaurant 🛏 No. of Guest Rooms 🕐 No. of Seats 🅿 Parking 🕐 Closed 🛗 Elevator

LIMAVADY

🏨 ROE PARK RESORT
$$
LIMAVADY
TEL 028/7772-2222
www.roeparkresort.com

A very well-appointed hotel in a beautiful location. Golfing fiends will find an 18-hole course, floodlit driving range, putting green, and a golf-training academy. Others will enjoy the wooded grounds, health and exercise facilities, and excellent fishing.

🛏 118 🅿 300 ⬛ 🏊
🅂 Major cards

🍴 THE LIME TREE
$$
60 CATHERINE ST.
TEL 028/7776-4300
limetreerest.com

A hospitable house where the cooking is solidly spot-on. The menu might include sirloin steaks in peppercorn sauce or perhaps a plate of sensational crab cakes.

🕐 Closed L, Sun.–Mon.
🅂 AE, MC, V

LONDONDERRY

🏨 BEECH HILL COUNTRY HOUSE HOTEL
$$$
32 ARDMORE RD.
TEL 028/7134-9279
beech-hill.com

An early Georgian mansion in wooded grounds, gardens, and waterfalls, offering well-furnished rooms and a stylish yet relaxed atmosphere.

🛏 17 plus 10 annex 🅿 75
🕐 Closed Christmas ⬛
🅂 Major cards

🏨 MALDRON HOTEL
$$–$$$
BUTCHER ST.
TEL 028/7137-1000
maldronhotelderry.com

This is a very stylish hotel, with

great views over the city from the upper floors. The public areas, which include a popular bistro and bar, are minimalistic, but there's no shortage of Irish hospitality from the staff.

🛏 93 🅿 25 ⬛
🅂 Major cards

MAGHERAFELT

🏨 LAUREL VILLA
$$
60 CHURCH ST.
TEL 028/7930-1459
laurel-villa.com

An absolute delight. Charming Gerardine Kielt supervises the immaculate bedrooms and cooks heavenly breakfasts, while her husband, Eugene, organizes poetry readings and tours of nearby Seamus Heaney Country (the Nobel Laureate poet was a local boy).

🛏 5 🕐 Call for off-season closings 🅂 MC, V

COUNTY TYRONE

DUNGANNON

🏨 GRANGE LODGE
$$
7 GRANGE RD.
TEL 028/8778-4212
grangelodgecountry house.com

This is one of the friendliest and most comfortable guesthouses in Ireland. Nothing is too much trouble for the hospitable Browns, and the home cooking is superb.

🛏 5 🅿 12 🕐 Closed mid-Dec.–Jan. 🅂 MC, V

GORTIN

🍴 THE HIDDEN PEARL RESTAURANT
$$
18 MAIN ST.
TEL 028/8164-8157

Handy while exploring the Sperrin Hills—soups, chowders, risotto, beef and venison dishes.

🅂 Major cards

OMAGH

🏨🍴 HAWTHORN COTTAGE
$
148 GREENCASTLE RD.
TEL 078/9994-2397
catrionamccullagh@hotmail.co.uk

This handsome Victorian house offers warm hospitality, comfortable rooms, and a high standard of cooking. Salmon, sole, and steaks are all good, and for vegetarians there are such delights as mushrooms with spinach and goat cheese.

🛏 5 🅿 65 🅂 Major cards

COUNTY FERMANAGH

ENNISKILLEN

🏨 KILLYHEVLIN LAKESIDE HOTEL & LODGE
$$$
ENNISKILLEN
TEL 028/6632-3481
killyhevlin.com

The hotel, with its modern, comfortable rooms, is surrounded by greenery on the outskirts of County Fermanagh's main town.

🛏 70 🅿 500 🕐 Closed Christmas 🅂 Major cards

🏨 CARRYBRIDGE LAKESIDE LODGE
$$
INISHMORE RD.
TEL 028/6638-1855
carrybridgelakesidelodge.com

Located south of the city on the quiet banks of the Upper Lough Erne, this charming hotel with its restaurant and bar enjoys a peaceful spot with a lake for fishing.

🛏 13 🕐 Closed Christmas 🅂 MC, V

⊞ ARCH HOUSE
$–$$

65 MARBLE ARCH RD.,
FLORENCECOURT
TEL 028/6634-8452
archhouse.com

This welcoming place offers superb mountain views and is a convenient base for visiting Florence Court House and Marble Arch Caves. Breakfast on kippers, homemade bread and scones, or a mighty fry.

🛈 6 ⊗ MC, V

⊞ DROMARD HOUSE
$

ENNISKILLEN
TEL 028/6638-7250
dromardhouse.com

Based in a beautiful old house, with bedrooms in a converted stable block, Dromard House offers Bed & Breakfast and self-catering accommodation. It stands in extensive grounds, and there are paths through the woods down to Lough Erne where you can fish.

🛈 4 🅿 4 ⊕ Closed Christmas
⊗ Major cards

IRVINESTOWN

⊞ MAHON'S HOTEL
$$

MILL ST.
TEL 028/6862-1656
mahonshotel.co.uk

Handy for Enniskillen, the islands of Lower Lough Erne, and the beautiful hilly country of southwest Tyrone, Mahon's is a friendly family-run hotel with comfortable, airy rooms.

🛈 24 🅿 40 ⊗ Major cards

COUNTY ARMAGH

ARMAGH CITY

⊞ NEWFORGE HOUSE
$$$$

58 NEWFORGE RD.,
MAGHERALIN
TEL 028/9261-1255

newforgehouse.com
Hosts John and Louise Mathers are the latest in six generations of the family at Newforge House, and there's an air of settled comfort and confidence about the place. Lovely grounds and fabulous cooking, with local ingredients and homegrown vegetables.

🛈 6 ⊕ Closed Christmas
⊗ Major cards

KEADY

⊞ DUNDRUM HOUSE
$

116 DUNDRUM RD.,
TASSAGH
TEL 028/3753-1257
dundrumhouse.com

Surrounded by 80 acres (32 ha) of its own farmland, this is a charming early 18th-century farmhouse with some splendid original features. It has been creatively restored, and the friendly hosts offer unlimited choices for breakfast.

🛈 3 🅿 5
⊗ MC, V

NEWRY

⊞ CANAL COURT HOTEL
$$$–$$$$

MERCHANT'S QUAY
TEL 028/3025-1234
canalcourthotel.com

With its dramatic frontage and lobby, this new hotel announces its status as a high-class place to stay. But there's an intimacy about it, and an emphasis on old-fashioned hospitality. Rooms have classic decor and king-size beds, and the restaurant offers fine dining.

🛈 51 🅿 60
⊕ Closed Christmas
⊟ ⊗ Major cards

PRICES

HOTELS
An indication of the cost of a double room in the high season is given by $ signs.

$$$$$	Over $330
$$$$	$200–$330
$$$	$150–$200
$$	$100–$150
$	Under $100

RESTAURANTS
An indication of the cost of a three-course meal without drinks is given by $ signs.

$$$$$	Over $80
$$$$	$50–$80
$$$	$35–$50
$$	$20–$35
$	Under $20

COUNTY DOWN

COMBER

⊞ 🍴 OLD SCHOOLHOUSE INN
$$–$$$

100 BALLYDRAIN RD.,
NEWTOWNARDS
TEL 028/9754-1182
theoldschoolhouseinn.com

There are 12 bedrooms, each named after an American president of Ulster descent, in this welcoming guesthouse. Enjoy a candlelit dinner of local specialties.

🛈 12 ♿ ⊕ Closed Mon.–Sat. L, Sun.–Mon. D, Christmas
⊗ AE, MC, V

DOWNPATRICK

⊞ 🍴 THE MILL AT BALLYDUGAN
$$

DRUMCULLEN RD.,

BALLYDUGAN
TEL 028/4461-3654
ballyduganmill.com

A really unusual place to stay—a lovingly restored flour mill eight floors high, offering characterful rooms and excellent food in either the **Wheelhouse Café** or the beamed restaurant.

🛈 12 🏧 Major cards

🏨 THE RIVER MILL B&B
$
BALLYCLANDER RD.,
ARDGLASS
TEL 028/4484-1988
the-river-mill.co.uk

This carefully restored 18th-century linen mill is traditional stone outside, cozily modernized within. It's located near Ardglass on the coast of St. Patrick's Country—tours of this lovely area are available.

🛈 5 🅿 🏧 Major cards

HOLYWOOD

🏨 THE COLONEL'S LODGE
$$$
23A BALLYMONEY RD.,
CRAIGANTLET,
NEWTOWNARDS
TEL 078/0114-0890

What used to be a granary has been converted into a country cottage, a welcoming haven with a sunlit patio—the ideal solution for a family that wants a relaxing vacation in the beautiful Irish countryside

🛈 1 🏧 Major cards

KILLINCHY

🍽 BALLOO HOUSE
$$$
1 COMBER RD.,
NEWTOWNARDS
TEL 028/9754-1210
ballooinns.com

A real treat. You can dine in style on langoustine and crab from Strangford Lough or

venison from nearby Finnebrogue, or in more casual bistro style on daily special dishes.

🕓 Closed Sun.–Mon.
🏧 MC, V

KILLYLEAGH

🍽 THE DUFFERIN ARMS
$$$
35 HIGH ST.
TEL 028/4482-1182
dufferinarms.com

With its castle and wonderful setting by Strangford Lough, Killyleagh makes a perfect escape from Belfast (half an hour away). This restaurant serves local produce with warmth and flair.

🏧 Major cards

KIRCUBBIN

🍽 SALTWATER BRIG
$
43 ROWREAGH RD.
TEL 028/4273-8435
saltwaterbrig.com

A pleasant pub and restaurant with an outdoor dining space to enjoy when the days are sunny.

🏧 Major cards

NEWTOWNARDS

🏨 BALLYNESTER HOUSE
$$
1A CARDY RD.,
GREYABBEY
TEL 028/4278-8386

A welcoming guesthouse in a beautiful location in the hills above Strangford Lough, with fine views. Choose from airy, comfortable bedrooms in the house, or the pitch pine beams and wooden ambience of the self-catering lodge next door.

🛈 3 🅿 9 🏧 MC, V

🏨 EDENVALE HOUSE
$$
130 PORTAFERRY RD.
TEL 028/4482-4881
edenvalehouse.com

Peace and quiet are the keynotes at this Georgian hideaway with its large gardens and views over Strangford Lough. Bedrooms are decorated and furnished in period style.

🛈 3 🅿 10 🕓 Closed Christmas 🏧 MC, V

PORTAFERRY

🏨🍽 PORTAFERRY HOTEL
$$$
10 THE STRAND
TEL 028/4272-8231
portaferryhotel.com

A very well run hotel right on the waterfront of charming Portaferry, overlooking the Narrows of Strangford Lough. The staff here is exceptionally pleasant, and the rooms with lough views are wonderful. It's the fish—especially the scallops—that bring people to the restaurant here from all over the neighborhood.

🛈 14 🅿 6 🕓 Closed Christmas 🏧 Major cards

STRANGFORD

🏨🍽 THE CUAN
$$
THE SQUARE
TEL 028/4488-1222
thecuan.com

A family-run hotel with a good friendly atmosphere and great food, locally sourced—try the seafood chowder, smoked haddock with champ, a casserole of local venison, or traditional liver and bacon.

🛈 18 🏧 Major cards

🚭 Nonsmoking 🔆 Air-conditioning 🏊 Indoor Pool 🏊 Outdoor Pool 💪 Health Club 📶 Wi-Fi 🏧 Credit Cards

SHOPPING

Think of shopping in Ireland, and the first things that spring to mind are usually superb crafts: Waterford crystal, Aran knitwear, Donegal tweed, Belleek pottery, Claddagh rings, Connemara marble, and Ulster linen, among others. Kilkenny is an acknowledged center of the best in Irish craftsmanship, and the major tourist information centers around the country usually have a good selection on sale. An excellent reminder of a trip to Ireland is some recorded traditional music, evoking happy evenings spent in pubs or at a *ceilidh*, or perhaps some poems by Seamus Heaney, a copy of *The Islandman* by Tomás O'Crohan, or an anthology of humorous articles by Flann O'Brien.

Irish food and drink specialties include Bailey's liqueur, Cork gin, and the famous Irish whiskeys (Bushmills, Powers, Jamesons, Paddy)—sure, you can buy all of these just about anywhere, but touring the distillery first makes it a very special shopping experience. There are also tasty farmhouse cheeses (try the Cashel Blue), smoked salmon, and delicious soda bread. More of an acquired taste, but certainly worth trying, is dulse, an interesting kind of dried seaweed snack.

For those visitors with a taste for kitsch, there are still plenty of outlets full of bright green, sham-rock-encrusted souvenirs, shillelaghs, and dancing leprechauns, along with various items of clothing that will declare in no uncertain terms to friends and neighbors back home that you have indeed been to the Emerald Isle.

You will also find plenty of religious memorabilia, from gaudy plastic Virgin Marys to tasteful and artistic replicas of Celtic crosses; these reach peak proportions in places where storekeepers can trade on various stories of visions and miracles, such as at Knock in County Mayo.

Visitors in search of their Irish roots will also find plenty of genealogy centers, many with computerized research facilities, offering documents to take home that give information about your family name.

■ DUBLIN

Dublin has long been a good place to shop, particularly fashionable south of the river, and there is apparently no limit to the choices available. Clothing includes classics, trendy designer innovations, and the latest streetwise and club-wear. Some of the finest arts and crafts in the world, and all manner of high-tech gadgetry, can be found here. Traditional-style department stores, reflecting a bygone age, stand alongside glittering malls and one-of-a-kind stores run by people who really know their stuff and don't mind how long it takes to tell you about it.

Grafton Street is undoubtedly the best place to start, full of character and bustling with shoppers and buskers. It leads to **Stephen's Green Shopping Centre** (stephensgreen.com), a bright and spacious mall. Side streets in the area have plenty of places to eat and interesting stores.

Powerscourt Centre (powers courtcentre.ie) is a unique mall, converted from a large town house, containing upscale stores and eating places.

The maze of narrow, cobbled lanes that comprise **Temple Bar** is a treasure trove of unique stores and galleries, interspersed with pubs and restaurants.

North of the river is not quite so glitzy, but it's been getting a face-lift, and wide **O'Connell Street** is full of character. The new **Liffey Board-walks** are worth a browse, and the street markets here give a true flavor of old Dublin.

There are a number of big shopping malls on the outskirts of the city—**Tallaght,** to the south, is the biggest.

Antiques

One of the best areas to shop for antiques is on and around **Francis Street.** There are also regular antiques fairs in the city, notably at **Newman House** (85–86 St. Stephen's Green) on alternate Sundays year-round. **Car Boot Shop** (21 Eden Quay, tel 086/679-8849) has a huge selection of silver, china, and curios.

Gerald Kenyon (6 Great Strand St., tel 01/873-0488) specializes in the sale and restoration of fine furniture.

Books

Chapters Bookstore (174 Parnell St., tel 01/879-2700, chapters.ie). For anyone looking for an enormous bookstore with second hand books, this is the place to be. Every floor is full of loaded bookshelves and the prices are extremely good. **Dubray Books** (36 Grafton St., tel 01/677-5568) has a vast selection of books, including Irish literature, novels, lesser known authors, and popular works. To enjoy a snack surrounded by books, go up to the little café on the last floor. **Eason's** (40 O'Connell St., tel 01/858-3800, easons.com) stocks some Irish books but mostly offers run-of-the-mill fiction, along with stationery and art supplies. **Hodges Figgis** (56–58 Dawson

St., tel 01/677-4754) is the largest bookstore in Dublin, a historic emporium that was mentioned by James Joyce in *Ulysses*. It has a huge range of books and there's a coffee shop upstairs.

Crafts

Designist *(68 South Great Georges St., tel. 01/475-8534, designist. ie)* offers a good selection of gift ideas and souvenirs as well as writing materials, candles, home accessories, and designer items, most of which are made by Irish brands.

Design Yard *(25 South Frederick St., Dublin 2, tel 01/474-1011, design-yard.ie)* is one of Ireland's leading showcases for modern quality arts, including an exceptional range of jewelry.

Irish Celtic Craftshop *(10–12 Lord Edward St., tel 01/679-9912, irish-celticcraftshop.com)* has a variety of crafts, including jewelry, knitwear, ceramics, and T-shirts with Celtic designs.

Kilkenny Shop *(6 Nassau St., tel 01/677-7066, kilkennyshop.com)* has a very upscale selection of quality knitwear, woven goods, designer clothing, and pottery.

Department Stores

Arnotts *(12 Henry St., tel 01/805-0400)*, a long-established institution, has three floors of clothing, home wares, sporting goods, and other items.

Brown Thomas *(88–95 Grafton St., tel 01/605-6666)* is by far the best and most exclusive department store in the city, with an aura of quality and class. Products include designer fashion, perfumes, crystal, and home wares.

Fashion

Design Centre *(Powerscourt Town-house Centre, 59 S. William St., tel 01/679-5718, designcentredublin. com)* is home to the best Irish

designers, including Roisín Linanne and Synan O'Mahony.

Louis Copeland *(39–41 Capel St., tel 01/872-1600, louiscopeland.com)* is the outlet for one of Europe's most renowned tailors, providing suits for the rich and famous, including some U.S. presidents.

Louise Kennedy *(56 Merrion Sq., tel 01/662-0056, louisekennedy.com)* offers exclusive designs for women such as Enya, Kylie Minogue, and Gwyneth Paltrow.

Jewelry

Appleby *(5–6 Johnson's Ct., Grafton St., tel 01/679-9572, appleby.ie)* is an exclusive jeweler with an excellent selection.

Weir & Sons *(96 Grafton St., tel 01/677-9678, weirandsons.ie)* has quality jewelry and watches, silver, and leather goods.

Markets

Wandering around the markets of Dublin offers a great insight into the day-to-day life of the city. Try the artisan food market on **Meeting House Square** in Temple Bar *(Sat.),* which has a great selection of cheeses, organic vegetables, fish, meat, and cakes; **Moore Street** market *(Mon.–Sat.)* is famous for fruit, vegetables, and footwear; **Georges Arcade** *(Mon.–Sun.)* has the same, plus clothing (new and secondhand) and fresh bread. There's a **book market** in Temple Bar Square on weekends.

Music

Claddagh Records *(2 Cecilia St., Temple Bar, tel 01/677-0262, claddaghrecords.com)* is an Aladdin's cave full of CDs, tapes, and vinyl. It carries traditional Irish music, including some rare recordings, bluegrass, blues, and world music.

Tower Records *(7 Dawson St., tel 01/677-0262, towerrecords.ie)* A vast assortment of CDs, vinyl

records, DVDs, and gadgets for music lovers and movie buffs.

■ EASTERN IRELAND

Antiques

Granny's Attic *(33 North Main St., Naas, Co. Kildare, tel 045/876-988)* is a treasure trove of antiques and curios.

Tara Antiques of Grennan Watermill *(Thomastown, Co. Kilkenny, tel 056/775-4077)* specializes in English and Irish furniture, art, clocks, and mirrors.

Books

Bridge Street Books *(Bridge St., Wicklow, tel 04/046-2240, bridge streetbooks.ie)* has a fine, wide selection of books.

The Book Centre *(10 High Street, Kilkenny, tel 056/776-2117, thebook centre.ie)* has an excellent selection of books and a very helpful staff.

Clothing

Padmore & Barnes of Kilkenny *(Wolf Tone St., Kilkenny, tel 056/772-1037, padmore-barnes.com)* specializes in handmade Irish shoes, exporting to the U.S., Canada, Japan, and Europe.

Crafts

Ardmore Pottery & Gallery *(The Cliff, Ardmore, Co. Waterford, tel 024/94-152, ardmorepottery. com)* sells spotted, striped, clever, and irresistible ware in gorgeous blues, reds, and yellows.

Avoca Handweavers *(Kilmacanogue, Co. Wicklow, tel 01/274-6939/6900, avoca.com)* sends their quality woven goods to craft outlets all over Ireland and have established themselves as the country's leading brand.

Irish Pewter Mill *(Timolin, near Moone, Co. Kildare, tel 087/909-0044)* has pewter jewelry, tableware, and gift items that are made here, in the mill of a 1,000-year-old nunnery.

Kilkenny is Ireland's principal center for top-quality original crafts, with many artists and artisans working in the area.

The **Kilkenny Design Centre** (tel 056/772-2118, kilkennydesign .com), in the Castle Yard, is their showcase, with all kinds of wares, including ceramics, carving, jewelry, and fabrics.

Lace Gallery (Carrigslaney, Kilbride, Co. Carlow, tel 059/915-5676, thelacegallery.com) is where Mary O'Neill makes, shows, and sells fine handmade lace.

Waterford Crystal (House of Waterford Crystal, 28 The Mall, Waterford, tel 051/317-000, waterfordvisitorcentre.com) is world famous for its glittering goblets, glasses, and chandeliers. See them made, then buy them here.

Jewelry

Murphy Jewellers of Kilkenny (High St., tel 056/772-1127, murphyjewellers.ie) has Irish-made Celtic gold and silver designs, diamond-set jewelry, and watches.

Markets

Kilkenny Farmers Market, in Market Yard on Friday and Saturday mornings, has home produce, home baking, crafts, and plants.

◼ SOUTHWEST IRELAND

This area is home to some of the finest craftspeople and some of the longest-established craft businesses, including Blarney Woollen Mills (see below). Cork city has plenty of outlets, as does Killarney, farther north, and there are little craft communities in various out-of-the-way places, like Ballydehob and Kinsale.

Antiques

Lynes & Lynes (Eastlink Business Park, Carrigtwohil, Cork, tel 021/438-9998, lynesandlynes.com)

offers fine pictures and antique furniture.

Books

Bookstór (1 Newman's Mall, Kinsale, Co. Cork, tel 021/477-4966) is an admirable independent bookshop, with a huge bargain selection and a monthly children's story time/sing-along at 10 a.m. on the first Saturday of the month.

Crafts

Blarney Woollen Mills (Blarney, Co. Cork, tel 021/451-6111, blarney .com) has one of the largest craft shops in Ireland, stocking not only the said woolens but also Waterford crystal, Royal Tara china, Belleek Pottery, Irish Dresden, and other crafts.

Kinsale Crystal (tel 021/477-4493, kinsalecrystal.ie) is run by Gerry Dale, ex-Waterford Crystal craftsman, who has a worldwide reputation.

Ladies View Industries (Ladies View, near Killarney, Co. Kerry, tel 064/663-3430, ladiesview.com) has a superb selection of lace and other crafts, and a wonderful view.

Weavers Shop (Green St., Dingle, Co. Kerry, tel 066/915-1688, lisbethmulcahy.com) has a range of Lisbeth Mulcahy's designs in woven scarves, wall hangings, and designer clothing, and you can watch handloom-weaving in action.

West Cork Crafts (61 Townshend St., Skibbereen, Co. Cork, tel 028/22-555, westcorkcrafts.ie) is an arts and crafts shop featuring the work of local artists—oil paintings, porcelain, wrought-iron work, knitwear, candles, jewelry.

Food

West Cork **cheese** is well known, and makers of quality include **Carrigaline Farmhouse Cheese** (carrigalinecheese.com), **Durrus Cheese** (durruscheese.com) from

just west of Bantry, and **Milleens** (milleenscheese.com), from the Beara Peninsula. And if you are in Clonakilty, County Cork, drop in at **Edward Twomey's** (clonakilty-blackpudding.ie) celebrated butcher store on Pearse Street and pick up a link or two of his tasty **black pudding** (blood pudding), made from a family recipe that dates back to the 1800s. **Mussels** are cultivated in Bantry Bay.

Jewelry

Brian de Staic (briandestaic.com) is a craftsman who produces beautiful pieces of Celtic jewelry. He has outlets in Dingle (Green St., Dingle, Co. Kerry, tel 066/915-1298) and Killarney (18 High St., Killarney, Co. Kerry, tel 066/915-1298).

Markets

The best shopping fun you are likely to have in Cork city is in the enclosed **English Market** (englishmarket.ie), with entrances off Grand Parade, Patrick Street, and Princes Street. It's an atmospheric place, brimming with goodies that include crafts, a delicatessen, and more mundane household items—with some good chat.

Most towns of any size in this area will have a general market once or twice a week. The market at **Skibbereen** (skibbereenmarket. com) is a colorful, vibrant event held every Saturday from 9.30 a.m. to 2 p.m. Vendors sell a little of everything from vegetables to cakes but also antique furniture, ceramics and household items.

Music

Everyone in search of music and/or instruments in Cork—electric guitarists, traditional music players, classical musicians—finds what they need at **Pro Musica** (20 Oliver Plunkett Street, Cork, tel 021/427-1659, promusica.ie).

THE WEST OF IRELAND

Galway is the main city, with the **Eyre Square Shopping Centre** (eyresquarecentre.com) at its heart and a cluster of shopping streets with lots of character. Country towns in this area, with their easy pace of life, no-pressure sales staff, and ready conversation, are a delight to stroll around: Try the narrow streets of **Ennis** in County Clare, or the Georgian thoroughfares of **Westport** in County Mayo.

A different shopping experience is to be found at **Bunratty Village Mills** (tel 061/364-321) in County Clare—a big, modern complex, catering to the tourists who flock here for the castle and folk park. Stores range from tasteful and expensive to kitschy.

If you're flying out of Shannon Airport, don't forget its **duty-free store** for souvenirs and gifts.

Antiques

Galway Antiques Trail (facebook .com/antiques.galway) brings together information on seven antique shops in Galway city.
Long Acre (Bridge St., Westport, Co. Mayo, tel 098/28-718, thelongacre. com) is a fine family-run emporium stuffed with collectibles and antiques.

Books

Since the famous Kenny's Bookshop moved out to an industrial estate, bookworms do their browsing at **Charlie Byrne's Bookshop** (Cornstore Mall, Middle St., Galway, tel 091/561-766, charliebyrne.com), a rambling secondhand treasure cave.

Clothing

The Co-op (Inishmaan, tel 099/73-010) produces Aran garments made by local knitters that are exported worldwide.
Mairéad Sharry (Lurgan Village,

Inis Oirr, Aran Islands, Co. Galway, tel 099/75-101) is a designer who incorporates traditional Aran stitches into gorgeous modern garments. Her shop also has Aran yarn, vintage tweed clothes, and books. Learning vacations and workshops are available as well.
Ó'Máille The Original House of Style (16 High St., Co. Galway, tel 095/562-696, omaille.com) has specialized for over 70 years in the sale of wool clothing and accessories: scarves, sweaters, and more.

Crafts

Connemara Marble Industries (at their quarry at Moycullen, Co. Galway, tel 091/555-102) produces beautiful craft and household items, including jewelry and gifts.
Kylemore Abbey Pottery (Kylemore Abbey, near Letterfrack, Co. Galway, tel 095/52-001 or 095/52-014, kylemoreabbey.com) has plenty going for it—a beautiful location, friendly workers, and its own gorgeous trademark fuchsia design.

Food

Connemara Smokehouse (Bally-conneely in western Connemara, tel 095/23-739, smokehouse.ie) is the place to buy wild, organic, smoked, or marinated salmon and other fish for your picnic or take-home present.
Sheridans Cheesemongers (14–16 Churchyard St., tel. 091/64-829, sheridanscheesemongers.com) is the ideal place to buy all types of Irish cheese (but not only).

Jewelry

The big item in Galway, of course, is the famous Claddagh ring, with its charming and distinctive motif of two hands encircling a heart, topped by a crown. Its long history is explained at the

little museum behind **Dillon's Claddagh Ring Shop** (1 Quay St., Galway, tel 091/566-365, claddaghring.ie), where you can buy rings in gold, silver, or platinum.

Markets

Every Saturday morning, **Galway** hosts a market near St. Nicholas Collegiate Church that is particularly strong on organic produce and homemade breads.

Music

Custy's Traditional Music Shop (Cookes Ln., Ennis, Co. Clare, tel 065/682-1727, custysmusic.com) has traditional instruments, including whistles, fiddles, and squeeze boxes.
Powells (53 The Four Corners, Williams St., Galway, tel 091/562-295, powellsmusic.ie) sells Irish music tapes and CDs, plus instruments and sheet music.
Roundstone Musical Instruments (IDA Craft Centre, Roundstone, Co. Galway, tel 095/35-808, bodhran.com) is most famous for the bodhrans (traditional Irish drums) that are made here. It also sells traditional music tapes and CDs.

NORTHWEST IRELAND

Sligo and **Donegal** towns have an enjoyable mix of upscale stores aimed at visitors and more down-to-earth shopping for locals, such as old-fashioned drapers and clothing stores (this is the home of Donegal tweed), plus traditional grocers and hardware stores with carved, wooden storefronts.

Antiques

The Gallery (Dunfanaghy, Co. Donegal, tel 074/913-6224, thegallerydunfanaghy.com), in a former fever hospital, has two stories of

antiques, paintings, and crafts.
Mourne Antiques (38 Upper Main Street, Letterkenny, Co. Donegal, tel 074/912-6457, mourneantiques .com) is crammed full of china, jewelry, silver, furniture, and other collectibles.

Crafts

Donegal Craft Village (tel 074/972-2225, donegalcraftvillage. com), just outside Donegal on the Sligo road, comprises a cluster of workshops where you can see artisans at work and buy unique items: metalwork, jewelry, sculpture, and batik, as well as uilleann pipes.
Glencolmcille Folk Village Shop (tel 074/973-0017, glenfolkvillage. com) makes a good stop-in for its fine range of knitted, crocheted, and other textile goods, and also crafts, jewelry, etc.—all made by locals.
Leitrim Design House (The Dock Arts Centre, Carrick-on-Shannon, Co. Leitrim, tel 071/965-0550, leitrim-designhouse.ie) is a retail showroom and gallery for Leitrim craftspeople and artists.

Department Stores

Magee's (The Diamond, Donegal town, tel 074/972-2660) is the place for tweed. You can watch a weaver at work before buying top-quality jackets and other tweed items.
McElhinney's (Main St., Ballybofey, tel 074/913-1217, mcelhinneys.com) is the largest department store in the northwest, with a wide selection of quality goods.

Food

The Organic Centre (Rossinver, tel 071/985-4338, theorganiccentre.ie) sells organic cheese, meat, herbs, vegetables, fruit, and candy.

Jewelry

The Cat and the Moon (4 Castle St., Sligo, tel 071/914-3686, thecatandthemoon.ie) is an all-encompassing craft and gift shop, including Celtic jewelry.

CENTRAL IRELAND

Books

The Old Bookshop (near Hill of Tara visitor center, Co. Meath) is packed with books on Celtic and mystical matters, some written by owner and Tara expert Michael Slavin.

Crafts

Carna Craft (Baltrasna, Ashbourne, Co. Meath, tel 01/835-0273) sells Michael Mulkerrin's sculptural figurines made of horseshoe nails.
Carrickmacross Lace Gallery (Market Square, Carrickmacross, Co. Monaghan, tel 042/966-4176, carrickmacrosslace.ie) has lace made in the traditional way; a lace-making demonstration is given by appointment.
Celtic Clays Workshop (Riverside, Carlingford, Co. Louth, tel 042/938-3996) is one of Ireland's leading studio potteries, producing stoneware with rich, earthy glazes.
Liz Christy (Swallow Studios, Annayalla, Castleblayney, Co. Monaghan, tel 042/974-6614, lizchristy.com) hand-weaves gorgeous scarves and stoles.

Jewelry

MC2 Jewellery & Giftware (Navan Town Centre, Navan, Co. Meath, tel 046/907-0550) has top-quality items, including Celtic designs.

NORTHERN IRELAND

In recent years, Northern Ireland, just like its neighbors to the south, has seen a growing development in its commerce sector with an increase of department stores in the capital and artisan shops in the smaller towns. Some of the most typical souvenirs are Belleek pottery, crystal ware from Tyrone and Fermanagh, linen, and Bushmills whiskey.

Belfast

There are many big places to shop in the city. The **CastleCourt Shopping Centre** (tel 028/9023-4591, castlecourt-uk.com), located on approximately 8.5 acres and three floors, is undoubtedly one of the most important shopping centers. The more recent **Victoria Square** (1 Victoria Sq., tel 028/9032-2277, victoriasquare.com) is an ultramodern structure that becomes a splendid tower of light at night. On the weekend, it pulsates with Irish visitors that flock to its boutiques and restaurants.

Antiques

Donegall Pass is the center of the antiques area of Belfast.
Oakland Antiques (135–137 Donegall Pass, tel 028/9023-0176, oaklandantiques.co.uk) is the city's largest antiques store, with Georgian, Victorian, and Edwardian furniture, silver, glass, porcelain, paintings, and many other items for sale.

Books

No Alibis Bookstore (83 Botanic Avenue, tel 028/9031-9601, noalibis.com) stocks U.K., U.S., and Irish crime fiction, and often has live music events. Another choice is **Waterstone's** (44–46 Fountain St., tel 028/9024-0159, waterstones. com), a major bookstore that somehow manages to be human and helpful.

Crafts

Conway Mill Craft Shop and Exhibition Centre (5–7 Conway St., tel 028/9032-6452), within a restored historic flax mill,

displays the work of the 22 craft workshops on site.
Workshops Collective for Arts and Crafts (1A Lawrence St., tel 028/9043-4993) has 12 workshops, a showroom, and a coffee shop in an old stable block off Botanic Avenue.

Fashion

The Bureau (B2, Portview, Newtownards Rd., tel 028/9046-0190, thebureaubelfast.com), once strictly a male preserve, now also has women's clothes for sale. Notable designers include Calvin Klein, Dries Van Noten, Katherine Hamnet, Miu-Miu, and others.
Office (2 High St., tel 028/9023-5189) is great for shoes that are a little bit naughty, a little bit nice.

Food

Aunt Sandra's Candy Factory (60 Castlereagh Rd., tel 028/9073-2868, auntsandras.com) sells handcrafted candy that you can watch being made.
Sawyers (5–6 Fountain Centre, College St., tel 028/9032-2021, sawersbelfast.com) is the best deli in town, with a huge range of cheeses, salamis, exotic meats (such as wild boar and ostrich), and pâtés, as well as fresh dulse (seaweed).

Jewelry

Fred J. Malcolm (641 Lisburn Rd., tel 028/9066-2666, & 18 Chichester St., Town Centre, tel 028/9032-1491, fredjmalcolm.com) offers tasteful diamond jewelry, watches, and antique pieces.

Music

HMV (3–6 Donegall Arcade, tel 084/321-0116, hmv.com) is one of the best stocked in the city with CDs, DVDs, and vinyl records as well as music or movie-themed gadgets, posters, and tee shirts.

Northern Ireland Counties

You'll find historic towns with traditional high streets, but there are also modern shopping facilities, such as the **Foyleside Shopping Centre** (foyleside.co.uk) in Derry, anchored by **Dunnes** (dunnesstores.com) and **Marks & Spencer** (marksandspencer.com).
Derry Craft Village (Inner City Trust, 31–33 Shipquay St., Co. Londonderry, tel 028/7126-0329, derrycraftvillage.com) Home to a variety of small shops whose wares range from handicrafts to accessories for Irish dance.

Antiques

Crannog Antiques (5 The Brook, Enniskillen, Co. Fermanagh, tel 028/6632-5850) has a lovely selection, including glass, china, furniture, jewelry, brass, and silver.

Books

As in the rest of Ireland, you'll find branches of **Eason's** in all the major towns and cities. Those listed below are alternatives that have good selections.
Foyle Books (12A Magazine St., Craft Village, Derry, Co. Londonderry, tel 028/7137-2530).
Little Acorns Bookstore (3–5 Society St., Derry, Co. Londonderry, 077/7611-7054).

Crafts

Belleek Pottery (Belleek, Co. Fermanagh, tel 028/6865-8501, belleek.com) is one of Ireland's top visitor attractions and is known worldwide for its delicate porcelain (see pp. 318–319).
Buttermarket Craft & Design Centre (Down St., Enniskillen, Co. Fermanagh, tel 028/6632-3117) Its workshops produce pottery, fishing tackle, sculptures, etc. and there is an exhibition space and a café.

Irish Linen Centre (Market Sq., Lisburn, Co. Antrim, tel 028/9266-3377) has an exhibition about the production of Irish linen, as well as a shop and café.
Island Turf Crafts (25 Coalisland Enterprise Centre, 51 Dungannon Rd., Coalisland, Co. Tyrone, tel 028/8774-9041, islandturfcrafts.com) makes statues, Celtic crosses, jewelry, and more out of Irish turf (peat).
The Steensons Workshop & Gallery (Seaview Hall, New Rd., Glenarm, Antrim Glens, Co. Antrim, tel 028/2884-1445, thesteensons.com) is a family-run goldsmiths on the Causeway Coast; watch rings, bracelets, necklaces, and brooches handcrafted, and buy on site.

Jewelry

Faller the Jeweller (12 Strand Rd., Derry, Co. Londonderry, tel 028/7136-2710, faller.com) is a family-run store with designer jewelry and gifts, including items made in their own workshop.
Inisor Jewellery (59 Molesworth St., Cookstown, Co. Tyrone, tel 028/8676-1606, inisor.com) produces handcrafted jewelry.

ENTERTAINMENT & ACTIVITIES

Anyone who spends time in Ireland needs no persuading that the Irish are natural entertainers—not in the "cap and bells" sense, but as a people absolutely in love with conversation, music, song, curiosity, argument, joking, and nonsense, the famous Irish *craic* (pronounced "crack"). And every town and village has a stage where anyone can be the star and everyone is part of the enthusiastically participating audience: the pub. There is so much recreation value in the pub that many don't bother looking elsewhere for their entertainment. An even more traditional venue for this kind of informal, come-all-ye gathering is the *ceilidh* (meeting) house, a cornerstone of community life before television and strangers would gather to chat, play music, and dance in some house known to be a venue for such goings-on. *Ceilidh* houses are enjoying something of a revival, and it's worth asking whether there is one in your locality.

The theater is extremely strong in Ireland, opera is gaining ground in the wake of the success of the annual Wexford Festival Opera, and Irish cinema has had extraordinary popularity in the past couple of decades.

Traditional culture is perpetuated in many forms, and apart from the informal music sessions in pubs, you'll find it in stage shows and tourist-oriented banquets.

Almost anywhere you look, there's some kind of festival going on: guzzling seaweed in Antrim or oysters in Galway; hooker (a kind of boat) racing in Connemara; poetry in Sligo; storytelling in Cork.

Nightlife in the big cities—Dublin, Belfast, Cork, Limerick, Galway—has kept pace with its European counterparts in the shape of extreme-noise dance clubs, comedy venues, and late-license bars. But in the smaller communities that make up Ireland's country towns and villages, where the majority of visitors spend most of their time, it is still the pub that offers the best of music, dancing, talk, and laughter.

When it comes to sports, a day at the racetrack (horses or greyhounds) is a long-established form of entertainment in Ireland, and Gaelic football, hurling, and soccer draw big crowds. Golf, fishing, boating, and horseback riding are popular activities, and walking is gaining ground, so to speak. The **Irish Heart Foundation** (*irishheart.ie*) lists around 70 walking clubs in the Republic.

■ DUBLIN

As the capital and a seedbed of a great literary tradition, Dublin is a cultured city with a long history of entertaining foreigners, vacationers, countryfolk, and Dubliners themselves. There are plenty of places where you can party until dawn. But Dublin has a lot more to offer than that.

Bars

Cool bars south of the river include **Café en Seine** (*40 Dawson St.*), a three-story art nouveau hive of bars and coffee hangouts; **Bison Bar** (*11 Wellington Quay, below The Workmans Club*) offers tangy Texan BBQ and more whiskeys than you can shake a Stetson at, while **Kinara Cocktail Bar** (*upstairs at Kinara Kitchen, 17 Ranelagh Village*) does stupendous cocktails, expertly. Moody **Dakota** (*9 South William St.*) is worth dropping into, if you're in the mood. North of the river, you could check out **The Church** (*junction of Mary St. & Jervis St., tel 01/828-0102*), a pub that inhabits—yes!—a former church.

City Walks

For guided or self guided walks around the city, from "Viking & Medieval Dublin" to the Literary Pub Crawl, visit **Dublin Tourism** website (*visitdublin.com/see-do/dublin-discovery-trails*).

Nightlife

Northside: **Pantibar** (formerly GUBU; *7–8 Capel St., 01/874-0710, pantibar.com*) is a flamboyant bar, primarily LGBT, but welcoming to all. Southside: **777** (*7 Castle House, South Great George's St., tel 01/425-4052, 777.ie*) has ear-crushing dancing and tequila brands to sample. **Bond** (*21–25 Harcourt St., tel 083/103-3519, russellcourthotel.ie/bond-nightclub*) has a more sophisticated air for over-30s who'd rather be stirred than shaken.

As far as other nightlife, if you're under 50 and looking for a lively time, you can scarcely escape the lure of **Temple Bar**. Clubs, pubs, sidewalk cafés, and other fun destinations seem to occupy all the buildings that don't house avant-garde or retro stores. Drinking and dancing places can change overnight in the trendiness pecking order, but currently the cool **Four Dame Lane** (*tel 01/679-0291*) on Dame Ln. and the **Turk's Head** (*paramounthotel.ie/dine-drinks*) on Parliament Street, are up in the popularity mix—as is **The Porterhouse** (*16–18 Parliament St., tel 01/679-8847, porterhousebrewco.ie*), a microbrewery that provides live music every night. There's more music at the fabulous **Sugar Club** (*8 Lower Leeson St., tel 01/678-7188*).

Pubs

Enjoy the art at the pub immortalized in James Joyce's *Ulysses*, **Davy Byrne's** (*21 Duke St.,*

davybyrnes.com) very fine establishment. You can eavesdrop on
conspiratorial politicians and
other city heavyweights in the
Victorian comfort of **Doheny &
Nesbitt's** (*dohenyandnesbitts.ie*) on
Lower Baggot Street. **Mulligan's**
(*Poolbeg St., mulligans.ie*) has long
claimed to serve the best Guinness in Ireland. The theatrical but
fun **Dublin Literary Pub Crawl**
(*nightly in summer; Thurs.–Sun. in
winter; tel 01/670-5602, dublin
pubcrawl.com*) starts at the Duke
pub on Duke Street and tours
famous literary pubs, with guides
who offer information about the
authors and act out scenes from
their work.

Theater

Three of Dublin's many theaters
well worth making an effort to get
to include the sometimes experi-
mental, always interesting **Project
Arts Centre** (*39 East Essex St.,
01/881-9613, projectartscentre.ie*)
and the well-regarded **Gate Theatre** (*Cavendish Row, Parnell Sq., tel
01/874-4045, gate-theatre.ie*). And,
of course, there's the one founded
by W. B. Yeats, J. M. Synge, Lady
Gregory, and others—the famous
Abbey Theatre (*26 Lower Abbey
St., tel 01/878-7222, abbeytheatre.
ie*), still putting on works by the
great classic playwrights as well as
newcomers.

Among other theaters are
Olympia Theatre (*2 Dame St., tel
01/679-3323, olympia.ie*), **Bord
Gáis Energy Theatre** (*Grand Canal
Square Dockland, tel 01/677-7999,
bordgaisenergytheatre.ie*). Opera and
symphonic concerts are held mostly
at **National Concert Hall** (*Earlsfort
Terrace, tel 01/2417-0000, nch.ie*).

Traditional Music

When it comes to finding the
best session of traditional music,
one really excellent venue is the
unpretentious but friendly **Cob-
blestone Bar** (*North King St., tel

01/872-1799) where the nightly
sessions are memorable. Also up
there in the ratings is the **Brazen
Head** (*20 Lower Bridge St., tel
01/679-186, brazenhead.com*), an
ancient pub (probably the city's
oldest) with great beer and an
exceptional atmosphere.

■ EASTERN IRELAND

Car Touring

Follow the **Gordon Bennett Touring Route** (*gordonbennettroute.com*),
a signposted trail of 104 miles (167
km) that takes you along quiet
back roads through Counties Carlow, Kildare, and Laois.

Golf

The east of Ireland, with its large
areas of level ground and low-
lying coasts, is great for golf, and
as in the rest of the country, there
are many championship courses.
Down on the coast of County
Waterford, there's the **Tramore
Golf Club** (*tel 051/386-170,
tramoregolfclub.com*), 10 miles
(16 km) south of Waterford town.

Horse Racing

Kildare is horse-racing country,
home to the **National Stud** (see
pp. 92–95) and the foremost racetrack—**The Curragh** (*tel 045/441-
205, curragh.ie*). Northeast of
Kildare town, off the N7, it's where
most of Ireland's classic races are
run. There are two tracks at Naas,
County Kildare—the **Punchestown**
track (*punchestown.com*) and the
Naas town track (*naasracecourse.
com*)—and one in **Leopardstown**
(*leopardstown.com*) in County
Dublin. Not quite so prominent,
but just as much fun, are the
Waterford & Tramore (*tramore-
racecourse.com*) and **Wexford**
(*wexfordraces.ie*) tracks.

Irish Culture

The **Bru Boru Heritage Centre**
(*tel 062/61-122, bruboru.ie*), in

Cashel, is a cultural enclave in the
shadow of the Rock of Cashel,
set up to study and portray Irish
music, song, dance, storytelling,
and theater. Its resident group of
musicians and artists are world
famous.

Opera

Don't miss **Wexford Festival Opera**
(see sidebar p. 114) if you like your
opera a little obscure and a lot
of fun.

Theater

The **Theatre Royal** (*The Mall,
Co. Waterford, tel 051/874-402, theatre
royal.ie*) is housed in the Georgian City
Hall and offers high-quality drama,
music, and dance from Irish and international companies.

Wexford Arts Centre (*tel
053/912-3764, wexfordartscentre.ie*), in
the Cornmarket, has a rich program
of music, theater, and film.

The **Watergate Theatre** (*Parliament St., Kilkenny, Co. Kilkenny, tel
056/776-1674, watergatetheatre.com*)
has a lovely, intimate auditorium
and a very interesting program of
quality drama, music, and children's
theater.

In Carlow, the new **Centre for
Contemporary Art** (*Old Dublin Rd.,
tel 059/917-2400, visualcarlow.ie*)
has a wide range of events, from
ballet and comedy to drama and
storytelling.

Traditional Music

There are countless pubs for good
traditional music. In St. Celbridge
in County Kildare, enjoyable music
sessions take place every week in
both Henry Grattan's restaurant and
lounge bar (*Maynooth Rd., tel 01/536-
7128, henrygrattans.ie*).

In the beautiful Vale of Avoca
in County Wicklow, **The Meetings**
(*tel 040/235-226, themeetings.ie*) has
music every weekend—every night
April–September—and has a traditional Irish *ceilidh* outdoors on summer Sunday afternoons.

In the north of County Tipperary, on the shores of Lough Derg, you'll find traditional music every night from June to October in **Larkin's** *(tel 067/23-232, larkins.ie)*, at Garrykennedy near Portroe.

One of the most famous places (so it's often crowded) is **Johnny Fox's** *(tel 01/295-5647, jfp.ie)* in Glencullen, high up in the Wicklow Mountains, where there is live music seven nights a week and on weekend afternoons, too (and also a dinner show with traditional dancers).

■ SOUTHWEST IRELAND
Concerts

The **National Events Centre** *(Gleneagle Hotel, Muchross Rd., Killarney, Co. Kerry, tel 064/667-1555, inec.ie)* is the largest venue in Ireland and hosts concerts, shows, and theater.

Gaelic Football

Purely Irish entertainment! You may well be the only foreigner in attendance if you turn up on Sunday to **Austin Stack Park** on John Joe Sheehy Road in Tralee, County Kerry, to watch a blisteringly exciting game of Gaelic football—like soccer, but with more thrills per minute.

Golf

Golf fiends can cosset their addiction in Kerry on several notable courses, all agreeably scenic, some spectacularly so—try **Ballybunion Golf Club** *(tel 068/27-146, ballybuniongolf club.ie)*, **Tralee Golf Club** *(tel 066/713-6379, traleegolfclub. com)*, **Beaufort Golf Club** *(tel 064/664-4440, beaufortgc.com)*, or **Ross Golf Club** *(tel 064/663-1125, killarneyraces.ie)*—the latter two near Killarney—or **Waterville Golf Links** on the Iveragh Peninsula's Ring of Kerry *(tel 066/947-4102, watervillegolflinks.*

ie). You could try two sports in one place at the **Killarney Golf and Fishing Club** *(tel 064/663-1034, killarneygolfclub.ie)*.

Greyhound Racing

Be prepared to stand up and shout your head off at the dogs on an evening out with a wallet of flutter money at **Cork Greyhound Stadium** *(tel 061/448-080, igb.ie)* in Curaheen Park on Curaheen Road.

Horse Racing

There are tracks at **Mallow** *(cork racecourse.ie)*, County Cork, and at **Killarney** *(killarneyraces.ie)* where you can enjoy the thrill of the sport among like-minded countryfolk.

Irish Culture

Tralee, in northern County Kerry, is where you'll find **Siamsa Tíre** *(Town Park, Denny St., tel 066/712-3055, siamsatire.com)*, the National Folk Theatre of Ireland. From May to October, the theater offers a program of entertainment based around Ireland's rich culture of music, dance, and folklore.

Pubs

For that longed-for relaxing pint and conversation, you can't do better than the cozy little first-floor **Hi-B Bar** opposite Cork city post office on Oliver Plunkett Street. Near Killarney, County Kerry, **Kate Kearney's Cottage** *(tel 064/44-146, katekearneys cottage.com)*, at the entrance to the Gap of Dunloe beauty spot, is a nice old pub.

Theater

Lime Tree Theatre *(69 O'Connell St., Limerick, tel 061/953-400, limetreetheatre.ie)* offers a program that ranges from plays and dance to comedy, musicals, concerts, and family shows. **Cork Opera House** *(Emmet Pl., Cork, tel 021/427-0022,*

corkoperahouse.ie) is a handsome city-center theater that can seat 1,000 people for opera, dance, and drama. The well-known **Everyman Palace Theatre** *(15 MacCurtain St., Cork, tel 021/450-1673, everyman cork.com)* is a restored 630-seat Victorian theater with a varied program, majoring in Irish drama during the summer.

Traditional Music

An Spailpín Fánac on South Main Street, Cork, opposite the Beamish brewery, is great for music—often traditional, but just about anything might emerge.

Music lovers are spoiled for choice in west Cork: **De Barra** *(debarra.ie)* in Clonakilty, **Jacob's Pub** in Baltimore, **Kitty Ó Sé's** in Kinsale, and **The Quays Bar** in Bantry are good options.

In County Kerry, traditional music in pubs is plentiful in Tralee—try **Paddy Mac's** on the Mall, **Baily's Corner** on Castle St., **Seán Óg's** *(sean-ogs.com)* on Bridge Street, or **Turner's** on Castle Street.

In Dingle town, head for **The Small Bridge**, **Dick Mack's** *(dickmacks pub.com)*, or the apparently tongue-tangling **Ua Flaithbheartaigh's** (don't panic—it's O'Flaherty's).

In Killarney, on High Street, **O'Connor's Traditional Pub** puts on traditional music, as does the **Laurels** *(thelaurelspub.com)* on Main Street.

In Limerick city, there's **Dolan's Pub & Restaurant** *(dolans.ie)* on Dock Road, or **Nancy Blakes** on Denmark Street.

■ THE WEST OF IRELAND
Clubbing

Halo Nightclub *(36 Abbeygate St., Galway city, tel 091/565-967, halonightclub.com)* caters for the smartly dressed over-23 crowd, while **Electric Garden** at the same address *(electricgalway.com)* is louder, younger, and more informal.

Greyhound Racing

Enjoy a bet on the dogs at **Galway Greyhound Track** *(tel 091/448-8080)* on College Road.

Horse Racing & Horseback Riding

Galway has **racing festivals** *(galway races.com)* in July and September each year, when the racing world mingles with enthusiasts and visitors for a memorable Irish experience. If you want to explore Connemara on a Connemara pony, there are plenty of places. Try **Errislannan Manor** *(tel 095/21-134, errislannan-manor-riding.com)* on the west coast, just south of Clifden, which offers riding and trekking for adults and children.

Medieval Banquets

In the west, especially in County Clare, there are lots of banquets, with groups of musicians and actors dressed in historical costume, often in castles and country houses. You really have to be in the mood, but when the *craic* and the company are right, they can be very good fun. Try **Bunratty Castle** *(tel 061/360-788, bunrattycastle.ie)*, where you feast (eating with your fingers) with the "Earl of Thomond," or take in a Riverdance-style show in the Corn Barn at **Knappogue Castle** *(tel 061/360-788, shannonheritage. com/KnappogueBanquet)* near Quin (eating irons provided here). Reservations advised.

Theater

In Galway city, theater lovers will make for the **Town Hall Theatre** *(tel 091/569-777, tht.ie)*, in Court House Square, or for the more adventurous, **Druid Theatre** *(tel 091/568-660, druid.ie)* nearby on Courthouse Lane.

Traditional Music

The **Glór Irish Music Centre** *(tel 065/684-3103, glor.ie)* in Ennis,

County Clare, puts on performances of traditional Irish music with some of the country's top musicians. If you prefer to take your chances in a Clare pub—and Clare is renowned for it—get down to Doolin and **McGann's** (mostly tunes) and **O'Connor's** (more songs), or the pubs in Kilfenora, Ennistymon, Lisdoonvarna, and many another town and village.

In Galway city, settle down with a pint at **Taaffe's** of Shop Street, **Brogan** on Prospect Hill, the **Róisín Dubh** *(roisindubh.net)* on Upper Dominick Street, or the atmospheric **Crane Bar** *(thecranebar.com)* on Sea Road on the west bank of the river, where you might find an Irish dancing session upstairs.

County Mayo is great for music, too—Westport is probably the cream of the crop, with really lively sessions in **Matt Molloy's** (the flautist with the Chieftains; *mattmolloy.com*), **Hoban's**, or **The Big Tree.**

■ NORTHWEST IRELAND

Boating

Little County Leitrim depends on its lakes and waterways to attract visitors, and there are a couple of enjoyable cruises to take: **Moon River Cruise** *(tel 071/962-1777, moonriver. ie)* on Main Street, Carrick-on-Shannon (floating bar and live music), and **Cruise-Ireland** *(The Marina St George's Terrace, Carrick-on-Shannon, tel 071/962-0236, cruise-ireland.com).*

Golf

For sheer scenic beauty, not to mention a respectable challenge, the **County Sligo Golf Club** *(tel 071/917-7134, countysligogolfclub.ie)*, known here as Rosses Point, is hard to beat—it was even immortalized by W. B. Yeats, who dedicated a poem to the view from the third tee.

Irish culture

Teac Jack *(tel 074/953-1173, teac jack.com)* is a cultural center at Derrybeg, by Gweedore in northwest County Donegal, where there are music sessions and ceilidh dancing. Sligo town gains tone from its associations with the famous Yeats brothers, hence its **Yeats International Summer School** (see sidebar p. 208) and **Sligo Live Music Festival** *(sligolive.ie).*

Seaweed Baths

If you want a unique experience, go to Enniscrone on the Sligo coast for a sloppy and refreshing slither in **Kilcullen's Seaweed Baths** (see sidebar p. 211; *tel 096/36-238, kilcullenseaweedbaths.net).*

Theater

High-quality musicals, classical concerts, and dramas are staged at the **Hawk's Well Theatre** *(tel 071/916-1518, hawkswell.com)* on Temple Street, Sligo. Letterkenny, County Donegal, offers **An Grianán Theatre** *(tel 074/912-0777, angrianan. com)* on Port Road, with regular music and drama.

Traditional Music

Furey's *(facebook.com/fureyssligo)* on the bridge is the best music pub in Sligo town, along with **Shoot the Crows** on Castle Street. In County Donegal, the friendliest, most spontaneous spot is the **Scotsman** on Bridge Street, Donegal town. **Peter Oliver's Corner House** in Ardara, **Cryan's Teach Ceoil** and **Anderson's Thatched Pub** in Carrick-on-Shannon, and **The Cottage** on Main Street, Letterkenny are great, too.

■ CENTRAL IRELAND

Entertainment tends to be less tourist-oriented here than in the rest of Ireland—for the simple reason that this dairying and bog area sees fewer visitors.

Fishing

In County Meath, you can fish in any of a hundred lakes and rivers. **Anglers World** (Balmoral Business Park, Kells Rd., Navan, tel 046/907-1866) offers permits and advice.

Golf

Meath is a great golfing county. Try the **Royal Tara Golf Club** (Bellinter near Navan, tel 046/902-5508, royaltaragolfclub.com), **Headfort Golf Club** (Navan Rd., Kells, tel 046/924-0146, headfort golfclub.ie), or **County Meath Golf Club** (Newtownmoynagh, Trim, tel 046/943-1463, countymeathgolf clubtrim.ie).

Greyhound Racing

In County Westmeath, small-town Ireland's passion for dog racing finds a noisy and enjoyable outlet in **Mullingar Greyhound Stadium** (tel 061/448-080) at Ballinderry near Mullingar.

Horse Racing & Horseback Riding

In County Meath, **Fairyhouse Racecourse** (Ratoath, tel 01/825-6167, fairyhouse.ie) is one of Ireland's major racetracks. There's a less formal, yet unique meeting at **Laytown** in June in which horses race along the beach while spectators watch from the dunes. If you want to ride, **Kells Equestrian Centre** (Normanstown, Carlanstown, near Kells, tel 046/924-6998 or 086/849-9201, kellsequestrian. com) is one place to go.

Irish Culture

At Ballyconnell in County Cavan, there's the **Ballyhugh Arts and Cultural Centre** (tel 049/952-6044) out on the Belturbet road, where exhibitions, live shows, and ceilidhs explore the native culture of west Cavan.

Theater

County Monaghan has the **Garage Theatre** (Monaghan Education Campus, Armagh Rd., Monaghan town, tel 047/39-777, garagetheatre.com), where you can catch a wide program of drama, dance, music, and comedy. In Drogheda, County Louth, there's the **Droichead Arts Centre** (tel 041/983-3946, droichead.com) on Stockwell St.. In Dundalk, the **Spirit Store** (tel 042/935-2697, spiritstore.ie), on Georges Quay, offers a varied mix of cultural activities.

Traditional Music

On Sunday nights in Dundalk there are traditional sessions downstairs in the **Spirit Store** (see Theater, above), and at **Courtney's Bar** on Park Street.

Walking the Slieve Bloom Mountains

The Slieve Bloom Mountains rise out of the agricultural plains, straddling the borders of Counties Laois and Offaly. They can't really claim to be mountains; they are more like rounded hills, packed tightly together. But there can't be a hill range in Ireland better provided with keen walkers.

Among several other initiatives, the local ramblers have founded the superb springtime **Slieve Bloom Walking Festival** (early May, slievebloom.ie). They've also devised a whole scattering of looped walks from trailheads in the skirts of the mountains. Some of these are part of the National Looped Walks scheme, and some are styled "eco-walks." Others are purely local initiatives. Best of all, the hospitable ramblers of the Slieve Bloom Walking Club are only too happy to have visitors along so they can show them just what it is they love about these hills, so you'll have your own expert guides to this beautiful part of the country.

■ NORTHERN IRELAND

Belfast

After years of apathy, neglect, and lack of investment brought about by the Troubles, Belfast has seized avidly on these more peaceful times to reinvent itself as just as much of a party city as Dublin. Every kind of entertainment is on offer here.

Concerts

The **Waterfront Hall** (2 Lanyon Pl., tel 028/9033-4455, www.waterfront .co.uk) and the nearby **SSE Arena** (2 Queen's Quay, tel 028/9073-9074, ssearenabelfast.com) stage megaconcerts and shows, while the **Ulster Hall** (34 Bedford St., tel 028/9033-4400) and **Eikon Exhibition Centre** (Balmoral Park, Sprucefield, Halftown Rd., Lisburn, tel 028/9066-5225, eikonexhibitioncentre.co.uk) host big music shows.

Nightlife

Belfast's trendiest nightclubs, restaurants, bars, and venues are in the Cathedral Quarter near St Anne's Cathedral.

Pubs

A great way to acquaint yourself with some of Belfast's oldest and most characterful pubs is ask for info at the Belfast Welcome Centre, in 8–9 Donegall Sq., or take part in a **Pub Walking Tour** (see sidebar p. 292; tel 028/9268-3665).

Theater

The **Backstage Theatre & Centre for the Arts** (Farneyhoogan, Longford, Co. Longford, tel 043/334-7888, backstage.ie) is a small, custom-built theater that offers an excellent, varied program, including touring international theater companies, Irish drama, comedy, and music.

Opera, musicals, pantomime, concerts, comedy shows, theater, and ballet can all be enjoyed in truly sumptuous surroundings at the **Grand Opera House** *(tel 028/9024-1919, goh.co.uk)* on Great Victoria Street. There's excellent repertory theater at the **Lyric Theatre** *(55 Ridgeway St., 028/9038-1081, lyrictheatre.co.uk)* on Stranmillis. The **Crescent Arts Centre** *(tel 028/9024-2338, crescentarts.org)* in the Golden Mile offers music, comedy, dance, and drama in a more intimate space.

Traditional Music
The Garrick *(29 Chichester St., 028/9032-1984, thegarrickbar.com)* has traditional music sessions on Wednesdays from 9:30 p.m. and Fridays from 5 p.m., Sundays in summer, too; also a singing session on the first Wednesday of each month at 9 p.m.

Northern Ireland Counties
Clubbing
Kelly's Complex *(tel 028/7082-6611, kellysportrush.co.uk)*, on Bushmills Road at Portrush, County Antrim, has seven bars, three dance floors, and a popular club known as **Lush.**

Fishing & Boating
Fermanagh offers fishing or boating on Lough Erne *(Fermanagh tourist office, tel 028/6632-5000)*. Fishermen in County Down could try for a trout in the Mourne Mountains' Shimna River. Obtain permits from **Four Seasons** *(47 Main St., Newcastle, tel 028/4372-5078)*.

Golf
Downpatrick offers golf at the 18-hole **St. Patrick's Golf Club** *(Saul Rd., Downpatrick, tel 028/4461-5947, stpatricksgolfclub. com)* and at **Ardglass Golf Club** *(tel 028/4484-1219, ardglass golfclub.com)*. One of the best (and

one of the oldest) courses is the **Royal County Down Golf Club** *(tel 028/4372-3314, royalcounty down.org)* at Newcastle, a championship links course beneath the Mourne Mountains.

Horse Racing
County Down is Northern Ireland's horse-racing base, with **Down Royal** *(downroyal.com)* and **Downpatrick** *(downpatrickrace course.co.uk)*, which bills itself as "the friendliest racecourse in Ireland."

Irish Culture
Two excellent County Tyrone venues are **Dún Uladh Heritage Centre** *(tel 028/8224-2777, dunuladh. ie)* on the outskirts of Omagh *(Sat. evenings from 10 p.m.)* and **An Creagán Visitor Centre** *(tel 028/8076-1112, an-creagan.com)*, east of Omagh, on the Cookstown road. In South Armagh, tradition comes into its own in the admirable **Tí Chulainn Cultural Activity Centre** (see sidebar p. 45; *tel 028/3088-8828, tichulainn.com)*, in the village of Mullaghbane, where the rich culture of the area is explored in music, song, and storytelling.

Nightlife
In Derry city, the **Gweedore Bar** *(61 Waterloo St., tel 028/7126-7295)* puts on live local bands and gets packed and sweaty.

If you're out on the town by night along the Down/Antrim border, try Lisburn's **Cardan Bar & Grill/Distil Night Club** *(41 Railway St., 028/9267-8065, thecardan.com)* for weekend clubbing.

Theater
County Antrim theaters include **Riverside Theatre** *(tel 028/7012-3123, ulster.ac.uk)*, on the University of Ulster campus at Coleraine, and the **McNeill Theatre** *(Larne Leisure Centre, tel 028/2826-2497, larneleisurecentre.*

com/mcneill-theatre), on Tower Road, Larne. In County Armagh, there's the **Market Place Theatre** *(tel 028/3752-1821, visitarmagh. com)* in Armagh city. In County Fermanagh, there's Enniskillen's **Ardhowen Theatre** *(tel 028/6632-5440, ardhowen.com)*, beside Lough Erne.

Traditional Music
In County Antrim, many of the small towns and villages have music pubs, in particular **McCollam's** (locally known as Johnny Joe's; *johnnyjoes.co.uk)* in Cushendall. In Derry city, **Peadar O'Donnells** *(tel 028/7126-7295)* is a characterful place with the decor of an old grocery store, famous for its traditional music sessions that take place every night of the week.

Traditional music and the delights of the ceilidh house have revived recently in County Tyrone. A ceilidh house might have music, dancing, jokes, stories, riddles—there's nothing planned, and nothing guaranteed but fun. **Teach Ceoil** *(tel 028/8164-8882)*, in Rouskey, is a ceilidh house in the foothills of the Sperrin Mountains, with a session usually held the last Saturday of every month.

In Enniskillen, County Fermanagh, you'll find live music at the **Crowe's Nest** on High Street. "**Blakes of the Hollow**," on Church Street, is a gem, and regular sessions here are among the best. In the village of Derrygonnelly, on the west side of Lower Lough Erne, try **McGovern's** or the **Cosy Bar.**

County Down boasts traditional music pubs in every town—a nice variant to the breakneck tunes is a sing-along session. Up in northwest Fermanagh, try **Belleek's Black Cat Cove** *(Main St., tel 028/6865-8942)* on a Thursday night.

INDEX

ILLUSTRATIONS CREDITS

2-3, S. McBride/AA Photo Library: 4, Will & Deni McIntyre/Corbis; 8, Courtesy Fáilte Ireland; 11, Chris Hill/chrishill@scenicireland.com; 12, holgs/iStockphoto.com; 14-15, Paul O'Connell/Getty Images; 16-17, Eoghan McNally/Shutterstock; 18, Alen MacWeeney/Corbis; 20, Martin McCullough/Rex USA; 20-21, faithie/123RF; 23, Michael Diggin; 25, Axiom Photographic; 26, Private Collection/Bridgeman Art Library; 28-29, Hulton Archive/Getty Images; 31, Hulton Archive/Getty Images; 32-33, Henri Burreau/Sygma/Corbis; 35, © Cathal McNaughton/Reuters/Corbis; 36, Ballymaloe Cookery School; 37, UnaPhoto/Shutterstock; 38-39, Courtesy of the Tourism Ireland; 43, © Paul Mohan/SPORTSFILE/Corbis; 44, S. L. Day/AA Photo Library; 46, Joan Marcus/Abhann Productions Ltd.; 47, Catherine Karnow; 48, Giancarlo Liguori/123RF; 50, Courtesy of the Tourism Ireland (Andrew Bradley); 52, Axiom Photographic; 54, Hulton Archive/Getty Images; 55, Hulton Archive/Getty Images; 56, The Ardagh Chalice, Reerasta, County Limerick, early 8th century, Celtic/National Museum of Ireland, Dublin/Photo © Boltin Picture Library/The Bridgeman Art Library; 58, National Museum of Ireland; 60, ©Gunold Brunbauer | Dreamstime.com; 62, S. Whitehorne/AA Photo Library; 63, S. L. Day/AA Photo Library; 64, S. L. Day/AA Photo Library; 66, Chester Beatty Library, Dublin/Bridgeman Art Library; 68, Axiom Photographic; 70, Courtesy of the Tourism Ireland (Sinead McCarthy); 71, Axiom Photographic; 72, maudis60/123RF; 73, Axiom Photographic; 74, Michael Corrigan/Axiom Photographic; 76-77, S. McBride/AA Photo Library; 79, S. McBride/AA Photo Library; 80, M. Short/AA Photo Library; 82, Axiom Photographic; 84, Courtesy of the Tourism Ireland (Brian Morrison); 86, Viking Splash Tours; 87, C. Coe/AA Photo Library; 90, Axiom Photographic; 94, Axiom Photographic; 96, Peter Zelei/iStockphoto; 102, Axiom Photographic; 104, Axiom Photographic; 106, Axiom Photographic; 108, Axiom Photographic; 111, Axiom Photographic; 113, S. L. Day/AA Photo Library; 115, Axiom Photographic; 116, P. Zoeller/AA Photo Library; 118, Axiom Photographic; 120, 121 Marian Porges; 122, S. McBride/AA Photo Library; 124, Axiom Photographic; 127, Axiom Photographic; 130, S. McBride/AA Photo Library; 132, Axiom Photographic; 134, Courtesy Fáilte Ireland; 136, walshphotos/Shutterstock; 138, Axiom Photographic; 141, Axiom Photographic; 142, S. McBride/AA Photo Library; 145, J. Blandford/AA Photo Library; 146, Axiom Photographic; 148, J. Blandford/AA Photo Library; 152, Michael Diggin; 154, Jim Kruger/iStockphoto.com; 157, Sam Abell/National Geographic Society; 158, Michael Diggin; 160, Patryk Kosmider/123RF; 161, Stephen Saks Photography/Alamy; 163, Axiom Photographic; 166, Axiom Photographic; 168, S. McBride/AA Photo Library; 170, Chris Hill/chrishill@scenicireland.com; 171, Ibsibs/Dreamstime.com; 174, Courtesy of the Tourism Ireland (Brian Morrison); 176, Colm Hogan; 178, S. Hill/AA Photo Library; 180, Axiom Photographic; 182, Axiom Photographic; 185, Jill Jennings/Chris Hill/chrishill@scenicireland.com; 186, Michael Diggin/AA Photo Library; 188, S. L. Day/AA Photo Library; 190, Axiom Photographic; 192, L. Blake/AA Photo Library; 194, Axiom Photographic; 196, Axiom Photographic; 199, Axiom Photographic; 200, S. L. Day/AA Photo Library; 202, Powerstock/Superstock; 203, Manuela Weschke/iStockphoto.com; 204, Axiom Photographic; 206, Peter Alexander/Alamy; 209, Axiom Photographic; 210, Axiom Photographic; 213, © Picade LLC/Alamy; 214, L. Blake/AA Photo Library; 216, C. Coe/AA Photo Library; 218, Axiom Photographic; 221, C. Coe/AA Photo Library; 222, Michael Diggin; 224, Jill Jennings/Chris Hill/chrishill@scenicireland.com; 226, Axiom Photographic; 228, David Lyons/Alamy; 230, Michael Walsh/123RF; 233, Chris Hill/chrishill@scenicireland.com; 236, Michael Diggin/AA Photo Library; 238, Axiom Photographic; 240, Axiom Photographic; 242, J. Jennings/AA Photo Library; 244, Gabriela Insuratelu/Shutterstock; 246, Michael Diggin; 248, Courtesy of the Tourism Ireland (Chris Hill); 250, Michael Diggin; 252, Axiom Photographic; 254, Phil Augustavo/iStockphoto.com; 255, walshphotos/Shutterstock; 256, M. Short/AA Photo Library; 258, Axiom Photographic; 260, Axiom Photographic; 262, Axiom Photographic; 264, Axiom Photographic; 266, UnaPhoto/Shutterstock; 268, Chris Hill/chrishill@scenicireland.com; 270, Axiom Photographic; 272, Michael Diggin; 275, AA Photo Library; 278, Chris Hill/National Geographic Creative; 280, Lawrence M. Porges; 283, Chris Hill/Axiom Photographic; 284, Axiom Photographic; 286, C. Coe/AA Photo Library; 287, Lawrence M. Porges; 288-289, Karen Martinez; 290, Khara Pringle/Chris Hill/chrishill@scenicireland.com; 293, RLWPhotos/iStockphoto.com; 294, Jill Jennings/Chris Hill/chrishill@scenicireland.com; 296, George Munday/Axiom Photographic; 298, Chris Hill/chrishill@scenicireland.com; 301, Nigel Carse/iStockphoto.com; 302, Jill Jennings/Chris Hill/chrishill@scenicireland.com; 304, © CATHAL MCNAUGHTON/Reuters/Corbis; 306, Sipa Press/Rex USA. 307, Jill Jennings/Chris Hill/chrishill@scenicireland.com; 308, Axiom Photographic; 310, Courtesy of the Tourism Ireland; 311, Axiom Photographic; 314, Axiom Photographic; 316, Axiom Photographic; 318, Jill Jennings/Chris Hill/chrishill@scenicireland.com; 320, Chris Hill/chrishill@scenicireland.com; 322, G. Munday/AA Photo Library; 323, C. Coe/AA Photo Library; 324, G. Munday/AA Photo Library; 326, Axiom Photographic; 328, Axiom Photographic; 330, Jill Jennings/Chris Hill/chrishill@scenicireland.com; 332, G. Munday/AA Photo Library; 334, Mary Evans Picture Library; 335, Mary Evans Picture Library; 336, Chris Hill/chrishill@scenicireland.com; 338, Martin Heaney/123RF; 340, Michael Diggin/AA Photo Library; 341, Sarah Hipwell/iStockphoto.com.

National Geographic
TRAVELER
Ireland
FIFTH EDITION

Since 1888, the National Geographic Society has funded more than 13,000 research, exploration, and preservation projects around the world. National Geographic Partners distributes a portion of the funds it receives from your purchase to National Geographic Society to support programs including the conservation of animals and their habitats.

National Geographic Partners, LLC
1145 17th Street NW
Washington, DC 20036-4688 USA

Get closer to National Geographic explorers and photographers, and connect with our global community. Join us today at nationalgeographic.com/join

For information about special discounts for bulk purchases, please contact National Geographic Books Special Sales: specialsales@natgeo.com

For rights or permissions inquiries, please contact National Geographic Books
Subsidiary Rights: bookrights@natgeo.com

Copyright © 2004, 2007, 2010, 2014, 2019 National Geographic Partners, LLC.
All rights reserved. Reproduction of the whole or any part of the contents without written permission from National Geographic Partners, LLC is prohibited.

NATIONAL GEOGRAPHIC and Yellow Border Design are trademarks of the National Geographic Society, used under license.

Map illustrations drawn by Chris Orr Associates, Southampton, England.
Cutaway illustrations drawn by Maltings Partnership, Derby, England.

Fifth edition edited by White Star s.r.l.
Licensee of National Geographic Partners, LLC.
Update by Iceigeo (Alessandra Mastroleo, Cynthia Anne Koeppe, Giulia Cassinari)

The information in this book has been carefully checked and to the best of our knowledge is accurate. However, details are subject to change, and the publisher cannot be responsible for such changes, or for errors or omissions. Assessments of sites, hotels, and restaurants are based on the author's subjective opinions, which do not necessarily reflect the publisher's opinion.

ISBN: 978-88-544-1513-3

Printed by
Rotolito S.p.A. - Seggiano di Pioltello (MI) - Italy

SOUTH COUNTRY LIBRARY

3 0614 00359 6055

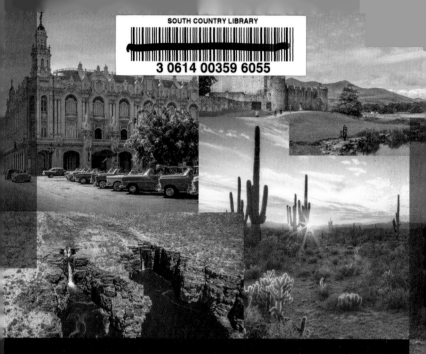

NATIONAL GEOGRAPHIC TRAVELER
THE BEST GUIDES BY YOUR SIDE

More than 80 destinations a

ARIZONA

AUSTRALIA

AVAILABLE WHEREVER BOOKS ARE SO
and at NationalGeographic.com/Books
 NatGeoBooks @NatGeoBooks